READER'S ADVISORY

AN UNSHELVED COLLECTION
BY BILL BARNES & GENE AMBAUM

OVERDUE
MEDIA
Seattle

Reprinting *Unshelved* comic strips originally published on the Unshelved website from February 17, 2008 to February 15, 2009, and *ALA CogNotes* newspapers in June 2008 and January 2009. Comic strips copyright © 2008 and 2009

The stories, characters, and incidents portrayed in this book are entirely fictional. Any resemblance to persons living or dead is entirely coincidental.

ISBN-10: 0-9740353-6-X
ISBN-13: 978-0-9740353-6-9

First printing: July 2009

Printed in Canada.

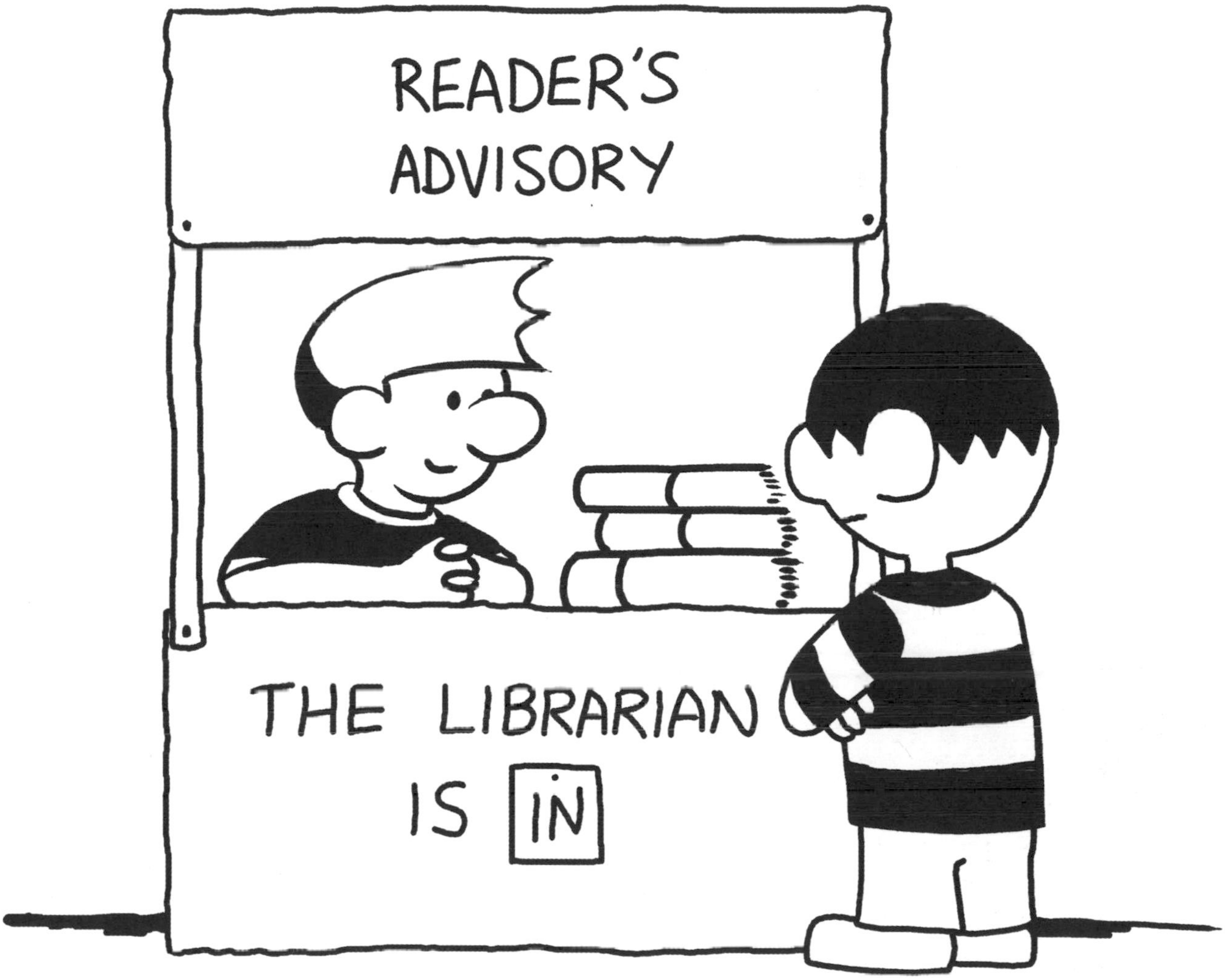
READER'S ADVISORY
THE LIBRARIAN IS IN

Other UNSHELVED collections by Bill Barnes & Gene Ambaum:

- **Unshelved**
- **What Would Dewey Do?**
- **Library Mascot Cage Match**
- **Book Club**
- **Read Responsibly**
- **Frequently Asked Questions**

FOREWORD

You know those carts in the library where you're supposed to set books for reshelving?

The staff doesn't trust patrons to put books back where they found them (with good reason, certainly) and so they leave those carts out there, in between aisles and tucked into the corners of reading rooms. They're like the little shelf atop the garbage can in a fast-food place where you leave your tray. You take the food, take the nourishment, take the good stuff into your body -- and leave the shell behind, so it can be put back where it goes.

After all, the book isn't the thing -- the stuff the book helps you put into your body is the thing. This is the magic of books as containers, of books as reminders, of books as outlines for ideas and concepts and emotions that we as people experience and share and recount.

Unshelved comics are like this too. When the reader identifies with a character, a phrase, a situation in the Mallville Public Library, it's not just Bill and Gene's story -- it's your story, it's my story, it's the story of everyone who's ever dealt with the public, it's the story of everyone who's ever wished they could snap off a witty comeback at just the right moment or blow off a numbskull boss with a clever retort.

And in that way, *Unshelved* comics are, like their namesakes sitting lonely on the re-shelving racks, just containers for experiences that we as readers share. The people and the place are real because you make it real. Bill and Gene are our daily guides to hidden cities in the jungle, hacking at vines and shining their flashlight at the treasures of human experience -- but it's up to us to open those gilded chests and devour all the chocolate doubloons within.

Okay my metaphor has now TOTALLY broken down. Enjoy these fine *Unshelved* candies!

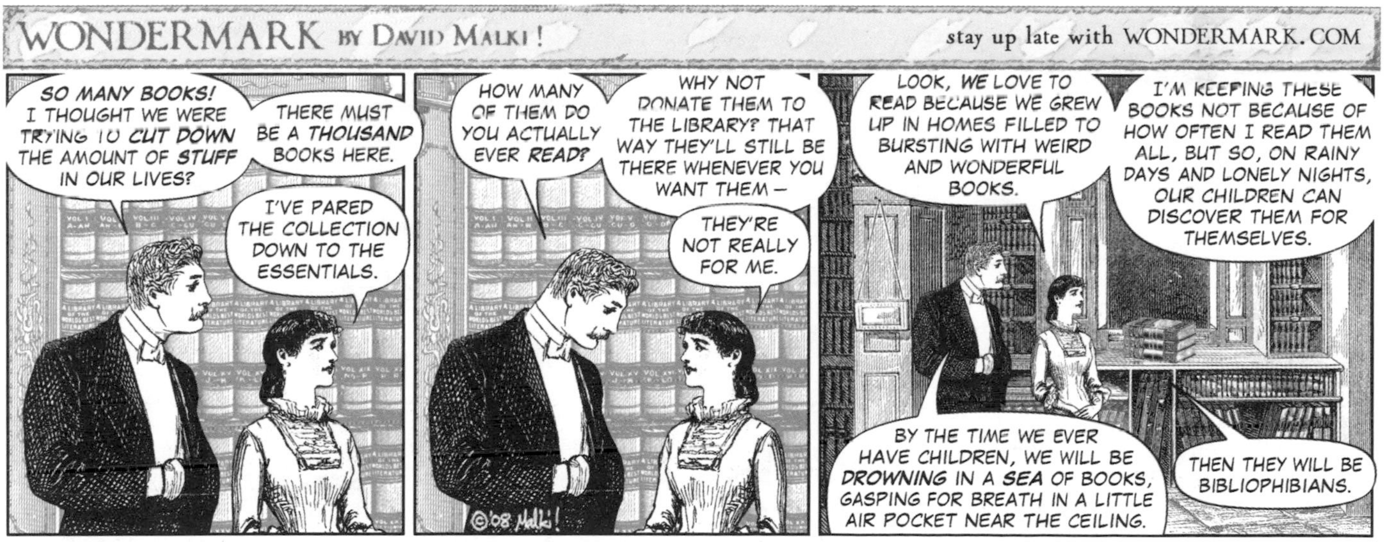
WONDERMARK BY DAVID MALKI !
stay up late with WONDERMARK.COM
SO MANY BOOKS! I THOUGHT WE WERE TRYING TO CUT DOWN THE AMOUNT OF STUFF IN OUR LIVES?
THERE MUST BE A THOUSAND BOOKS HERE.
I'VE PARED THE COLLECTION DOWN TO THE ESSENTIALS.
HOW MANY OF THEM DO YOU ACTUALLY EVER READ?
WHY NOT DONATE THEM TO THE LIBRARY? THAT WAY THEY'LL STILL BE THERE WHENEVER YOU WANT THEM —
THEY'RE NOT REALLY FOR ME.
©'08 Malki !
LOOK, WE LOVE TO READ BECAUSE WE GREW UP IN HOMES FILLED TO BURSTING WITH WEIRD AND WONDERFUL BOOKS.
I'M KEEPING THESE BOOKS NOT BECAUSE OF HOW OFTEN I READ THEM ALL, BUT SO, ON RAINY DAYS AND LONELY NIGHTS, OUR CHILDREN CAN DISCOVER THEM FOR THEMSELVES.
BY THE TIME WE EVER HAVE CHILDREN, WE WILL BE DROWNING IN A SEA OF BOOKS, GASPING FOR BREATH IN A LITTLE AIR POCKET NEAR THE CEILING.
THEN THEY WILL BE BIBLIOPHIBIANS.

DAVID MALKI collects nineteenth-century woodcuts and painstakingly edits them, adding his own words and sensibilities, until they become something new. Something terrible. A comic strip called *Wondermark*. Read it online at **wondermark.com** and in *Beards of our Forefathers* and *Clever Tricks to Stave Off Death* from Dark Horse Books. He's also a filmmaker and pilot. And, who knows, probably a brain surgeon or something too.

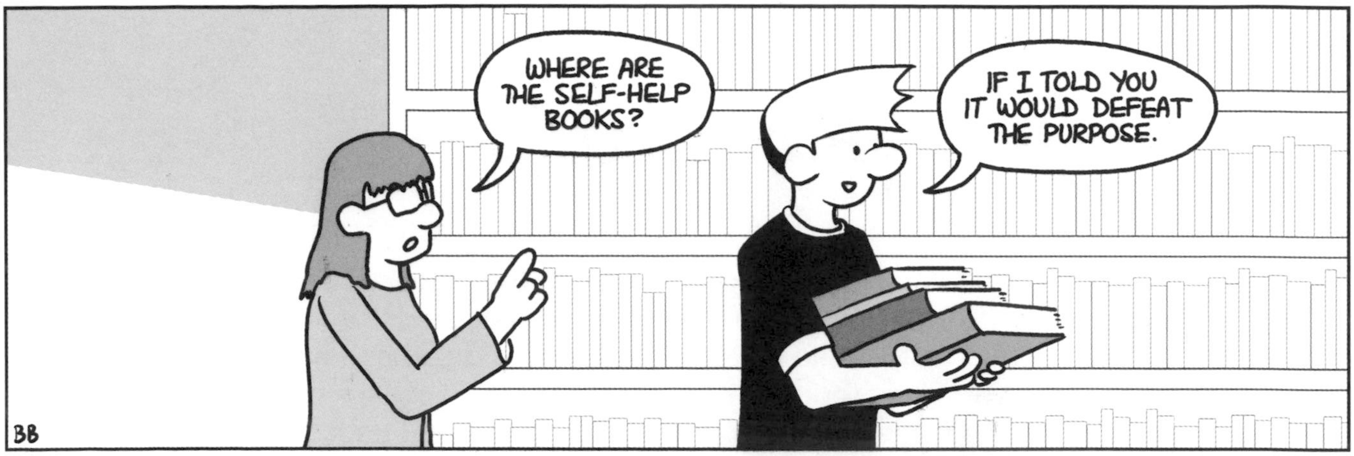
WHERE ARE THE SELF-HELP BOOKS?
IF I TOLD YOU IT WOULD DEFEAT THE PURPOSE.
BB

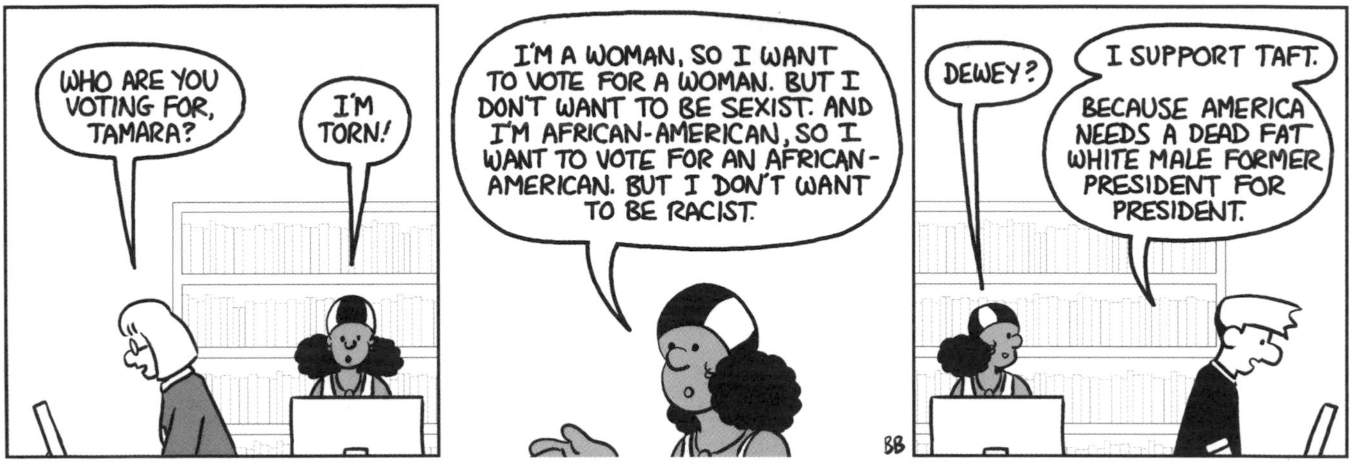
WHO ARE YOU VOTING FOR, TAMARA?
I'M TORN!
I'M A WOMAN, SO I WANT TO VOTE FOR A WOMAN. BUT I DON'T WANT TO BE SEXIST. AND I'M AFRICAN-AMERICAN, SO I WANT TO VOTE FOR AN AFRICAN-AMERICAN. BUT I DON'T WANT TO BE RACIST.
DEWEY?
I SUPPORT TAFT.
BECAUSE AMERICA NEEDS A DEAD FAT WHITE MALE FORMER PRESIDENT FOR PRESIDENT.
BB

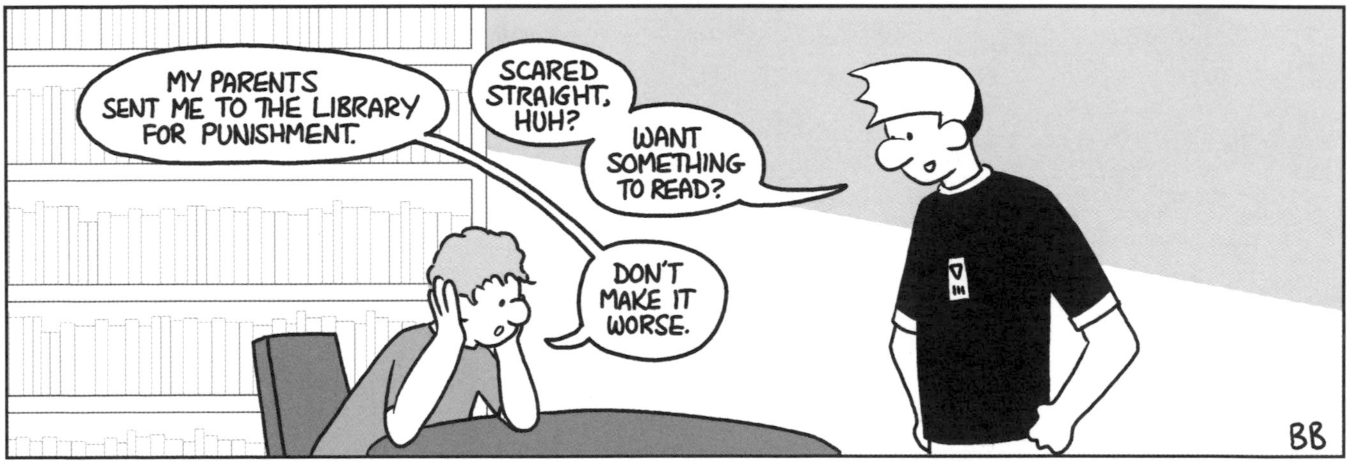
MY PARENTS SENT ME TO THE LIBRARY FOR PUNISHMENT.
SCARED STRAIGHT, HUH?
WANT SOMETHING TO READ?
DON'T MAKE IT WORSE.
BB

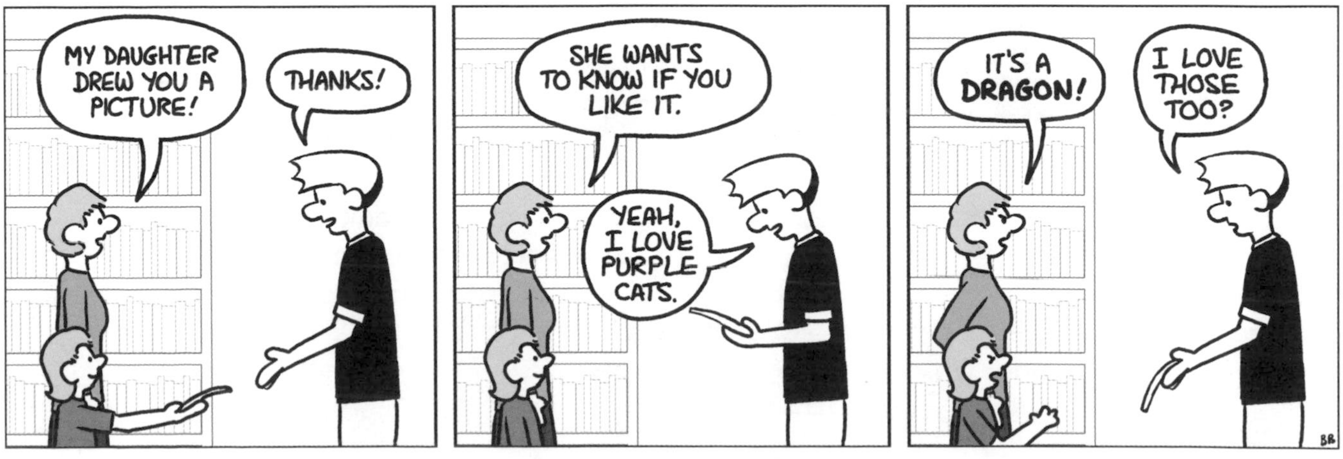
MY DAUGHTER DREW YOU A PICTURE!
THANKS!
SHE WANTS TO KNOW IF YOU LIKE IT.
YEAH, I LOVE PURPLE CATS.
IT'S A **DRAGON**!
I LOVE THOSE TOO?
BB

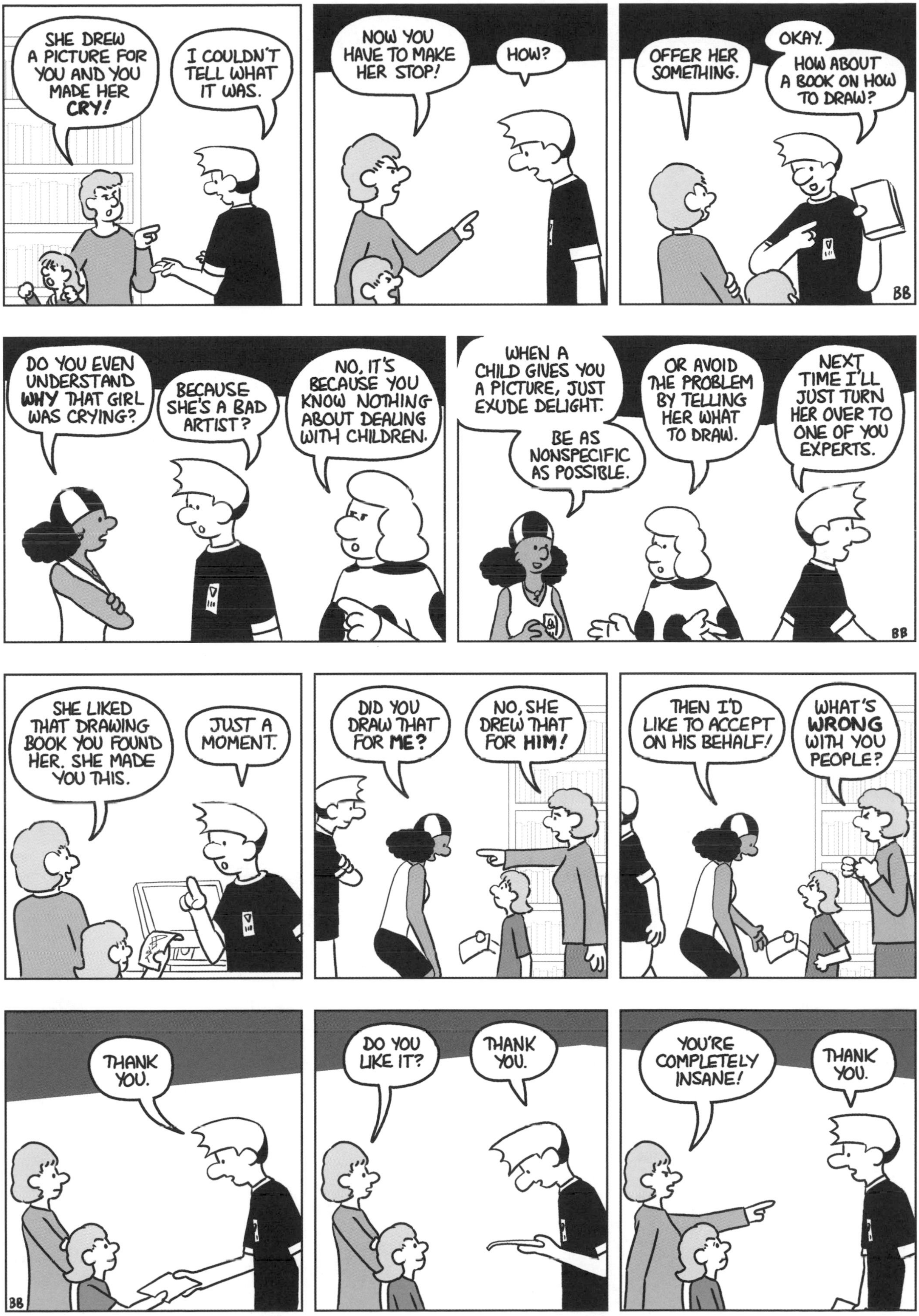
SHE DREW A PICTURE FOR YOU AND YOU MADE HER **CRY**!
I COULDN'T TELL WHAT IT WAS.
NOW YOU HAVE TO MAKE HER STOP!
HOW?
OFFER HER SOMETHING.
OKAY.
HOW ABOUT A BOOK ON HOW TO DRAW?
BB
DO YOU EVEN UNDERSTAND **WHY** THAT GIRL WAS CRYING?
BECAUSE SHE'S A BAD ARTIST?
NO, IT'S BECAUSE YOU KNOW NOTHING ABOUT DEALING WITH CHILDREN.
WHEN A CHILD GIVES YOU A PICTURE, JUST EXUDE DELIGHT.
BE AS NONSPECIFIC AS POSSIBLE.
OR AVOID THE PROBLEM BY TELLING HER WHAT TO DRAW.
NEXT TIME I'LL JUST TURN HER OVER TO ONE OF YOU EXPERTS.
BB
SHE LIKED THAT DRAWING BOOK YOU FOUND HER. SHE MADE YOU THIS.
JUST A MOMENT.
DID YOU DRAW THAT FOR **ME?**
NO, SHE DREW THAT FOR **HIM**!
THEN I'D LIKE TO ACCEPT ON HIS BEHALF!
WHAT'S **WRONG** WITH YOU PEOPLE?
THANK YOU.
BB
DO YOU LIKE IT?
THANK YOU.
YOU'RE COMPLETELY INSANE!
THANK YOU.

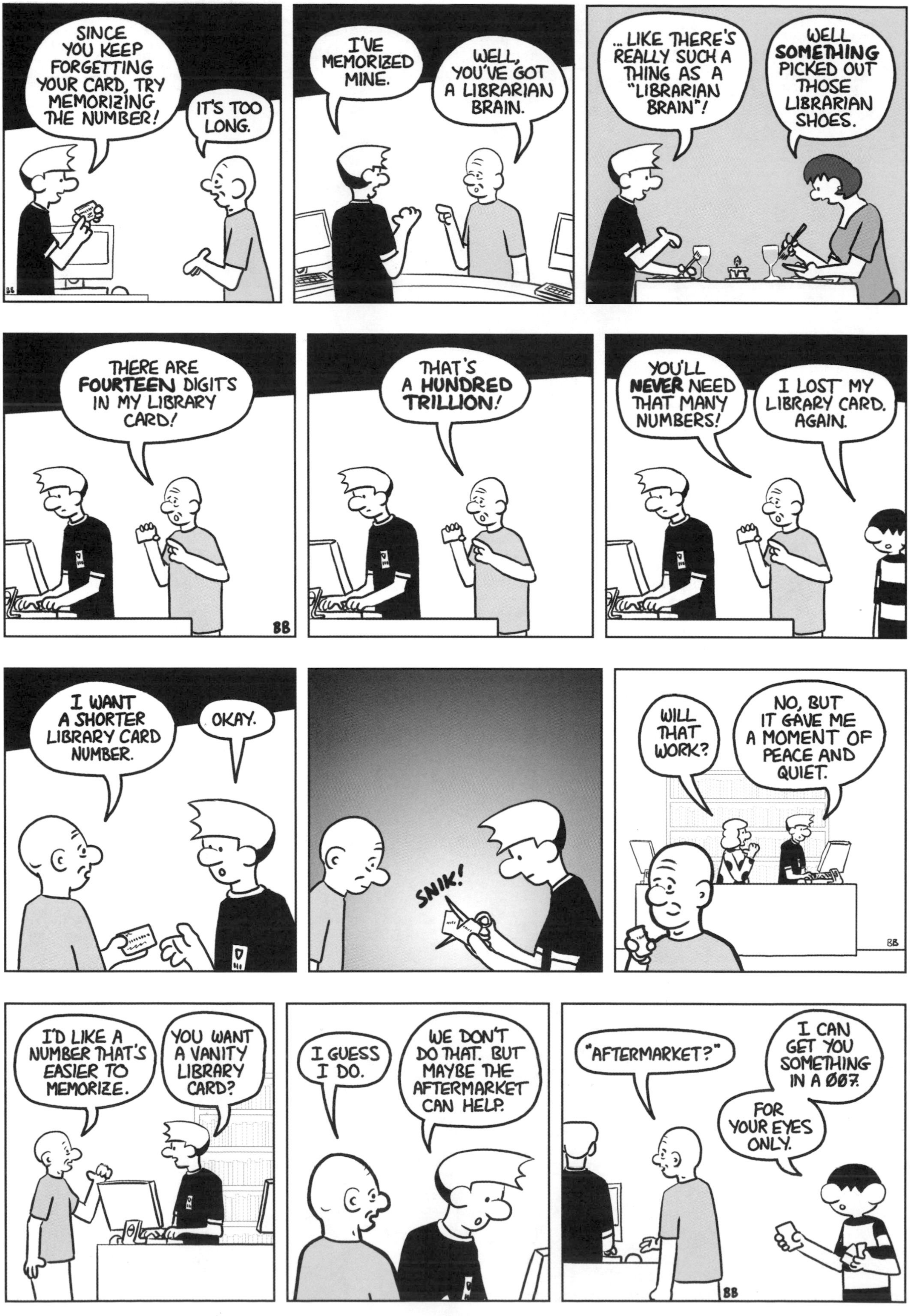
SINCE YOU KEEP FORGETTING YOUR CARD, TRY MEMORIZING THE NUMBER!
IT'S TOO LONG.
I'VE MEMORIZED MINE.
WELL, YOU'VE GOT A LIBRARIAN BRAIN.
...LIKE THERE'S REALLY SUCH A THING AS A "LIBRARIAN BRAIN"!
WELL **SOMETHING** PICKED OUT THOSE LIBRARIAN SHOES.
THERE ARE **FOURTEEN** DIGITS IN MY LIBRARY CARD!
THAT'S A **HUNDRED TRILLION**!
YOU'LL **NEVER** NEED THAT MANY NUMBERS!
I LOST MY LIBRARY CARD. AGAIN.
I WANT A SHORTER LIBRARY CARD NUMBER.
OKAY.
SNIK!
WILL THAT WORK?
NO, BUT IT GAVE ME A MOMENT OF PEACE AND QUIET.
I'D LIKE A NUMBER THAT'S EASIER TO MEMORIZE.
YOU WANT A VANITY LIBRARY CARD?
I GUESS I DO.
WE DON'T DO THAT. BUT MAYBE THE AFTERMARKET CAN HELP.
"AFTERMARKET?"
I CAN GET YOU SOMETHING IN A ØØ7.
FOR YOUR EYES ONLY.

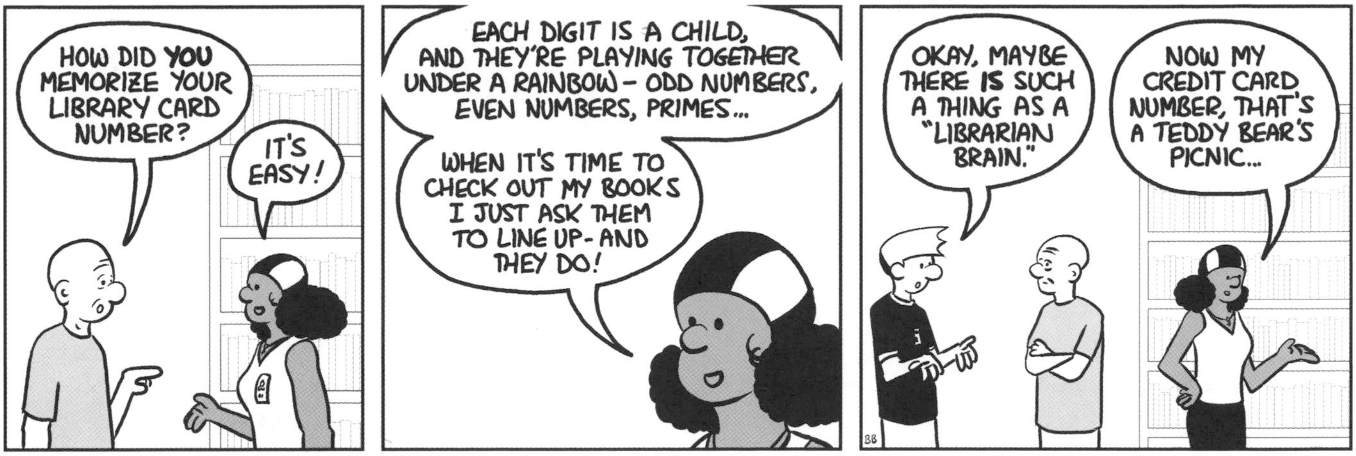
HOW DID **YOU** MEMORIZE YOUR LIBRARY CARD NUMBER?
IT'S EASY!
EACH DIGIT IS A CHILD, AND THEY'RE PLAYING TOGETHER UNDER A RAINBOW - ODD NUMBERS, EVEN NUMBERS, PRIMES...
WHEN IT'S TIME TO CHECK OUT MY BOOKS I JUST ASK THEM TO LINE UP - AND THEY DO!
OKAY, MAYBE THERE **IS** SUCH A THING AS A "LIBRARIAN BRAIN."
NOW MY CREDIT CARD NUMBER, THAT'S A TEDDY BEAR'S PICNIC...
BB

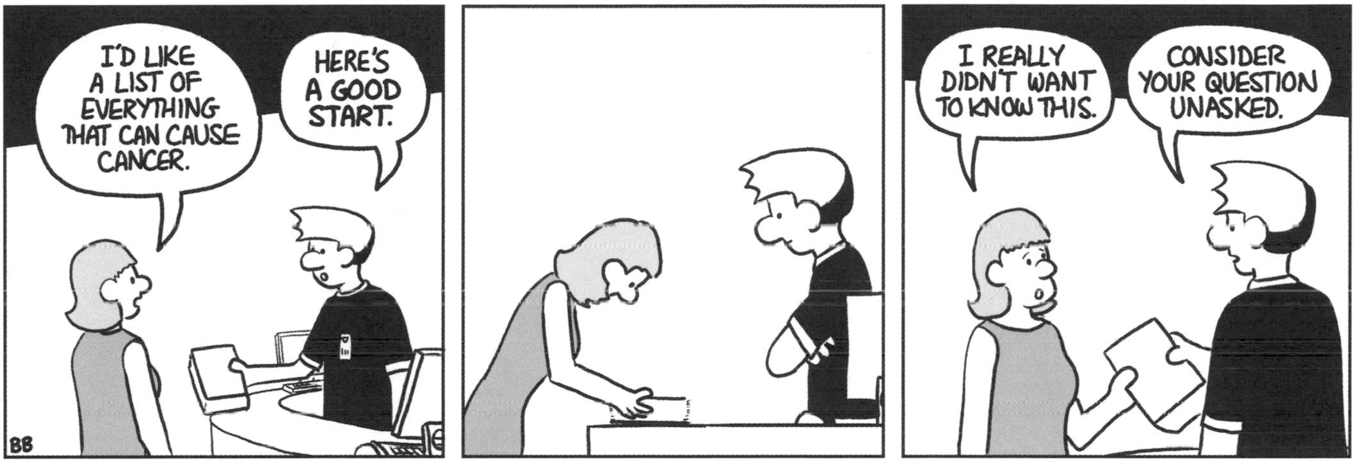
I'D LIKE A LIST OF EVERYTHING THAT CAN CAUSE CANCER.
HERE'S A GOOD START.
BB
I REALLY DIDN'T WANT TO KNOW THIS.
CONSIDER YOUR QUESTION UNASKED.

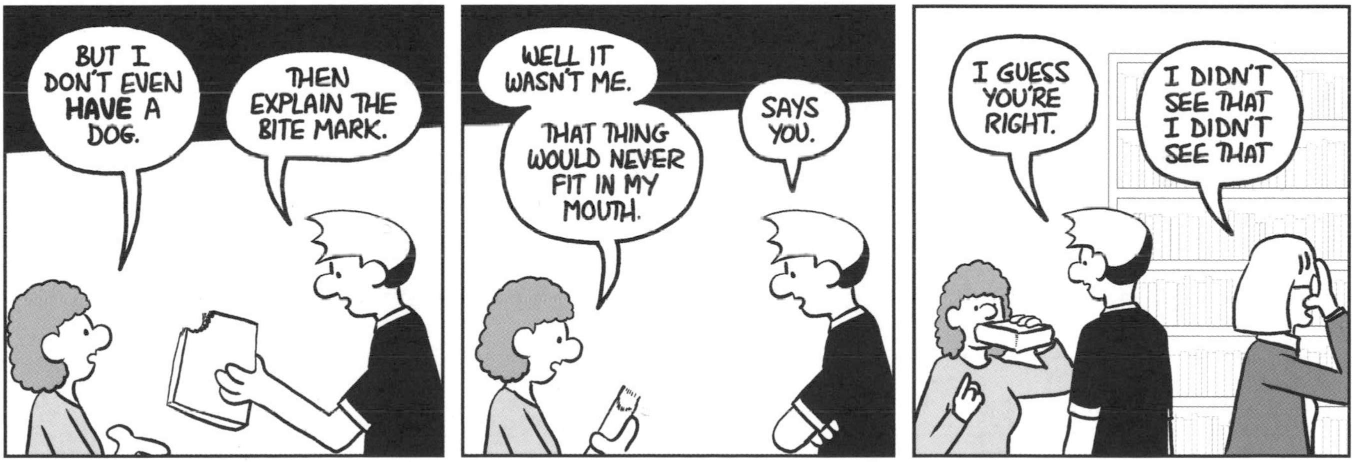
BUT I DON'T EVEN **HAVE** A DOG.
THEN EXPLAIN THE BITE MARK.
WELL IT WASN'T ME.
THAT THING WOULD NEVER FIT IN MY MOUTH.
SAYS YOU.
I GUESS YOU'RE RIGHT.
I DIDN'T SEE THAT I DIDN'T SEE THAT

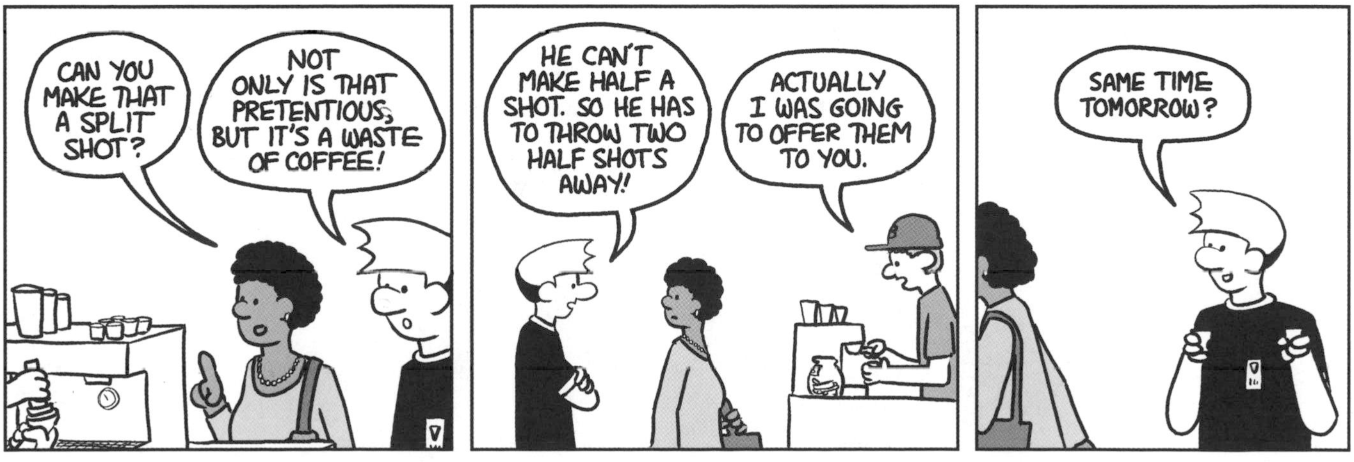
CAN YOU MAKE THAT A SPLIT SHOT?
NOT ONLY IS THAT PRETENTIOUS, BUT IT'S A WASTE OF COFFEE!
HE CAN'T MAKE HALF A SHOT. SO HE HAS TO THROW TWO HALF SHOTS AWAY!
ACTUALLY I WAS GOING TO OFFER THEM TO YOU.
SAME TIME TOMORROW?

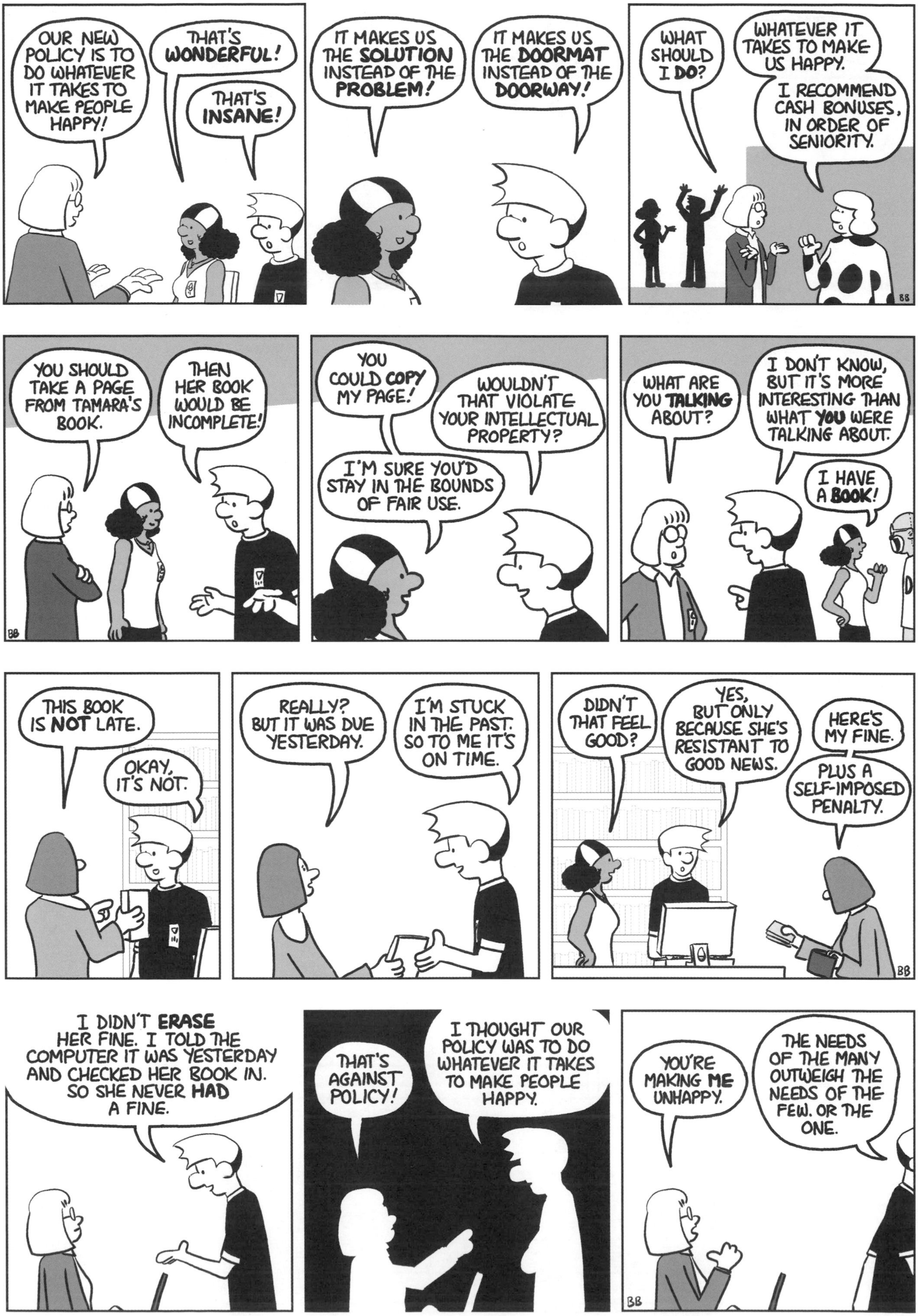
OUR NEW POLICY IS TO DO WHATEVER IT TAKES TO MAKE PEOPLE HAPPY!
THAT'S WONDERFUL!
THAT'S INSANE!
IT MAKES US THE SOLUTION INSTEAD OF THE PROBLEM!
IT MAKES US THE DOORMAT INSTEAD OF THE DOORWAY!
WHAT SHOULD I DO?
WHATEVER IT TAKES TO MAKE US HAPPY.
I RECOMMEND CASH BONUSES, IN ORDER OF SENIORITY.
BB
YOU SHOULD TAKE A PAGE FROM TAMARA'S BOOK.
THEN HER BOOK WOULD BE INCOMPLETE!
BB
YOU COULD COPY MY PAGE!
WOULDN'T THAT VIOLATE YOUR INTELLECTUAL PROPERTY?
I'M SURE YOU'D STAY IN THE BOUNDS OF FAIR USE.
WHAT ARE YOU TALKING ABOUT?
I DON'T KNOW, BUT IT'S MORE INTERESTING THAN WHAT YOU WERE TALKING ABOUT.
I HAVE A BOOK!
THIS BOOK IS NOT LATE.
OKAY, IT'S NOT.
REALLY? BUT IT WAS DUE YESTERDAY.
I'M STUCK IN THE PAST. SO TO ME IT'S ON TIME.
DIDN'T THAT FEEL GOOD?
YES, BUT ONLY BECAUSE SHE'S RESISTANT TO GOOD NEWS.
HERE'S MY FINE.
PLUS A SELF-IMPOSED PENALTY.
BB
I DIDN'T ERASE HER FINE. I TOLD THE COMPUTER IT WAS YESTERDAY AND CHECKED HER BOOK IN. SO SHE NEVER HAD A FINE.
THAT'S AGAINST POLICY!
I THOUGHT OUR POLICY WAS TO DO WHATEVER IT TAKES TO MAKE PEOPLE HAPPY.
YOU'RE MAKING ME UNHAPPY.
THE NEEDS OF THE MANY OUTWEIGH THE NEEDS OF THE FEW. OR THE ONE.
BB

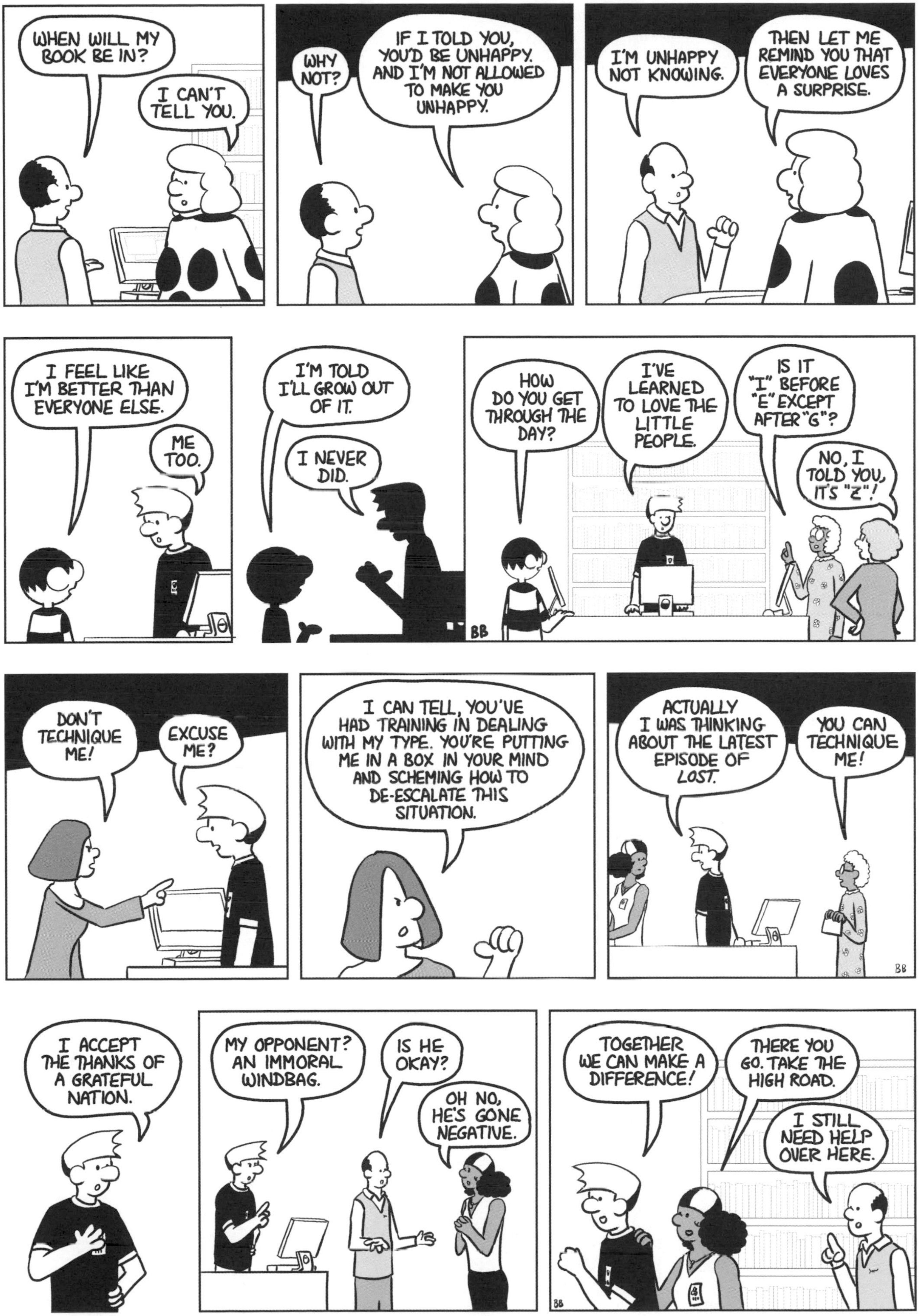
WHEN WILL MY BOOK BE IN?
I CAN'T TELL YOU.
WHY NOT?
IF I TOLD YOU, YOU'D BE UNHAPPY. AND I'M NOT ALLOWED TO MAKE YOU UNHAPPY.
I'M UNHAPPY NOT KNOWING.
THEN LET ME REMIND YOU THAT EVERYONE LOVES A SURPRISE.
I FEEL LIKE I'M BETTER THAN EVERYONE ELSE.
ME TOO.
I'M TOLD I'LL GROW OUT OF IT.
I NEVER DID.
HOW DO YOU GET THROUGH THE DAY?
I'VE LEARNED TO LOVE THE LITTLE PEOPLE.
IS IT "I" BEFORE "E" EXCEPT AFTER "G"?
NO, I TOLD YOU, IT'S "Z"!
BB
DON'T TECHNIQUE ME!
EXCUSE ME?
I CAN TELL, YOU'VE HAD TRAINING IN DEALING WITH MY TYPE. YOU'RE PUTTING ME IN A BOX IN YOUR MIND AND SCHEMING HOW TO DE-ESCALATE THIS SITUATION.
ACTUALLY I WAS THINKING ABOUT THE LATEST EPISODE OF LOST.
YOU CAN TECHNIQUE ME!
BB
I ACCEPT THE THANKS OF A GRATEFUL NATION.
MY OPPONENT? AN IMMORAL WINDBAG.
IS HE OKAY?
OH NO, HE'S GONE NEGATIVE.
TOGETHER WE CAN MAKE A DIFFERENCE!
THERE YOU GO. TAKE THE HIGH ROAD.
I STILL NEED HELP OVER HERE.
BB

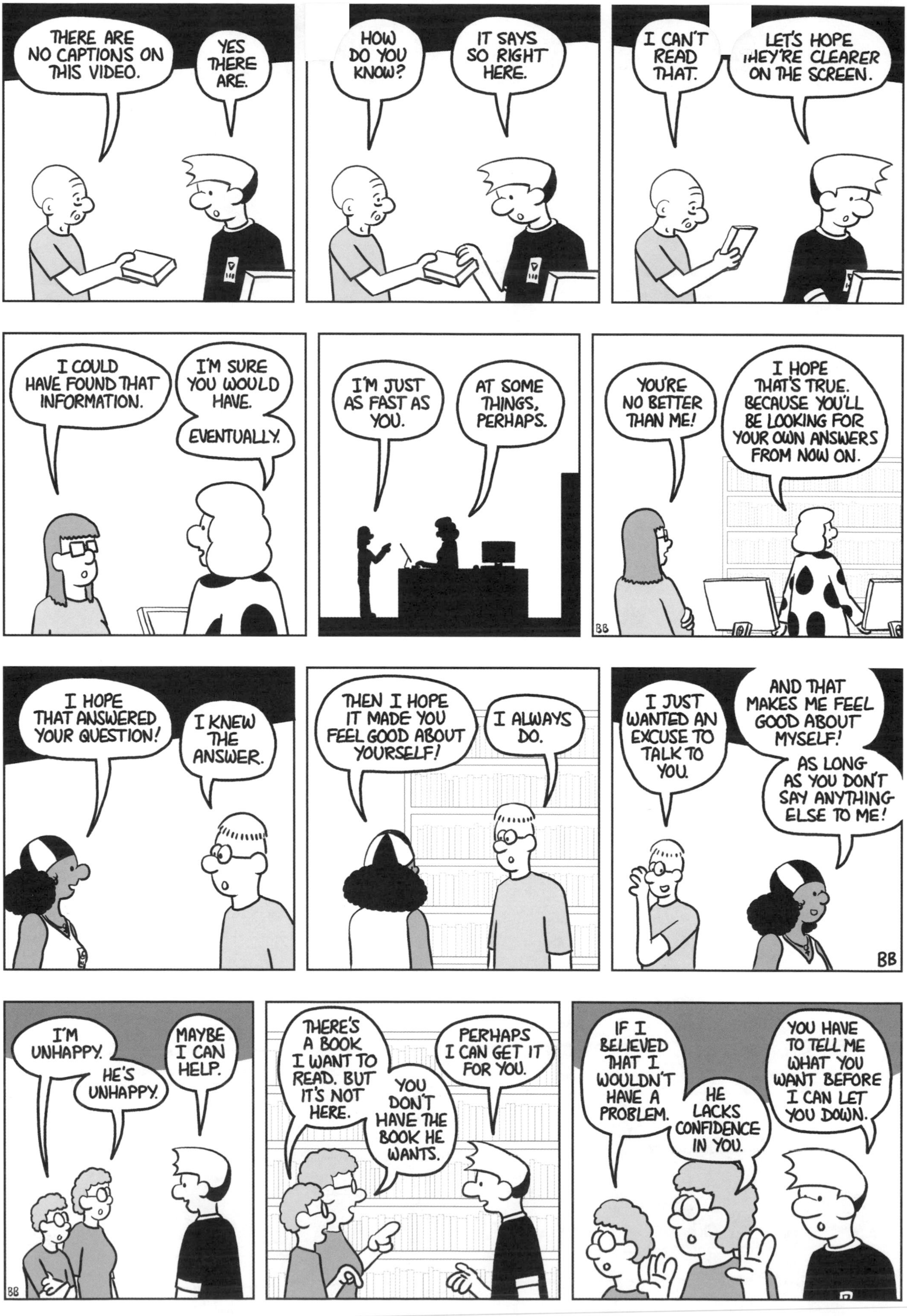
THERE ARE NO CAPTIONS ON THIS VIDEO.
YES THERE ARE.
HOW DO YOU KNOW?
IT SAYS SO RIGHT HERE.
I CAN'T READ THAT.
LET'S HOPE THEY'RE CLEARER ON THE SCREEN.
I COULD HAVE FOUND THAT INFORMATION.
I'M SURE YOU WOULD HAVE.
EVENTUALLY.
I'M JUST AS FAST AS YOU.
AT SOME THINGS, PERHAPS.
YOU'RE NO BETTER THAN ME!
I HOPE THAT'S TRUE. BECAUSE YOU'LL BE LOOKING FOR YOUR OWN ANSWERS FROM NOW ON.
BB
I HOPE THAT ANSWERED YOUR QUESTION!
I KNEW THE ANSWER.
THEN I HOPE IT MADE YOU FEEL GOOD ABOUT YOURSELF!
I ALWAYS DO.
I JUST WANTED AN EXCUSE TO TALK TO YOU.
AND THAT MAKES ME FEEL GOOD ABOUT MYSELF!
AS LONG AS YOU DON'T SAY ANYTHING ELSE TO ME!
BB
I'M UNHAPPY.
HE'S UNHAPPY.
MAYBE I CAN HELP.
BB
THERE'S A BOOK I WANT TO READ. BUT IT'S NOT HERE.
YOU DON'T HAVE THE BOOK HE WANTS.
PERHAPS I CAN GET IT FOR YOU.
IF I BELIEVED THAT I WOULDN'T HAVE A PROBLEM.
HE LACKS CONFIDENCE IN YOU.
YOU HAVE TO TELL ME WHAT YOU WANT BEFORE I CAN LET YOU DOWN.

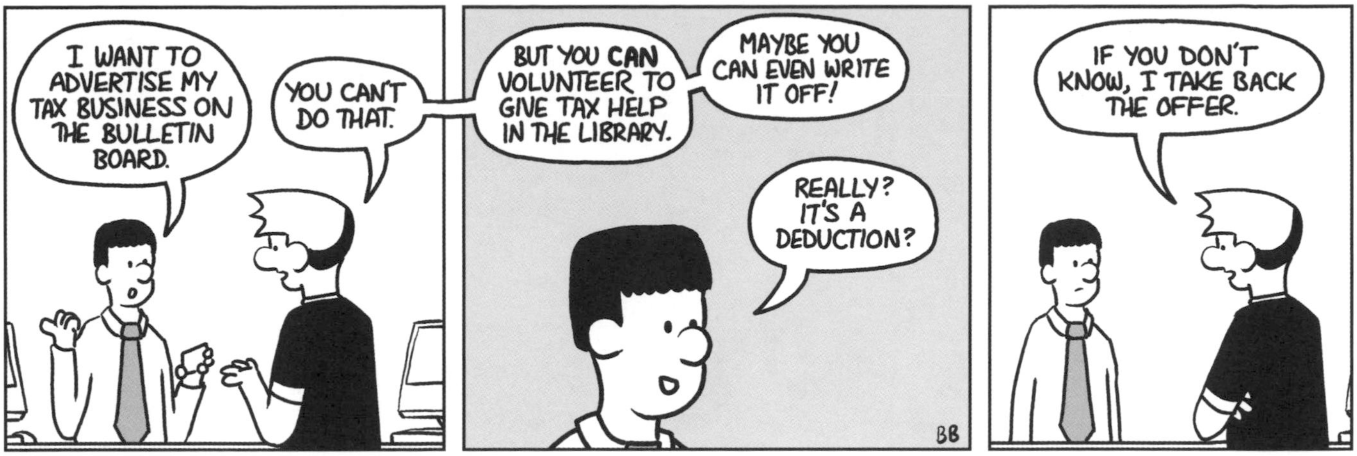
I WANT TO ADVERTISE MY TAX BUSINESS ON THE BULLETIN BOARD.
YOU CAN'T DO THAT.
BUT YOU **CAN** VOLUNTEER TO GIVE TAX HELP IN THE LIBRARY.
MAYBE YOU CAN EVEN WRITE IT OFF!
REALLY? IT'S A DEDUCTION?
IF YOU DON'T KNOW, I TAKE BACK THE OFFER.
BB

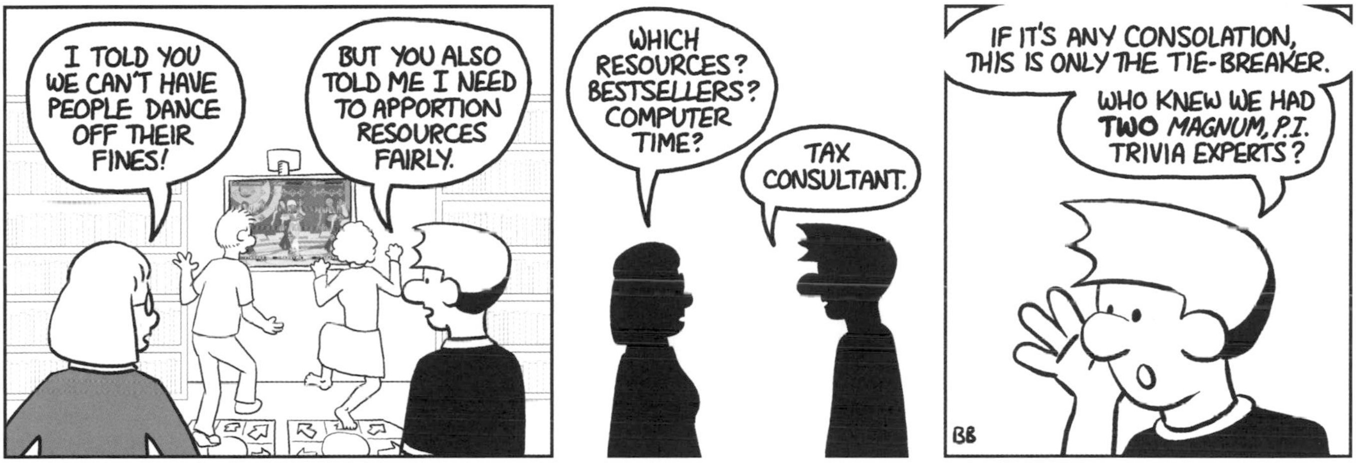
I TOLD YOU WE CAN'T HAVE PEOPLE DANCE OFF THEIR FINES!
BUT YOU ALSO TOLD ME I NEED TO APPORTION RESOURCES FAIRLY.
WHICH RESOURCES? BESTSELLERS? COMPUTER TIME?
TAX CONSULTANT.
IF IT'S ANY CONSOLATION, THIS IS ONLY THE TIE-BREAKER.
WHO KNEW WE HAD **TWO** *MAGNUM, P.I.* TRIVIA EXPERTS?
BB

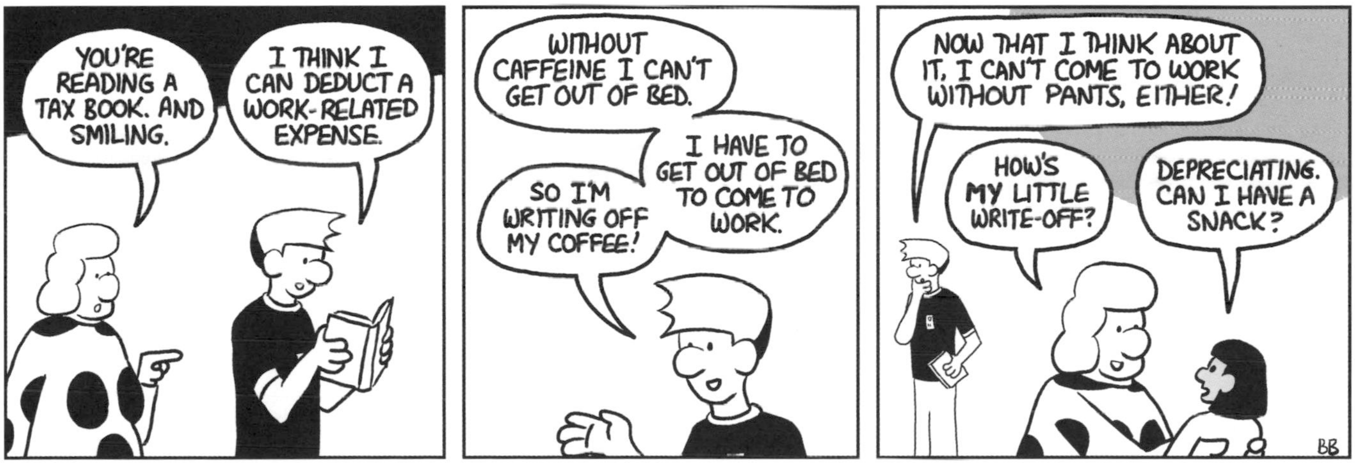
YOU'RE READING A TAX BOOK. AND SMILING.
I THINK I CAN DEDUCT A WORK-RELATED EXPENSE.
WITHOUT CAFFEINE I CAN'T GET OUT OF BED.
I HAVE TO GET OUT OF BED TO COME TO WORK.
SO I'M WRITING OFF MY COFFEE!
NOW THAT I THINK ABOUT IT, I CAN'T COME TO WORK WITHOUT PANTS, EITHER!
HOW'S **MY** LITTLE WRITE-OFF?
DEPRECIATING. CAN I HAVE A SNACK?
BB

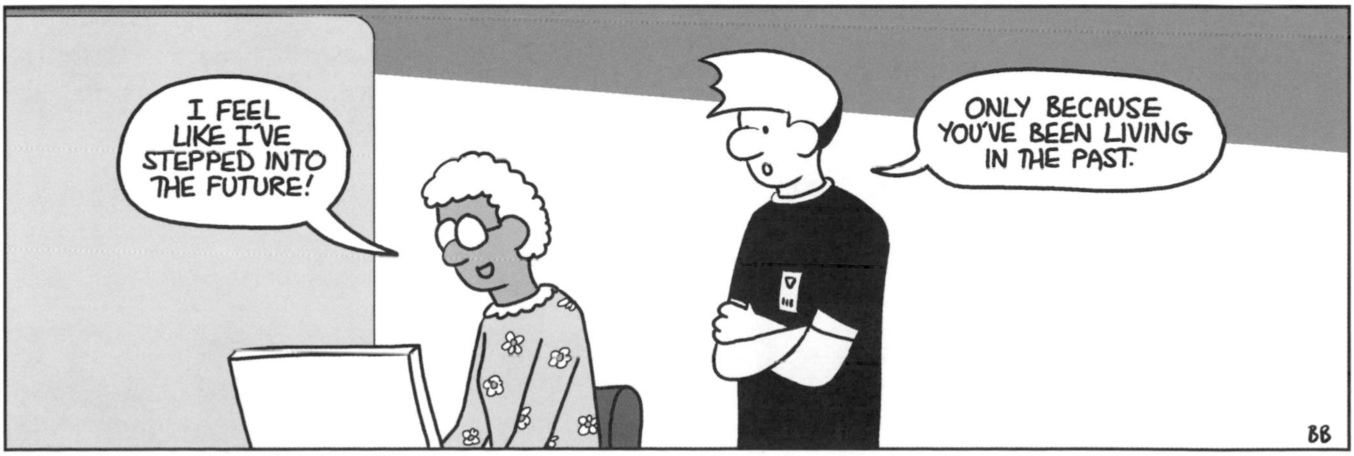
I FEEL LIKE I'VE STEPPED INTO THE FUTURE!
ONLY BECAUSE YOU'VE BEEN LIVING IN THE PAST.
BB

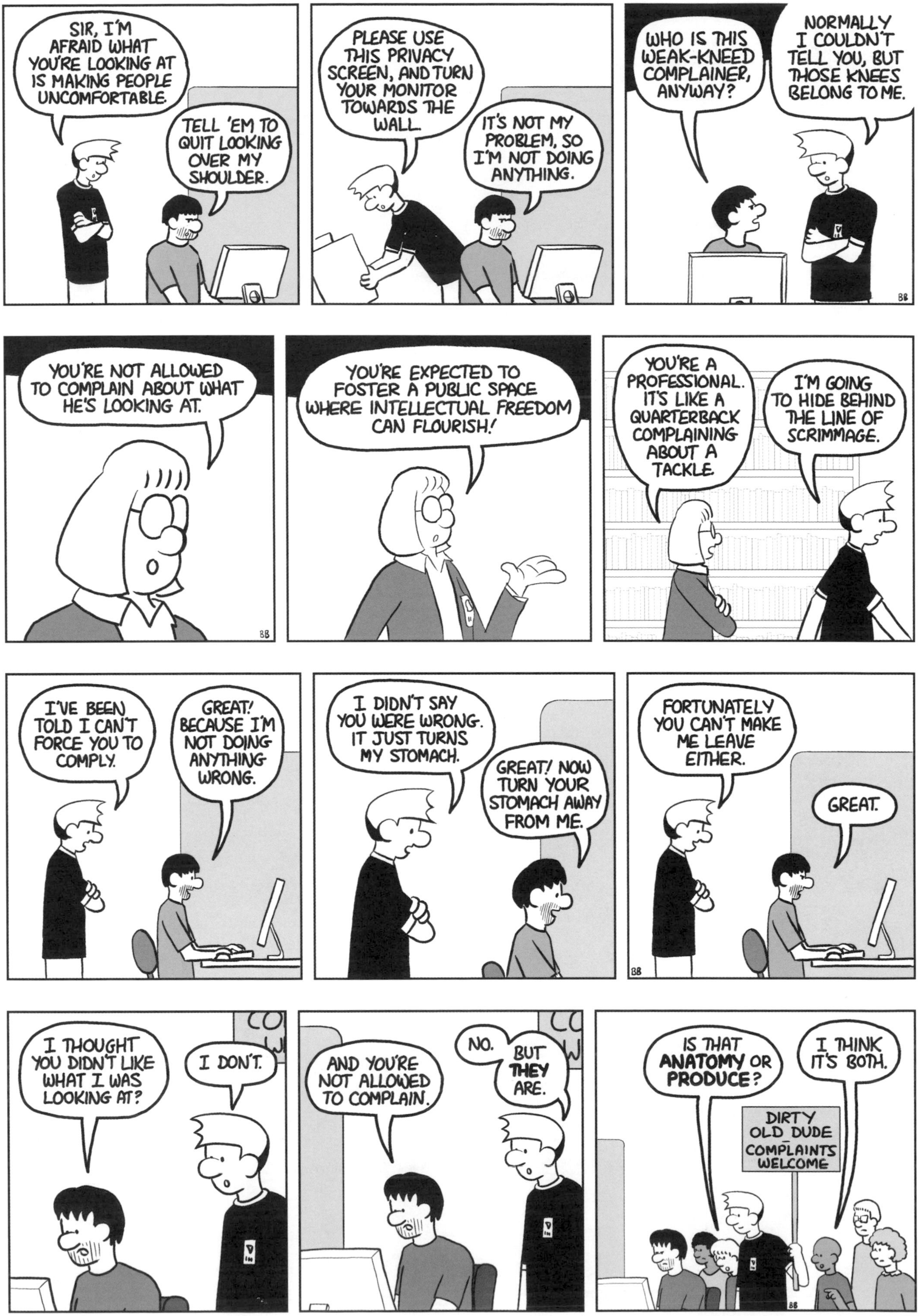
SIR, I'M AFRAID WHAT YOU'RE LOOKING AT IS MAKING PEOPLE UNCOMFORTABLE.
TELL 'EM TO QUIT LOOKING OVER MY SHOULDER.
PLEASE USE THIS PRIVACY SCREEN, AND TURN YOUR MONITOR TOWARDS THE WALL.
IT'S NOT MY PROBLEM, SO I'M NOT DOING ANYTHING.
WHO IS THIS WEAK-KNEED COMPLAINER, ANYWAY?
NORMALLY I COULDN'T TELL YOU, BUT THOSE KNEES BELONG TO ME.
BB
YOU'RE NOT ALLOWED TO COMPLAIN ABOUT WHAT HE'S LOOKING AT.
BB
YOU'RE EXPECTED TO FOSTER A PUBLIC SPACE WHERE INTELLECTUAL FREEDOM CAN FLOURISH!
YOU'RE A PROFESSIONAL. IT'S LIKE A QUARTERBACK COMPLAINING ABOUT A TACKLE.
I'M GOING TO HIDE BEHIND THE LINE OF SCRIMMAGE.
I'VE BEEN TOLD I CAN'T FORCE YOU TO COMPLY.
GREAT! BECAUSE I'M NOT DOING ANYTHING WRONG.
I DIDN'T SAY YOU WERE WRONG. IT JUST TURNS MY STOMACH.
GREAT! NOW TURN YOUR STOMACH AWAY FROM ME.
FORTUNATELY YOU CAN'T MAKE ME LEAVE EITHER.
GREAT.
BB
I THOUGHT YOU DIDN'T LIKE WHAT I WAS LOOKING AT?
I DON'T.
AND YOU'RE NOT ALLOWED TO COMPLAIN.
NO.
BUT **THEY** ARE.
IS THAT **ANATOMY** OR **PRODUCE**?
I THINK IT'S BOTH.
DIRTY OLD DUDE COMPLAINTS WELCOME
BB

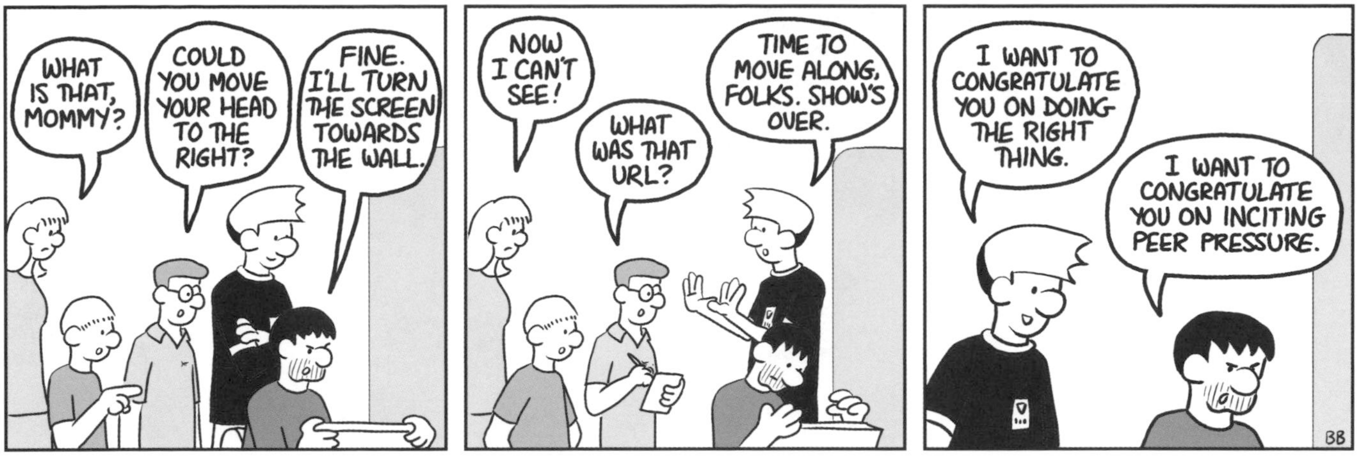
WHAT IS THAT, MOMMY?
COULD YOU MOVE YOUR HEAD TO THE RIGHT?
FINE. I'LL TURN THE SCREEN TOWARDS THE WALL.
NOW I CAN'T SEE!
WHAT WAS THAT URL?
TIME TO MOVE ALONG, FOLKS. SHOW'S OVER.
I WANT TO CONGRATULATE YOU ON DOING THE RIGHT THING.
I WANT TO CONGRATULATE YOU ON INCITING PEER PRESSURE.
BB

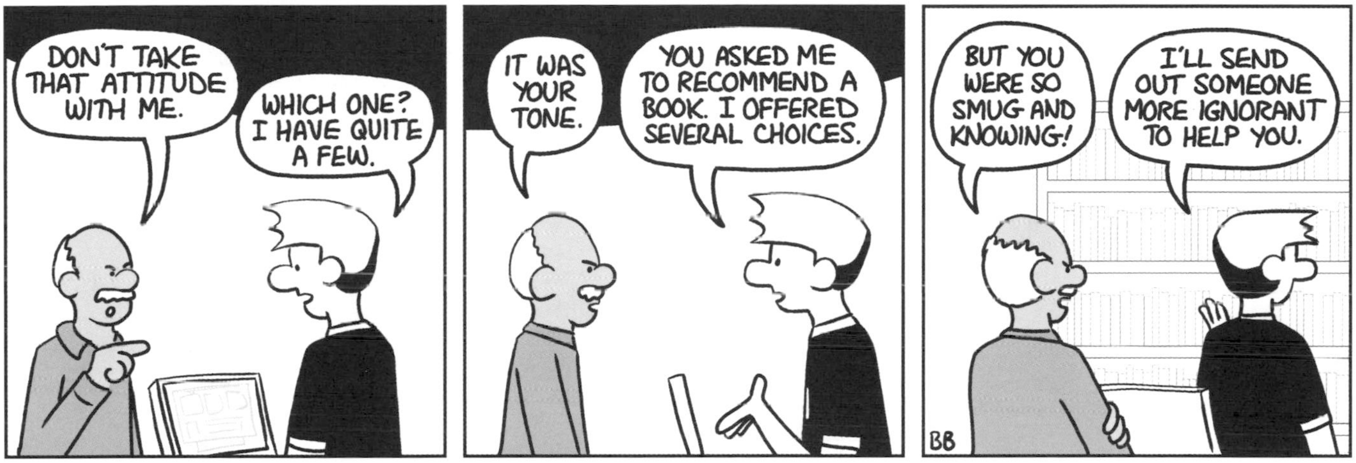
DON'T TAKE THAT ATTITUDE WITH ME.
WHICH ONE? I HAVE QUITE A FEW.
IT WAS YOUR TONE.
YOU ASKED ME TO RECOMMEND A BOOK. I OFFERED SEVERAL CHOICES.
BUT YOU WERE SO SMUG AND KNOWING!
I'LL SEND OUT SOMEONE MORE IGNORANT TO HELP YOU.
BB

LIBRARY TIP #41: DON'T TOUCH THE LIBRARIAN

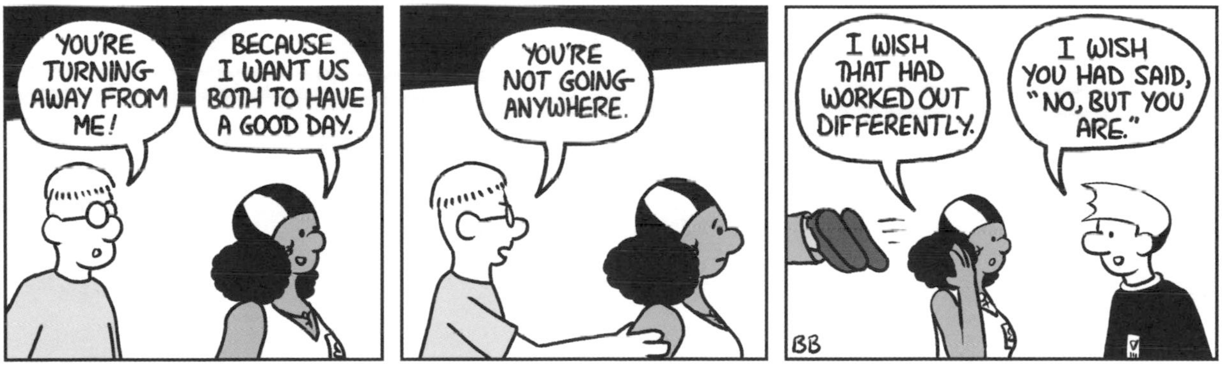
YOU'RE TURNING AWAY FROM ME!
BECAUSE I WANT US BOTH TO HAVE A GOOD DAY.
YOU'RE NOT GOING ANYWHERE.
I WISH THAT HAD WORKED OUT DIFFERENTLY.
I WISH YOU HAD SAID, "NO, BUT YOU ARE."
BB

LIBRARY TIP #42: PRESS F1

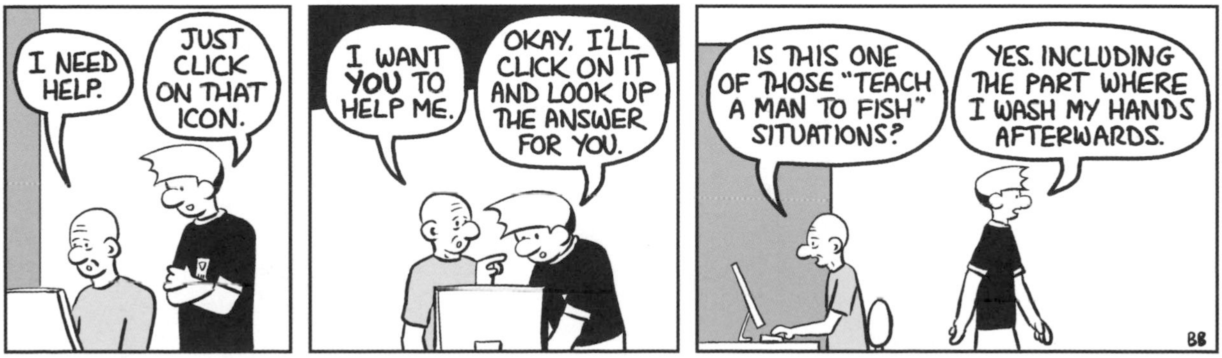
I NEED HELP.
JUST CLICK ON THAT ICON.
I WANT YOU TO HELP ME.
OKAY. I'LL CLICK ON IT AND LOOK UP THE ANSWER FOR YOU.
IS THIS ONE OF THOSE "TEACH A MAN TO FISH" SITUATIONS?
YES. INCLUDING THE PART WHERE I WASH MY HANDS AFTERWARDS.
BB

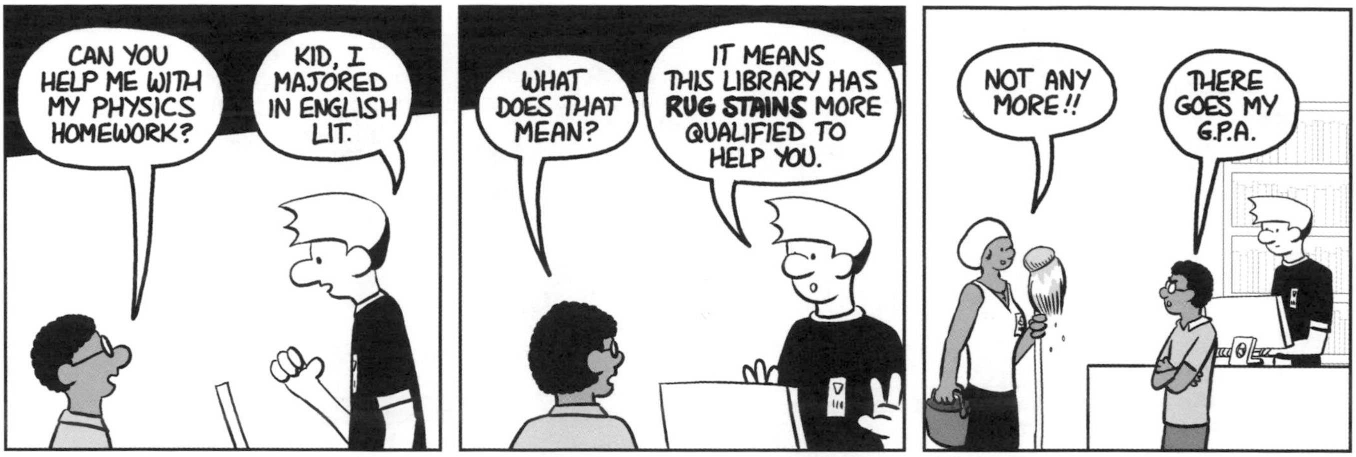
CAN YOU HELP ME WITH MY PHYSICS HOMEWORK?
KID, I MAJORED IN ENGLISH LIT.
WHAT DOES THAT MEAN?
IT MEANS THIS LIBRARY HAS **RUG STAINS** MORE QUALIFIED TO HELP YOU.
NOT ANY MORE!!
THERE GOES MY G.P.A.

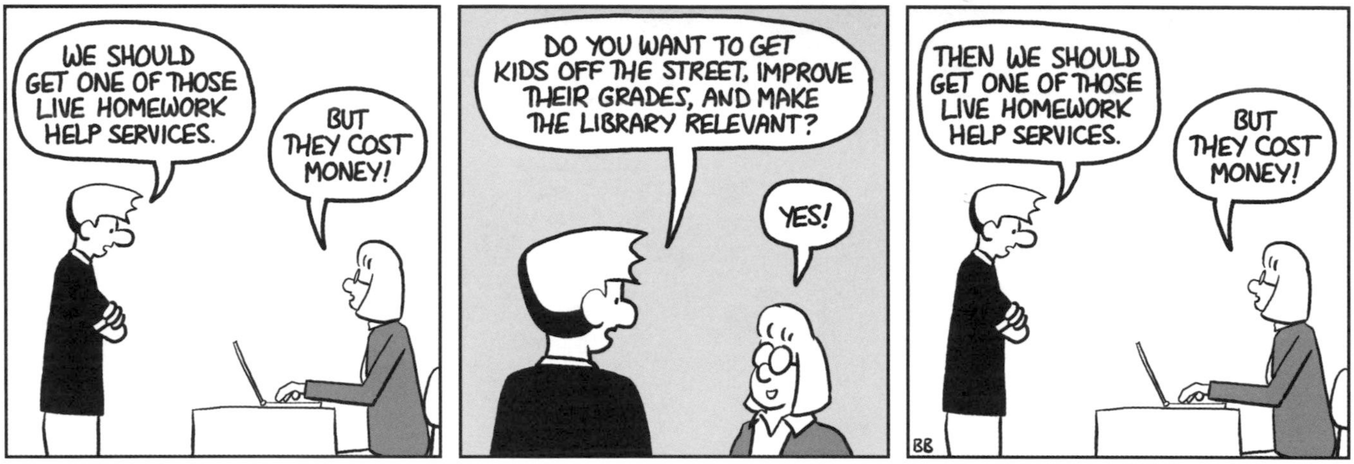
WE SHOULD GET ONE OF THOSE LIVE HOMEWORK HELP SERVICES.
BUT THEY COST MONEY!
DO YOU WANT TO GET KIDS OFF THE STREET, IMPROVE THEIR GRADES, AND MAKE THE LIBRARY RELEVANT?
YES!
THEN WE SHOULD GET ONE OF THOSE LIVE HOMEWORK HELP SERVICES.
BUT THEY COST MONEY!
BB

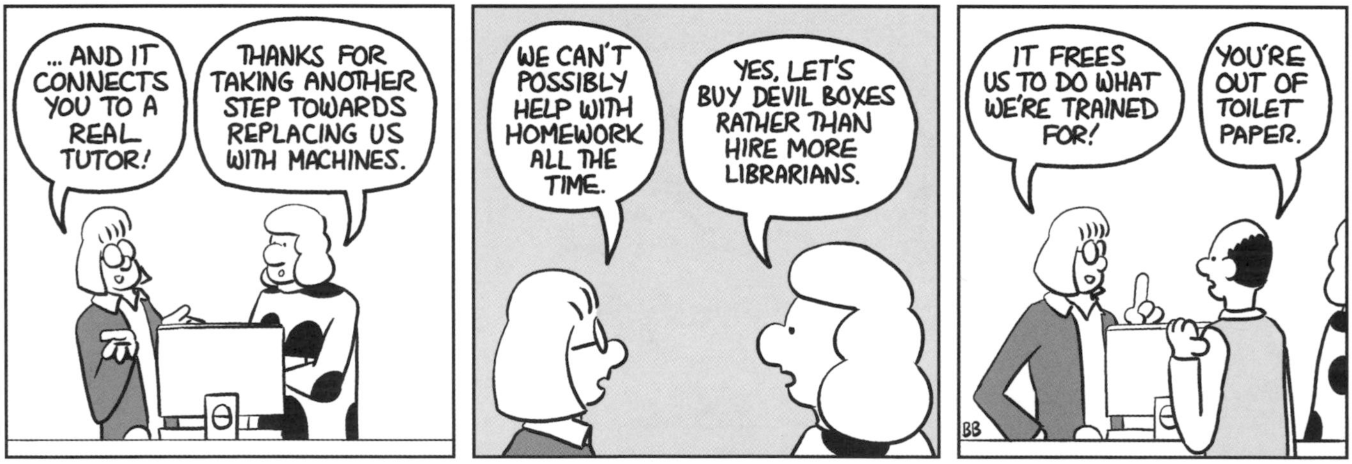
... AND IT CONNECTS YOU TO A REAL TUTOR!
THANKS FOR TAKING ANOTHER STEP TOWARDS REPLACING US WITH MACHINES.
WE CAN'T POSSIBLY HELP WITH HOMEWORK ALL THE TIME.
YES, LET'S BUY DEVIL BOXES RATHER THAN HIRE MORE LIBRARIANS.
IT FREES US TO DO WHAT WE'RE TRAINED FOR!
YOU'RE OUT OF TOILET PAPER.
BB

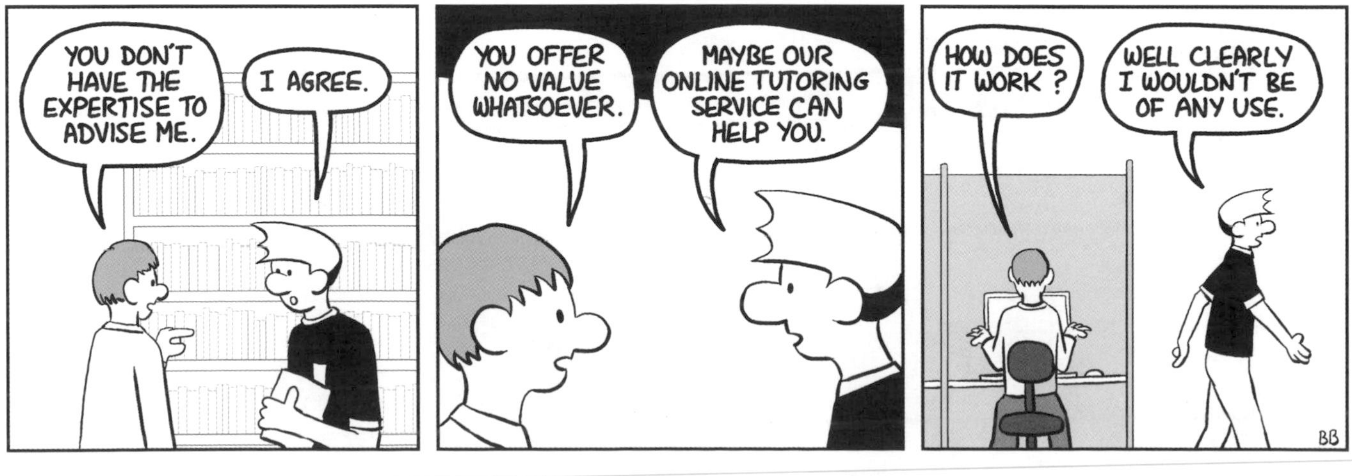
YOU DON'T HAVE THE EXPERTISE TO ADVISE ME.
I AGREE.
YOU OFFER NO VALUE WHATSOEVER.
MAYBE OUR ONLINE TUTORING SERVICE CAN HELP YOU.
HOW DOES IT WORK ?
WELL CLEARLY I WOULDN'T BE OF ANY USE.
BB

TRY THIS. IT USES CHAT TO ANSWER YOUR QUESTIONS.

I DON'T LIKE CHAT.

IT'S A WASTE OF TIME. PEOPLE TALK ABOUT THINGS THAT AREN'T RELEVANT. THEY GO ON AND ON AND ON ABOUT [...], RIGHT? THEY KEEP ON [...] THEY JUST REPEA[...]. I'M NOT LIKE TH[...] GET TO THE PO[...].

I JUST WANT TO GET DOWN TO BUSINESS.

I'M SURE THEY'LL APPRECIATE THAT.

I HAVE A COMPLAINT ABOUT THIS SO-CALLED "HOMEWORK HELP"

THIS IS THE ALWAYS THE MOST EXCITING PART ABOUT LAUNCHING A NEW SERVICE.

YOU'RE **EXCLUDING** THOSE WHO DON'T HAVE ACCESS TO COMPUTERS!

WE HAVE COMPUTERS HERE. FREE FOR ALL.

SOME PEOPLE DON'T **LIKE** COMPUTERS.

BUT I HAPPEN TO KNOW YOU'RE NOT ONE OF THEM.

I INSIST YOU CATER TO EVERY HYPOTHETICAL SCENARIO I CAN DREAM UP!

AREN'T YOU GOING TO DO SOMETHING ABOUT THIS COMPUTER?

OUT OF ORDER

I MADE A SIGN. THAT ALREADY EXCEEDS MY JOB DESCRIPTION.

SCRAM!

"SCRAM"?

I NEED TO CHECK MY EMAIL.

AND I NEED TO PLAY THIS GAME TO WORK THROUGH THE VIOLENCE THAT PLAGUES MY INTERNAL WORLD.

BUT IF YOU'D RATHER I EXTERNALIZED IT...

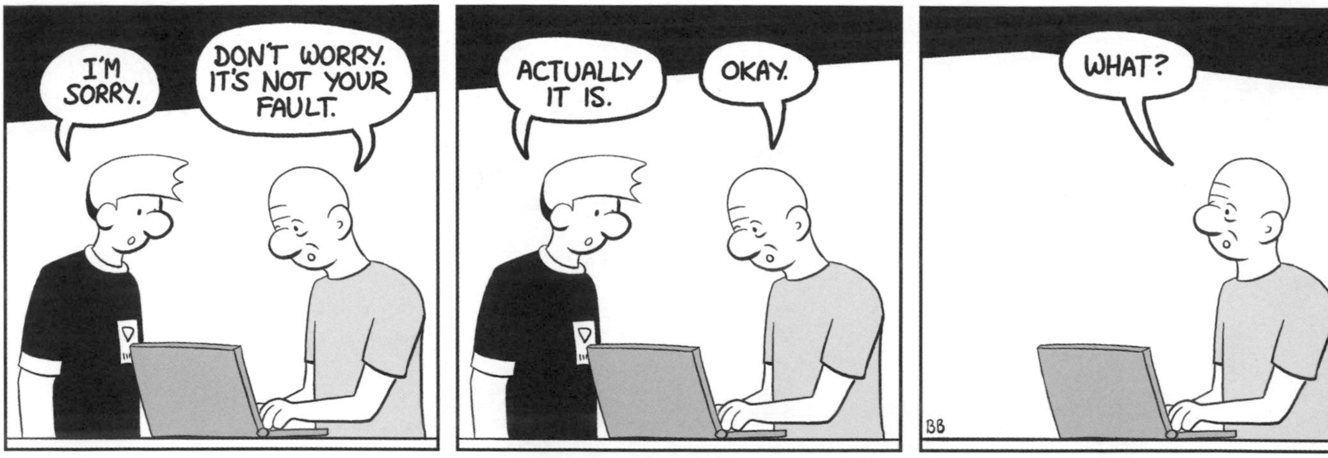
I'M SORRY.
DON'T WORRY. IT'S NOT YOUR FAULT.
ACTUALLY IT IS.
OKAY.
WHAT?
BB

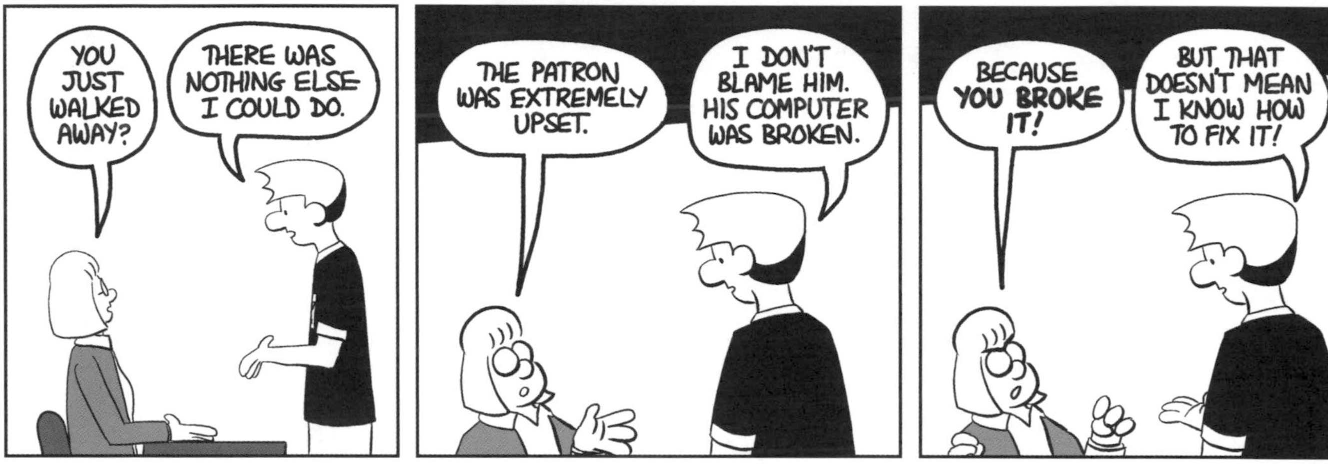
YOU JUST WALKED AWAY?
THERE WAS NOTHING ELSE I COULD DO.
THE PATRON WAS EXTREMELY UPSET.
I DON'T BLAME HIM. HIS COMPUTER WAS BROKEN.
BECAUSE YOU BROKE IT!
BUT THAT DOESN'T MEAN I KNOW HOW TO FIX IT!

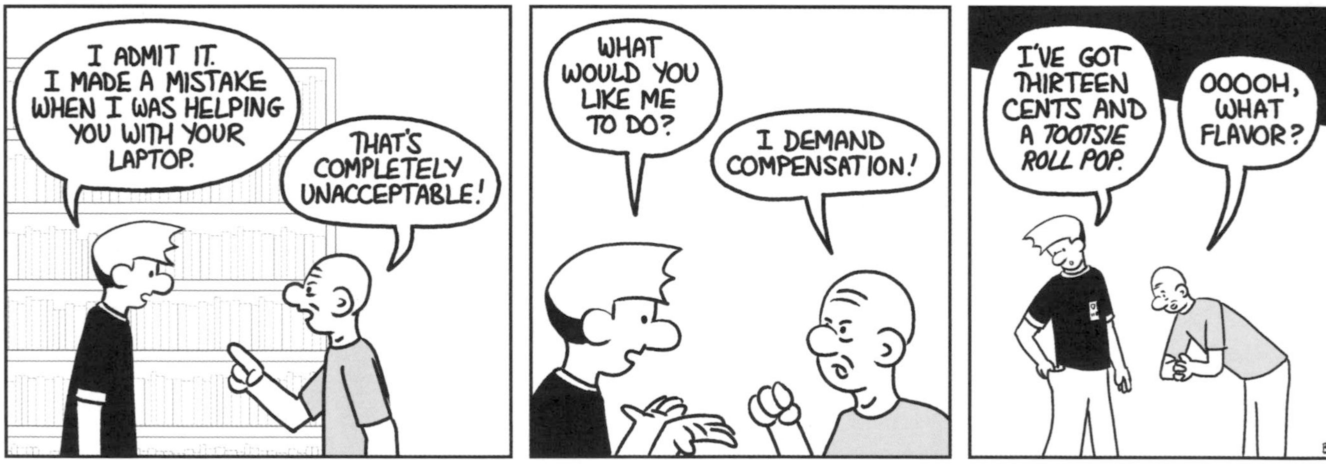
I ADMIT IT. I MADE A MISTAKE WHEN I WAS HELPING YOU WITH YOUR LAPTOP.
THAT'S COMPLETELY UNACCEPTABLE!
WHAT WOULD YOU LIKE ME TO DO?
I DEMAND COMPENSATION!
I'VE GOT THIRTEEN CENTS AND A TOOTSIE ROLL POP.
OOOOH, WHAT FLAVOR?
BB

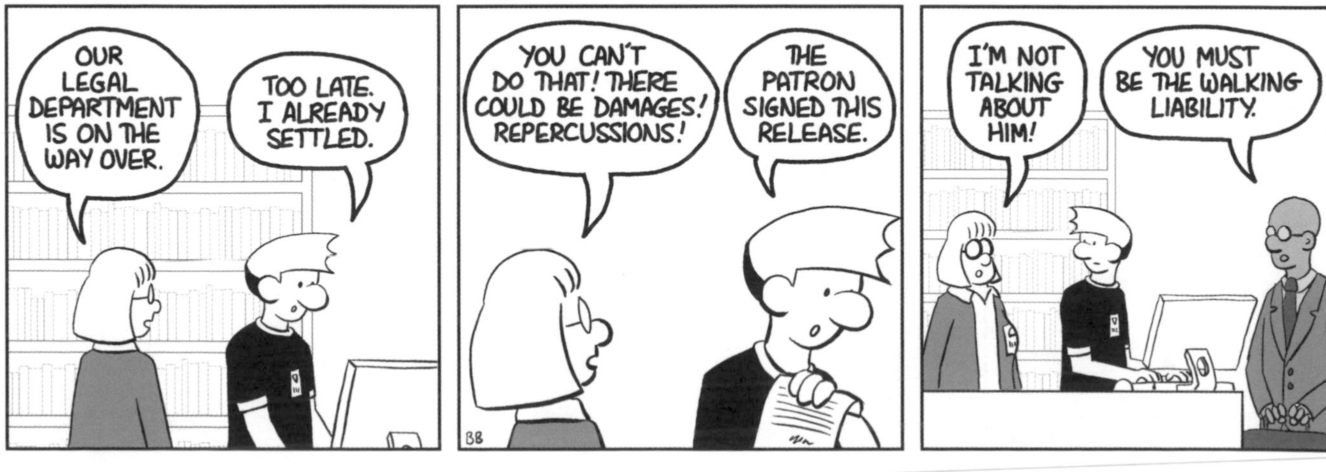
OUR LEGAL DEPARTMENT IS ON THE WAY OVER.
TOO LATE. I ALREADY SETTLED.
YOU CAN'T DO THAT! THERE COULD BE DAMAGES! REPERCUSSIONS!
THE PATRON SIGNED THIS RELEASE.
BB
I'M NOT TALKING ABOUT HIM!
YOU MUST BE THE WALKING LIABILITY.

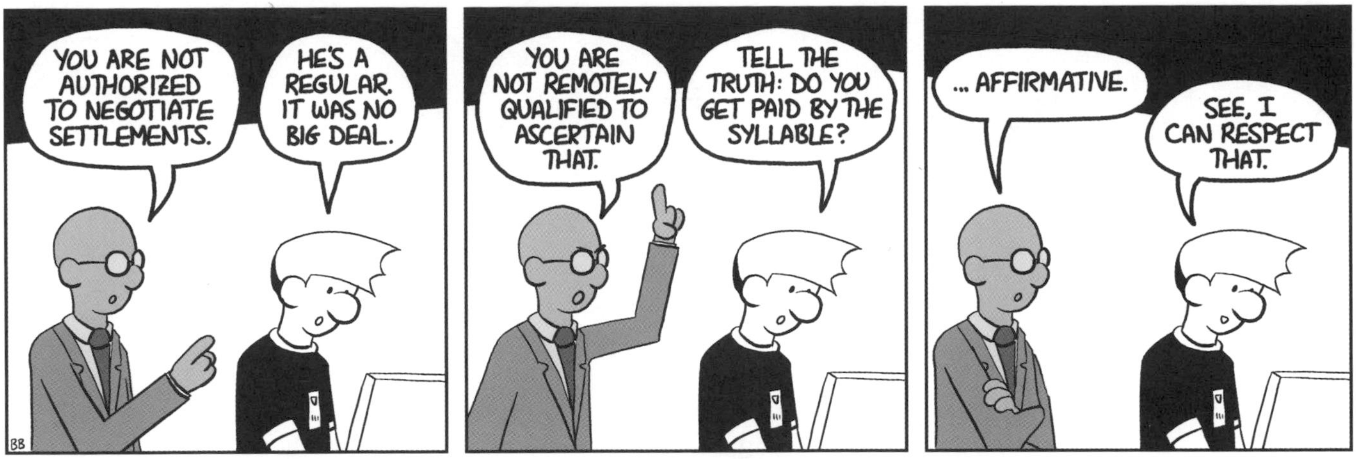
YOU ARE NOT AUTHORIZED TO NEGOTIATE SETTLEMENTS.
HE'S A REGULAR. IT WAS NO BIG DEAL.
YOU ARE NOT REMOTELY QUALIFIED TO ASCERTAIN THAT.
TELL THE TRUTH: DO YOU GET PAID BY THE SYLLABLE?
... AFFIRMATIVE.
SEE, I CAN RESPECT THAT.
BB

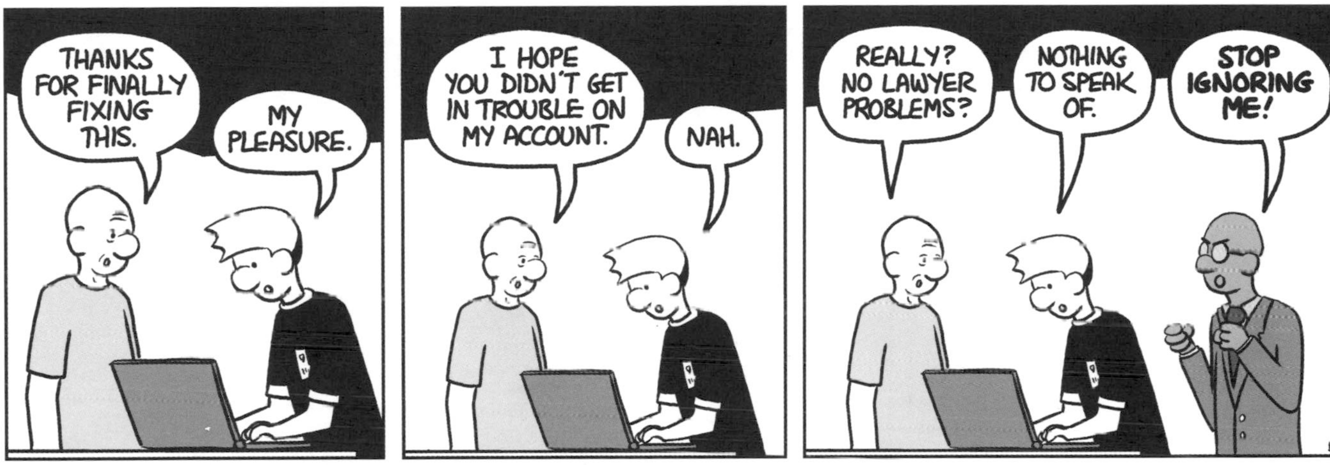
THANKS FOR FINALLY FIXING THIS.
MY PLEASURE.
I HOPE YOU DIDN'T GET IN TROUBLE ON MY ACCOUNT.
NAH.
REALLY? NO LAWYER PROBLEMS?
NOTHING TO SPEAK OF.
STOP IGNORING ME!
BB

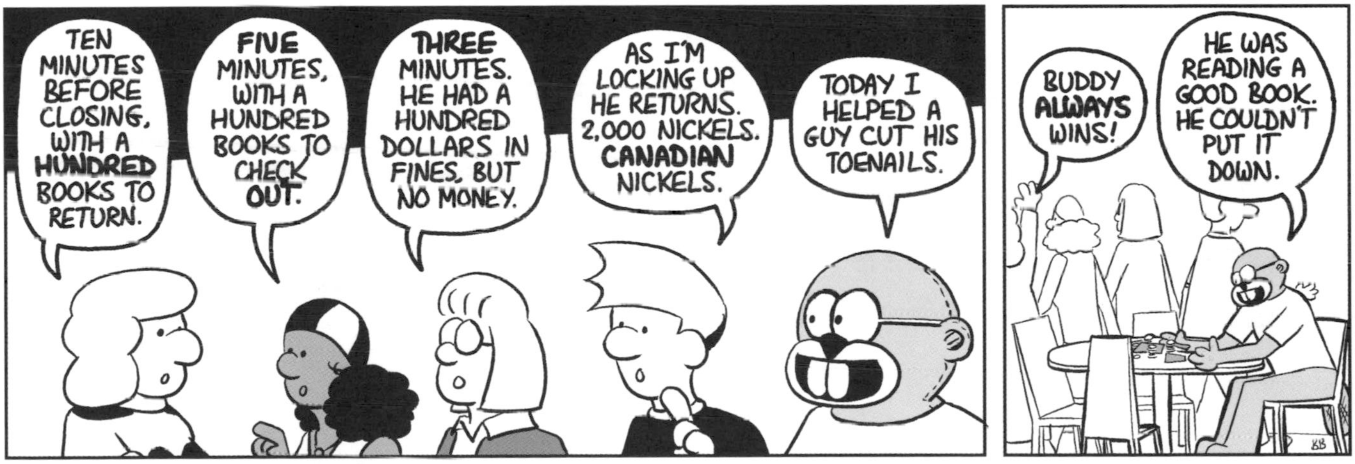
TEN MINUTES BEFORE CLOSING, WITH A **HUNDRED** BOOKS TO RETURN.
FIVE MINUTES, WITH A HUNDRED BOOKS TO CHECK **OUT**.
THREE MINUTES. HE HAD A HUNDRED DOLLARS IN FINES, BUT NO MONEY.
AS I'M LOCKING UP HE RETURNS. 2,000 NICKELS. **CANADIAN** NICKELS.
TODAY I HELPED A GUY CUT HIS TOENAILS.
BUDDY **ALWAYS** WINS!
HE WAS READING A GOOD BOOK. HE COULDN'T PUT IT DOWN.
BB

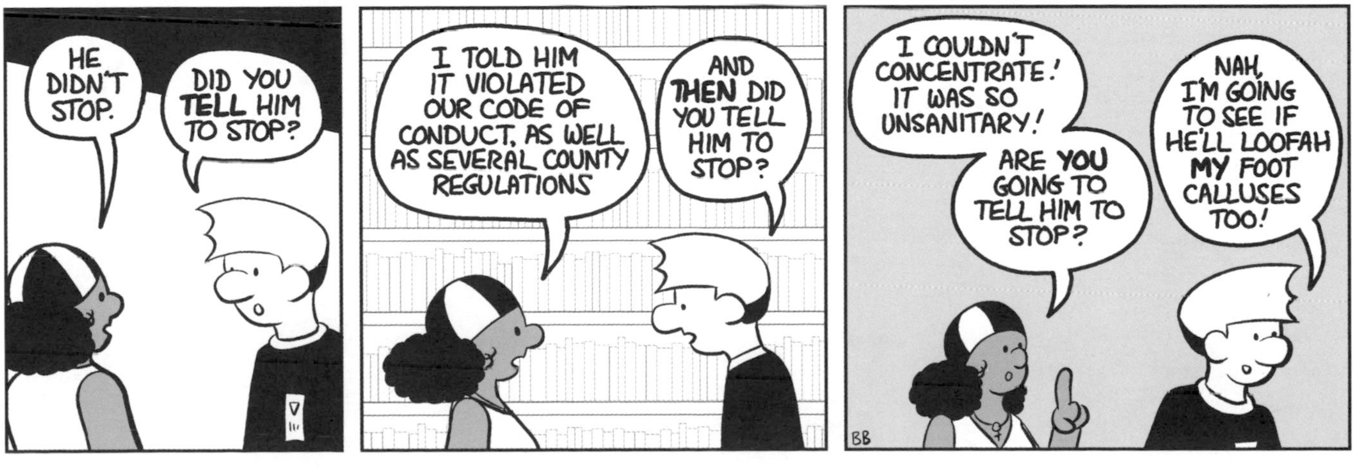
HE DIDN'T STOP.
DID YOU **TELL** HIM TO STOP?
I TOLD HIM IT VIOLATED OUR CODE OF CONDUCT, AS WELL AS SEVERAL COUNTY REGULATIONS
AND **THEN** DID YOU TELL HIM TO STOP?
I COULDN'T CONCENTRATE! IT WAS SO UNSANITARY!
ARE **YOU** GOING TO TELL HIM TO STOP?
NAH, I'M GOING TO SEE IF HE'LL LOOFAH **MY** FOOT CALLUSES TOO!
BB

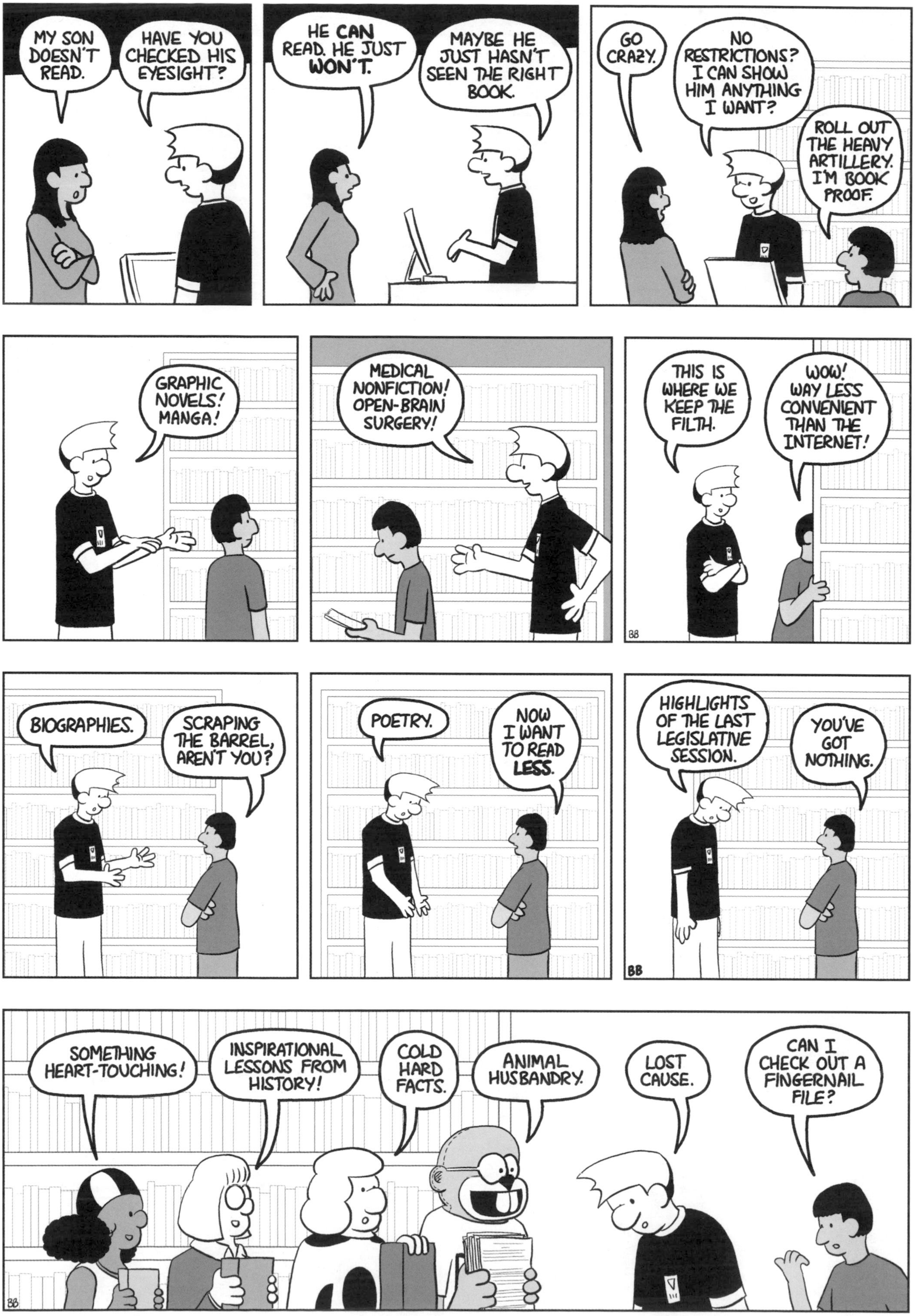
MY SON DOESN'T READ.
HAVE YOU CHECKED HIS EYESIGHT?
HE CAN READ. HE JUST WON'T.
MAYBE HE JUST HASN'T SEEN THE RIGHT BOOK.
GO CRAZY.
NO RESTRICTIONS? I CAN SHOW HIM ANYTHING I WANT?
ROLL OUT THE HEAVY ARTILLERY. I'M BOOK PROOF.
GRAPHIC NOVELS! MANGA!
MEDICAL NONFICTION! OPEN-BRAIN SURGERY!
THIS IS WHERE WE KEEP THE FILTH.
WOW! WAY LESS CONVENIENT THAN THE INTERNET!
BB
BIOGRAPHIES.
SCRAPING THE BARREL, AREN'T YOU?
POETRY.
NOW I WANT TO READ LESS.
HIGHLIGHTS OF THE LAST LEGISLATIVE SESSION.
YOU'VE GOT NOTHING.
BB
SOMETHING HEART-TOUCHING!
INSPIRATIONAL LESSONS FROM HISTORY!
COLD HARD FACTS.
ANIMAL HUSBANDRY.
LOST CAUSE.
CAN I CHECK OUT A FINGERNAIL FILE?
BB

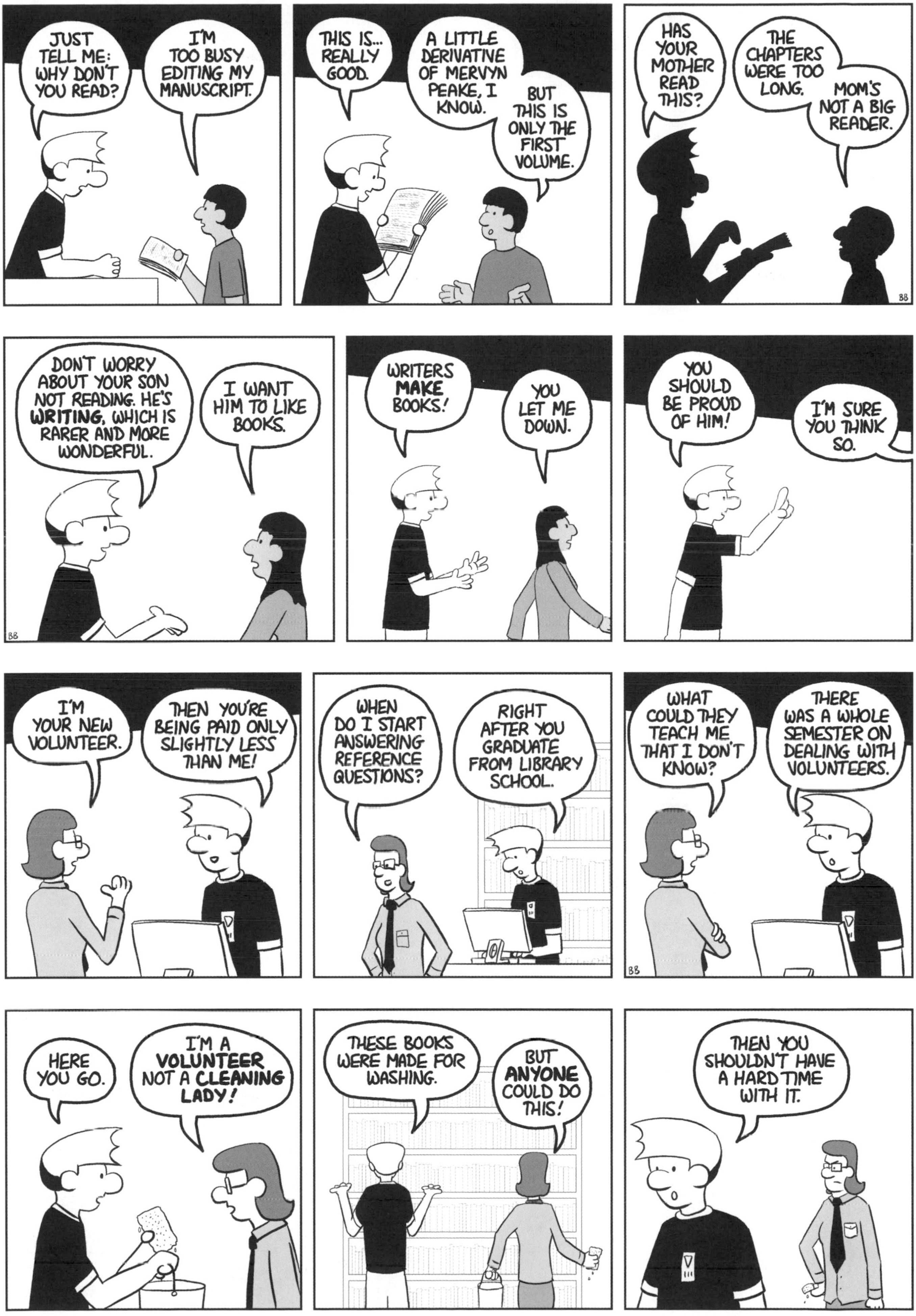
JUST TELL ME: WHY DON'T YOU READ?
I'M TOO BUSY EDITING MY MANUSCRIPT.
THIS IS... REALLY GOOD.
A LITTLE DERIVATIVE OF MERVYN PEAKE, I KNOW.
BUT THIS IS ONLY THE FIRST VOLUME.
HAS YOUR MOTHER READ THIS?
THE CHAPTERS WERE TOO LONG.
MOM'S NOT A BIG READER.
BB
DON'T WORRY ABOUT YOUR SON NOT READING. HE'S **WRITING**, WHICH IS RARER AND MORE WONDERFUL.
I WANT HIM TO LIKE BOOKS.
BB
WRITERS **MAKE** BOOKS!
YOU LET ME DOWN.
YOU SHOULD BE PROUD OF HIM!
I'M SURE YOU THINK SO.
I'M YOUR NEW VOLUNTEER.
THEN YOU'RE BEING PAID ONLY SLIGHTLY LESS THAN ME!
WHEN DO I START ANSWERING REFERENCE QUESTIONS?
RIGHT AFTER YOU GRADUATE FROM LIBRARY SCHOOL.
WHAT COULD THEY TEACH ME THAT I DON'T KNOW?
THERE WAS A WHOLE SEMESTER ON DEALING WITH VOLUNTEERS.
BB
HERE YOU GO.
I'M A **VOLUNTEER** NOT A **CLEANING LADY**!
THESE BOOKS WERE MADE FOR WASHING.
BUT **ANYONE** COULD DO THIS!
THEN YOU SHOULDN'T HAVE A HARD TIME WITH IT.

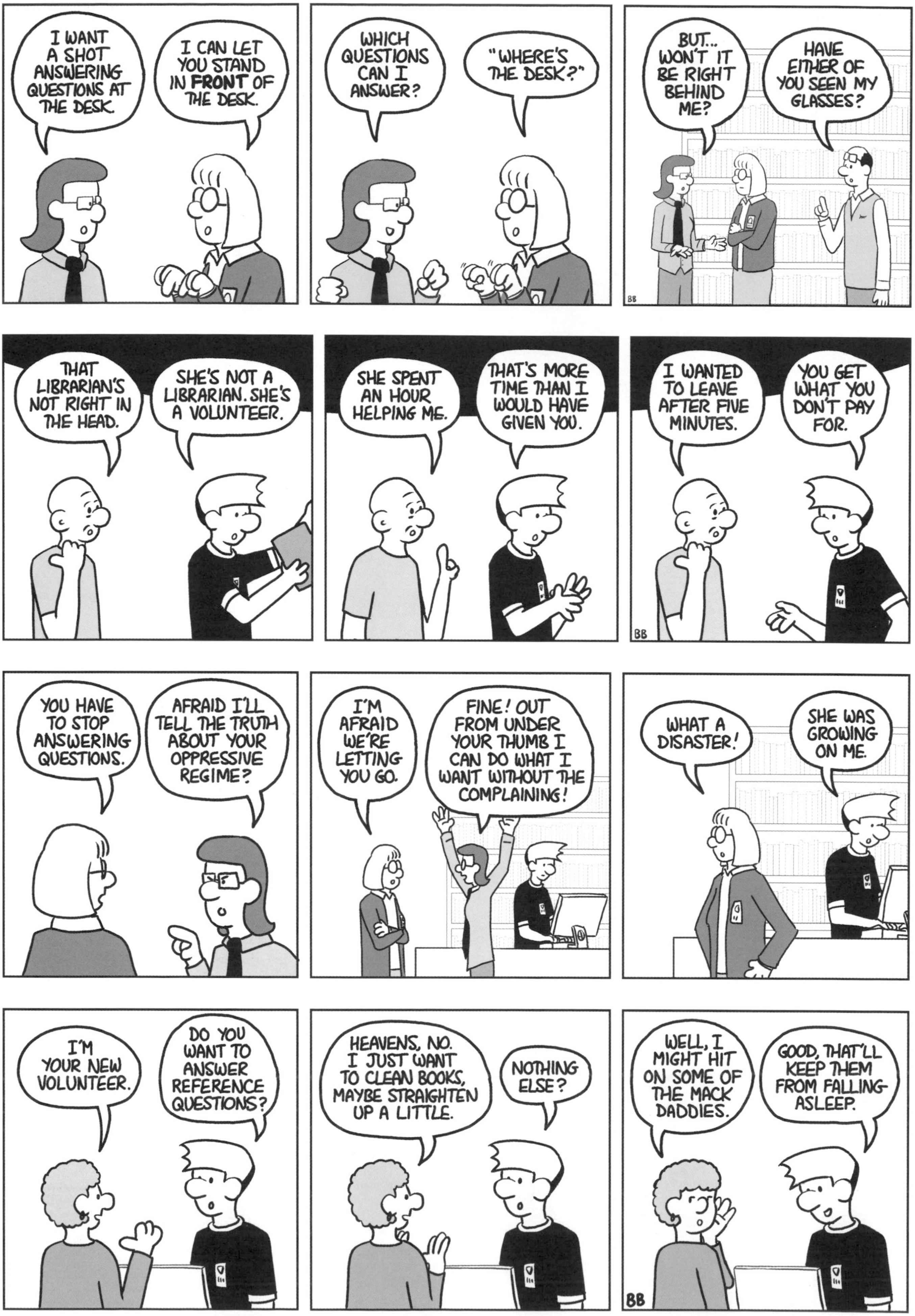
I WANT A SHOT ANSWERING QUESTIONS AT THE DESK.
I CAN LET YOU STAND IN FRONT OF THE DESK.
WHICH QUESTIONS CAN I ANSWER?
"WHERE'S THE DESK?"
BUT... WON'T IT BE RIGHT BEHIND ME?
HAVE EITHER OF YOU SEEN MY GLASSES?
BB
THAT LIBRARIAN'S NOT RIGHT IN THE HEAD.
SHE'S NOT A LIBRARIAN. SHE'S A VOLUNTEER.
SHE SPENT AN HOUR HELPING ME.
THAT'S MORE TIME THAN I WOULD HAVE GIVEN YOU.
I WANTED TO LEAVE AFTER FIVE MINUTES.
YOU GET WHAT YOU DON'T PAY FOR.
BB
YOU HAVE TO STOP ANSWERING QUESTIONS.
AFRAID I'LL TELL THE TRUTH ABOUT YOUR OPPRESSIVE REGIME?
I'M AFRAID WE'RE LETTING YOU GO.
FINE! OUT FROM UNDER YOUR THUMB I CAN DO WHAT I WANT WITHOUT THE COMPLAINING!
WHAT A DISASTER!
SHE WAS GROWING ON ME.
I'M YOUR NEW VOLUNTEER.
DO YOU WANT TO ANSWER REFERENCE QUESTIONS?
HEAVENS, NO. I JUST WANT TO CLEAN BOOKS, MAYBE STRAIGHTEN UP A LITTLE.
NOTHING ELSE?
WELL, I MIGHT HIT ON SOME OF THE MACK DADDIES.
GOOD, THAT'LL KEEP THEM FROM FALLING ASLEEP.
BB

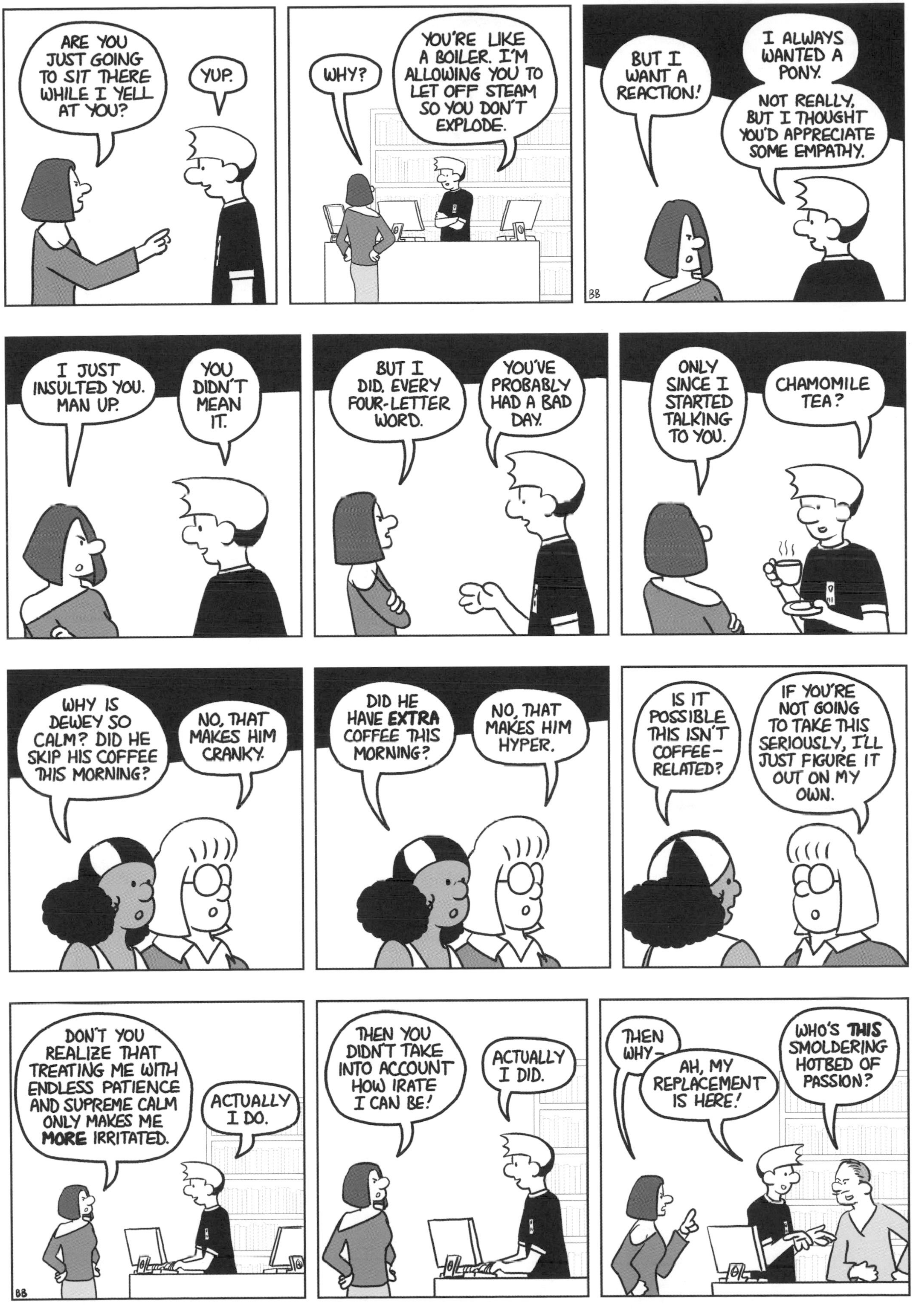

ARE YOU JUST GOING TO SIT THERE WHILE I YELL AT YOU?
YUP.
WHY?
YOU'RE LIKE A BOILER. I'M ALLOWING YOU TO LET OFF STEAM SO YOU DON'T EXPLODE.
BUT I WANT A REACTION!
I ALWAYS WANTED A PONY.
NOT REALLY, BUT I THOUGHT YOU'D APPRECIATE SOME EMPATHY.
BB
I JUST INSULTED YOU. MAN UP.
YOU DIDN'T MEAN IT.
BUT I DID. EVERY FOUR-LETTER WORD.
YOU'VE PROBABLY HAD A BAD DAY.
ONLY SINCE I STARTED TALKING TO YOU.
CHAMOMILE TEA?
WHY IS DEWEY SO CALM? DID HE SKIP HIS COFFEE THIS MORNING?
NO, THAT MAKES HIM CRANKY.
DID HE HAVE **EXTRA** COFFEE THIS MORNING?
NO, THAT MAKES HIM HYPER.
IS IT POSSIBLE THIS ISN'T COFFEE-RELATED?
IF YOU'RE NOT GOING TO TAKE THIS SERIOUSLY, I'LL JUST FIGURE IT OUT ON MY OWN.
DON'T YOU REALIZE THAT TREATING ME WITH ENDLESS PATIENCE AND SUPREME CALM ONLY MAKES ME **MORE** IRRITATED.
ACTUALLY I DO.
BB
THEN YOU DIDN'T TAKE INTO ACCOUNT HOW IRATE I CAN BE!
ACTUALLY I DID.
THEN WHY—
AH, MY REPLACEMENT IS HERE!
WHO'S **THIS** SMOLDERING HOTBED OF PASSION?

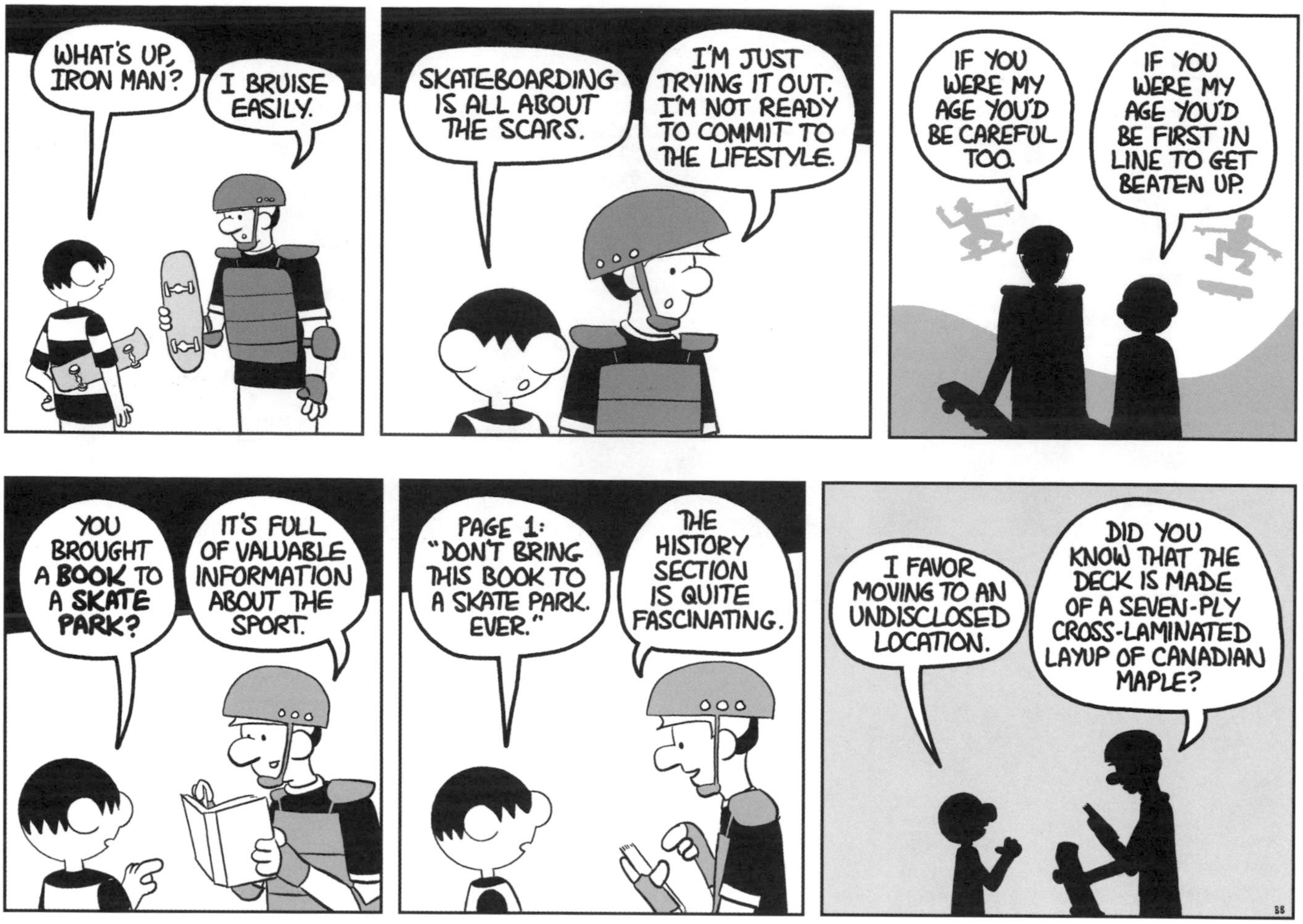
WHAT'S UP, IRON MAN?
I BRUISE EASILY.
SKATEBOARDING IS ALL ABOUT THE SCARS.
I'M JUST TRYING IT OUT. I'M NOT READY TO COMMIT TO THE LIFESTYLE.
IF YOU WERE MY AGE YOU'D BE CAREFUL TOO.
IF YOU WERE MY AGE YOU'D BE FIRST IN LINE TO GET BEATEN UP.
YOU BROUGHT A **BOOK** TO A **SKATE PARK**?
IT'S FULL OF VALUABLE INFORMATION ABOUT THE SPORT.
PAGE 1: "DON'T BRING THIS BOOK TO A SKATE PARK. EVER."
THE HISTORY SECTION IS QUITE FASCINATING.
I FAVOR MOVING TO AN UNDISCLOSED LOCATION.
DID YOU KNOW THAT THE DECK IS MADE OF A SEVEN-PLY CROSS-LAMINATED LAYUP OF CANADIAN MAPLE?
BB

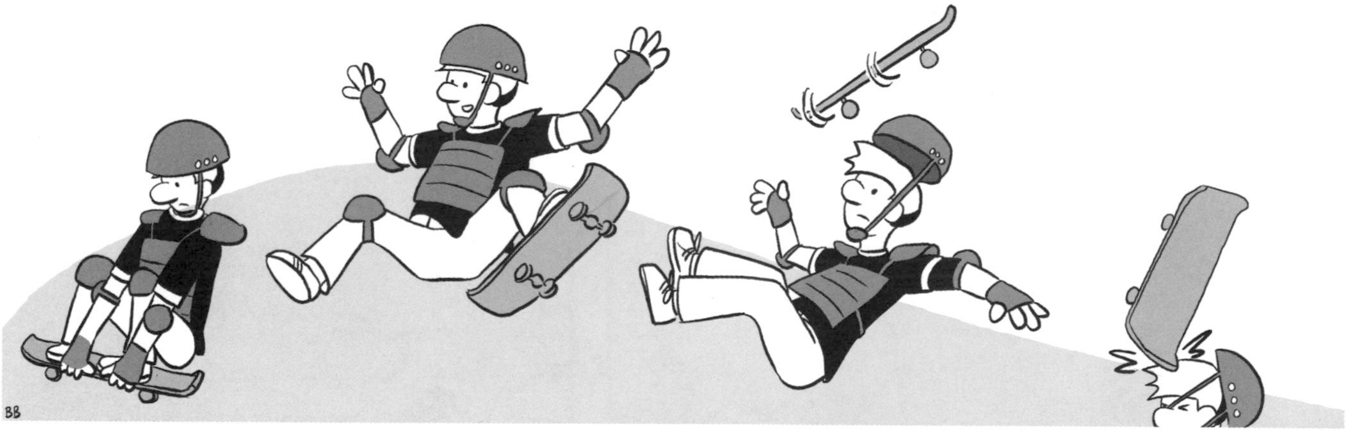
BB

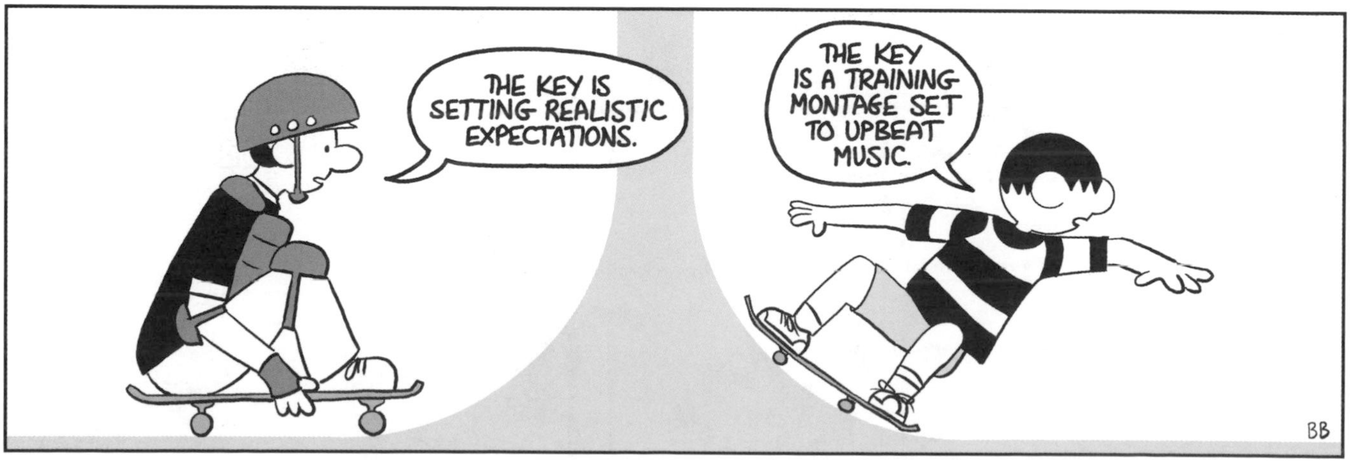
THE KEY IS SETTING REALISTIC EXPECTATIONS.
THE KEY IS A TRAINING MONTAGE SET TO UPBEAT MUSIC.
BB

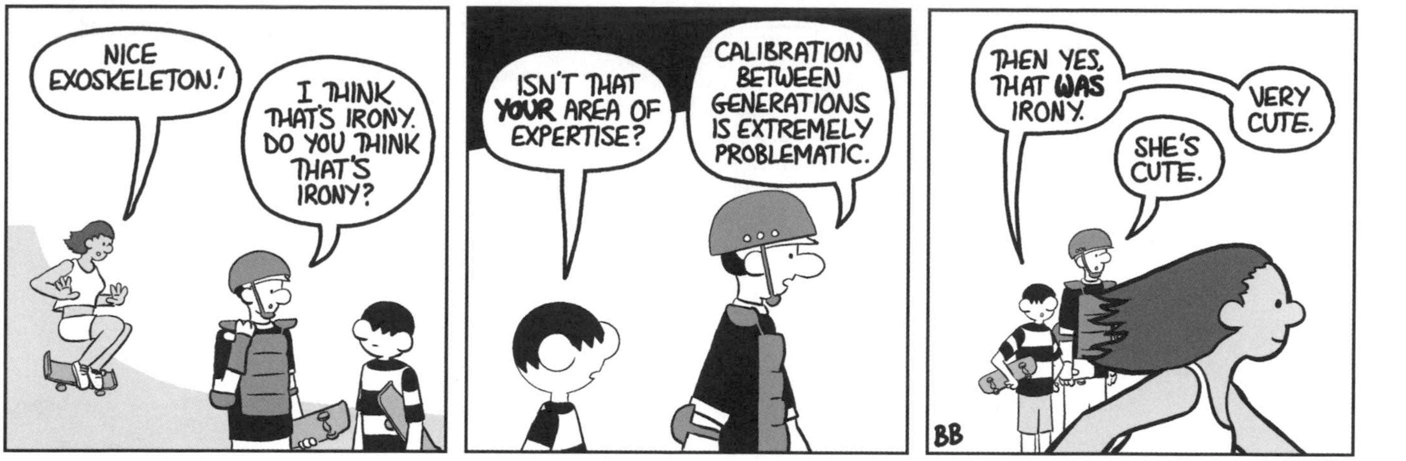
NICE EXOSKELETON!
I THINK THAT'S IRONY. DO YOU THINK THAT'S IRONY?
ISN'T THAT **YOUR** AREA OF EXPERTISE?
CALIBRATION BETWEEN GENERATIONS IS EXTREMELY PROBLEMATIC.
THEN YES, THAT **WAS** IRONY.
VERY CUTE.
SHE'S CUTE.
BB

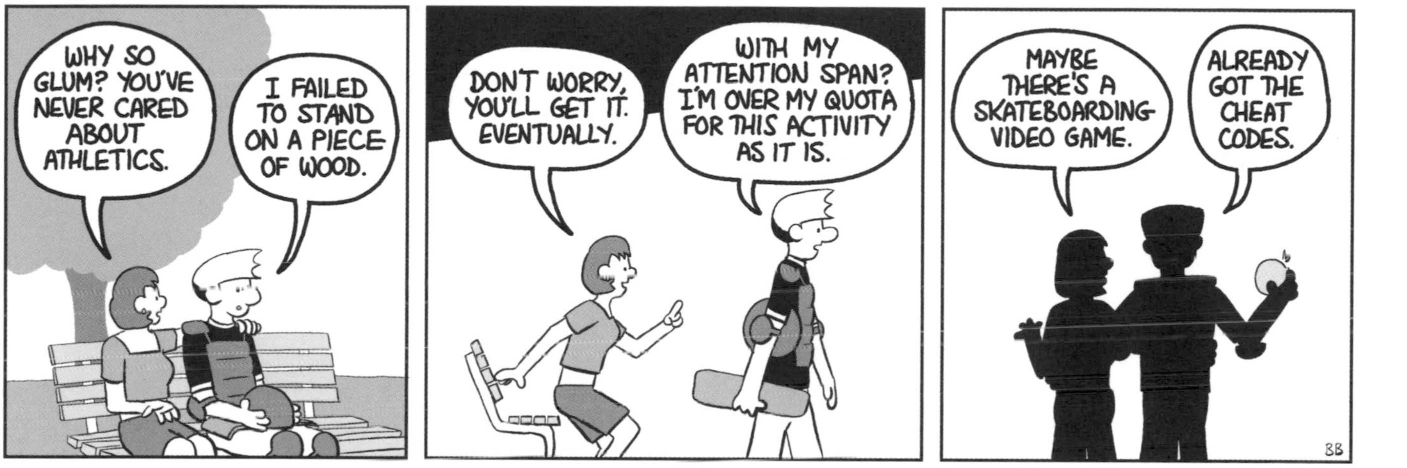
WHY SO GLUM? YOU'VE NEVER CARED ABOUT ATHLETICS.
I FAILED TO STAND ON A PIECE OF WOOD.
DON'T WORRY, YOU'LL GET IT. EVENTUALLY.
WITH MY ATTENTION SPAN? I'M OVER MY QUOTA FOR THIS ACTIVITY AS IT IS.
MAYBE THERE'S A SKATEBOARDING VIDEO GAME.
ALREADY GOT THE CHEAT CODES.
BB

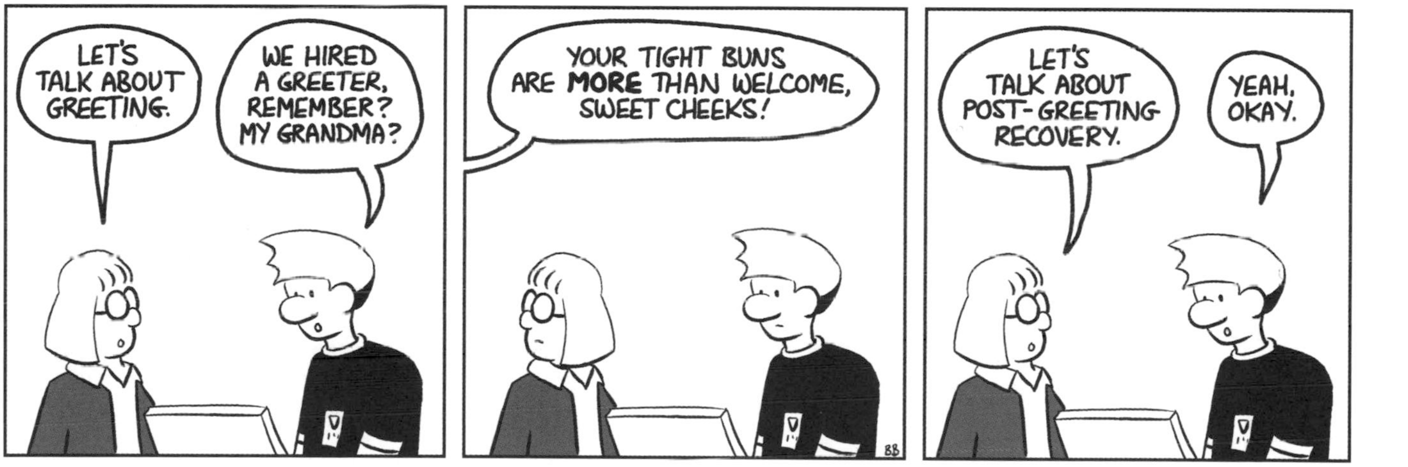
LET'S TALK ABOUT GREETING.
WE HIRED A GREETER, REMEMBER? MY GRANDMA?
YOUR TIGHT BUNS ARE **MORE** THAN WELCOME, SWEET CHEEKS!
BB
LET'S TALK ABOUT POST-GREETING RECOVERY.
YEAH, OKAY.

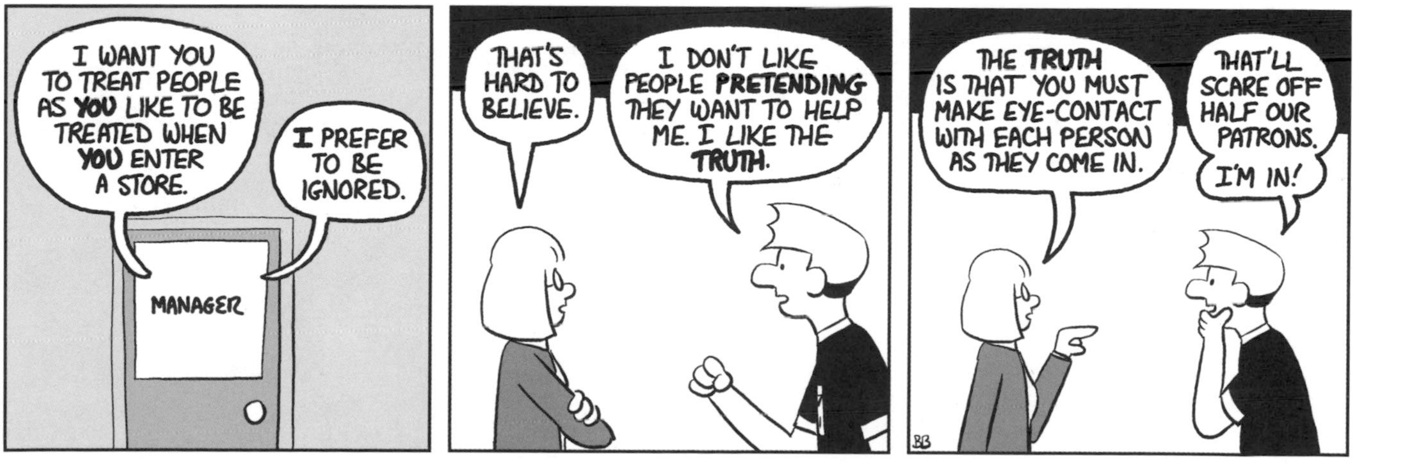
I WANT YOU TO TREAT PEOPLE AS **YOU** LIKE TO BE TREATED WHEN **YOU** ENTER A STORE.
I PREFER TO BE IGNORED.
MANAGER
THAT'S HARD TO BELIEVE.
I DON'T LIKE PEOPLE **PRETENDING** THEY WANT TO HELP ME. I LIKE THE **TRUTH**.
THE **TRUTH** IS THAT YOU MUST MAKE EYE-CONTACT WITH EACH PERSON AS THEY COME IN.
THAT'LL SCARE OFF HALF OUR PATRONS.
I'M IN!
BB

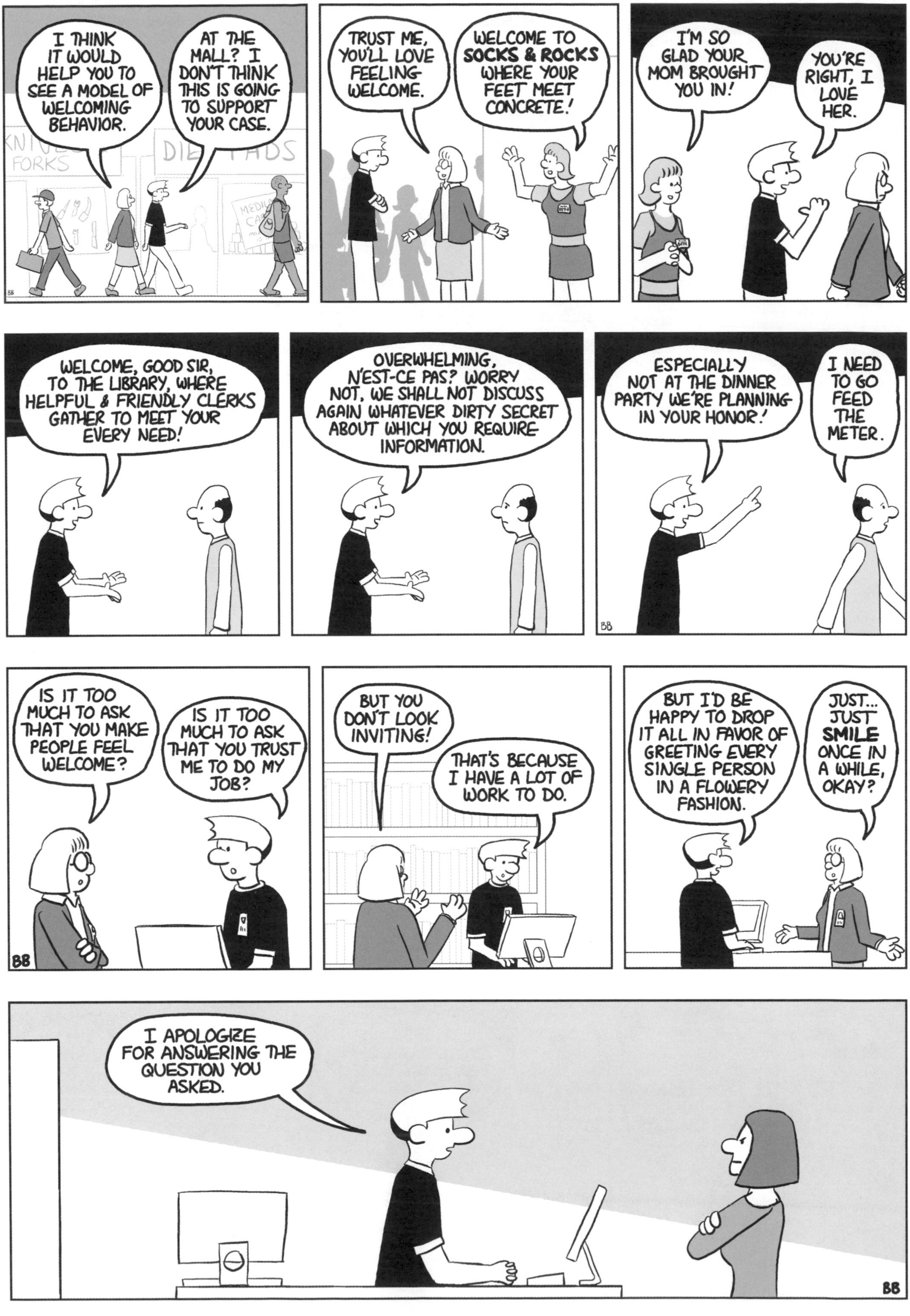
I THINK IT WOULD HELP YOU TO SEE A MODEL OF WELCOMING BEHAVIOR.
AT THE MALL? I DON'T THINK THIS IS GOING TO SUPPORT YOUR CASE.
TRUST ME, YOU'LL LOVE FEELING WELCOME.
WELCOME TO **SOCKS & ROCKS** WHERE YOUR FEET MEET CONCRETE!
I'M SO GLAD YOUR MOM BROUGHT YOU IN!
YOU'RE RIGHT, I LOVE HER.
WELCOME, GOOD SIR, TO THE LIBRARY, WHERE HELPFUL & FRIENDLY CLERKS GATHER TO MEET YOUR EVERY NEED!
OVERWHELMING, N'EST-CE PAS? WORRY NOT, WE SHALL NOT DISCUSS AGAIN WHATEVER DIRTY SECRET ABOUT WHICH YOU REQUIRE INFORMATION.
ESPECIALLY NOT AT THE DINNER PARTY WE'RE PLANNING IN YOUR HONOR!
I NEED TO GO FEED THE METER.
IS IT TOO MUCH TO ASK THAT YOU MAKE PEOPLE FEEL WELCOME?
IS IT TOO MUCH TO ASK THAT YOU TRUST ME TO DO MY JOB?
BUT YOU DON'T LOOK INVITING!
THAT'S BECAUSE I HAVE A LOT OF WORK TO DO.
BUT I'D BE HAPPY TO DROP IT ALL IN FAVOR OF GREETING EVERY SINGLE PERSON IN A FLOWERY FASHION.
JUST... JUST **SMILE** ONCE IN A WHILE, OKAY?
I APOLOGIZE FOR ANSWERING THE QUESTION YOU ASKED.

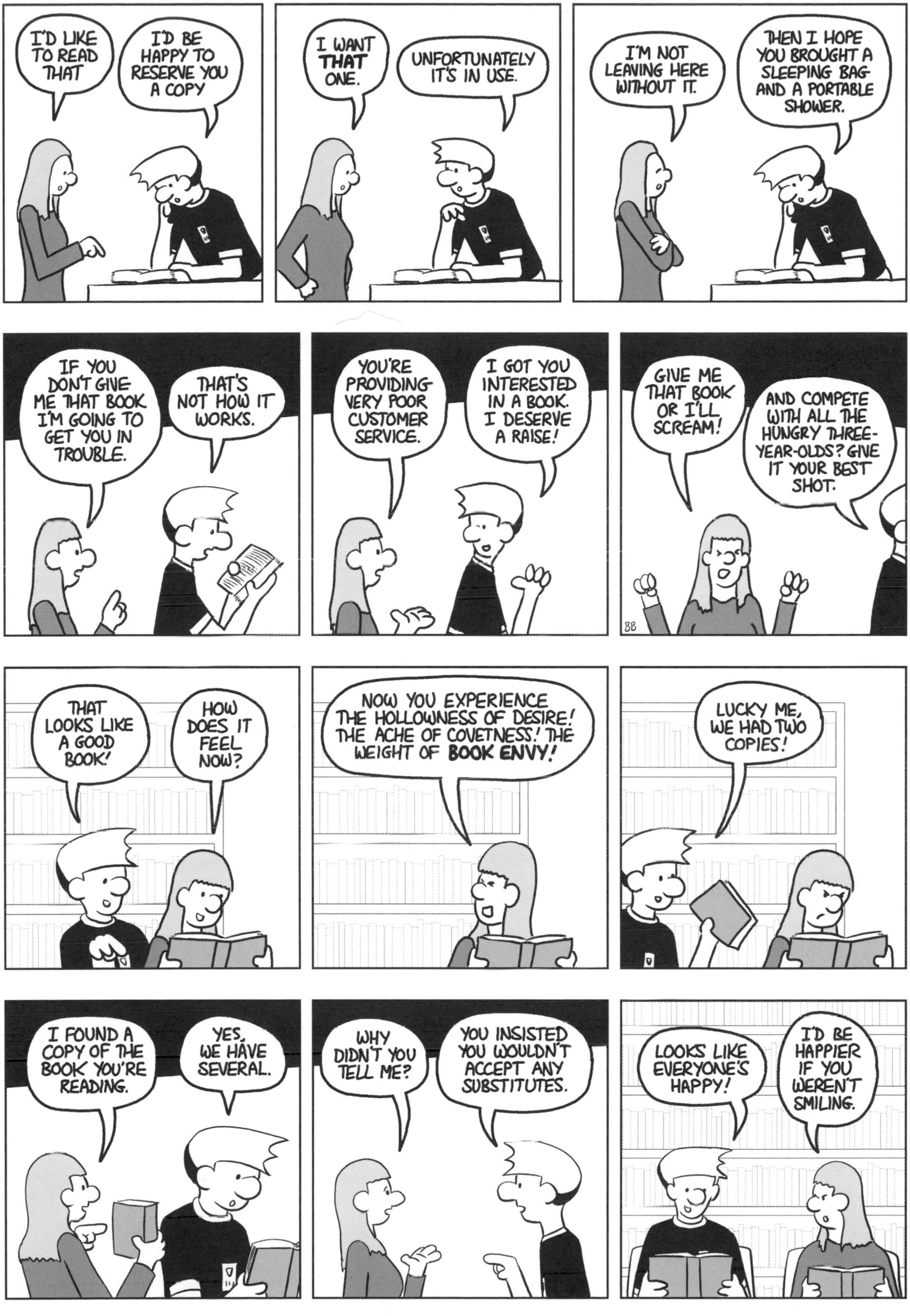
I'D LIKE TO READ THAT
I'D BE HAPPY TO RESERVE YOU A COPY
I WANT **THAT** ONE.
UNFORTUNATELY IT'S IN USE.
I'M NOT LEAVING HERE WITHOUT IT.
THEN I HOPE YOU BROUGHT A SLEEPING BAG AND A PORTABLE SHOWER.
IF YOU DON'T GIVE ME THAT BOOK I'M GOING TO GET YOU IN TROUBLE.
THAT'S NOT HOW IT WORKS.
YOU'RE PROVIDING VERY POOR CUSTOMER SERVICE.
I GOT YOU INTERESTED IN A BOOK. I DESERVE A RAISE!
GIVE ME THAT BOOK OR I'LL SCREAM!
AND COMPETE WITH ALL THE HUNGRY THREE-YEAR-OLDS? GIVE IT YOUR BEST SHOT.
BB
THAT LOOKS LIKE A GOOD BOOK!
HOW DOES IT FEEL NOW?
NOW YOU EXPERIENCE THE HOLLOWNESS OF DESIRE! THE ACHE OF COVETNESS! THE WEIGHT OF **BOOK ENVY**!
LUCKY ME, WE HAD TWO COPIES!
I FOUND A COPY OF THE BOOK YOU'RE READING.
YES, WE HAVE SEVERAL.
WHY DIDN'T YOU TELL ME?
YOU INSISTED YOU WOULDN'T ACCEPT ANY SUBSTITUTES.
LOOKS LIKE EVERYONE'S HAPPY!
I'D BE HAPPIER IF YOU WEREN'T SMILING.

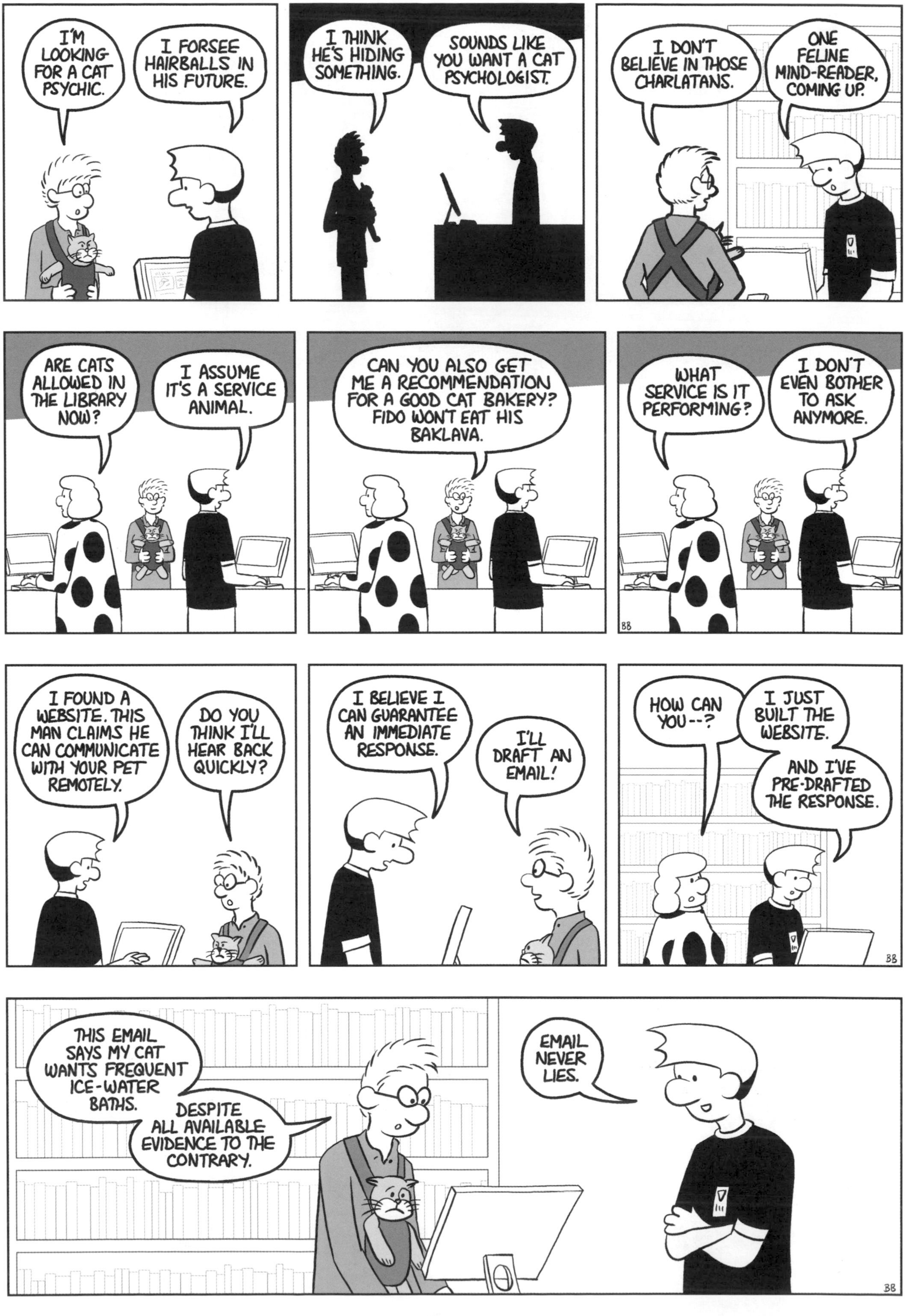

I'M LOOKING FOR A CAT PSYCHIC.
I FORSEE HAIRBALLS IN HIS FUTURE.
I THINK HE'S HIDING SOMETHING.
SOUNDS LIKE YOU WANT A CAT PSYCHOLOGIST.
I DON'T BELIEVE IN THOSE CHARLATANS.
ONE FELINE MIND-READER, COMING UP.
ARE CATS ALLOWED IN THE LIBRARY NOW?
I ASSUME IT'S A SERVICE ANIMAL.
CAN YOU ALSO GET ME A RECOMMENDATION FOR A GOOD CAT BAKERY? FIDO WON'T EAT HIS BAKLAVA.
WHAT SERVICE IS IT PERFORMING?
I DON'T EVEN BOTHER TO ASK ANYMORE.
BB
I FOUND A WEBSITE. THIS MAN CLAIMS HE CAN COMMUNICATE WITH YOUR PET REMOTELY.
DO YOU THINK I'LL HEAR BACK QUICKLY?
I BELIEVE I CAN GUARANTEE AN IMMEDIATE RESPONSE.
I'LL DRAFT AN EMAIL!
HOW CAN YOU--?
I JUST BUILT THE WEBSITE.
AND I'VE PRE-DRAFTED THE RESPONSE.
BB
THIS EMAIL SAYS MY CAT WANTS FREQUENT ICE-WATER BATHS.
DESPITE ALL AVAILABLE EVIDENCE TO THE CONTRARY.
EMAIL NEVER LIES.
BB

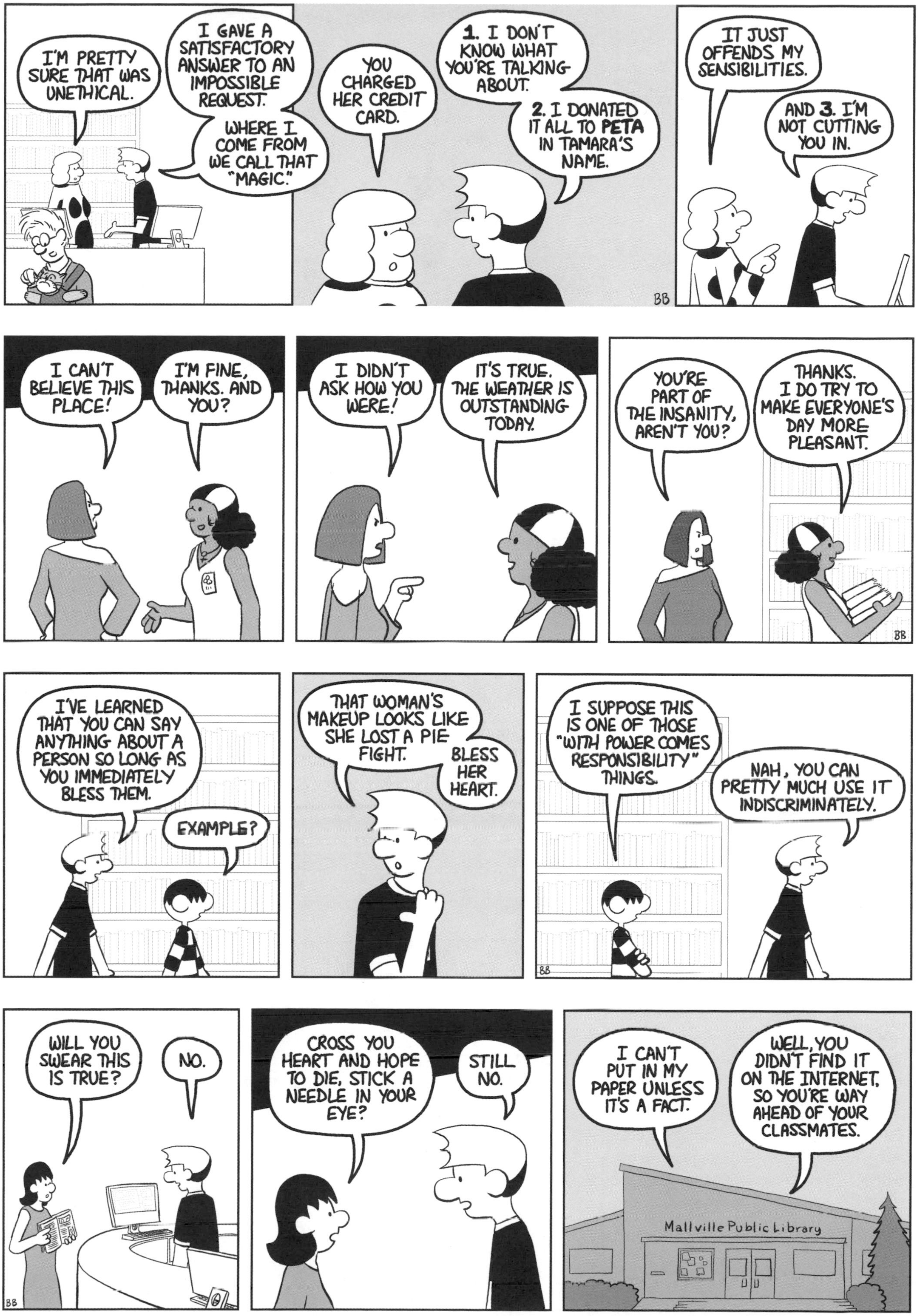
I'M PRETTY SURE THAT WAS UNETHICAL.
I GAVE A SATISFACTORY ANSWER TO AN IMPOSSIBLE REQUEST.
WHERE I COME FROM WE CALL THAT "MAGIC."
YOU CHARGED HER CREDIT CARD.
1. I DON'T KNOW WHAT YOU'RE TALKING ABOUT.
2. I DONATED IT ALL TO PETA IN TAMARA'S NAME.
IT JUST OFFENDS MY SENSIBILITIES.
AND 3. I'M NOT CUTTING YOU IN.
BB
I CAN'T BELIEVE THIS PLACE!
I'M FINE, THANKS. AND YOU?
I DIDN'T ASK HOW YOU WERE!
IT'S TRUE. THE WEATHER IS OUTSTANDING TODAY.
YOU'RE PART OF THE INSANITY, AREN'T YOU?
THANKS. I DO TRY TO MAKE EVERYONE'S DAY MORE PLEASANT.
BB
I'VE LEARNED THAT YOU CAN SAY ANYTHING ABOUT A PERSON SO LONG AS YOU IMMEDIATELY BLESS THEM.
EXAMPLE?
THAT WOMAN'S MAKEUP LOOKS LIKE SHE LOST A PIE FIGHT.
BLESS HER HEART.
I SUPPOSE THIS IS ONE OF THOSE "WITH POWER COMES RESPONSIBILITY" THINGS.
NAH, YOU CAN PRETTY MUCH USE IT INDISCRIMINATELY.
BB
WILL YOU SWEAR THIS IS TRUE?
NO.
CROSS YOU HEART AND HOPE TO DIE, STICK A NEEDLE IN YOUR EYE?
STILL NO.
I CAN'T PUT IN MY PAPER UNLESS IT'S A FACT.
WELL, YOU DIDN'T FIND IT ON THE INTERNET, SO YOU'RE WAY AHEAD OF YOUR CLASSMATES.
Mallville Public Library
BB

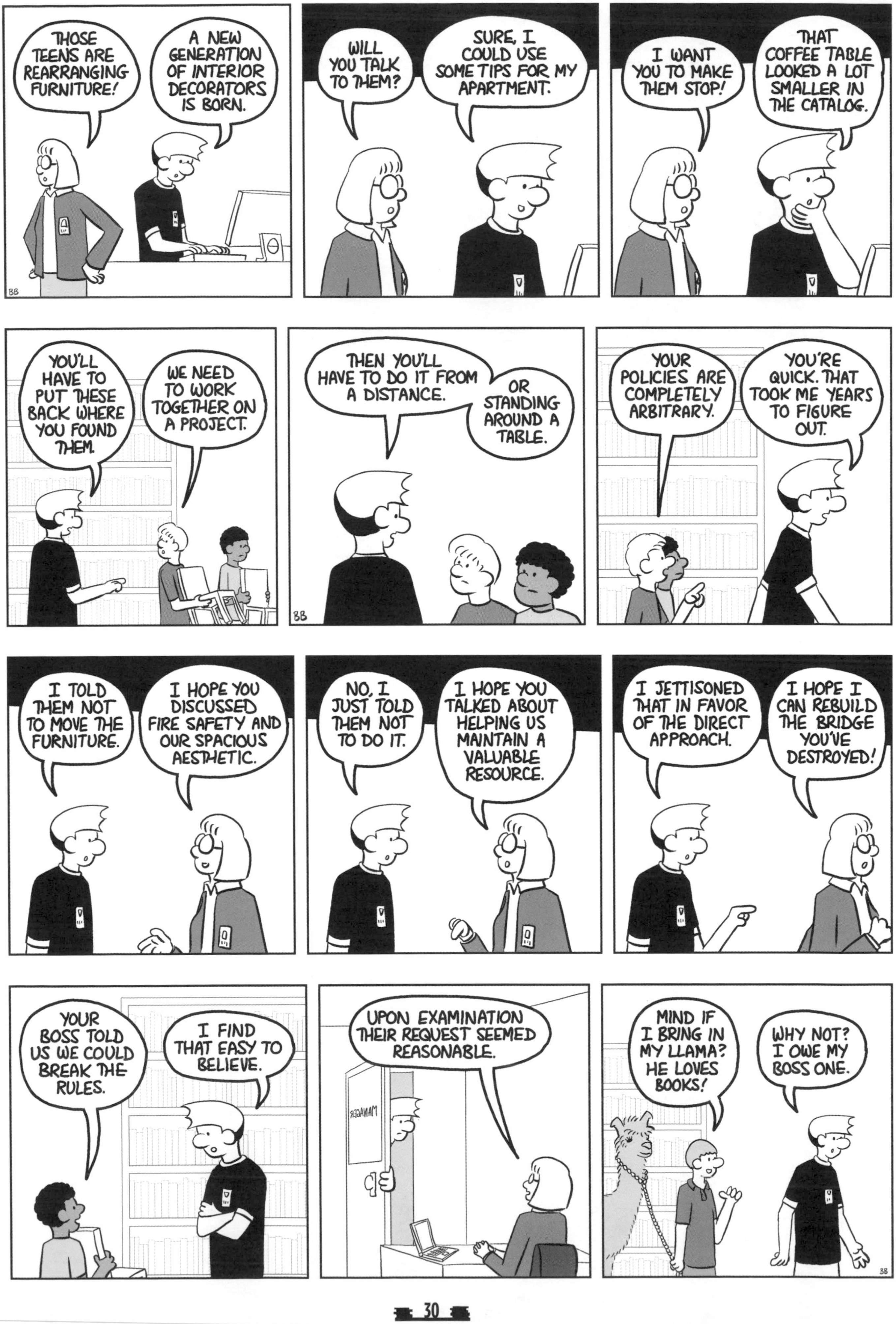
THOSE TEENS ARE REARRANGING FURNITURE!
A NEW GENERATION OF INTERIOR DECORATORS IS BORN.
WILL YOU TALK TO THEM?
SURE, I COULD USE SOME TIPS FOR MY APARTMENT.
I WANT YOU TO MAKE THEM STOP!
THAT COFFEE TABLE LOOKED A LOT SMALLER IN THE CATALOG.
YOU'LL HAVE TO PUT THESE BACK WHERE YOU FOUND THEM.
WE NEED TO WORK TOGETHER ON A PROJECT.
THEN YOU'LL HAVE TO DO IT FROM A DISTANCE.
OR STANDING AROUND A TABLE.
YOUR POLICIES ARE COMPLETELY ARBITRARY.
YOU'RE QUICK. THAT TOOK ME YEARS TO FIGURE OUT.
I TOLD THEM NOT TO MOVE THE FURNITURE.
I HOPE YOU DISCUSSED FIRE SAFETY AND OUR SPACIOUS AESTHETIC.
NO, I JUST TOLD THEM NOT TO DO IT.
I HOPE YOU TALKED ABOUT HELPING US MAINTAIN A VALUABLE RESOURCE.
I JETTISONED THAT IN FAVOR OF THE DIRECT APPROACH.
I HOPE I CAN REBUILD THE BRIDGE YOU'VE DESTROYED!
YOUR BOSS TOLD US WE COULD BREAK THE RULES.
I FIND THAT EASY TO BELIEVE.
MANAGER
UPON EXAMINATION THEIR REQUEST SEEMED REASONABLE.
MIND IF I BRING IN MY LLAMA? HE LOVES BOOKS!
WHY NOT? I OWE MY BOSS ONE.

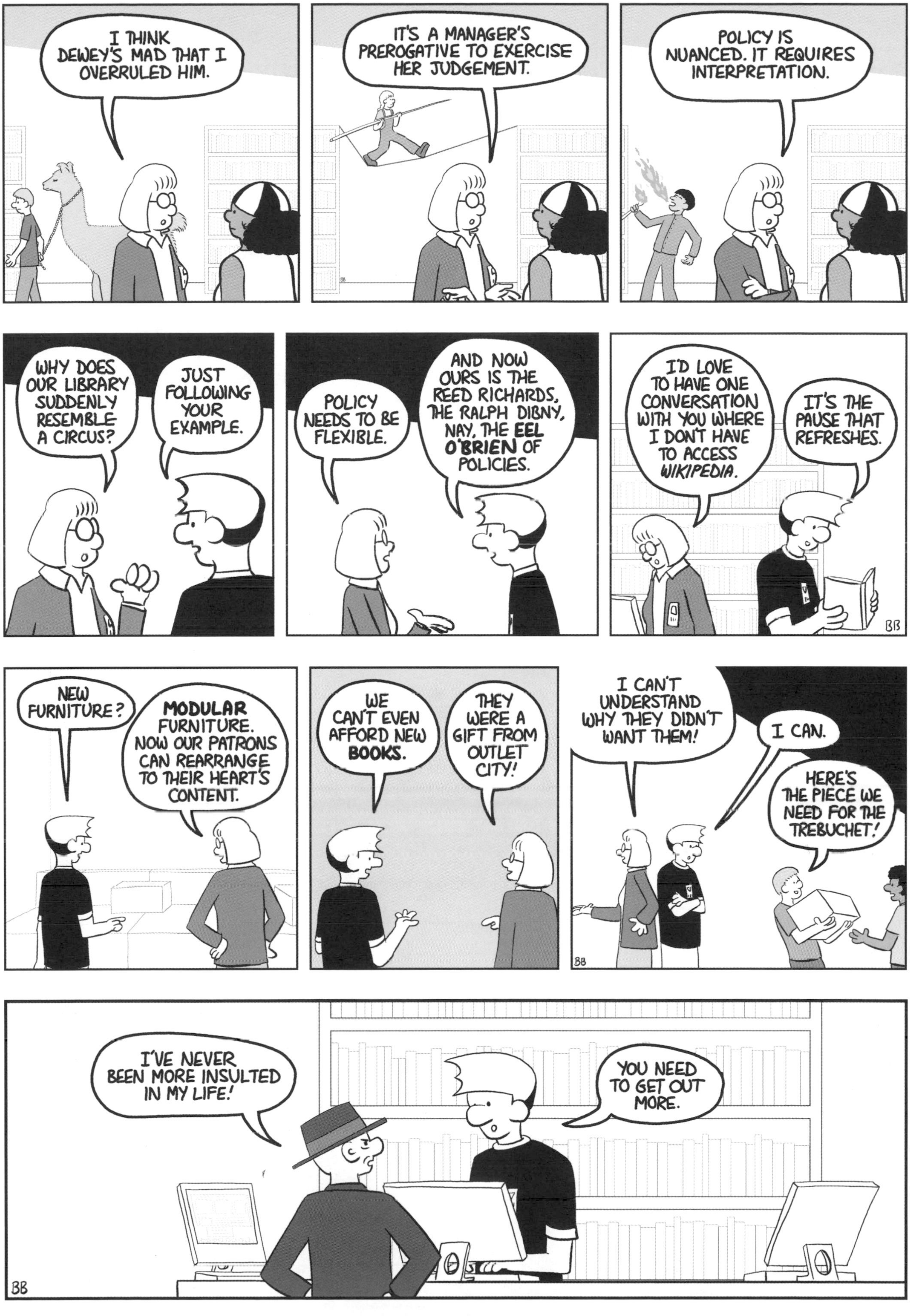
I THINK DEWEY'S MAD THAT I OVERRULED HIM.
IT'S A MANAGER'S PREROGATIVE TO EXERCISE HER JUDGEMENT.
POLICY IS NUANCED. IT REQUIRES INTERPRETATION.
WHY DOES OUR LIBRARY SUDDENLY RESEMBLE A CIRCUS?
JUST FOLLOWING YOUR EXAMPLE.
POLICY NEEDS TO BE FLEXIBLE.
AND NOW OURS IS THE REED RICHARDS, THE RALPH DIBNY, NAY, THE **EEL O'BRIEN** OF POLICIES.
I'D LOVE TO HAVE ONE CONVERSATION WITH YOU WHERE I DON'T HAVE TO ACCESS *WIKIPEDIA*.
IT'S THE PAUSE THAT REFRESHES.
NEW FURNITURE?
MODULAR FURNITURE. NOW OUR PATRONS CAN REARRANGE TO THEIR HEART'S CONTENT.
WE CAN'T EVEN AFFORD NEW **BOOKS**.
THEY WERE A GIFT FROM OUTLET CITY!
I CAN'T UNDERSTAND WHY THEY DIDN'T WANT THEM!
I CAN.
HERE'S THE PIECE WE NEED FOR THE TREBUCHET!
I'VE NEVER BEEN MORE INSULTED IN MY LIFE!
YOU NEED TO GET OUT MORE.

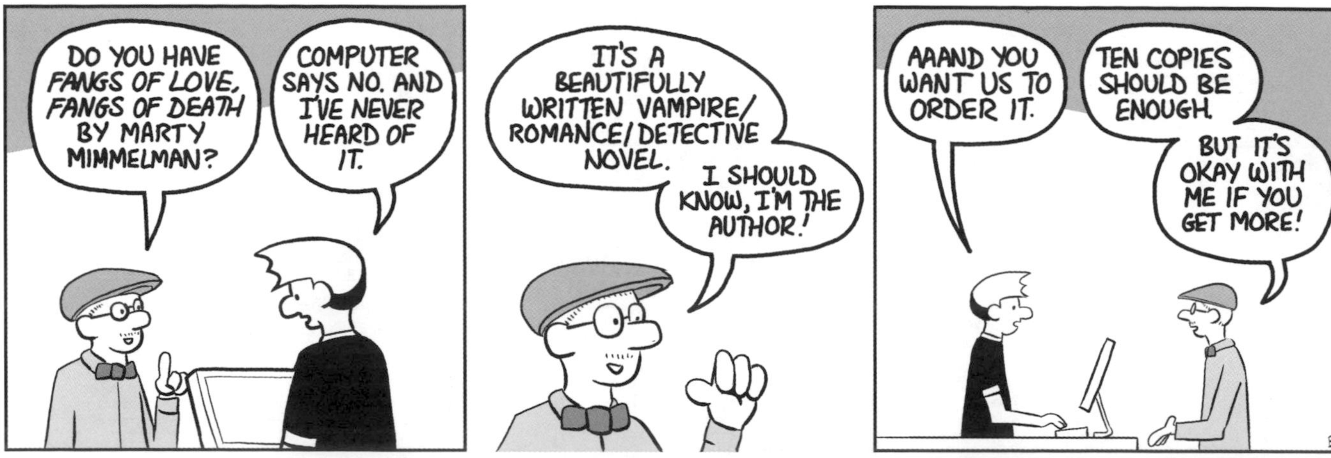
DO YOU HAVE *FANGS OF LOVE, FANGS OF DEATH* BY MARTY MIMMELMAN?
COMPUTER SAYS NO. AND I'VE NEVER HEARD OF IT.
IT'S A BEAUTIFULLY WRITTEN VAMPIRE/ ROMANCE/ DETECTIVE NOVEL.
I SHOULD KNOW, I'M THE AUTHOR!
AAAND YOU WANT US TO ORDER IT.
TEN COPIES SHOULD BE ENOUGH.
BUT IT'S OKAY WITH ME IF YOU GET MORE!
BB

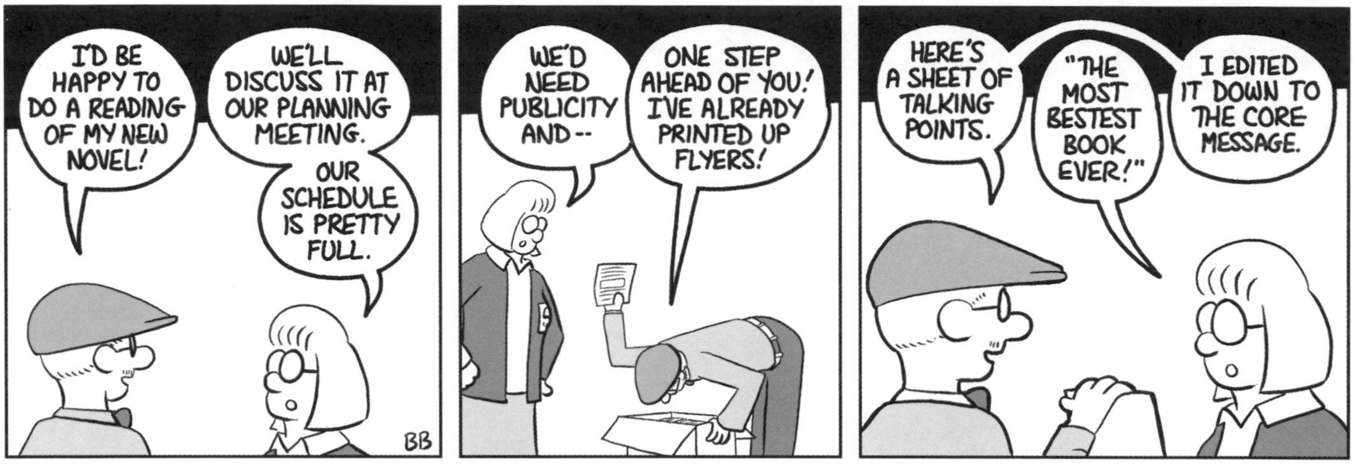
I'D BE HAPPY TO DO A READING OF MY NEW NOVEL!
WE'LL DISCUSS IT AT OUR PLANNING MEETING.
OUR SCHEDULE IS PRETTY FULL.
BB
WE'D NEED PUBLICITY AND--
ONE STEP AHEAD OF YOU! I'VE ALREADY PRINTED UP FLYERS!
HERE'S A SHEET OF TALKING POINTS.
"THE MOST BESTEST BOOK EVER!"
I EDITED IT DOWN TO THE CORE MESSAGE.

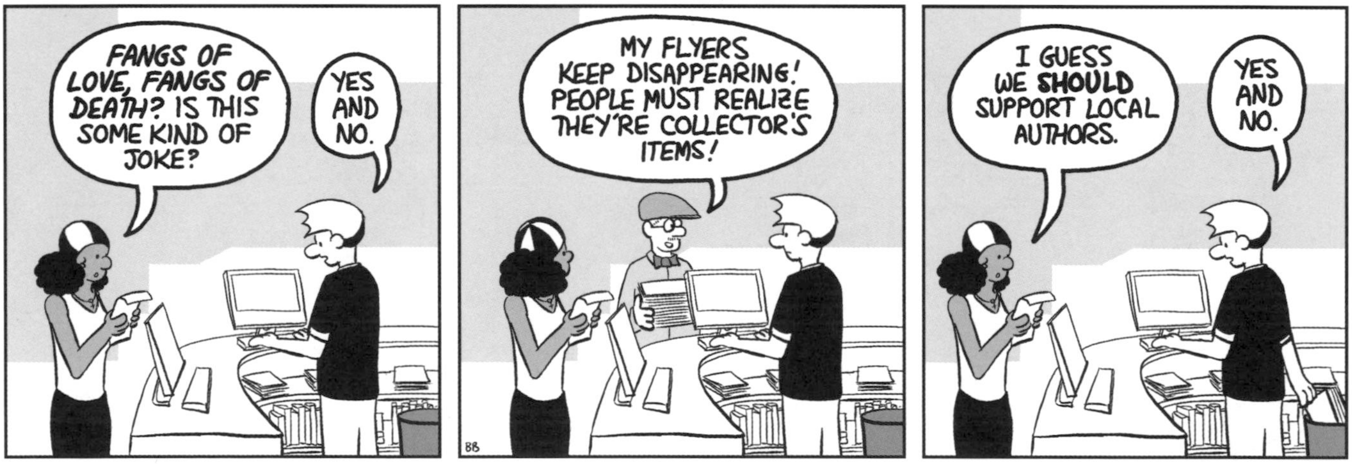
FANGS OF LOVE, FANGS OF DEATH? IS THIS SOME KIND OF JOKE?
YES AND NO.
BB
MY FLYERS KEEP DISAPPEARING! PEOPLE MUST REALIZE THEY'RE COLLECTOR'S ITEMS!
I GUESS WE **SHOULD** SUPPORT LOCAL AUTHORS.
YES AND NO.

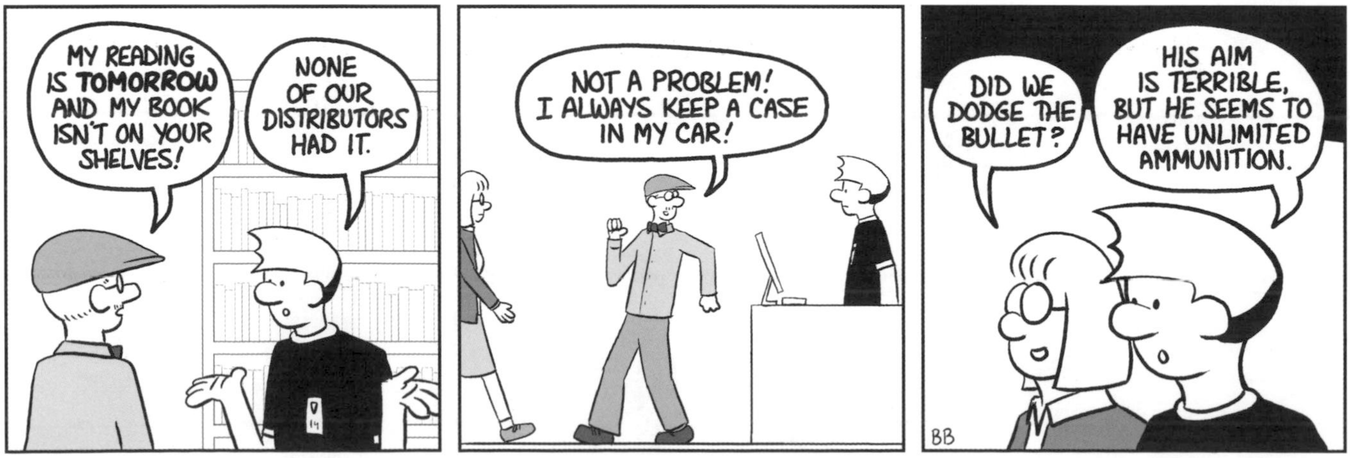
MY READING IS **TOMORROW** AND MY BOOK ISN'T ON YOUR SHELVES!
NONE OF OUR DISTRIBUTORS HAD IT.
NOT A PROBLEM! I ALWAYS KEEP A CASE IN MY CAR!
DID WE DODGE THE BULLET?
HIS AIM IS TERRIBLE, BUT HE SEEMS TO HAVE UNLIMITED AMMUNITION.
BB

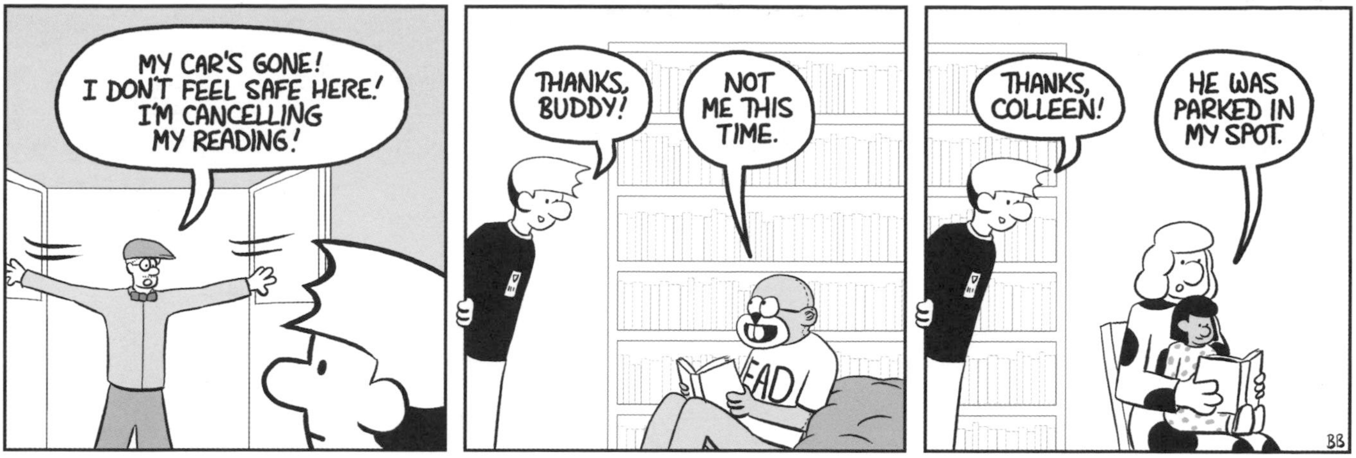
MY CAR'S GONE! I DON'T FEEL SAFE HERE! I'M CANCELLING MY READING!
THANKS, BUDDY!
NOT ME THIS TIME.
THANKS, COLLEEN!
HE WAS PARKED IN MY SPOT.
BB

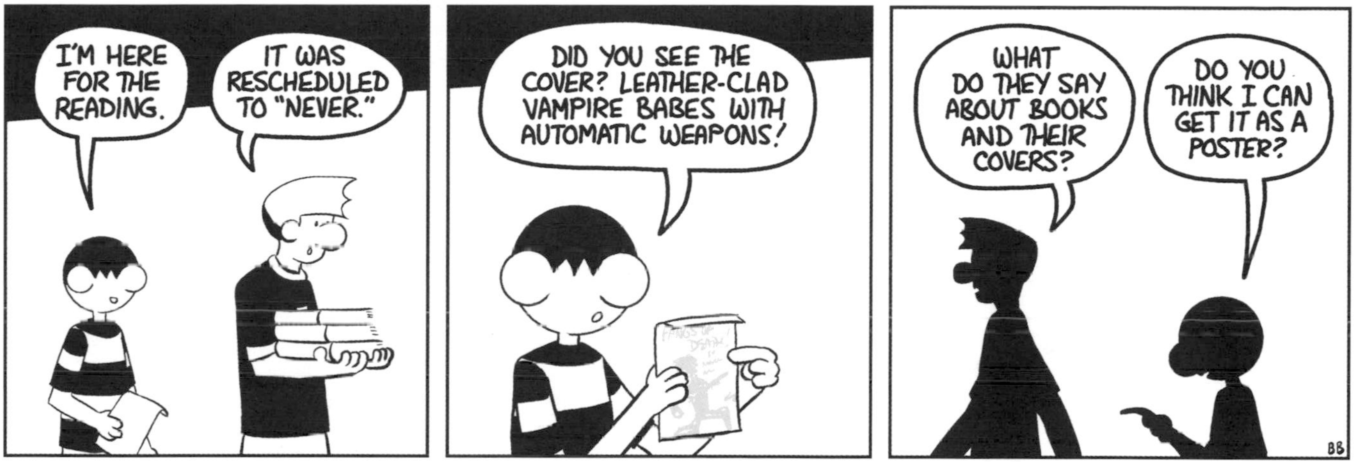
I'M HERE FOR THE READING.
IT WAS RESCHEDULED TO "NEVER."
DID YOU SEE THE COVER? LEATHER-CLAD VAMPIRE BABES WITH AUTOMATIC WEAPONS!
WHAT DO THEY SAY ABOUT BOOKS AND THEIR COVERS?
DO YOU THINK I CAN GET IT AS A POSTER?
BB

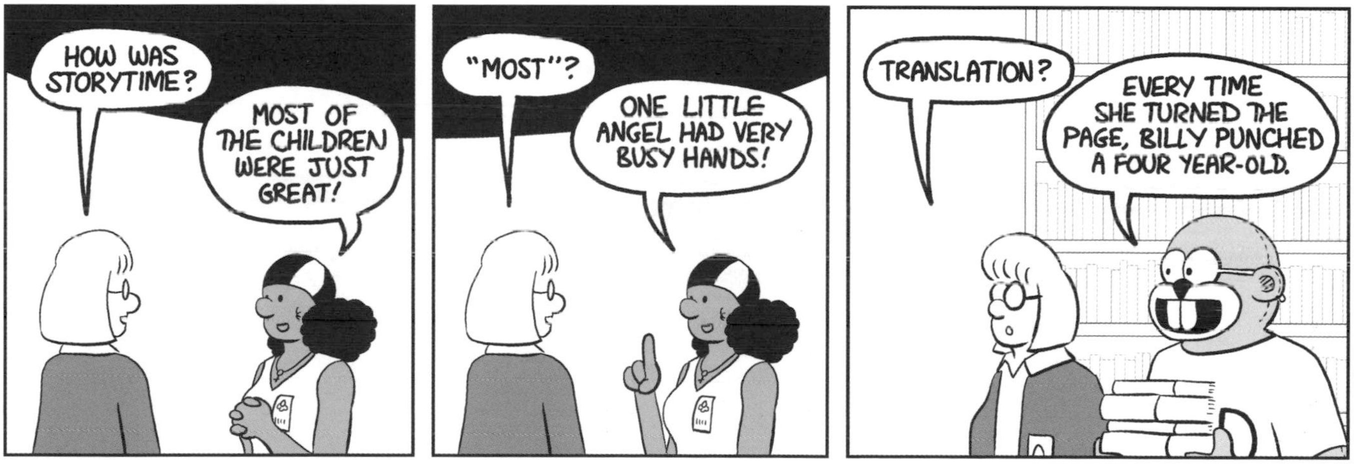
HOW WAS STORYTIME?
MOST OF THE CHILDREN WERE JUST GREAT!
"MOST"?
ONE LITTLE ANGEL HAD VERY BUSY HANDS!
TRANSLATION?
EVERY TIME SHE TURNED THE PAGE, BILLY PUNCHED A FOUR YEAR-OLD.

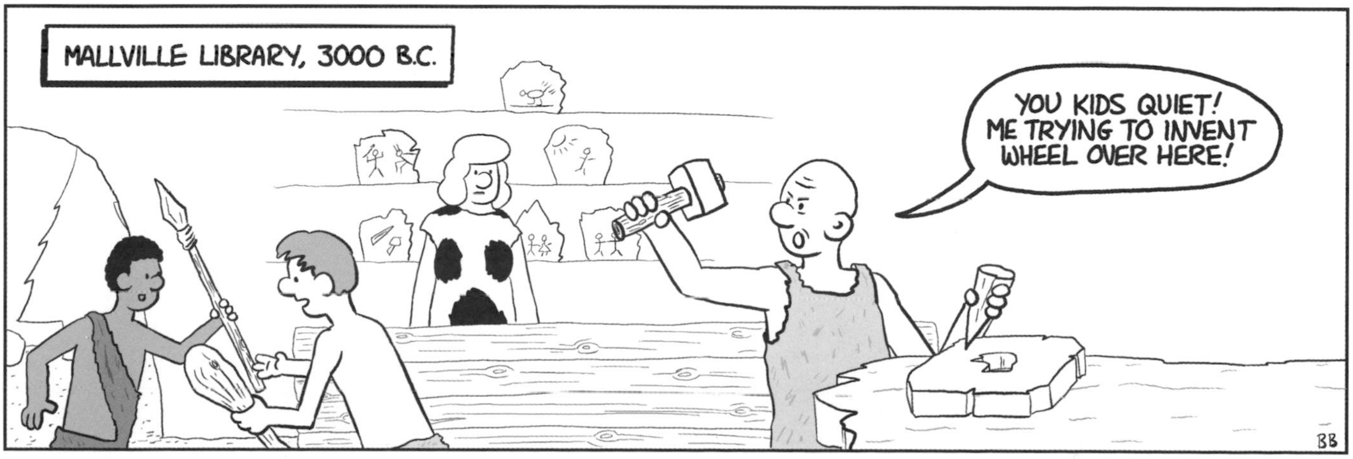
MALLVILLE LIBRARY, 3000 B.C.
YOU KIDS QUIET! ME TRYING TO INVENT WHEEL OVER HERE!
BB

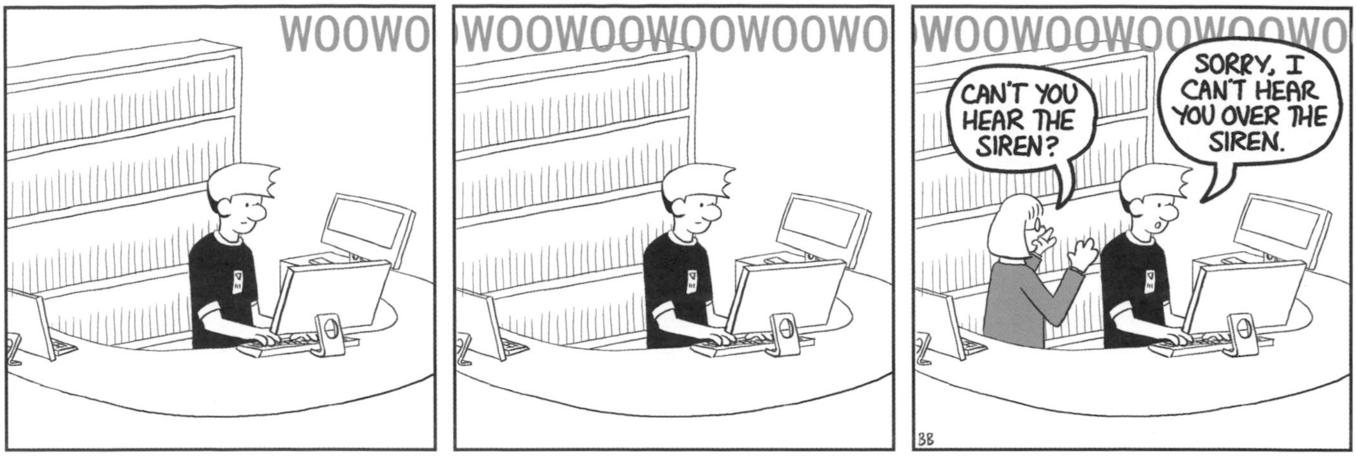
WOOWO
WOOWOOWOOWOOWO
WOOWOOWOOWOOWO
CAN'T YOU HEAR THE SIREN?
SORRY, I CAN'T HEAR YOU OVER THE SIREN.
BB

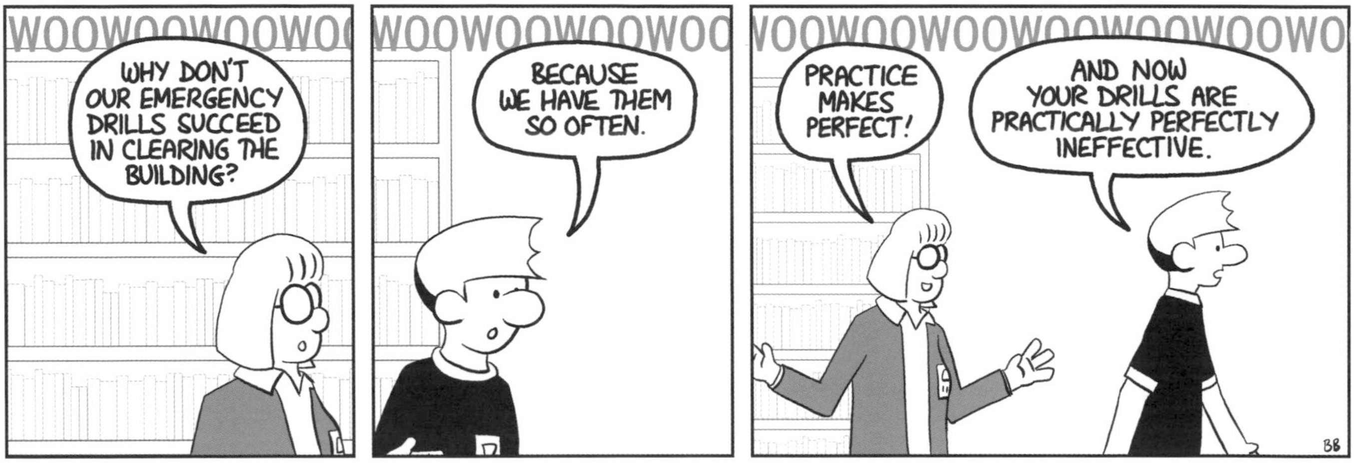
WOOWOOWOOWO
WHY DON'T OUR EMERGENCY DRILLS SUCCEED IN CLEARING THE BUILDING?
WOOWOOWOOWOO
BECAUSE WE HAVE THEM SO OFTEN.
WOOWOOWOOWOOWOOWO
PRACTICE MAKES PERFECT!
AND NOW YOUR DRILLS ARE PRACTICALLY PERFECTLY INEFFECTIVE.
BB

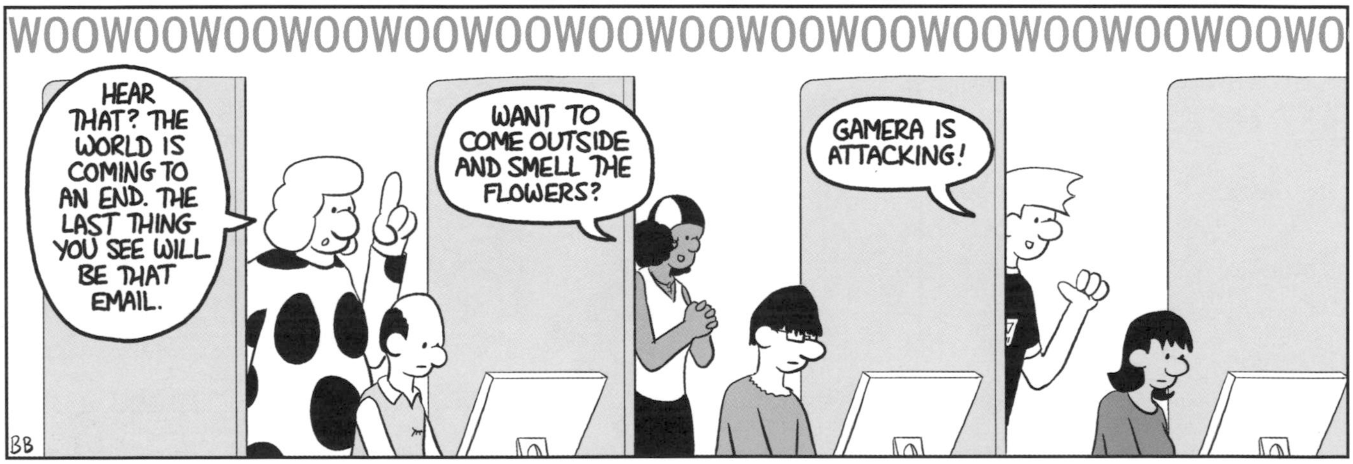
WOOWOOWOOWOOWOOWOOWOOWOOWOOWOOWOOWOOWOOWO
HEAR THAT? THE WORLD IS COMING TO AN END. THE LAST THING YOU SEE WILL BE THAT EMAIL.
WANT TO COME OUTSIDE AND SMELL THE FLOWERS?
GAMERA IS ATTACKING!
BB

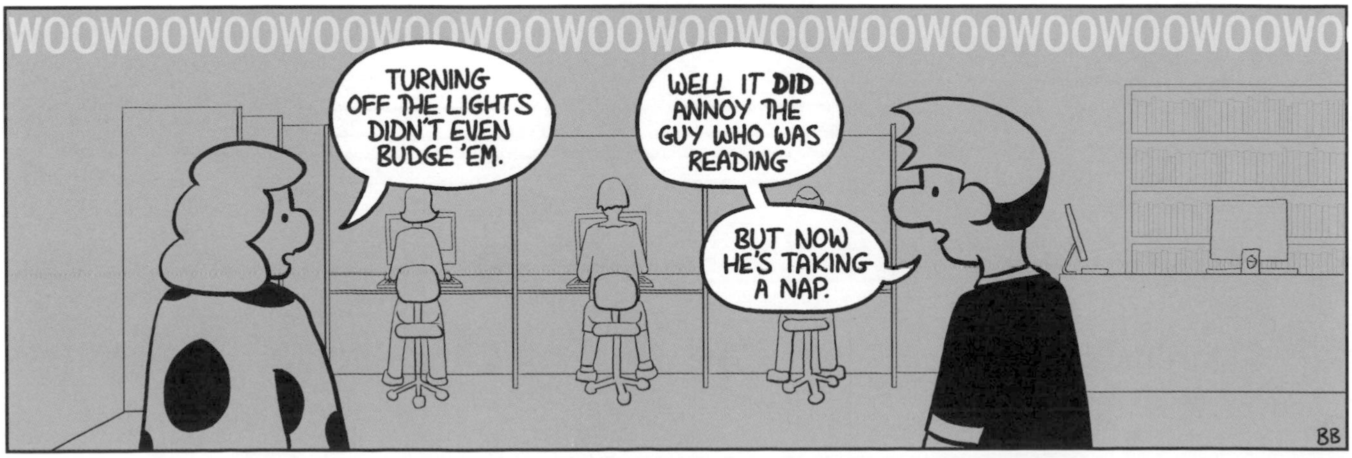
WOOWOOWOOWOOWOOWOOWOOWOOWOOWOOWOOWOOWOOWO
TURNING OFF THE LIGHTS DIDN'T EVEN BUDGE 'EM.
WELL IT **DID** ANNOY THE GUY WHO WAS READING
BUT NOW HE'S TAKING A NAP.
BB

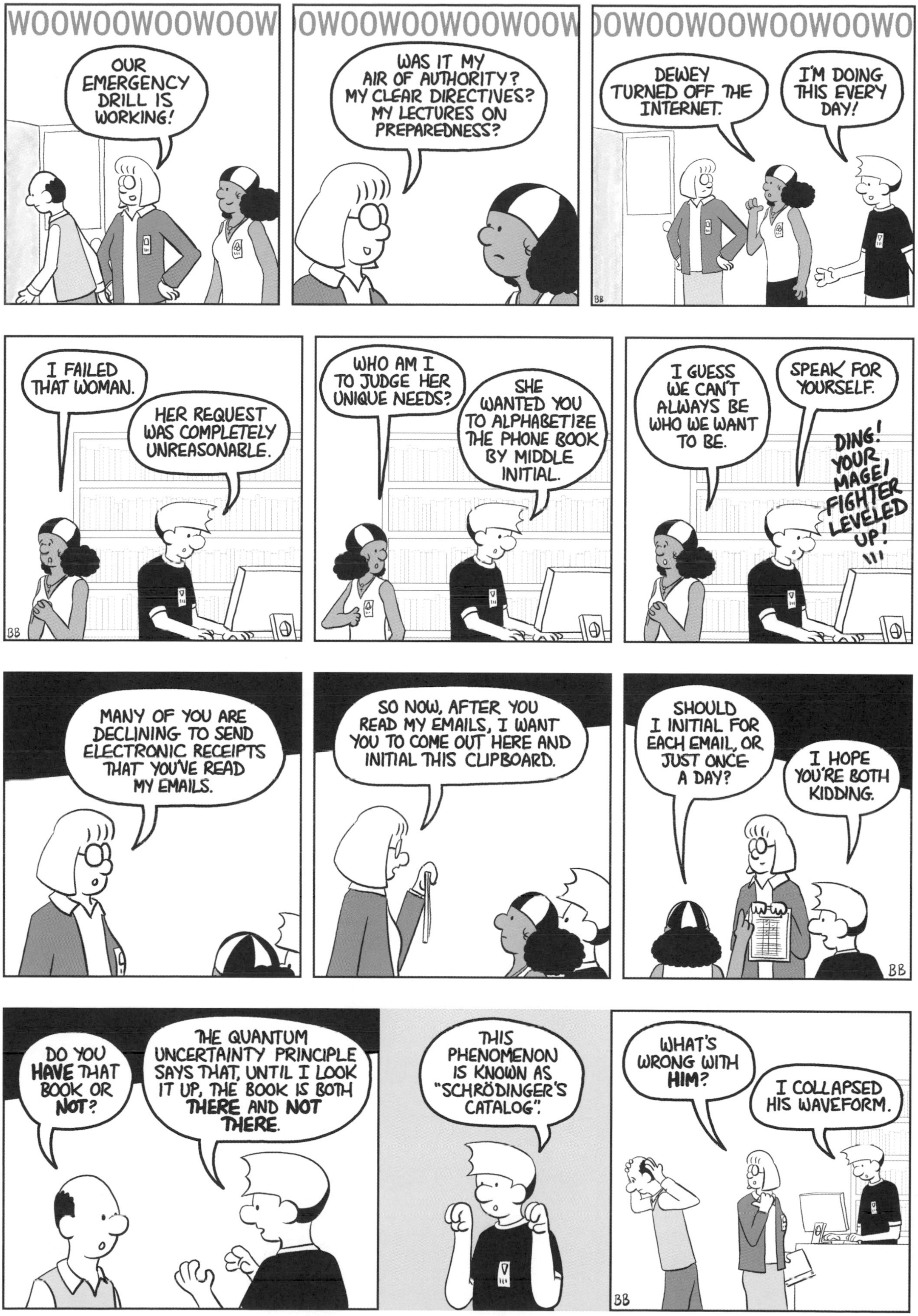
WOOWOOWOOWOOW
OUR EMERGENCY DRILL IS WORKING!
OWOOWOOWOOWOOW
WAS IT MY AIR OF AUTHORITY? MY CLEAR DIRECTIVES? MY LECTURES ON PREPAREDNESS?
OOWOOWOOWOOWOOWO
DEWEY TURNED OFF THE INTERNET.
I'M DOING THIS EVERY DAY!
BB
I FAILED THAT WOMAN.
HER REQUEST WAS COMPLETELY UNREASONABLE.
BB
WHO AM I TO JUDGE HER UNIQUE NEEDS?
SHE WANTED YOU TO ALPHABETIZE THE PHONE BOOK BY MIDDLE INITIAL.
I GUESS WE CAN'T ALWAYS BE WHO WE WANT TO BE.
SPEAK FOR YOURSELF.
DING! YOUR MAGE/FIGHTER LEVELED UP!
MANY OF YOU ARE DECLINING TO SEND ELECTRONIC RECEIPTS THAT YOU'VE READ MY EMAILS.
SO NOW, AFTER YOU READ MY EMAILS, I WANT YOU TO COME OUT HERE AND INITIAL THIS CLIPBOARD.
SHOULD I INITIAL FOR EACH EMAIL, OR JUST ONCE A DAY?
I HOPE YOU'RE BOTH KIDDING.
BB
DO YOU **HAVE** THAT BOOK OR **NOT**?
THE QUANTUM UNCERTAINTY PRINCIPLE SAYS THAT, UNTIL I LOOK IT UP, THE BOOK IS BOTH **THERE** AND **NOT THERE**.
THIS PHENOMENON IS KNOWN AS "SCHRÖDINGER'S CATALOG".
WHAT'S WRONG WITH **HIM**?
I COLLAPSED HIS WAVEFORM.
BB

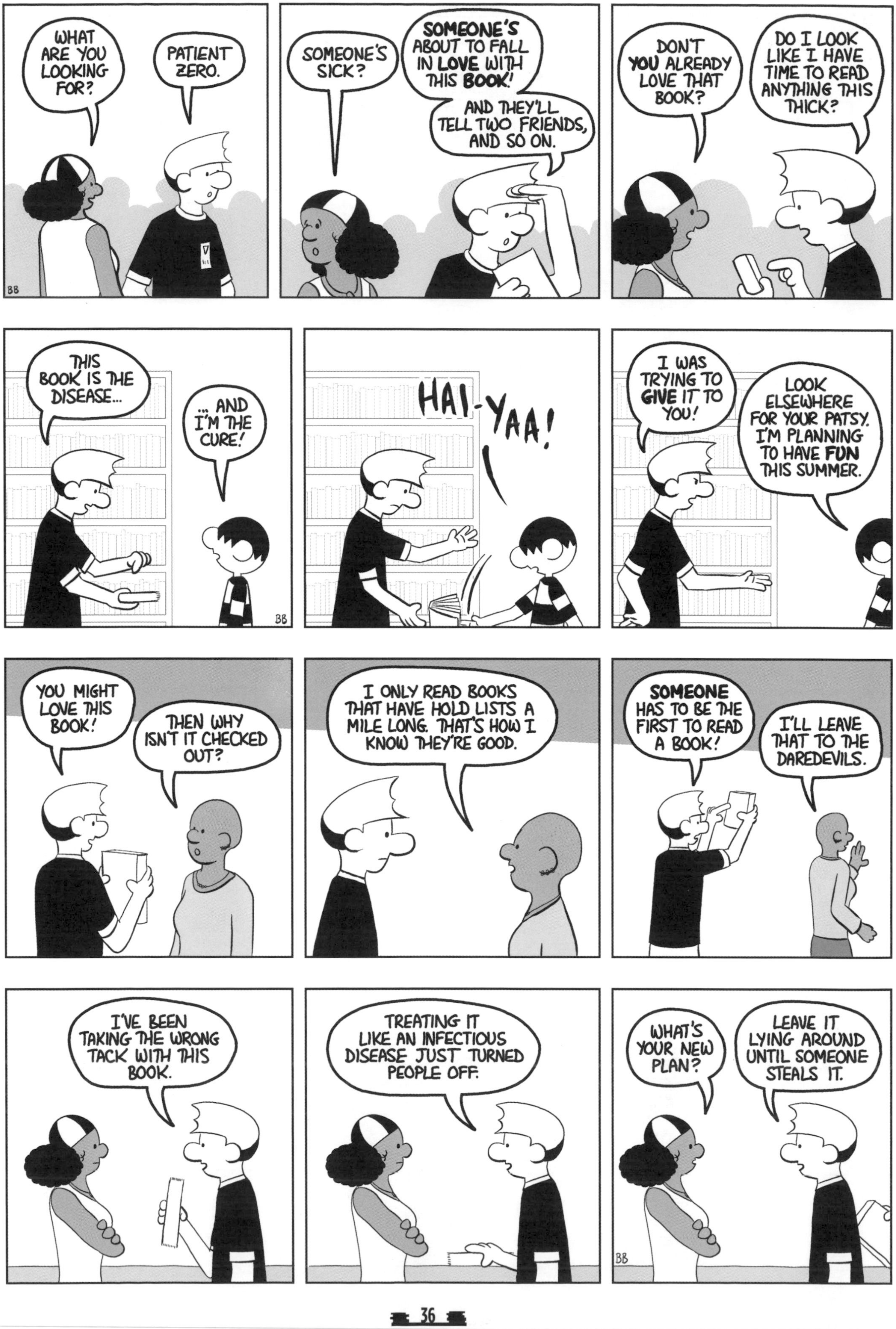

BB
WHAT ARE YOU LOOKING FOR?
PATIENT ZERO.
SOMEONE'S SICK?
SOMEONE'S ABOUT TO FALL IN **LOVE** WITH THIS **BOOK**!
AND THEY'LL TELL TWO FRIENDS, AND SO ON.
DON'T **YOU** ALREADY LOVE THAT BOOK?
DO I LOOK LIKE I HAVE TIME TO READ ANYTHING THIS THICK?
THIS BOOK IS THE DISEASE...
... AND I'M THE CURE!
BB
HAI-YAA!
I WAS TRYING TO **GIVE** IT TO YOU!
LOOK ELSEWHERE FOR YOUR PATSY. I'M PLANNING TO HAVE **FUN** THIS SUMMER.
YOU MIGHT LOVE THIS BOOK!
THEN WHY ISN'T IT CHECKED OUT?
I ONLY READ BOOKS THAT HAVE HOLD LISTS A MILE LONG. THAT'S HOW I KNOW THEY'RE GOOD.
SOMEONE HAS TO BE THE FIRST TO READ A BOOK!
I'LL LEAVE THAT TO THE DAREDEVILS.
I'VE BEEN TAKING THE WRONG TACK WITH THIS BOOK.
TREATING IT LIKE AN INFECTIOUS DISEASE JUST TURNED PEOPLE OFF.
WHAT'S YOUR NEW PLAN?
LEAVE IT LYING AROUND UNTIL SOMEONE STEALS IT.
BB

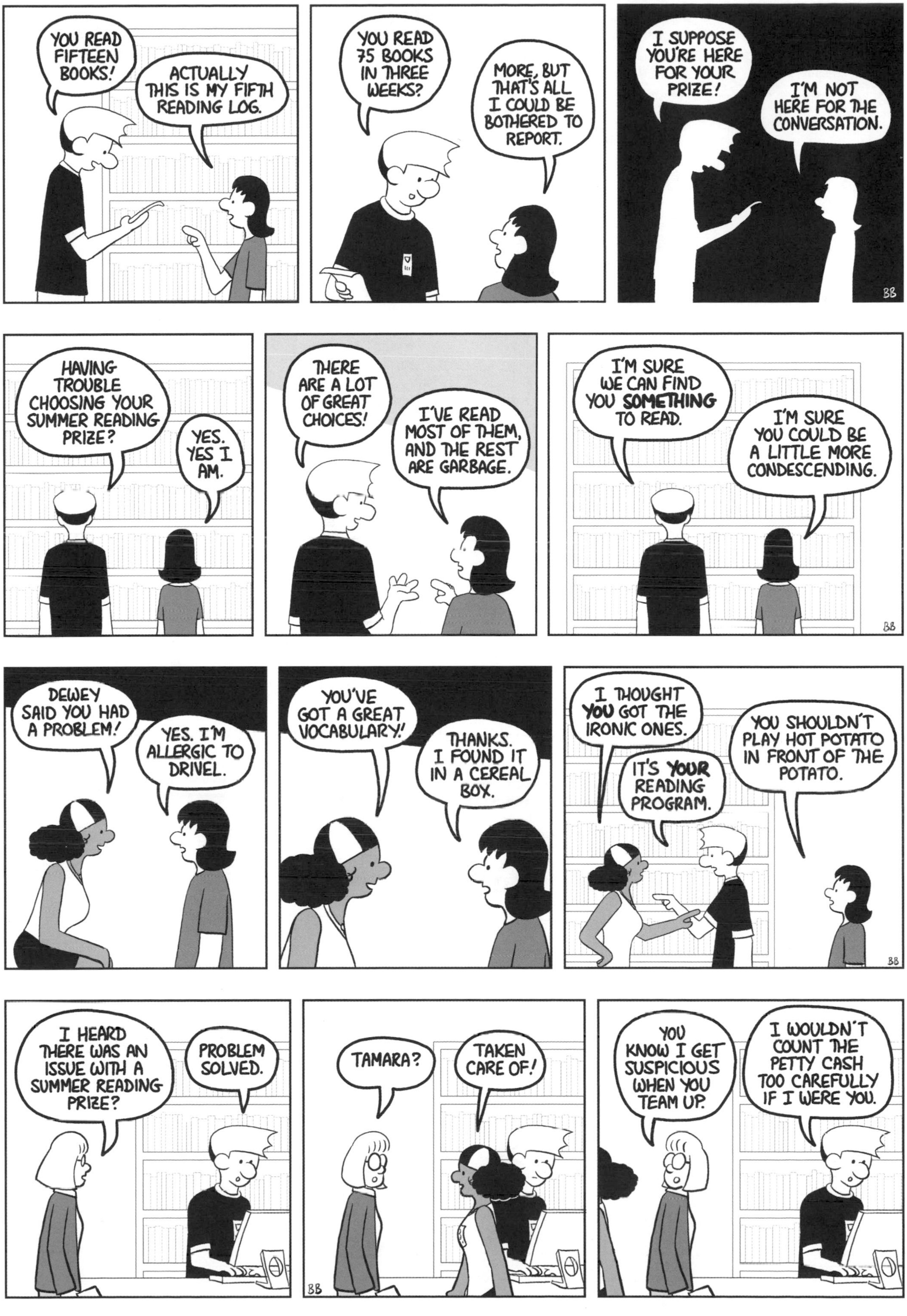
YOU READ FIFTEEN BOOKS!
ACTUALLY THIS IS MY FIFTH READING LOG.
YOU READ 75 BOOKS IN THREE WEEKS?
MORE, BUT THAT'S ALL I COULD BE BOTHERED TO REPORT.
I SUPPOSE YOU'RE HERE FOR YOUR PRIZE!
I'M NOT HERE FOR THE CONVERSATION.
BB
HAVING TROUBLE CHOOSING YOUR SUMMER READING PRIZE?
YES. YES I AM.
THERE ARE A LOT OF GREAT CHOICES!
I'VE READ MOST OF THEM, AND THE REST ARE GARBAGE.
I'M SURE WE CAN FIND YOU **SOMETHING** TO READ.
I'M SURE YOU COULD BE A LITTLE MORE CONDESCENDING.
BB
DEWEY SAID YOU HAD A PROBLEM!
YES. I'M ALLERGIC TO DRIVEL.
YOU'VE GOT A GREAT VOCABULARY!
THANKS. I FOUND IT IN A CEREAL BOX.
I THOUGHT **YOU** GOT THE IRONIC ONES.
IT'S **YOUR** READING PROGRAM.
YOU SHOULDN'T PLAY HOT POTATO IN FRONT OF THE POTATO.
BB
I HEARD THERE WAS AN ISSUE WITH A SUMMER READING PRIZE?
PROBLEM SOLVED.
BB
TAMARA?
TAKEN CARE OF!
YOU KNOW I GET SUSPICIOUS WHEN YOU TEAM UP.
I WOULDN'T COUNT THE PETTY CASH TOO CAREFULLY IF I WERE YOU.

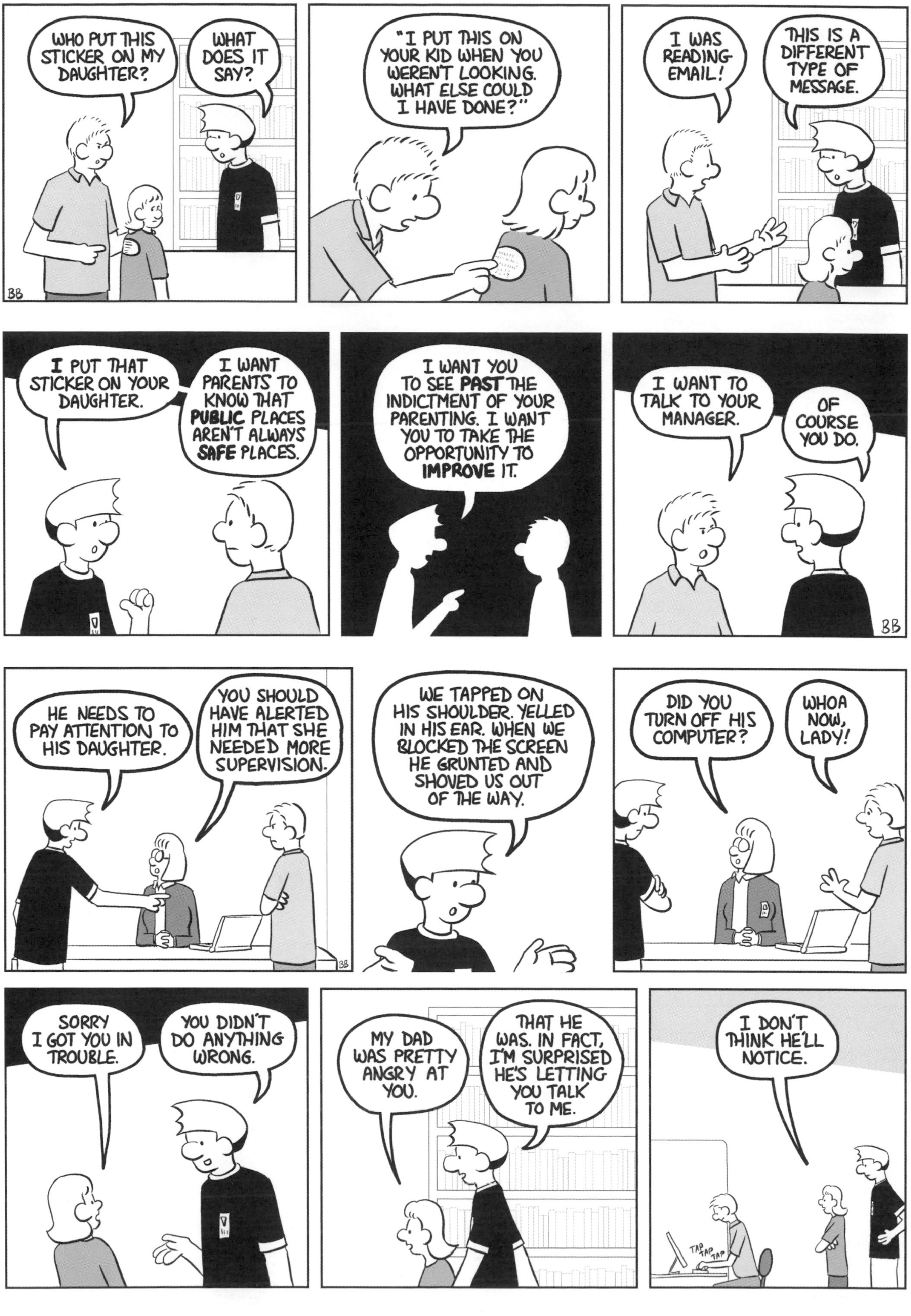
BB
WHO PUT THIS STICKER ON MY DAUGHTER?
WHAT DOES IT SAY?
"I PUT THIS ON YOUR KID WHEN YOU WEREN'T LOOKING. WHAT ELSE COULD I HAVE DONE?"
I WAS READING EMAIL!
THIS IS A DIFFERENT TYPE OF MESSAGE.
I PUT THAT STICKER ON YOUR DAUGHTER.
I WANT PARENTS TO KNOW THAT PUBLIC PLACES AREN'T ALWAYS SAFE PLACES.
I WANT YOU TO SEE PAST THE INDICTMENT OF YOUR PARENTING. I WANT YOU TO TAKE THE OPPORTUNITY TO IMPROVE IT.
I WANT TO TALK TO YOUR MANAGER.
OF COURSE YOU DO.
BB
HE NEEDS TO PAY ATTENTION TO HIS DAUGHTER.
YOU SHOULD HAVE ALERTED HIM THAT SHE NEEDED MORE SUPERVISION.
BB
WE TAPPED ON HIS SHOULDER. YELLED IN HIS EAR. WHEN WE BLOCKED THE SCREEN HE GRUNTED AND SHOVED US OUT OF THE WAY.
DID YOU TURN OFF HIS COMPUTER?
WHOA NOW, LADY!
SORRY I GOT YOU IN TROUBLE.
YOU DIDN'T DO ANYTHING WRONG.
MY DAD WAS PRETTY ANGRY AT YOU.
THAT HE WAS. IN FACT, I'M SURPRISED HE'S LETTING YOU TALK TO ME.
I DON'T THINK HE'LL NOTICE.
TAP TAP TAP

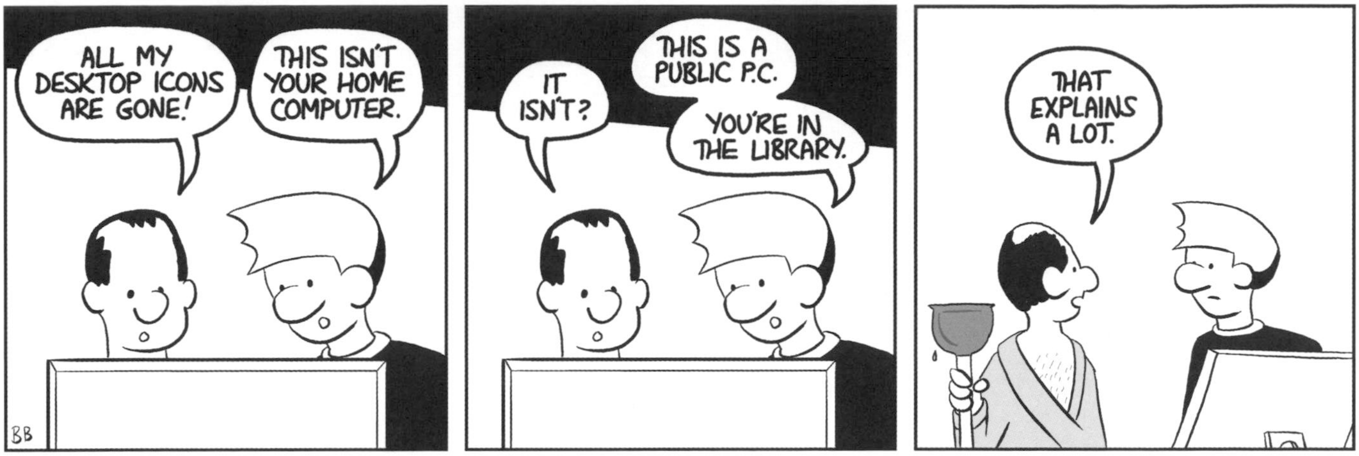
ALL MY DESKTOP ICONS ARE GONE!
THIS ISN'T YOUR HOME COMPUTER.
IT ISN'T?
THIS IS A PUBLIC P.C.
YOU'RE IN THE LIBRARY.
THAT EXPLAINS A LOT.
BB

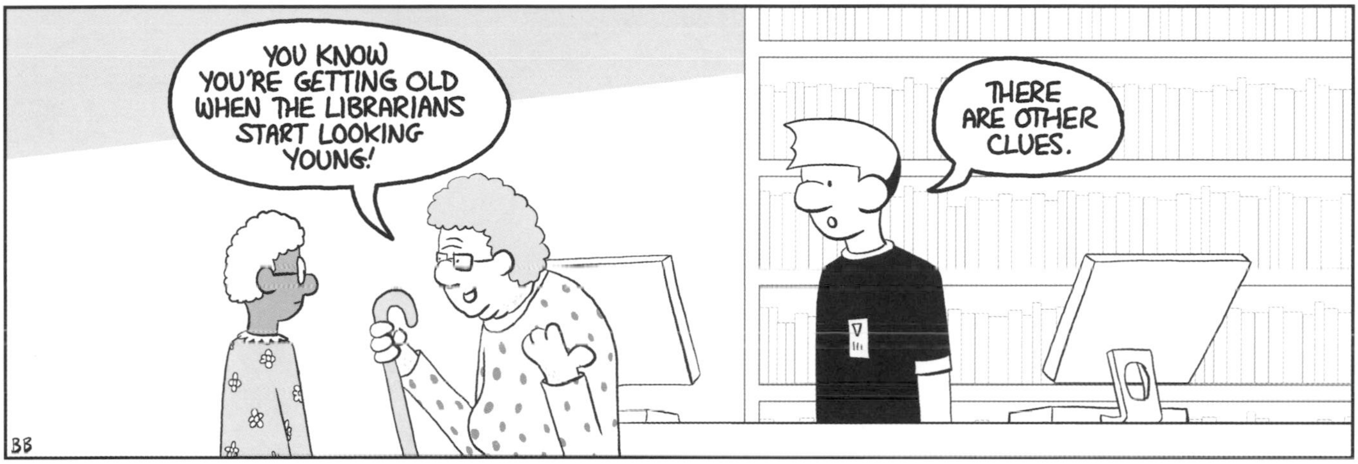
YOU KNOW YOU'RE GETTING OLD WHEN THE LIBRARIANS START LOOKING YOUNG!
THERE ARE OTHER CLUES.
BB

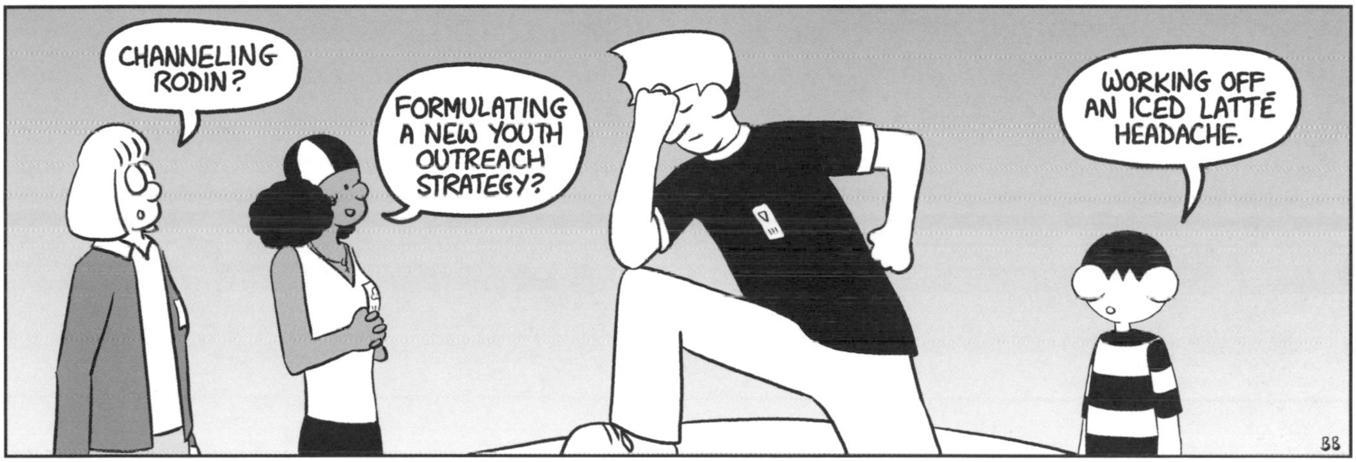
CHANNELING RODIN?
FORMULATING A NEW YOUTH OUTREACH STRATEGY?
WORKING OFF AN ICED LATTÉ HEADACHE.
BB

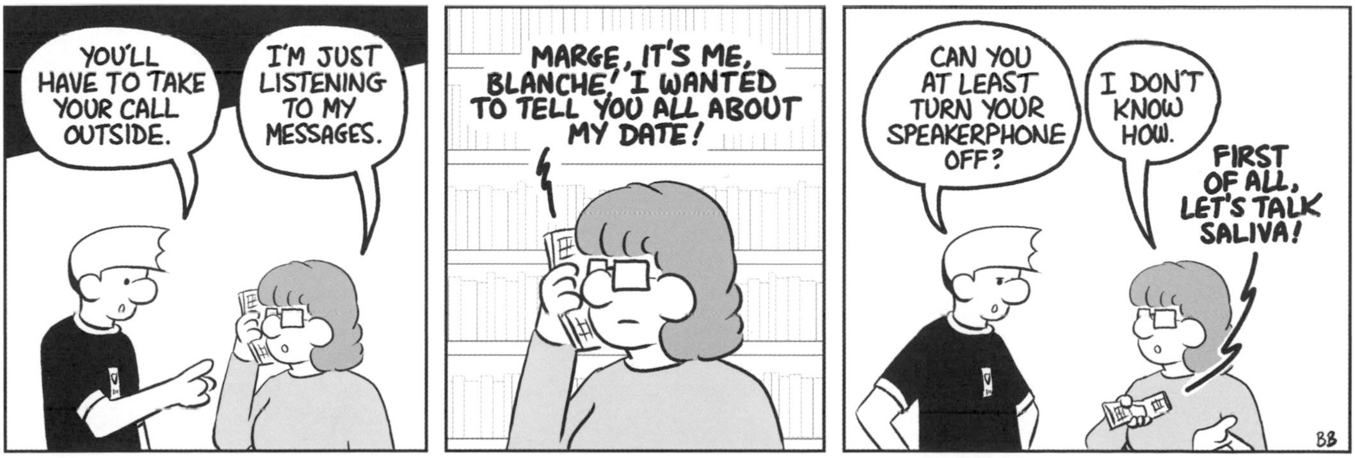
YOU'LL HAVE TO TAKE YOUR CALL OUTSIDE.
I'M JUST LISTENING TO MY MESSAGES.
MARGE, IT'S ME, BLANCHE! I WANTED TO TELL YOU ALL ABOUT MY DATE!
CAN YOU AT LEAST TURN YOUR SPEAKERPHONE OFF?
I DON'T KNOW HOW.
FIRST OF ALL, LET'S TALK SALIVA!
BB

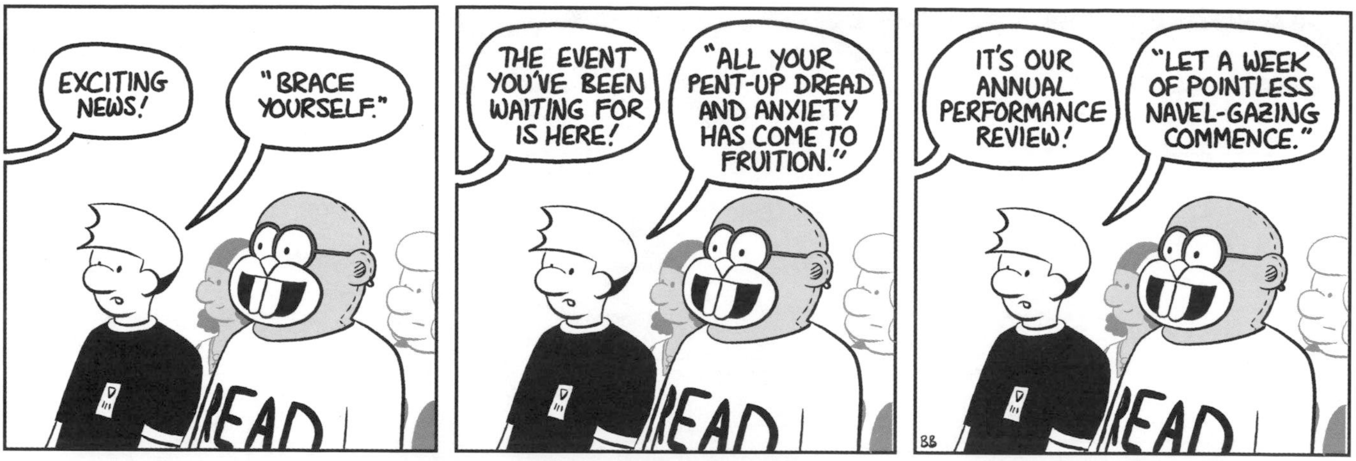
EXCITING NEWS!
"BRACE YOURSELF."
THE EVENT YOU'VE BEEN WAITING FOR IS HERE!
"ALL YOUR PENT-UP DREAD AND ANXIETY HAS COME TO FRUITION."
IT'S OUR ANNUAL PERFORMANCE REVIEW!
"LET A WEEK OF POINTLESS NAVEL-GAZING COMMENCE."
BB

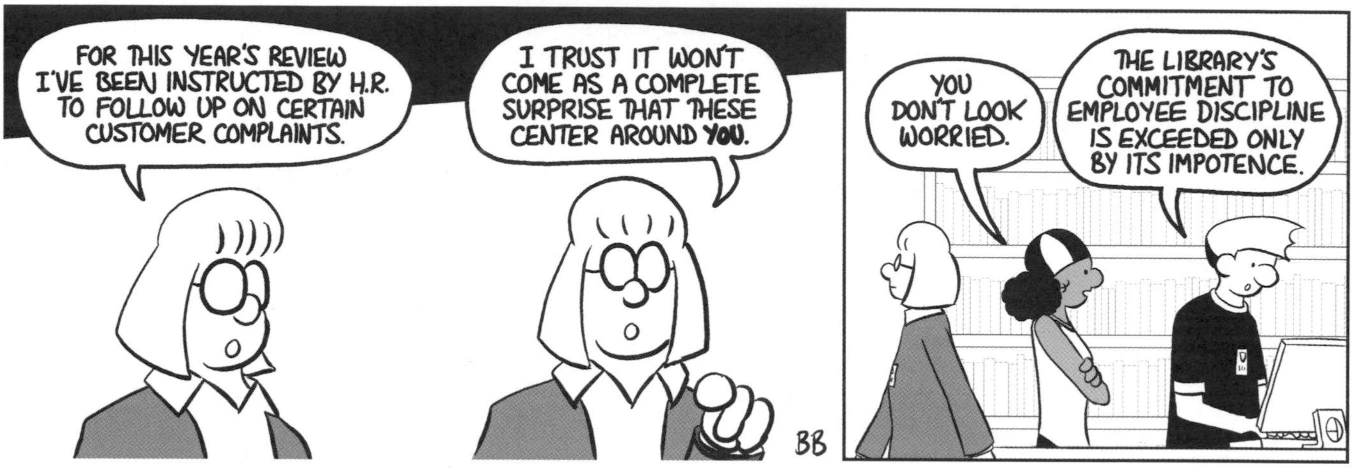
FOR THIS YEAR'S REVIEW I'VE BEEN INSTRUCTED BY H.R. TO FOLLOW UP ON CERTAIN CUSTOMER COMPLAINTS.
I TRUST IT WON'T COME AS A COMPLETE SURPRISE THAT THESE CENTER AROUND **YOU**.
BB
YOU DON'T LOOK WORRIED.
THE LIBRARY'S COMMITMENT TO EMPLOYEE DISCIPLINE IS EXCEEDED ONLY BY ITS IMPOTENCE.

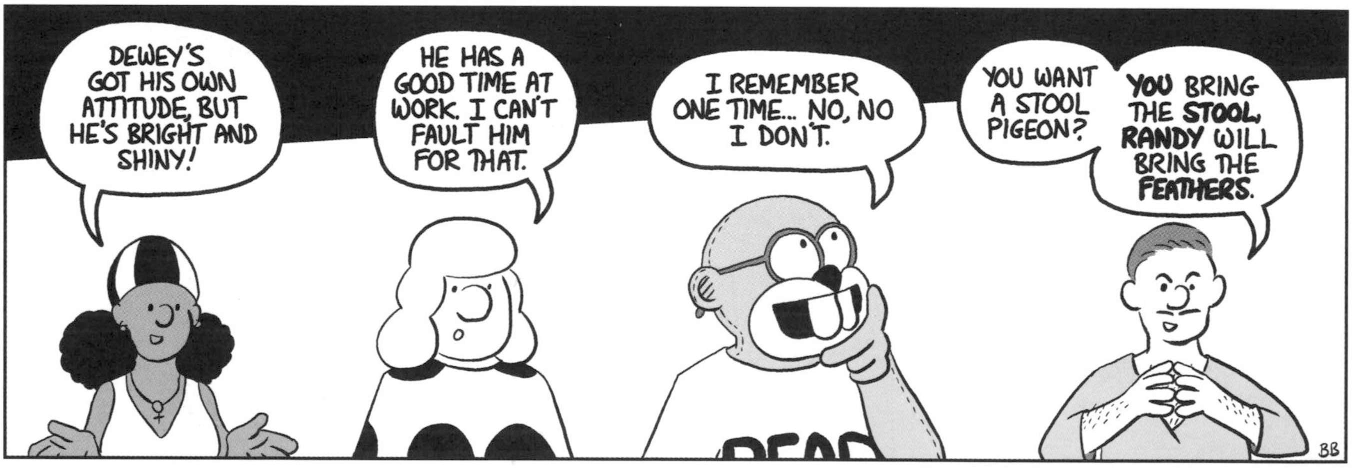
DEWEY'S GOT HIS OWN ATTITUDE, BUT HE'S BRIGHT AND SHINY!
HE HAS A GOOD TIME AT WORK. I CAN'T FAULT HIM FOR THAT.
I REMEMBER ONE TIME... NO, NO I DON'T.
YOU WANT A STOOL PIGEON?
YOU BRING THE **STOOL**, **RANDY** WILL BRING THE **FEATHERS**.
BB

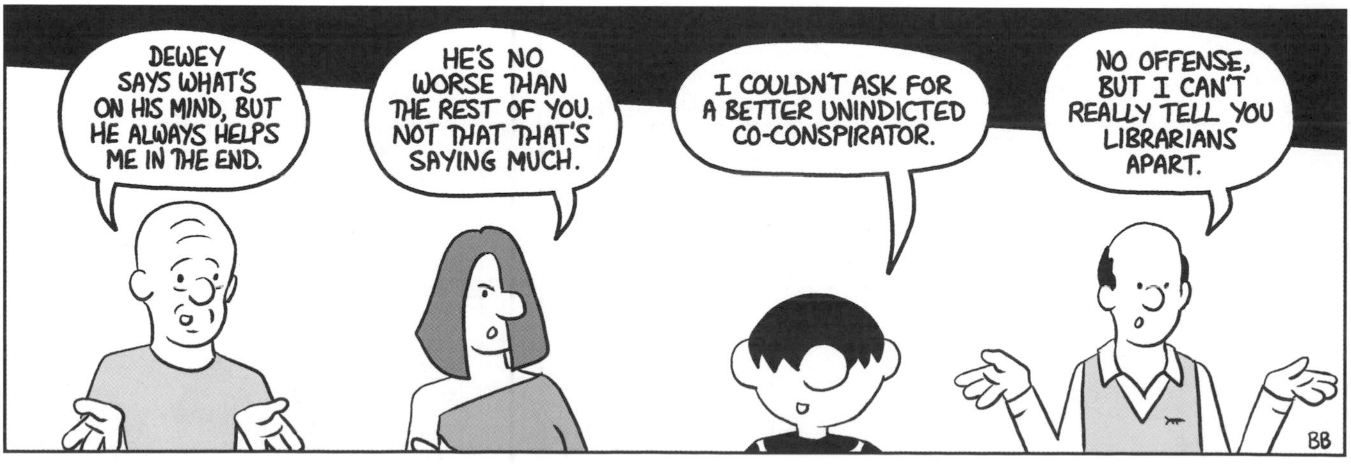
DEWEY SAYS WHAT'S ON HIS MIND, BUT HE ALWAYS HELPS ME IN THE END.
HE'S NO WORSE THAN THE REST OF YOU. NOT THAT THAT'S SAYING MUCH.
I COULDN'T ASK FOR A BETTER UNINDICTED CO-CONSPIRATOR.
NO OFFENSE, BUT I CAN'T REALLY TELL YOU LIBRARIANS APART.
BB

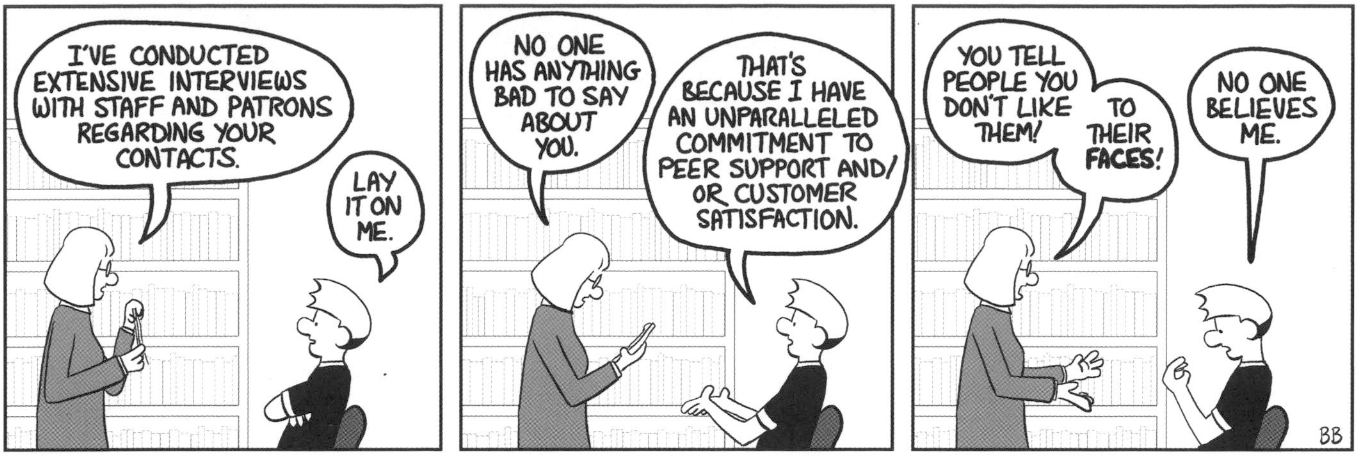

I'VE CONDUCTED EXTENSIVE INTERVIEWS WITH STAFF AND PATRONS REGARDING YOUR CONTACTS.
LAY IT ON ME.
NO ONE HAS ANYTHING BAD TO SAY ABOUT YOU.
THAT'S BECAUSE I HAVE AN UNPARALLELED COMMITMENT TO PEER SUPPORT AND/OR CUSTOMER SATISFACTION.
YOU TELL PEOPLE YOU DON'T LIKE THEM!
TO THEIR **FACES**!
NO ONE BELIEVES ME.
BB

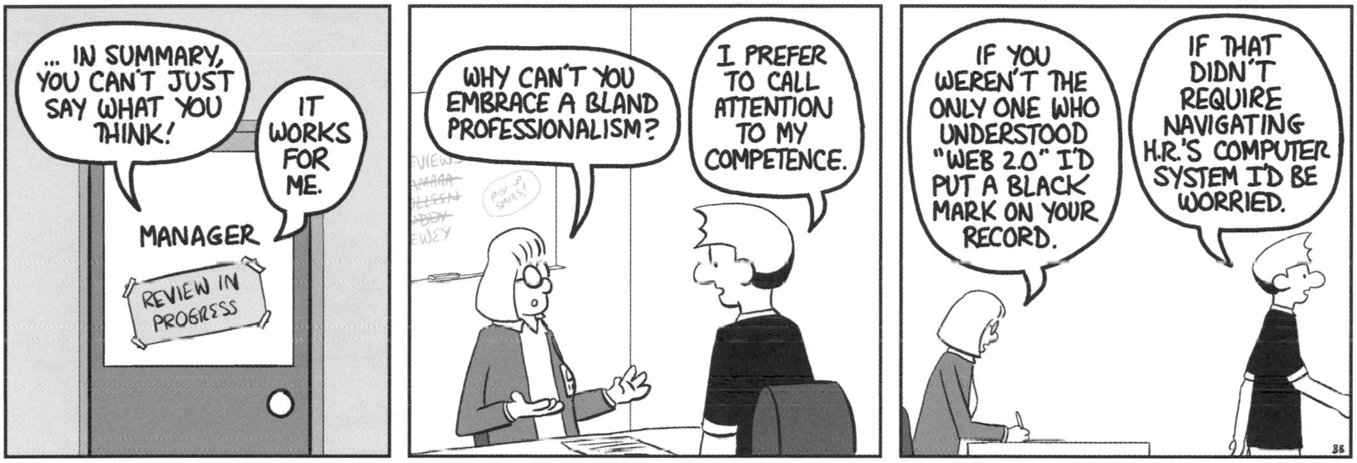

... IN SUMMARY, YOU CAN'T JUST SAY WHAT YOU THINK!
IT WORKS FOR ME.
MANAGER
REVIEW IN PROGRESS
WHY CAN'T YOU EMBRACE A BLAND PROFESSIONALISM?
I PREFER TO CALL ATTENTION TO MY COMPETENCE.
IF YOU WEREN'T THE ONLY ONE WHO UNDERSTOOD "WEB 2.0" I'D PUT A BLACK MARK ON YOUR RECORD.
IF THAT DIDN'T REQUIRE NAVIGATING H.R.'S COMPUTER SYSTEM I'D BE WORRIED.
BB

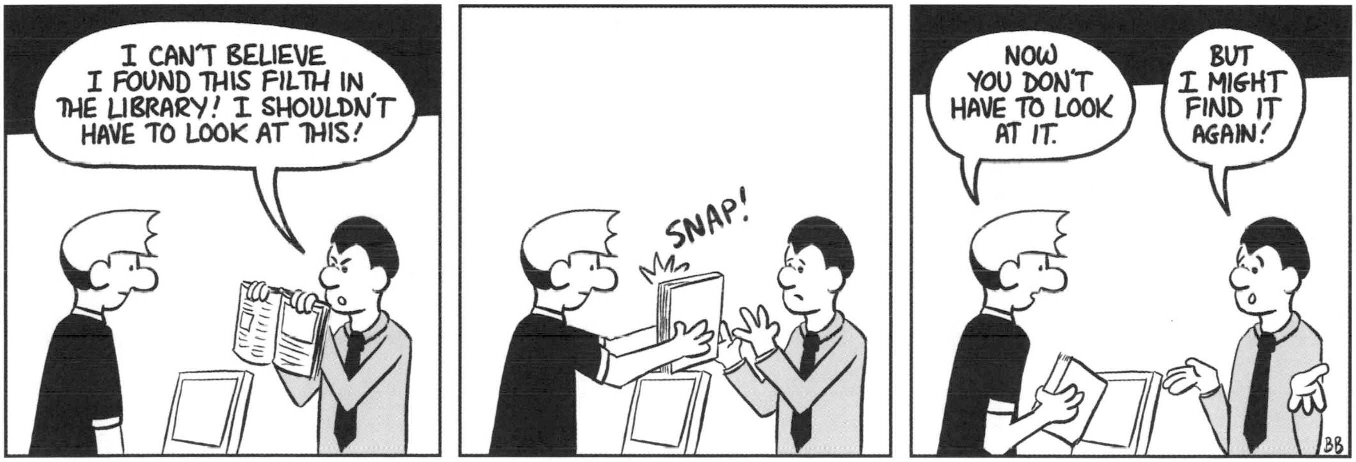

I CAN'T BELIEVE I FOUND THIS FILTH IN THE LIBRARY! I SHOULDN'T HAVE TO LOOK AT THIS!
SNAP!
NOW YOU DON'T HAVE TO LOOK AT IT.
BUT I MIGHT FIND IT AGAIN!
BB

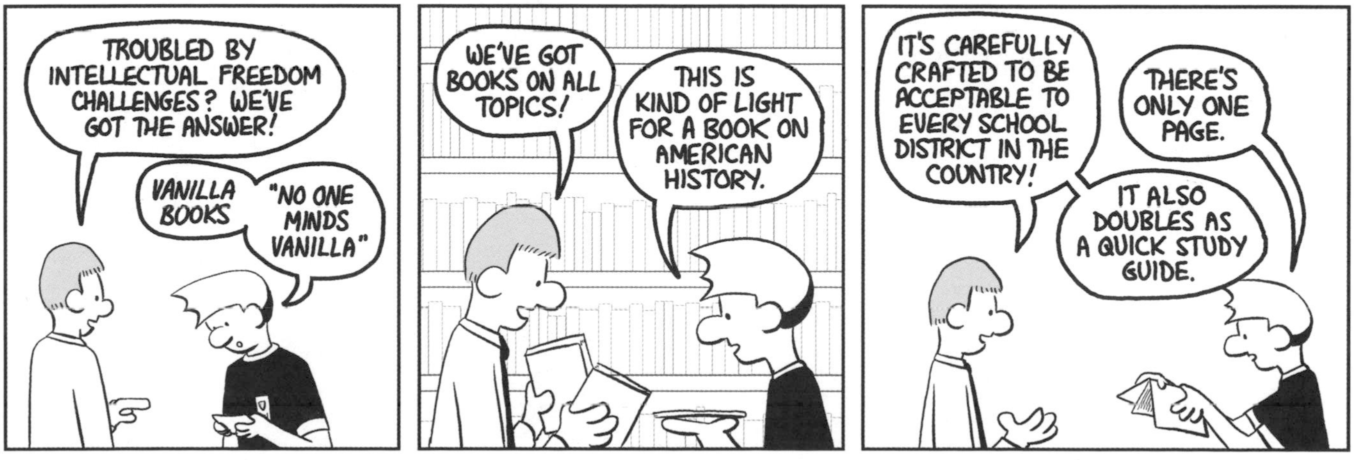

TROUBLED BY INTELLECTUAL FREEDOM CHALLENGES? WE'VE GOT THE ANSWER!
VANILLA BOOKS
"NO ONE MINDS VANILLA"
WE'VE GOT BOOKS ON ALL TOPICS!
THIS IS KIND OF LIGHT FOR A BOOK ON AMERICAN HISTORY.
IT'S CAREFULLY CRAFTED TO BE ACCEPTABLE TO EVERY SCHOOL DISTRICT IN THE COUNTRY!
THERE'S ONLY ONE PAGE.
IT ALSO DOUBLES AS A QUICK STUDY GUIDE.

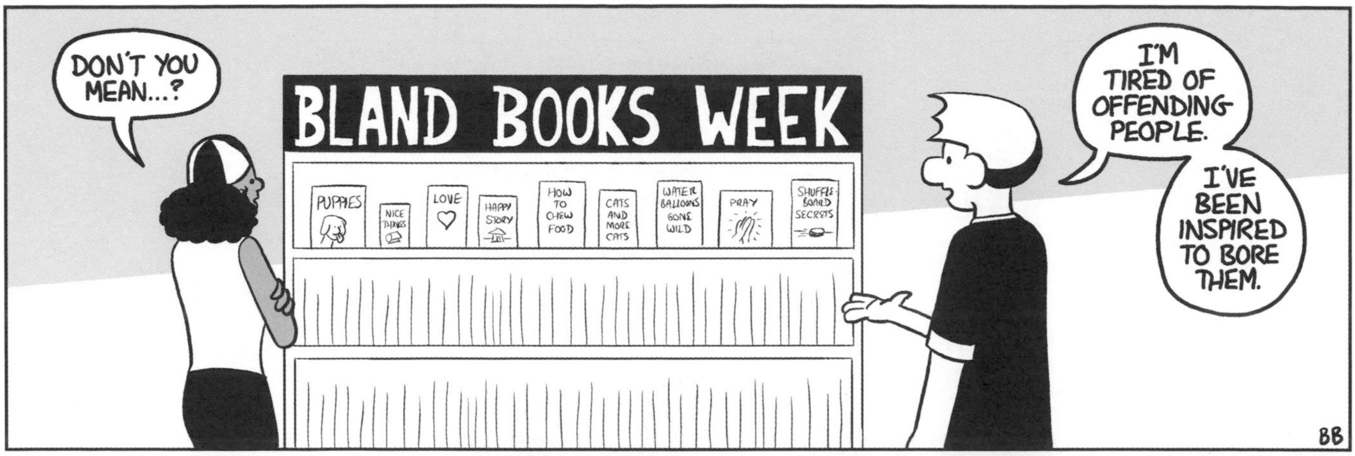
DON'T YOU MEAN...?
BLAND BOOKS WEEK
PUPPIES
NICE THINGS
LOVE
HAPPY STORY
HOW TO CHEW FOOD
CATS AND MORE CATS
WATER BALLOONS GONE WILD
PRAY
SHUFFLEBOARD SECRETS
I'M TIRED OF OFFENDING PEOPLE.
I'VE BEEN INSPIRED TO BORE THEM.
BB

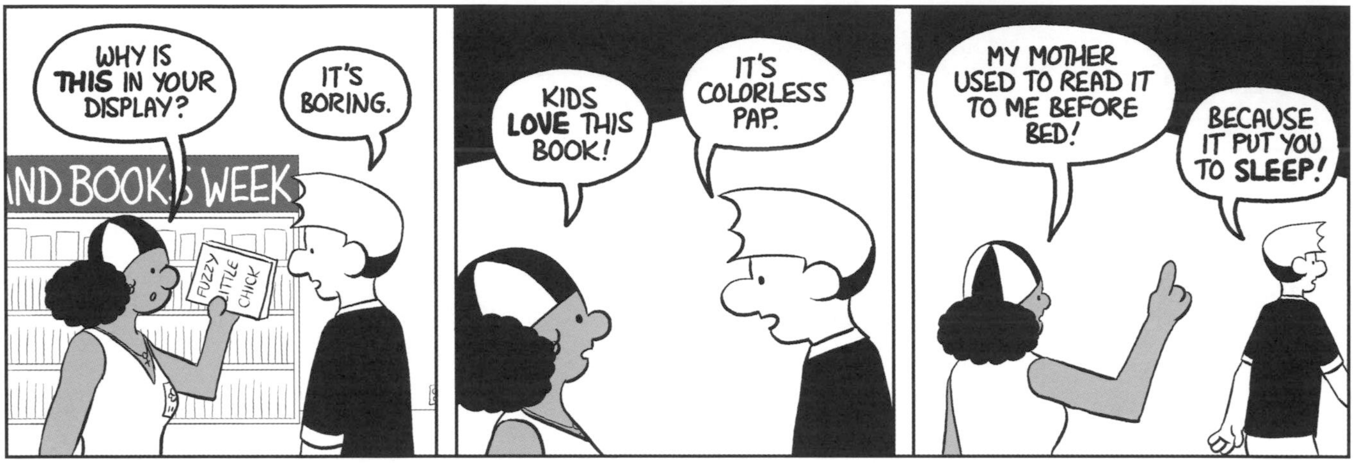
WHY IS **THIS** IN YOUR DISPLAY?
IT'S BORING.
FUZZY LITTLE CHICK
KIDS **LOVE** THIS BOOK!
IT'S COLORLESS PAP.
MY MOTHER USED TO READ IT TO ME BEFORE BED!
BECAUSE IT PUT YOU TO **SLEEP**!

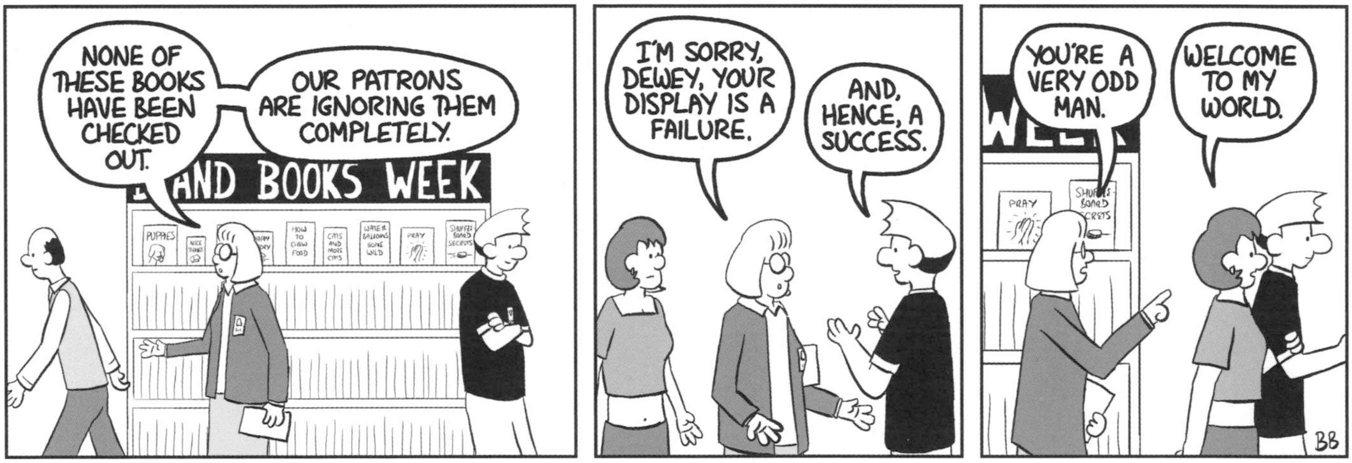
NONE OF THESE BOOKS HAVE BEEN CHECKED OUT.
OUR PATRONS ARE IGNORING THEM COMPLETELY.
I'M SORRY, DEWEY, YOUR DISPLAY IS A FAILURE.
AND, HENCE, A SUCCESS.
YOU'RE A VERY ODD MAN.
WELCOME TO MY WORLD.
BB

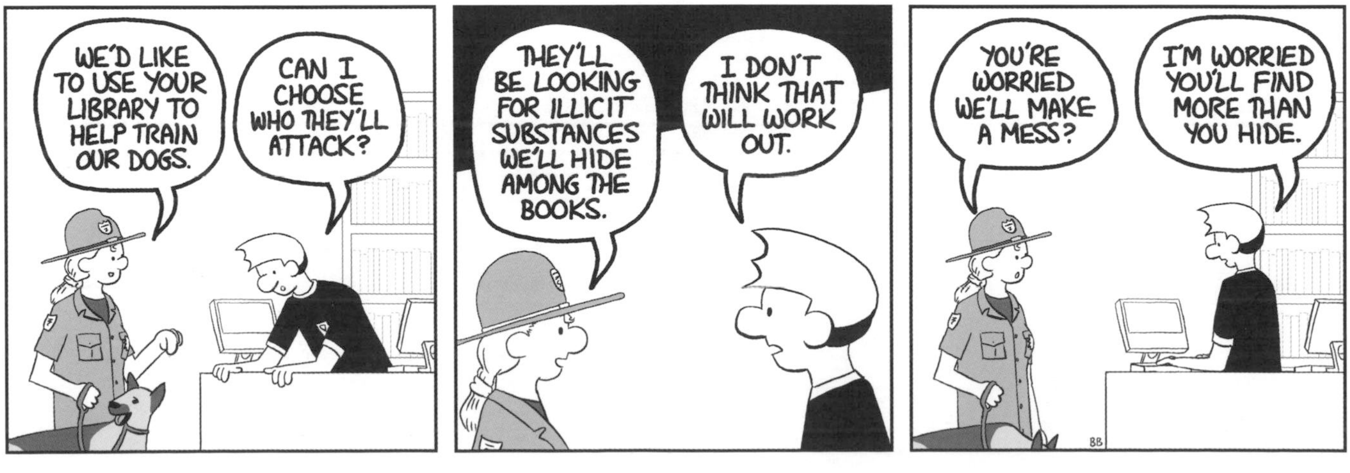
WE'D LIKE TO USE YOUR LIBRARY TO HELP TRAIN OUR DOGS.
CAN I CHOOSE WHO THEY'LL ATTACK?
THEY'LL BE LOOKING FOR ILLICIT SUBSTANCES WE'LL HIDE AMONG THE BOOKS.
I DON'T THINK THAT WILL WORK OUT.
YOU'RE WORRIED WE'LL MAKE A MESS?
I'M WORRIED YOU'LL FIND MORE THAN YOU HIDE.
BB

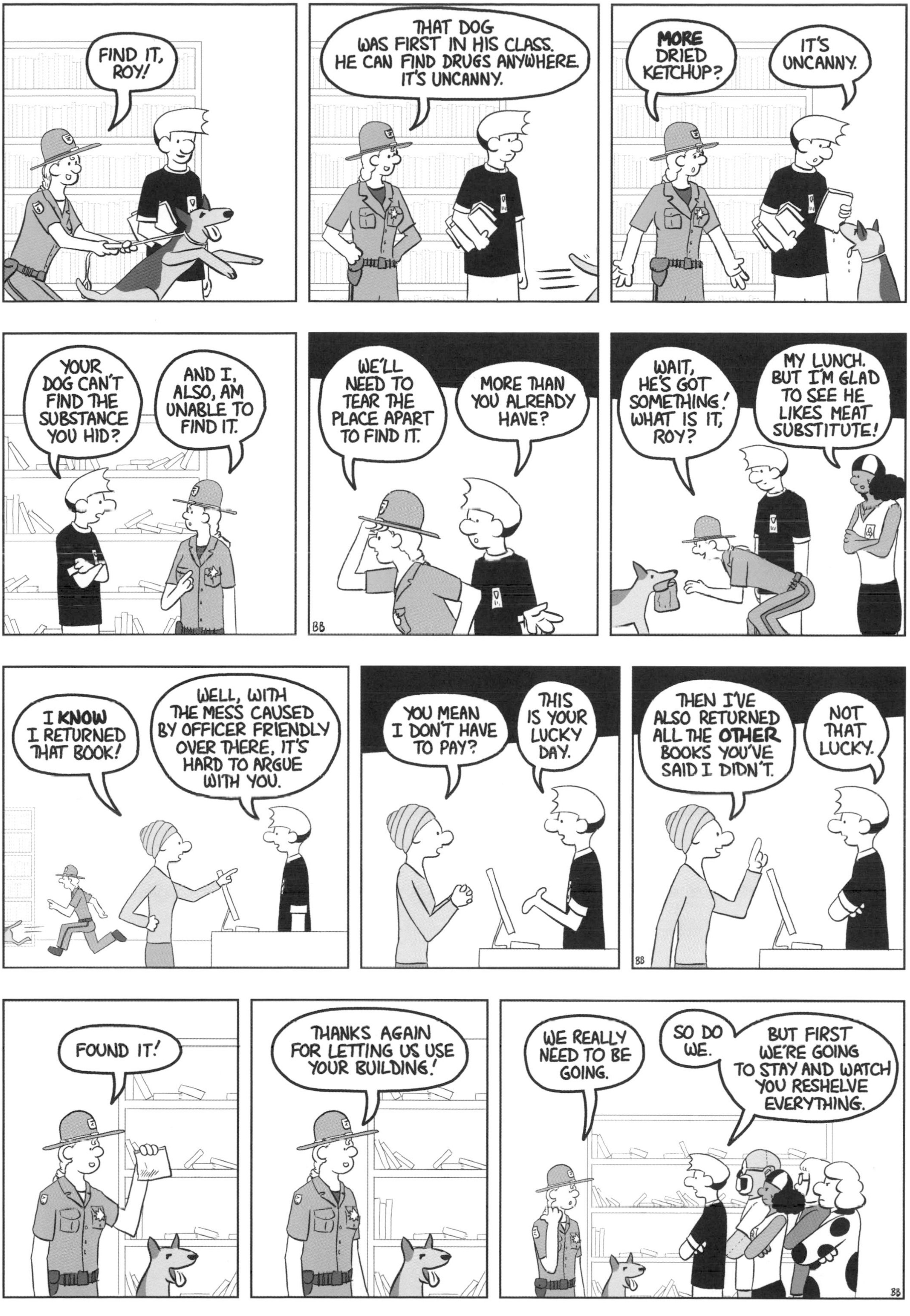
FIND IT, ROY!
THAT DOG WAS FIRST IN HIS CLASS. HE CAN FIND DRUGS ANYWHERE. IT'S UNCANNY.
MORE DRIED KETCHUP?
IT'S UNCANNY.
YOUR DOG CAN'T FIND THE SUBSTANCE YOU HID?
AND I, ALSO, AM UNABLE TO FIND IT.
WE'LL NEED TO TEAR THE PLACE APART TO FIND IT.
MORE THAN YOU ALREADY HAVE?
BB
WAIT, HE'S GOT SOMETHING! WHAT IS IT, ROY?
MY LUNCH. BUT I'M GLAD TO SEE HE LIKES MEAT SUBSTITUTE!
I KNOW I RETURNED THAT BOOK!
WELL, WITH THE MESS CAUSED BY OFFICER FRIENDLY OVER THERE, IT'S HARD TO ARGUE WITH YOU.
YOU MEAN I DON'T HAVE TO PAY?
THIS IS YOUR LUCKY DAY.
THEN I'VE ALSO RETURNED ALL THE OTHER BOOKS YOU'VE SAID I DIDN'T.
NOT THAT LUCKY.
BB
FOUND IT!
THANKS AGAIN FOR LETTING US USE YOUR BUILDING!
WE REALLY NEED TO BE GOING.
SO DO WE.
BUT FIRST WE'RE GOING TO STAY AND WATCH YOU RESHELVE EVERYTHING.
BB

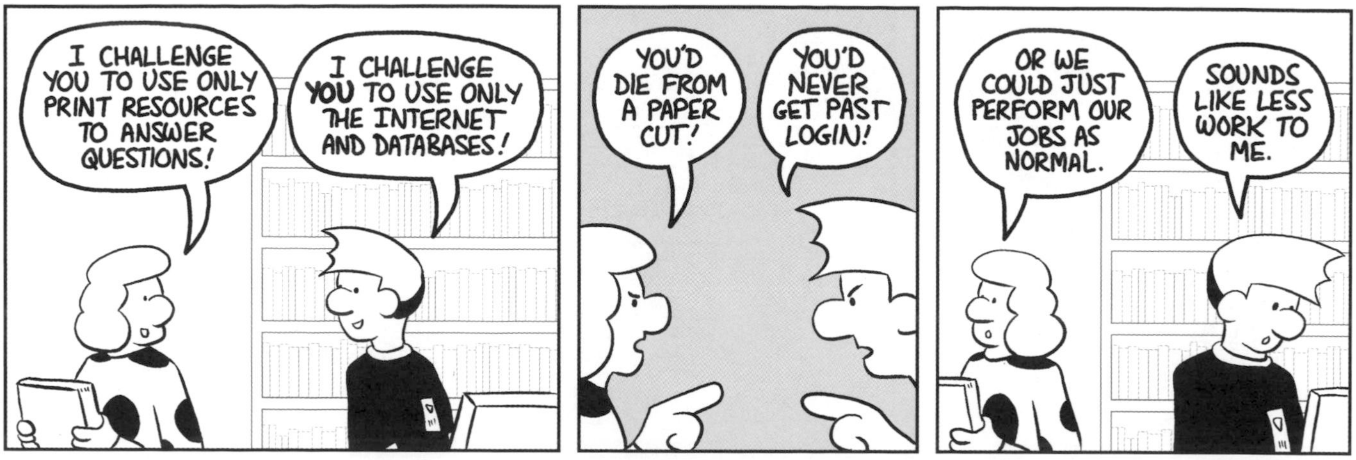
I CHALLENGE YOU TO USE ONLY PRINT RESOURCES TO ANSWER QUESTIONS!
I CHALLENGE **YOU** TO USE ONLY THE INTERNET AND DATABASES!
YOU'D DIE FROM A PAPER CUT!
YOU'D NEVER GET PAST LOGIN!
OR WE COULD JUST PERFORM OUR JOBS AS NORMAL.
SOUNDS LIKE LESS WORK TO ME.

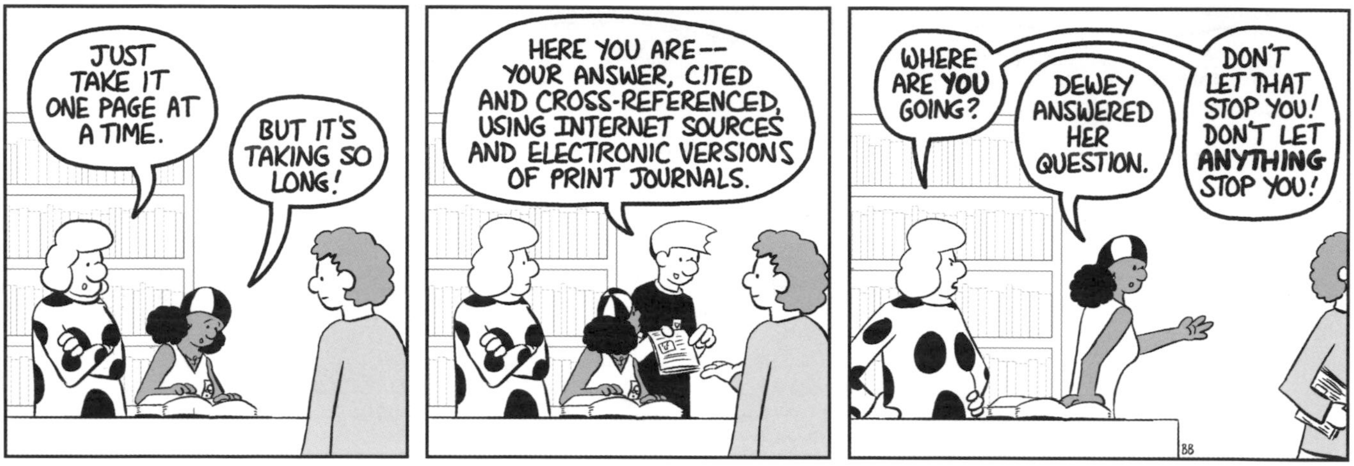
JUST TAKE IT ONE PAGE AT A TIME.
BUT IT'S TAKING SO LONG!
HERE YOU ARE-- YOUR ANSWER, CITED AND CROSS-REFERENCED, USING INTERNET SOURCES AND ELECTRONIC VERSIONS OF PRINT JOURNALS.
WHERE ARE **YOU** GOING?
DEWEY ANSWERED HER QUESTION.
DON'T LET THAT STOP YOU! DON'T LET **ANYTHING** STOP YOU!
BB

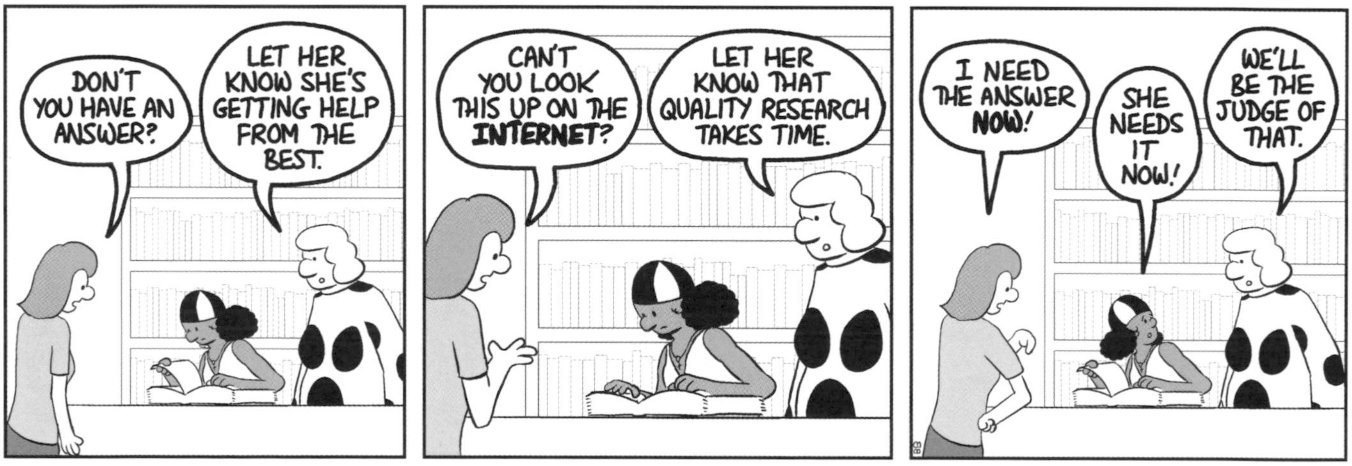
DON'T YOU HAVE AN ANSWER?
LET HER KNOW SHE'S GETTING HELP FROM THE BEST.
CAN'T YOU LOOK THIS UP ON THE **INTERNET**?
LET HER KNOW THAT QUALITY RESEARCH TAKES TIME.
I NEED THE ANSWER **NOW**!
SHE NEEDS IT NOW!
WE'LL BE THE JUDGE OF THAT.
BB

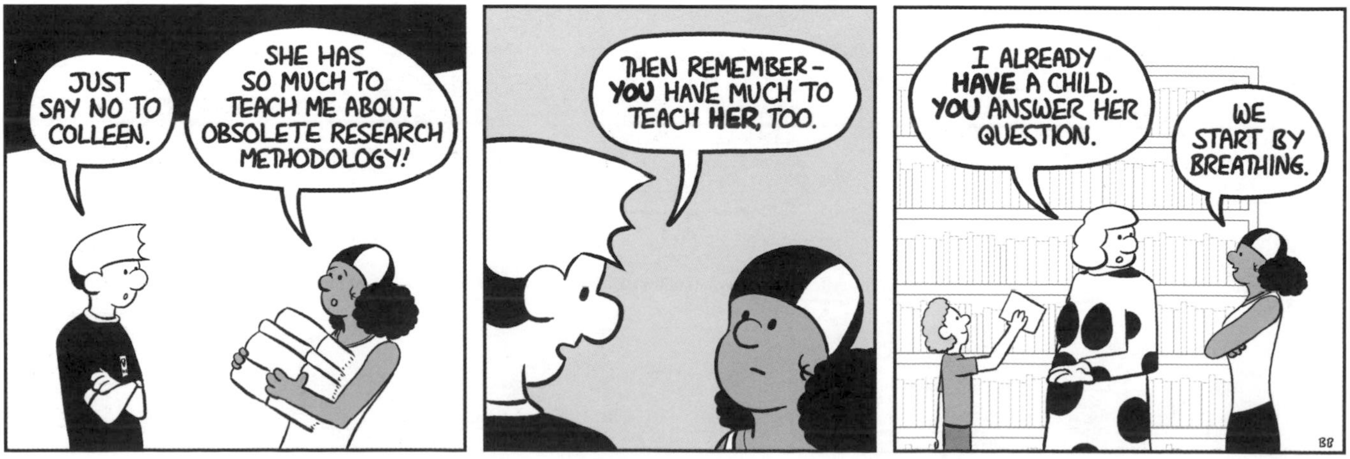
JUST SAY NO TO COLLEEN.
SHE HAS SO MUCH TO TEACH ME ABOUT OBSOLETE RESEARCH METHODOLOGY!
THEN REMEMBER- **YOU** HAVE MUCH TO TEACH **HER**, TOO.
I ALREADY **HAVE** A CHILD. **YOU** ANSWER HER QUESTION.
WE START BY BREATHING.
BB

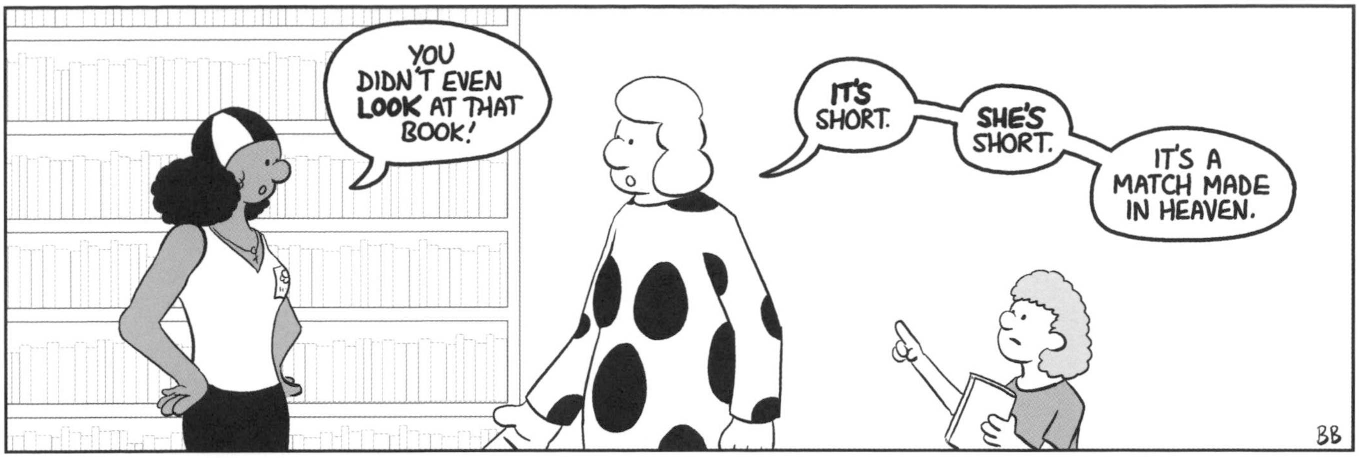
YOU DIDN'T EVEN **LOOK** AT THAT BOOK!
IT'S SHORT.
SHE'S SHORT.
IT'S A MATCH MADE IN HEAVEN.
BB

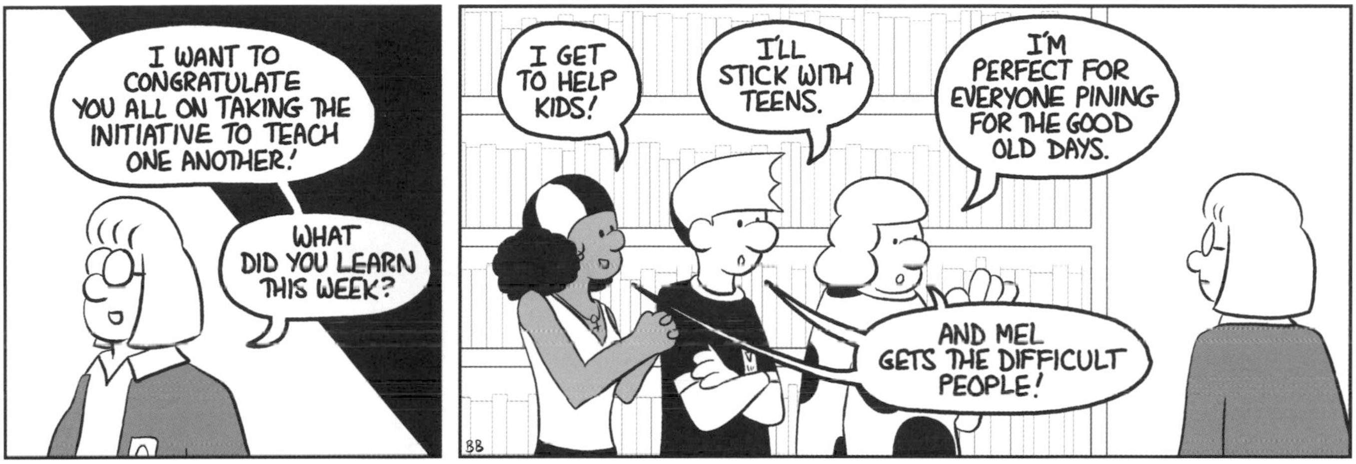
I WANT TO CONGRATULATE YOU ALL ON TAKING THE INITIATIVE TO TEACH ONE ANOTHER!
WHAT DID YOU LEARN THIS WEEK?
BB
I GET TO HELP KIDS!
I'LL STICK WITH TEENS.
I'M PERFECT FOR EVERYONE PINING FOR THE GOOD OLD DAYS.
AND MEL GETS THE DIFFICULT PEOPLE!

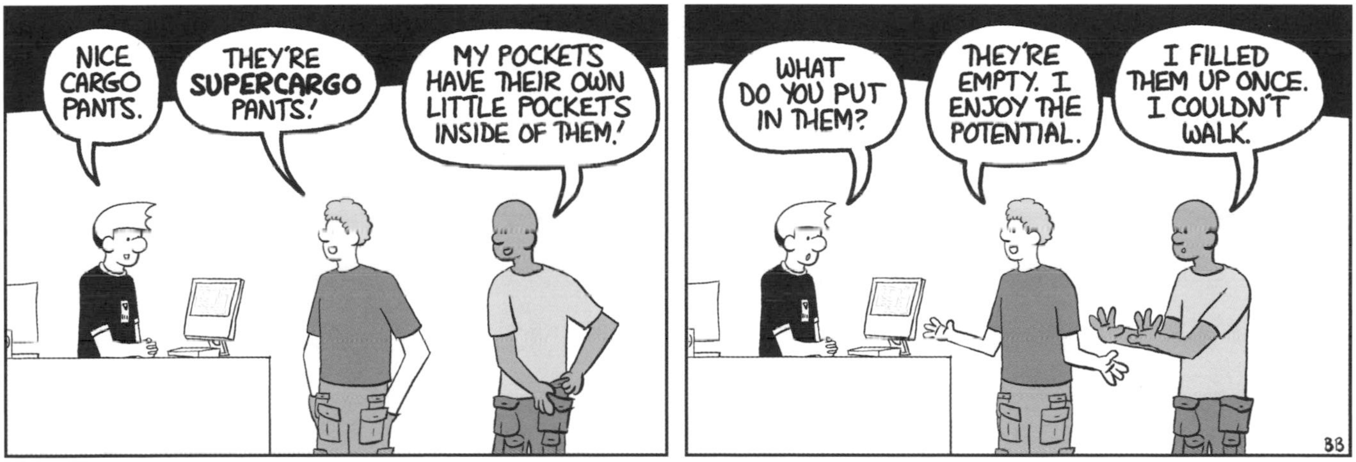
NICE CARGO PANTS.
THEY'RE **SUPERCARGO** PANTS!
MY POCKETS HAVE THEIR OWN LITTLE POCKETS INSIDE OF THEM!
WHAT DO YOU PUT IN THEM?
THEY'RE EMPTY. I ENJOY THE POTENTIAL.
I FILLED THEM UP ONCE. I COULDN'T WALK.
BB

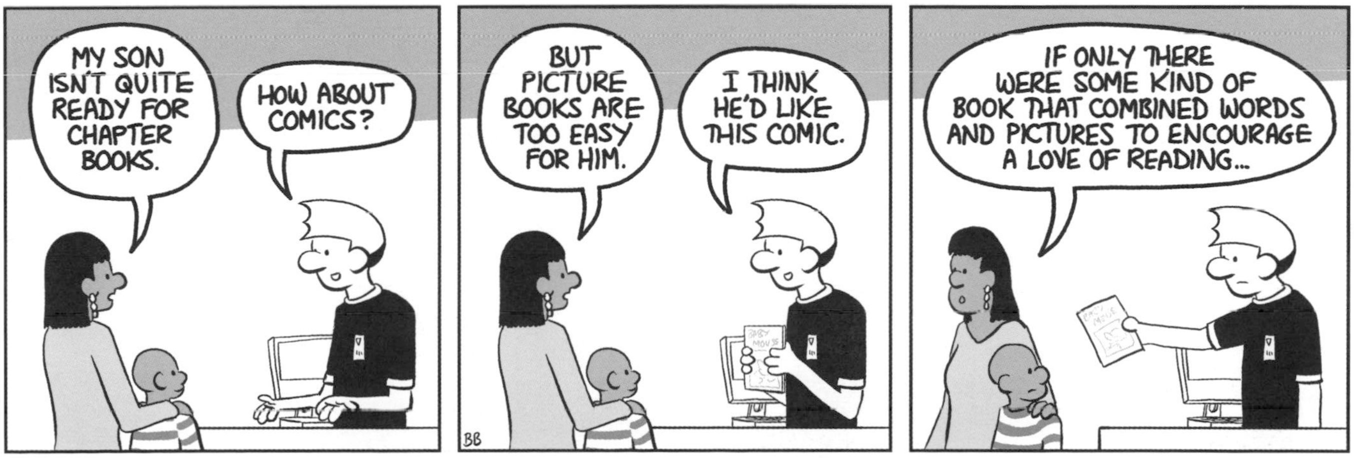
MY SON ISN'T QUITE READY FOR CHAPTER BOOKS.
HOW ABOUT COMICS?
BUT PICTURE BOOKS ARE TOO EASY FOR HIM.
I THINK HE'D LIKE THIS COMIC.
BB
IF ONLY THERE WERE SOME KIND OF BOOK THAT COMBINED WORDS AND PICTURES TO ENCOURAGE A LOVE OF READING...

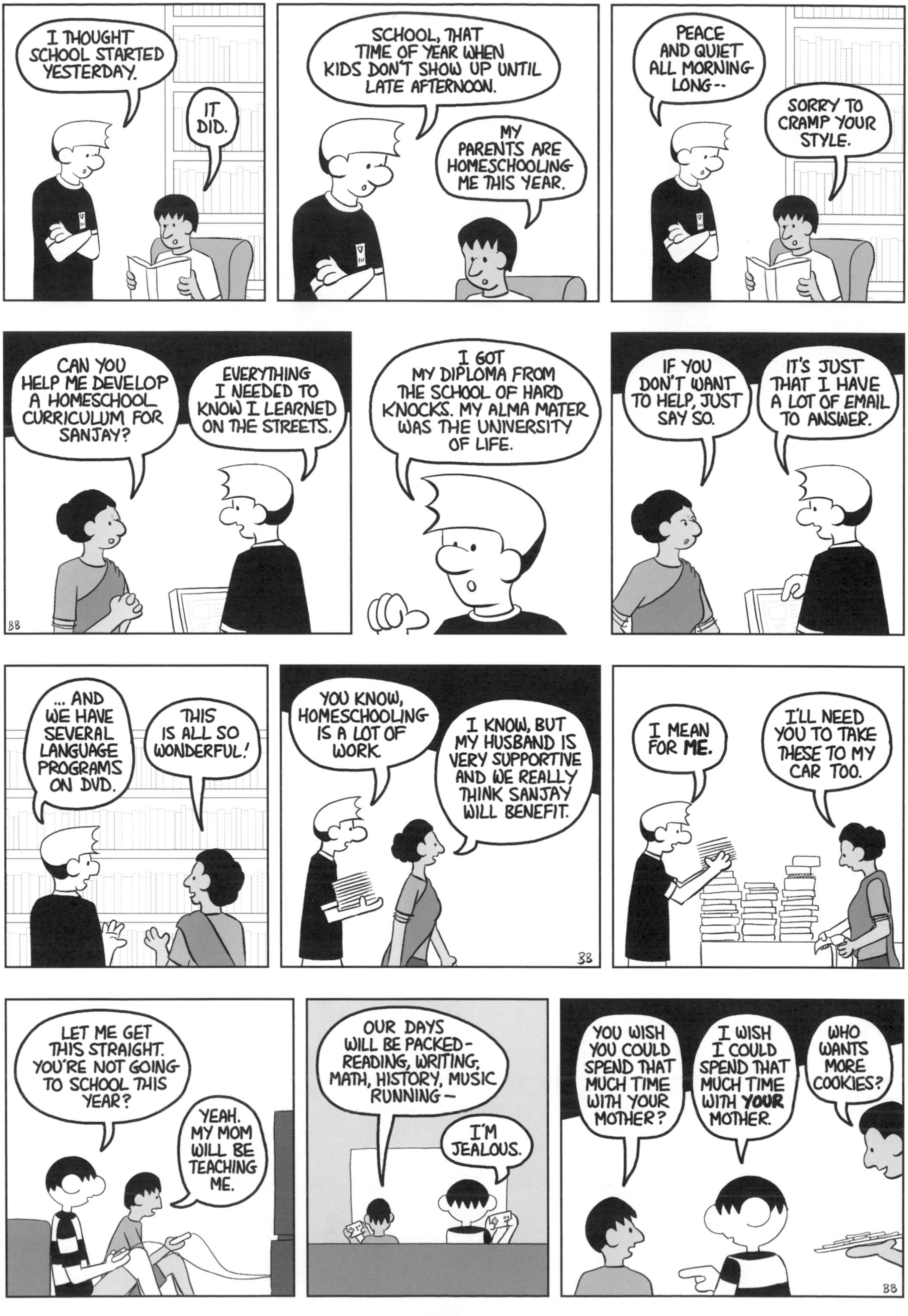
I THOUGHT SCHOOL STARTED YESTERDAY.
IT DID.
SCHOOL, THAT TIME OF YEAR WHEN KIDS DON'T SHOW UP UNTIL LATE AFTERNOON.
MY PARENTS ARE HOMESCHOOLING ME THIS YEAR.
PEACE AND QUIET ALL MORNING LONG--
SORRY TO CRAMP YOUR STYLE.
CAN YOU HELP ME DEVELOP A HOMESCHOOL CURRICULUM FOR SANJAY?
EVERYTHING I NEEDED TO KNOW I LEARNED ON THE STREETS.
I GOT MY DIPLOMA FROM THE SCHOOL OF HARD KNOCKS. MY ALMA MATER WAS THE UNIVERSITY OF LIFE.
IF YOU DON'T WANT TO HELP, JUST SAY SO.
IT'S JUST THAT I HAVE A LOT OF EMAIL TO ANSWER.
... AND WE HAVE SEVERAL LANGUAGE PROGRAMS ON DVD.
THIS IS ALL SO WONDERFUL!
YOU KNOW, HOMESCHOOLING IS A LOT OF WORK.
I KNOW, BUT MY HUSBAND IS VERY SUPPORTIVE AND WE REALLY THINK SANJAY WILL BENEFIT.
I MEAN FOR **ME**.
I'LL NEED YOU TO TAKE THESE TO MY CAR TOO.
LET ME GET THIS STRAIGHT. YOU'RE NOT GOING TO SCHOOL THIS YEAR?
YEAH. MY MOM WILL BE TEACHING ME.
OUR DAYS WILL BE PACKED- READING, WRITING, MATH, HISTORY, MUSIC RUNNING—
I'M JEALOUS.
YOU WISH YOU COULD SPEND THAT MUCH TIME WITH YOUR MOTHER?
I WISH I COULD SPEND THAT MUCH TIME WITH **YOUR** MOTHER.
WHO WANTS MORE COOKIES?

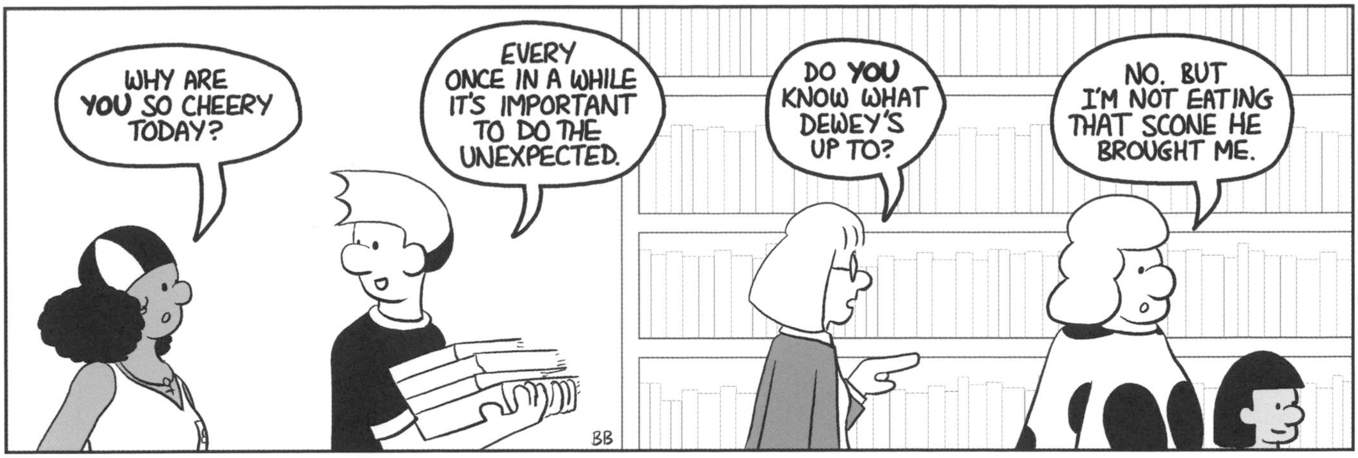
WHY ARE YOU SO CHEERY TODAY?
EVERY ONCE IN A WHILE IT'S IMPORTANT TO DO THE UNEXPECTED.
DO YOU KNOW WHAT DEWEY'S UP TO?
NO. BUT I'M NOT EATING THAT SCONE HE BROUGHT ME.
BB

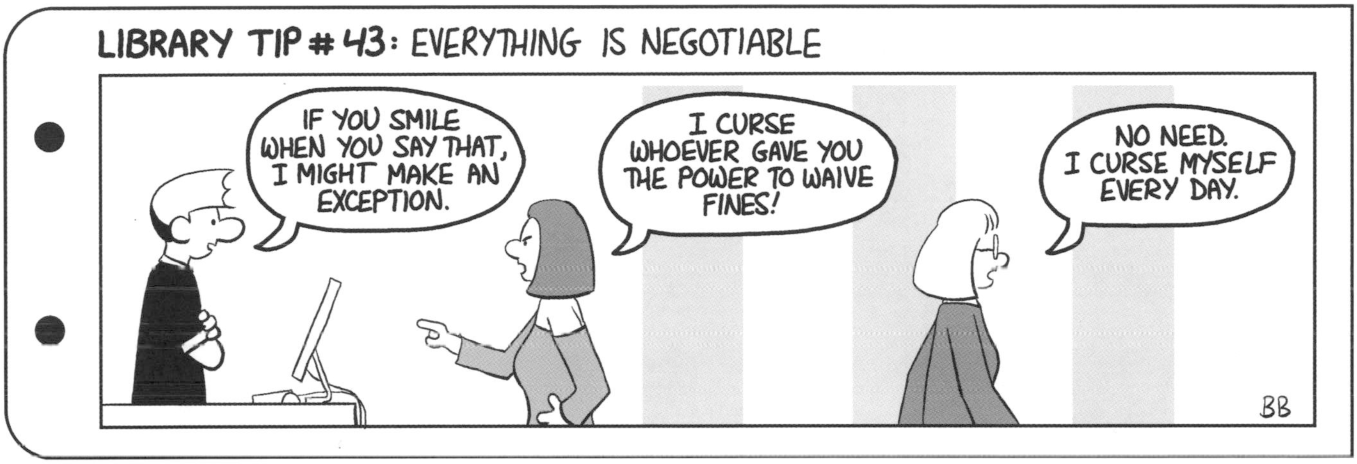
LIBRARY TIP # 43: EVERYTHING IS NEGOTIABLE
IF YOU SMILE WHEN YOU SAY THAT, I MIGHT MAKE AN EXCEPTION.
I CURSE WHOEVER GAVE YOU THE POWER TO WAIVE FINES!
NO NEED. I CURSE MYSELF EVERY DAY.
BB

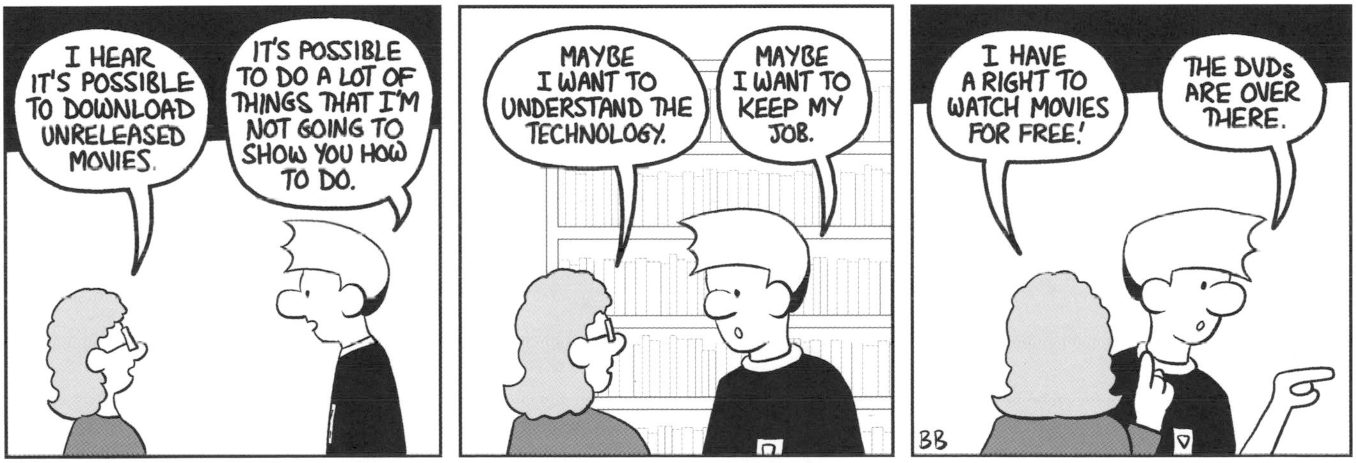
I HEAR IT'S POSSIBLE TO DOWNLOAD UNRELEASED MOVIES.
IT'S POSSIBLE TO DO A LOT OF THINGS THAT I'M NOT GOING TO SHOW YOU HOW TO DO.
MAYBE I WANT TO UNDERSTAND THE TECHNOLOGY.
MAYBE I WANT TO KEEP MY JOB.
I HAVE A RIGHT TO WATCH MOVIES FOR FREE!
THE DVDs ARE OVER THERE.
BB

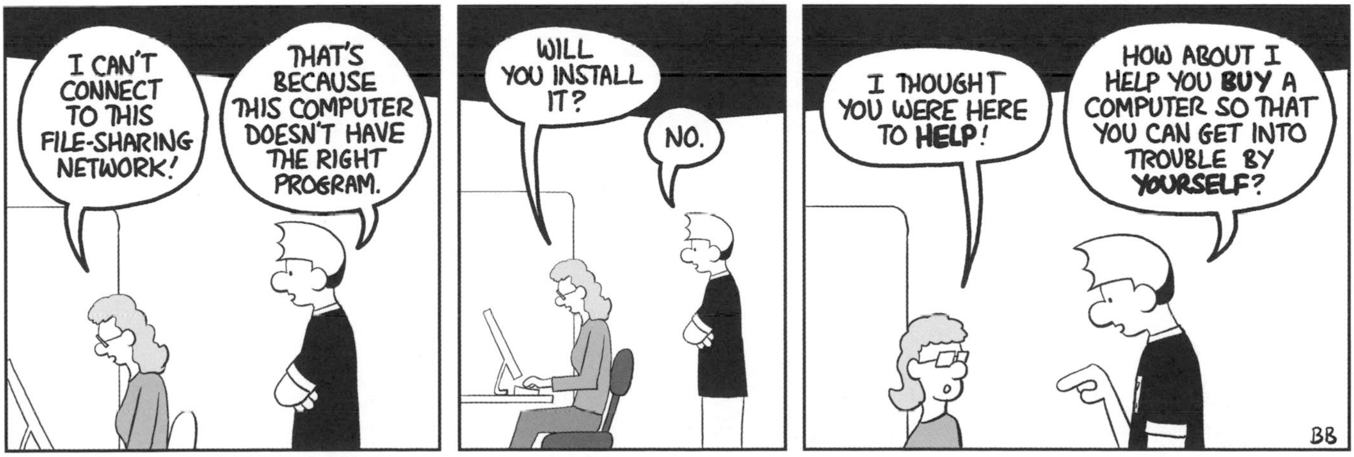
I CAN'T CONNECT TO THIS FILE-SHARING NETWORK!
THAT'S BECAUSE THIS COMPUTER DOESN'T HAVE THE RIGHT PROGRAM.
WILL YOU INSTALL IT?
NO.
I THOUGHT YOU WERE HERE TO HELP!
HOW ABOUT I HELP YOU BUY A COMPUTER SO THAT YOU CAN GET INTO TROUBLE BY YOURSELF?
BB

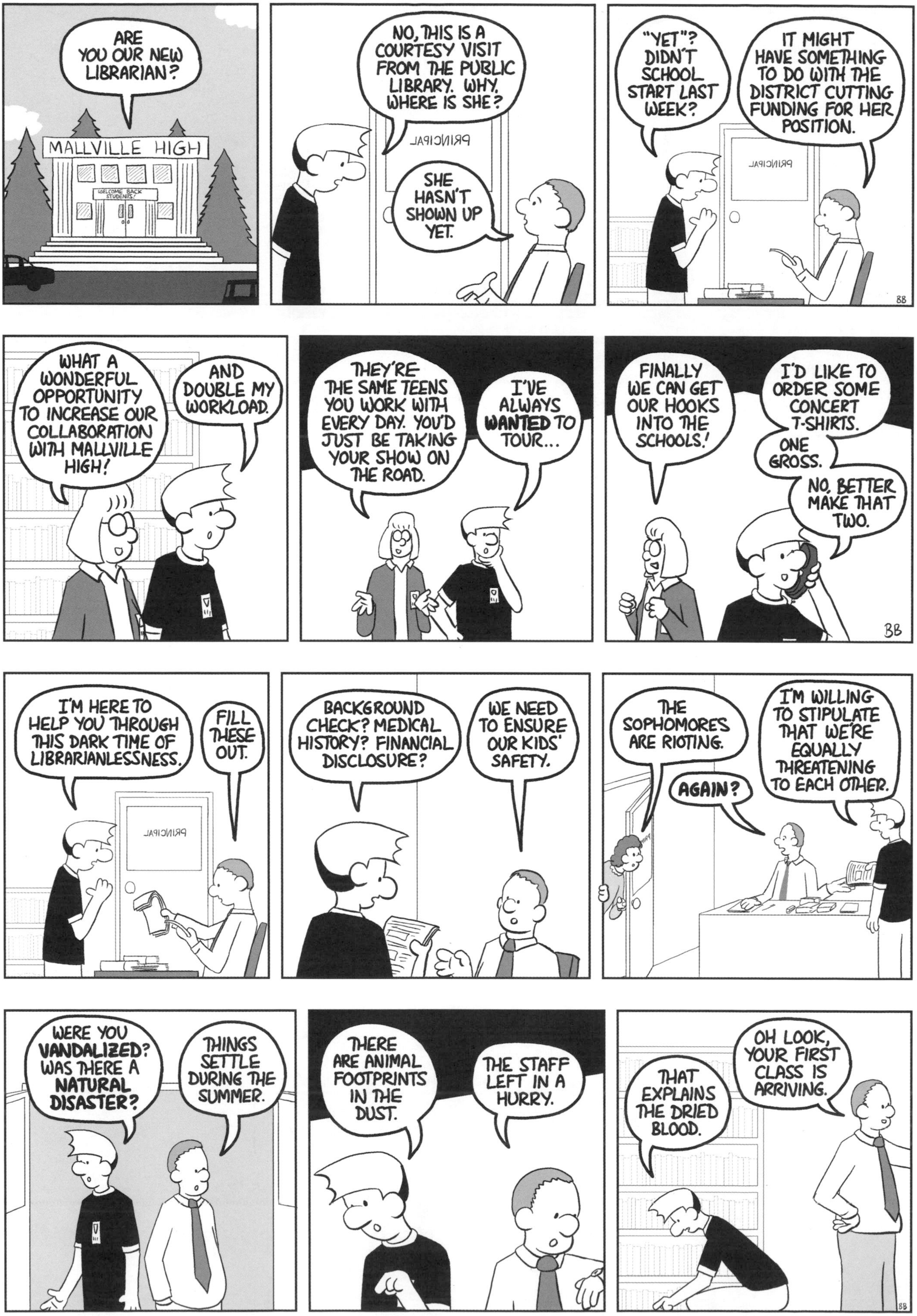

ARE YOU OUR NEW LIBRARIAN?
MALLVILLE HIGH
WELCOME BACK STUDENTS!
NO, THIS IS A COURTESY VISIT FROM THE PUBLIC LIBRARY. WHY, WHERE IS SHE?
PRINCIPAL
SHE HASN'T SHOWN UP YET.
"YET"? DIDN'T SCHOOL START LAST WEEK?
IT MIGHT HAVE SOMETHING TO DO WITH THE DISTRICT CUTTING FUNDING FOR HER POSITION.
BB
WHAT A WONDERFUL OPPORTUNITY TO INCREASE OUR COLLABORATION WITH MALLVILLE HIGH!
AND DOUBLE MY WORKLOAD.
THEY'RE THE SAME TEENS YOU WORK WITH EVERY DAY. YOU'D JUST BE TAKING YOUR SHOW ON THE ROAD.
I'VE ALWAYS WANTED TO TOUR...
FINALLY WE CAN GET OUR HOOKS INTO THE SCHOOLS!
I'D LIKE TO ORDER SOME CONCERT T-SHIRTS.
ONE GROSS.
NO, BETTER MAKE THAT TWO.
BB
I'M HERE TO HELP YOU THROUGH THIS DARK TIME OF LIBRARIANLESSNESS.
FILL THESE OUT.
PRINCIPAL
BACKGROUND CHECK? MEDICAL HISTORY? FINANCIAL DISCLOSURE?
WE NEED TO ENSURE OUR KIDS' SAFETY.
THE SOPHOMORES ARE RIOTING.
AGAIN?
I'M WILLING TO STIPULATE THAT WE'RE EQUALLY THREATENING TO EACH OTHER.
WERE YOU VANDALIZED? WAS THERE A NATURAL DISASTER?
THINGS SETTLE DURING THE SUMMER.
THERE ARE ANIMAL FOOTPRINTS IN THE DUST.
THE STAFF LEFT IN A HURRY.
THAT EXPLAINS THE DRIED BLOOD.
OH LOOK, YOUR FIRST CLASS IS ARRIVING.
BB

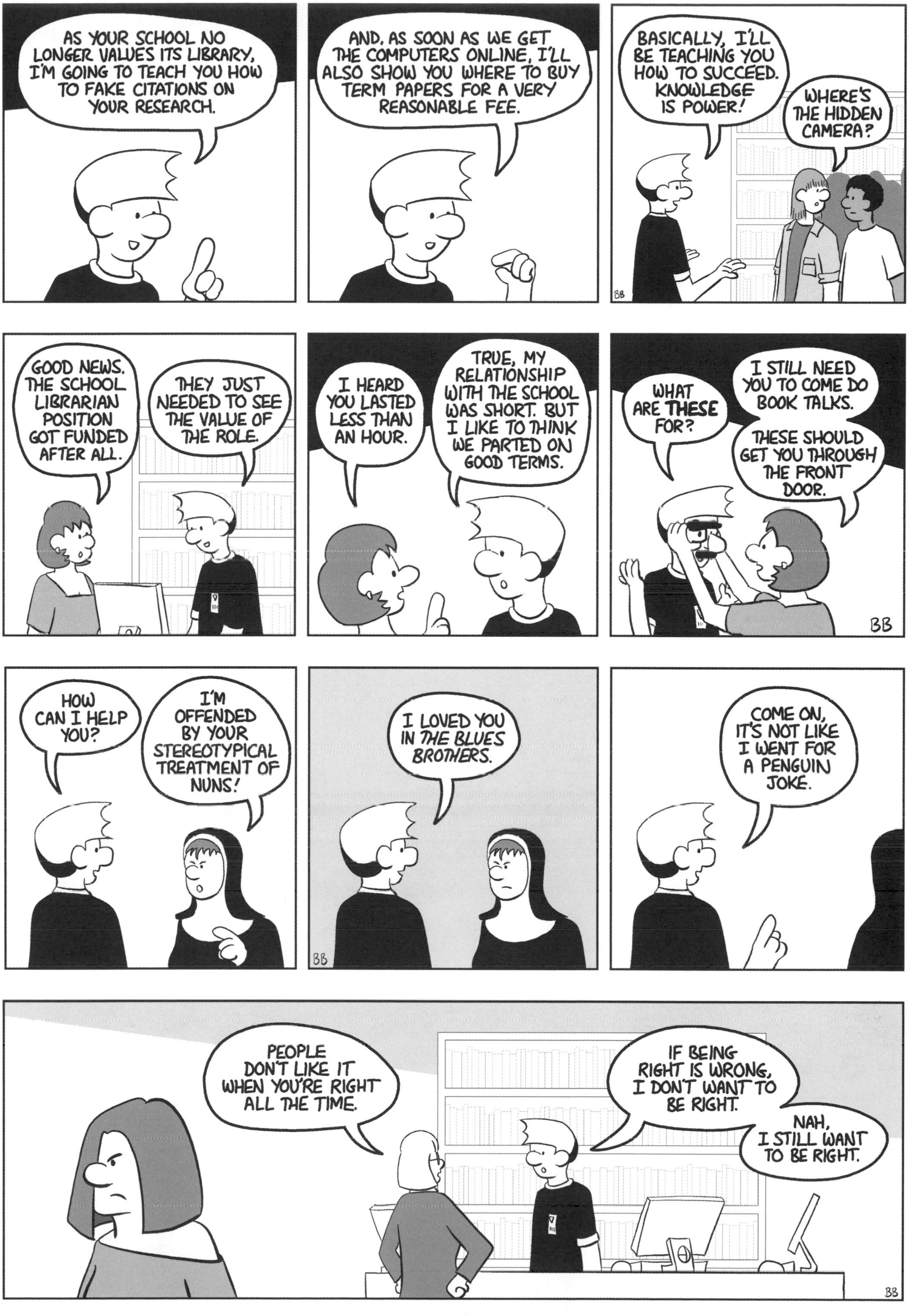
AS YOUR SCHOOL NO LONGER VALUES ITS LIBRARY, I'M GOING TO TEACH YOU HOW TO FAKE CITATIONS ON YOUR RESEARCH.
AND, AS SOON AS WE GET THE COMPUTERS ONLINE, I'LL ALSO SHOW YOU WHERE TO BUY TERM PAPERS FOR A VERY REASONABLE FEE.
BASICALLY, I'LL BE TEACHING YOU HOW TO SUCCEED. KNOWLEDGE IS POWER!
WHERE'S THE HIDDEN CAMERA?
BB
GOOD NEWS. THE SCHOOL LIBRARIAN POSITION GOT FUNDED AFTER ALL.
THEY JUST NEEDED TO SEE THE VALUE OF THE ROLE.
I HEARD YOU LASTED LESS THAN AN HOUR.
TRUE, MY RELATIONSHIP WITH THE SCHOOL WAS SHORT. BUT I LIKE TO THINK WE PARTED ON GOOD TERMS.
WHAT ARE **THESE** FOR?
I STILL NEED YOU TO COME DO BOOK TALKS.
THESE SHOULD GET YOU THROUGH THE FRONT DOOR.
BB
HOW CAN I HELP YOU?
I'M OFFENDED BY YOUR STEREOTYPICAL TREATMENT OF NUNS!
I LOVED YOU IN *THE BLUES BROTHERS*.
BB
COME ON, IT'S NOT LIKE I WENT FOR A PENGUIN JOKE.
PEOPLE DON'T LIKE IT WHEN YOU'RE RIGHT ALL THE TIME.
IF BEING RIGHT IS WRONG, I DON'T WANT TO BE RIGHT.
NAH, I STILL WANT TO BE RIGHT.
BB

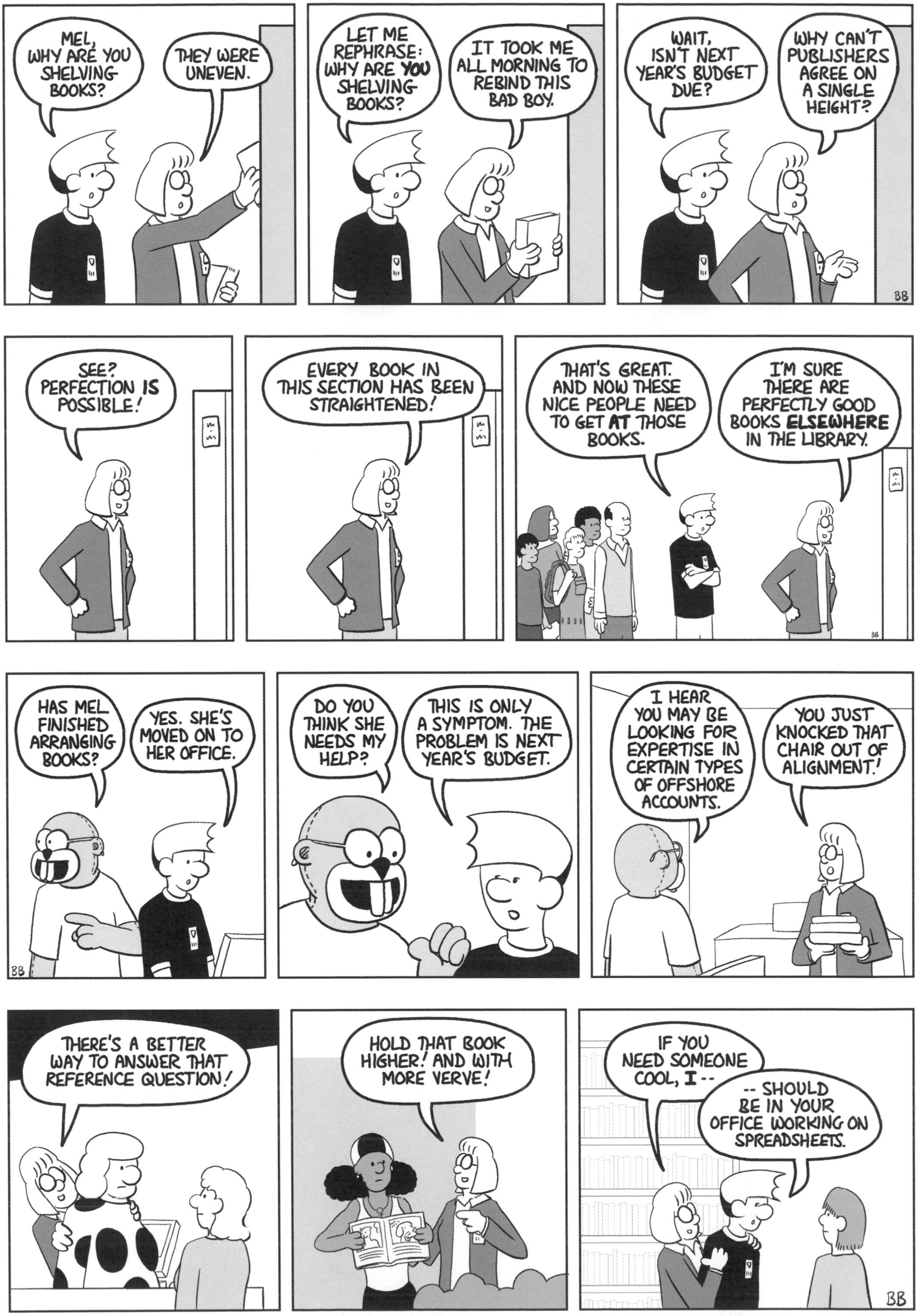
MEL, WHY ARE YOU SHELVING BOOKS?
THEY WERE UNEVEN.
LET ME REPHRASE: WHY ARE **YOU** SHELVING BOOKS?
IT TOOK ME ALL MORNING TO REBIND THIS BAD BOY.
WAIT, ISN'T NEXT YEAR'S BUDGET DUE?
WHY CAN'T PUBLISHERS AGREE ON A SINGLE HEIGHT?
BB
SEE? PERFECTION **IS** POSSIBLE!
EVERY BOOK IN THIS SECTION HAS BEEN STRAIGHTENED!
THAT'S GREAT. AND NOW THESE NICE PEOPLE NEED TO GET **AT** THOSE BOOKS.
I'M SURE THERE ARE PERFECTLY GOOD BOOKS **ELSEWHERE** IN THE LIBRARY.
BB
HAS MEL FINISHED ARRANGING BOOKS?
YES. SHE'S MOVED ON TO HER OFFICE.
BB
DO YOU THINK SHE NEEDS MY HELP?
THIS IS ONLY A SYMPTOM. THE PROBLEM IS NEXT YEAR'S BUDGET.
I HEAR YOU MAY BE LOOKING FOR EXPERTISE IN CERTAIN TYPES OF OFFSHORE ACCOUNTS.
YOU JUST KNOCKED THAT CHAIR OUT OF ALIGNMENT!
THERE'S A BETTER WAY TO ANSWER THAT REFERENCE QUESTION!
HOLD THAT BOOK HIGHER! AND WITH MORE VERVE!
IF YOU NEED SOMEONE COOL, **I** --
-- SHOULD BE IN YOUR OFFICE WORKING ON SPREADSHEETS.
BB

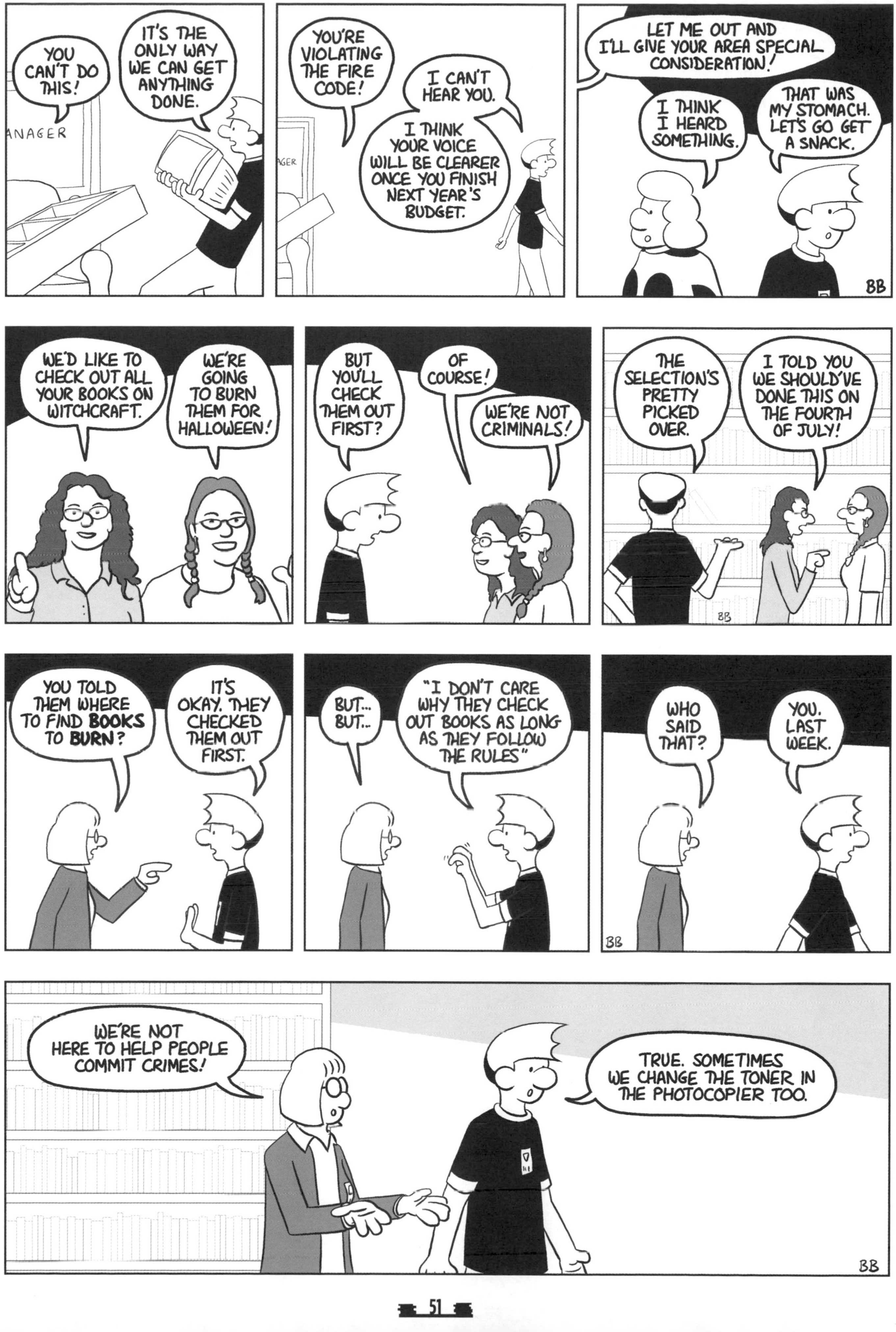
YOU CAN'T DO THIS!
IT'S THE ONLY WAY WE CAN GET ANYTHING DONE.
YOU'RE VIOLATING THE FIRE CODE!
I CAN'T HEAR YOU.
I THINK YOUR VOICE WILL BE CLEARER ONCE YOU FINISH NEXT YEAR'S BUDGET.
LET ME OUT AND I'LL GIVE YOUR AREA SPECIAL CONSIDERATION!
I THINK I HEARD SOMETHING.
THAT WAS MY STOMACH. LET'S GO GET A SNACK.
BB
WE'D LIKE TO CHECK OUT ALL YOUR BOOKS ON WITCHCRAFT.
WE'RE GOING TO BURN THEM FOR HALLOWEEN!
BUT YOU'LL CHECK THEM OUT FIRST?
OF COURSE!
WE'RE NOT CRIMINALS!
THE SELECTION'S PRETTY PICKED OVER.
I TOLD YOU WE SHOULD'VE DONE THIS ON THE FOURTH OF JULY!
BB
YOU TOLD THEM WHERE TO FIND **BOOKS** TO **BURN**?
IT'S OKAY. THEY CHECKED THEM OUT FIRST.
BUT... BUT...
"I DON'T CARE WHY THEY CHECK OUT BOOKS AS LONG AS THEY FOLLOW THE RULES"
WHO SAID THAT?
YOU. LAST WEEK.
BB
WE'RE NOT HERE TO HELP PEOPLE COMMIT CRIMES!
TRUE. SOMETIMES WE CHANGE THE TONER IN THE PHOTOCOPIER TOO.
BB

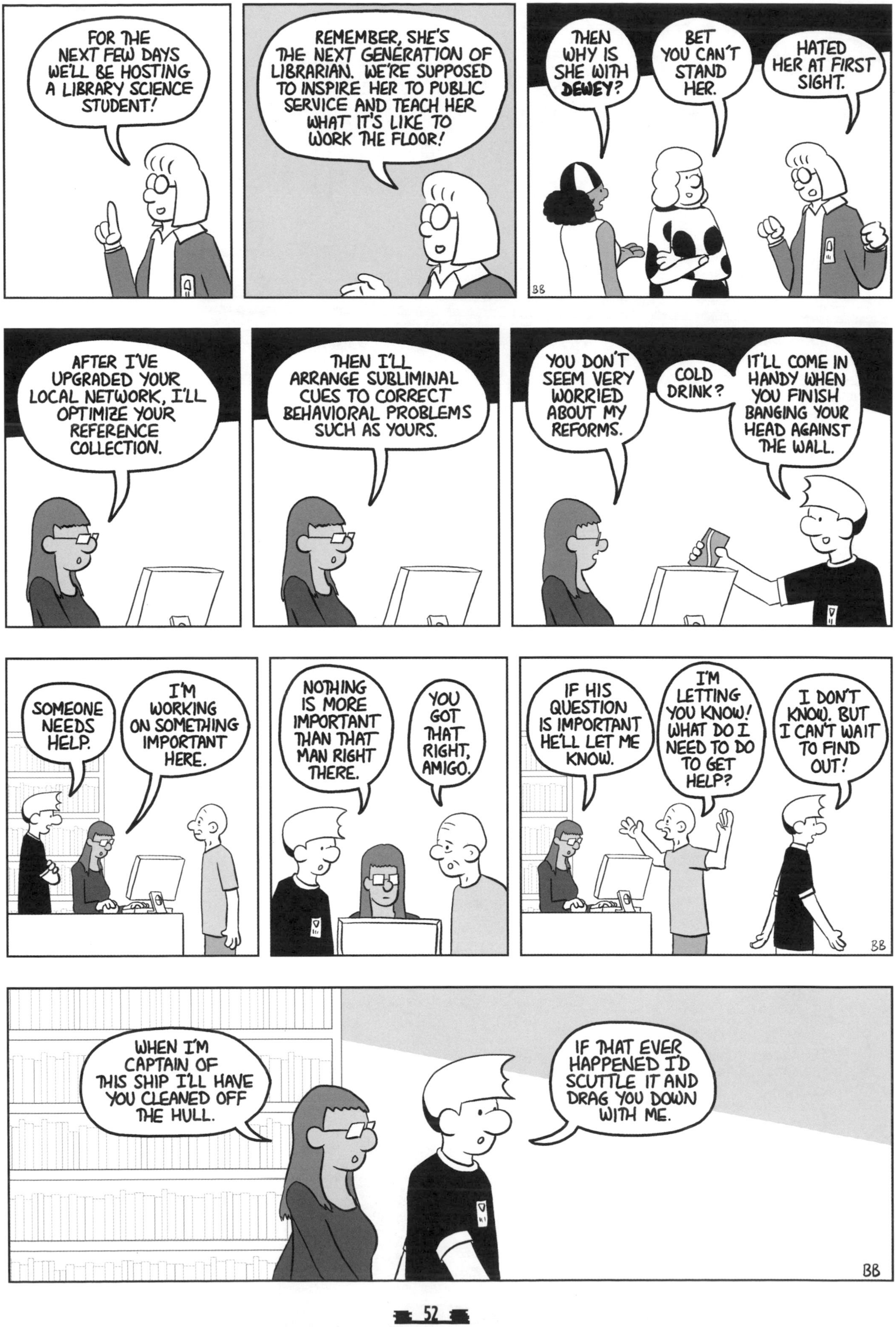
FOR THE NEXT FEW DAYS WE'LL BE HOSTING A LIBRARY SCIENCE STUDENT!
REMEMBER, SHE'S THE NEXT GENERATION OF LIBRARIAN. WE'RE SUPPOSED TO INSPIRE HER TO PUBLIC SERVICE AND TEACH HER WHAT IT'S LIKE TO WORK THE FLOOR!
THEN WHY IS SHE WITH **DEWEY**?
BET YOU CAN'T STAND HER.
HATED HER AT FIRST SIGHT.
BB
AFTER I'VE UPGRADED YOUR LOCAL NETWORK, I'LL OPTIMIZE YOUR REFERENCE COLLECTION.
THEN I'LL ARRANGE SUBLIMINAL CUES TO CORRECT BEHAVIORAL PROBLEMS SUCH AS YOURS.
YOU DON'T SEEM VERY WORRIED ABOUT MY REFORMS.
COLD DRINK?
IT'LL COME IN HANDY WHEN YOU FINISH BANGING YOUR HEAD AGAINST THE WALL.
SOMEONE NEEDS HELP.
I'M WORKING ON SOMETHING IMPORTANT HERE.
NOTHING IS MORE IMPORTANT THAN THAT MAN RIGHT THERE.
YOU GOT THAT RIGHT, AMIGO.
IF HIS QUESTION IS IMPORTANT HE'LL LET ME KNOW.
I'M LETTING YOU KNOW! WHAT DO I NEED TO DO TO GET HELP?
I DON'T KNOW. BUT I CAN'T WAIT TO FIND OUT!
BB
WHEN I'M CAPTAIN OF THIS SHIP I'LL HAVE YOU CLEANED OFF THE HULL.
IF THAT EVER HAPPENED I'D SCUTTLE IT AND DRAG YOU DOWN WITH ME.
BB

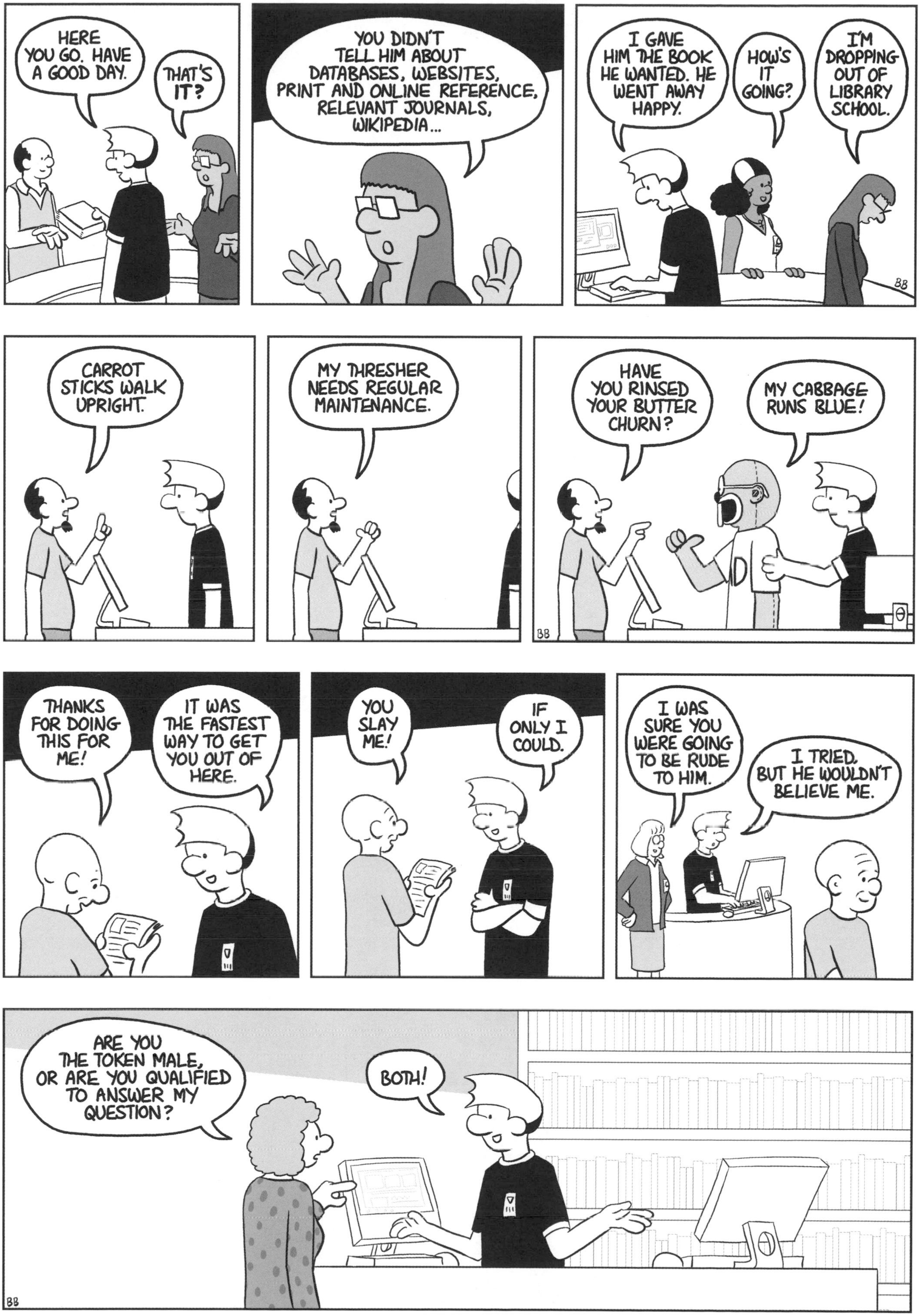
HERE YOU GO. HAVE A GOOD DAY.
THAT'S IT?
YOU DIDN'T TELL HIM ABOUT DATABASES, WEBSITES, PRINT AND ONLINE REFERENCE, RELEVANT JOURNALS, WIKIPEDIA...
I GAVE HIM THE BOOK HE WANTED. HE WENT AWAY HAPPY.
HOW'S IT GOING?
I'M DROPPING OUT OF LIBRARY SCHOOL.
BB
CARROT STICKS WALK UPRIGHT.
MY THRESHER NEEDS REGULAR MAINTENANCE.
HAVE YOU RINSED YOUR BUTTER CHURN?
MY CABBAGE RUNS BLUE!
BB
THANKS FOR DOING THIS FOR ME!
IT WAS THE FASTEST WAY TO GET YOU OUT OF HERE.
YOU SLAY ME!
IF ONLY I COULD.
I WAS SURE YOU WERE GOING TO BE RUDE TO HIM.
I TRIED. BUT HE WOULDN'T BELIEVE ME.
ARE YOU THE TOKEN MALE, OR ARE YOU QUALIFIED TO ANSWER MY QUESTION?
BOTH!
BB

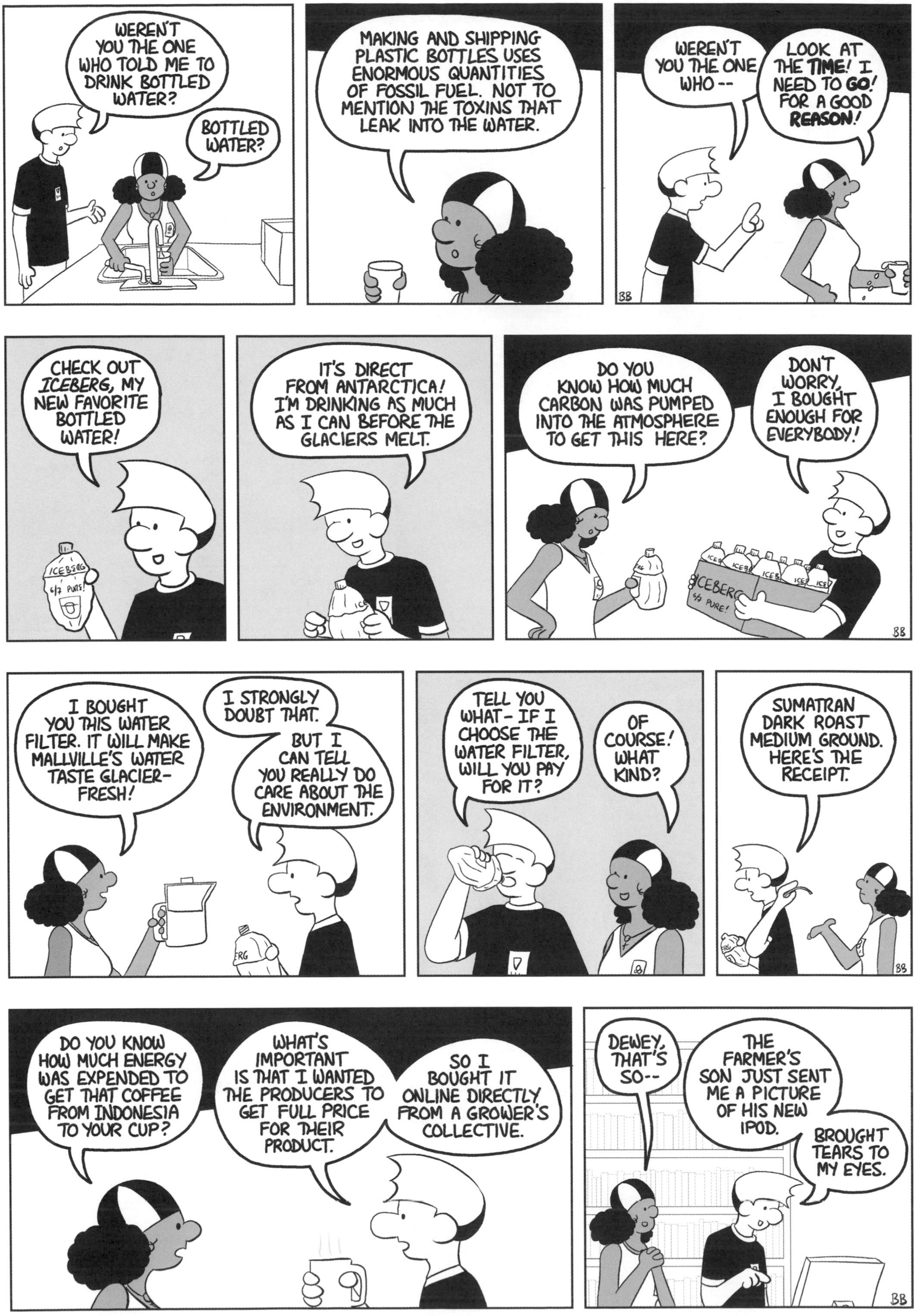
WEREN'T YOU THE ONE WHO TOLD ME TO DRINK BOTTLED WATER?
BOTTLED WATER?
MAKING AND SHIPPING PLASTIC BOTTLES USES ENORMOUS QUANTITIES OF FOSSIL FUEL. NOT TO MENTION THE TOXINS THAT LEAK INTO THE WATER.
WEREN'T YOU THE ONE WHO--
LOOK AT THE TIME! I NEED TO GO! FOR A GOOD REASON!
BB
CHECK OUT ICEBERG, MY NEW FAVORITE BOTTLED WATER!
ICEBERG
6/7 PURE!
IT'S DIRECT FROM ANTARCTICA! I'M DRINKING AS MUCH AS I CAN BEFORE THE GLACIERS MELT.
DO YOU KNOW HOW MUCH CARBON WAS PUMPED INTO THE ATMOSPHERE TO GET THIS HERE?
DON'T WORRY, I BOUGHT ENOUGH FOR EVERYBODY!
ICEBERG
6/7 PURE!
BB
I BOUGHT YOU THIS WATER FILTER. IT WILL MAKE MALLVILLE'S WATER TASTE GLACIER-FRESH!
I STRONGLY DOUBT THAT.
BUT I CAN TELL YOU REALLY DO CARE ABOUT THE ENVIRONMENT.
TELL YOU WHAT- IF I CHOOSE THE WATER FILTER, WILL YOU PAY FOR IT?
OF COURSE! WHAT KIND?
SUMATRAN DARK ROAST MEDIUM GROUND. HERE'S THE RECEIPT.
BB
DO YOU KNOW HOW MUCH ENERGY WAS EXPENDED TO GET THAT COFFEE FROM INDONESIA TO YOUR CUP?
WHAT'S IMPORTANT IS THAT I WANTED THE PRODUCERS TO GET FULL PRICE FOR THEIR PRODUCT.
SO I BOUGHT IT ONLINE DIRECTLY FROM A GROWER'S COLLECTIVE.
DEWEY, THAT'S SO--
THE FARMER'S SON JUST SENT ME A PICTURE OF HIS NEW IPOD.
BROUGHT TEARS TO MY EYES.
BB

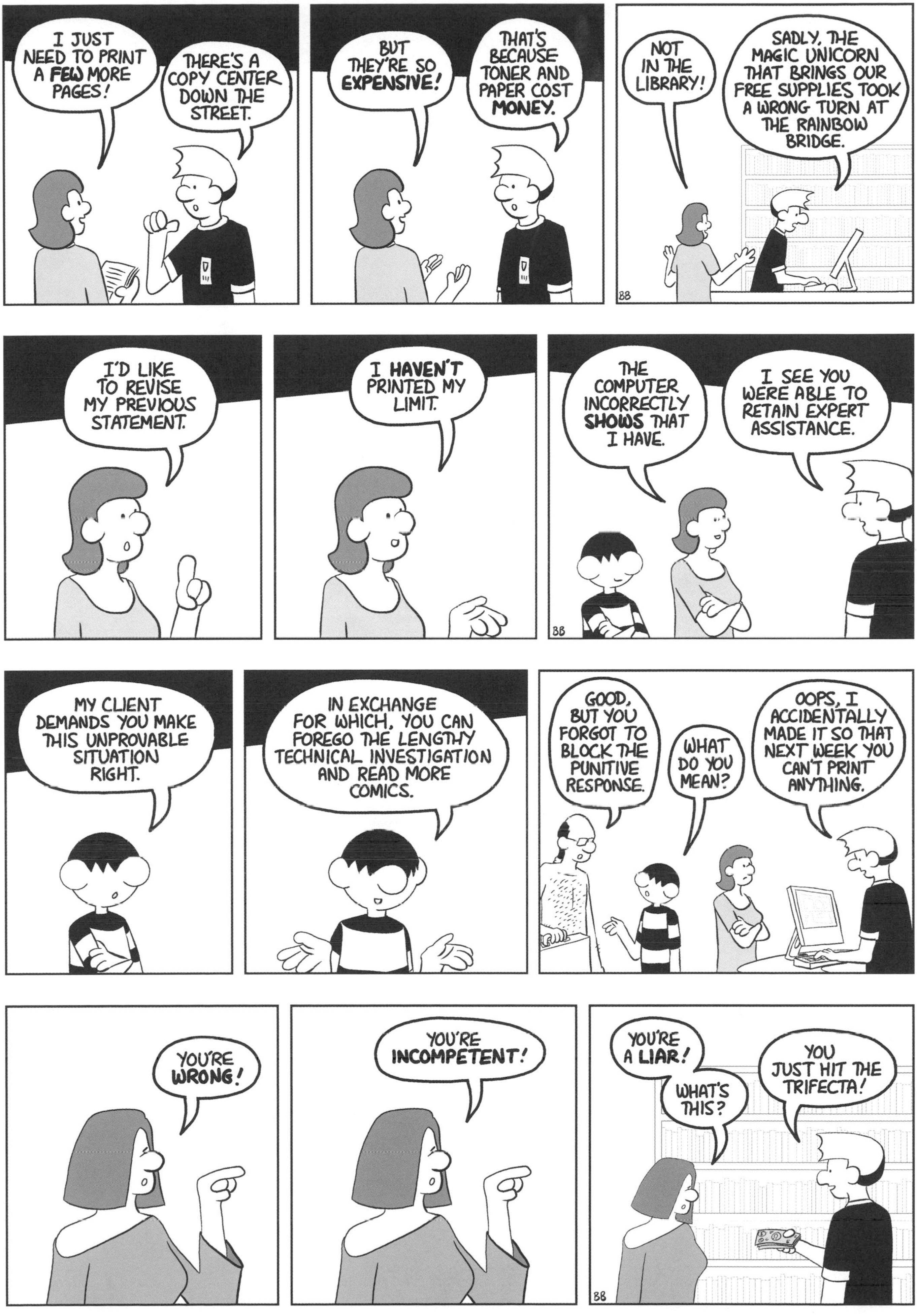
I JUST NEED TO PRINT A **FEW** MORE PAGES!
THERE'S A COPY CENTER DOWN THE STREET.
BUT THEY'RE SO **EXPENSIVE**!
THAT'S BECAUSE TONER AND PAPER COST **MONEY**.
NOT IN THE LIBRARY!
SADLY, THE MAGIC UNICORN THAT BRINGS OUR FREE SUPPLIES TOOK A WRONG TURN AT THE RAINBOW BRIDGE.
BB
I'D LIKE TO REVISE MY PREVIOUS STATEMENT.
I **HAVEN'T** PRINTED MY LIMIT.
THE COMPUTER INCORRECTLY **SHOWS** THAT I HAVE.
I SEE YOU WERE ABLE TO RETAIN EXPERT ASSISTANCE.
BB
MY CLIENT DEMANDS YOU MAKE THIS UNPROVABLE SITUATION RIGHT.
IN EXCHANGE FOR WHICH, YOU CAN FOREGO THE LENGTHY TECHNICAL INVESTIGATION AND READ MORE COMICS.
GOOD, BUT YOU FORGOT TO BLOCK THE PUNITIVE RESPONSE.
WHAT DO YOU MEAN?
OOPS, I ACCIDENTALLY MADE IT SO THAT NEXT WEEK YOU CAN'T PRINT ANYTHING.
YOU'RE **WRONG**!
YOU'RE **INCOMPETENT**!
YOU'RE A **LIAR**!
WHAT'S THIS?
YOU JUST HIT THE TRIFECTA!
BB

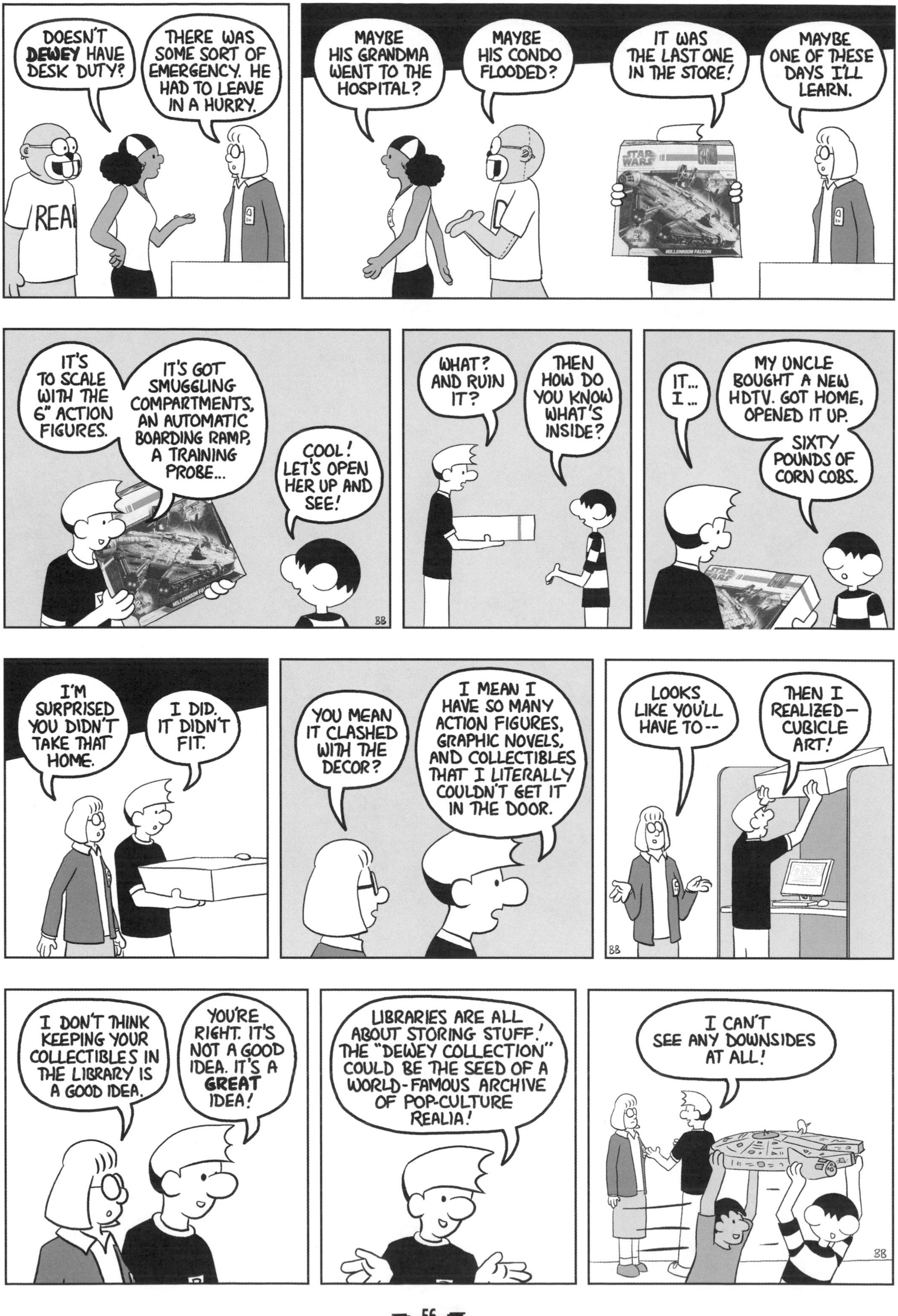
DOESN'T **DEWEY** HAVE DESK DUTY?
THERE WAS SOME SORT OF EMERGENCY. HE HAD TO LEAVE IN A HURRY.
MAYBE HIS GRANDMA WENT TO THE HOSPITAL?
MAYBE HIS CONDO FLOODED?
IT WAS THE LAST ONE IN THE STORE!
MAYBE ONE OF THESE DAYS I'LL LEARN.
IT'S TO SCALE WITH THE 6" ACTION FIGURES.
IT'S GOT SMUGGLING COMPARTMENTS, AN AUTOMATIC BOARDING RAMP, A TRAINING PROBE...
COOL! LET'S OPEN HER UP AND SEE!
BB
WHAT? AND RUIN IT?
THEN HOW DO YOU KNOW WHAT'S INSIDE?
IT... I...
MY UNCLE BOUGHT A NEW HDTV. GOT HOME, OPENED IT UP.
SIXTY POUNDS OF CORN COBS.
I'M SURPRISED YOU DIDN'T TAKE THAT HOME.
I DID. IT DIDN'T FIT.
YOU MEAN IT CLASHED WITH THE DECOR?
I MEAN I HAVE SO MANY ACTION FIGURES, GRAPHIC NOVELS, AND COLLECTIBLES THAT I LITERALLY COULDN'T GET IT IN THE DOOR.
LOOKS LIKE YOU'LL HAVE TO--
THEN I REALIZED— CUBICLE ART!
BB
I DON'T THINK KEEPING YOUR COLLECTIBLES IN THE LIBRARY IS A GOOD IDEA.
YOU'RE RIGHT. IT'S NOT A GOOD IDEA. IT'S A **GREAT** IDEA!
LIBRARIES ARE ALL ABOUT STORING STUFF! THE "DEWEY COLLECTION" COULD BE THE SEED OF A WORLD-FAMOUS ARCHIVE OF POP-CULTURE REALIA!
I CAN'T SEE ANY DOWNSIDES AT ALL!
BB

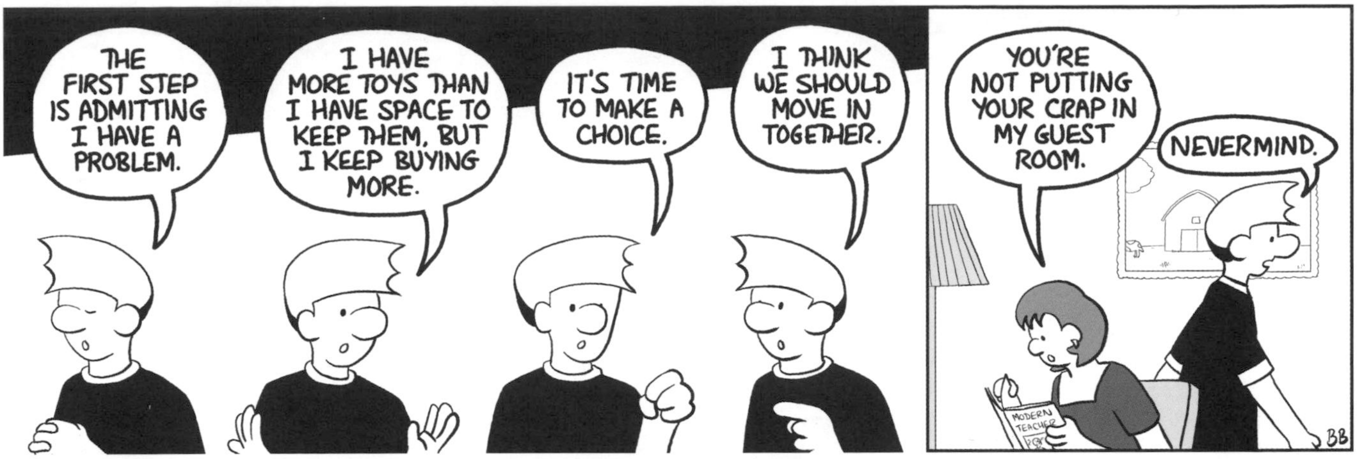
THE FIRST STEP IS ADMITTING I HAVE A PROBLEM.
I HAVE MORE TOYS THAN I HAVE SPACE TO KEEP THEM, BUT I KEEP BUYING MORE.
IT'S TIME TO MAKE A CHOICE.
I THINK WE SHOULD MOVE IN TOGETHER.
YOU'RE NOT PUTTING YOUR CRAP IN MY GUEST ROOM.
NEVERMIND.
MODERN TEACHER
BB

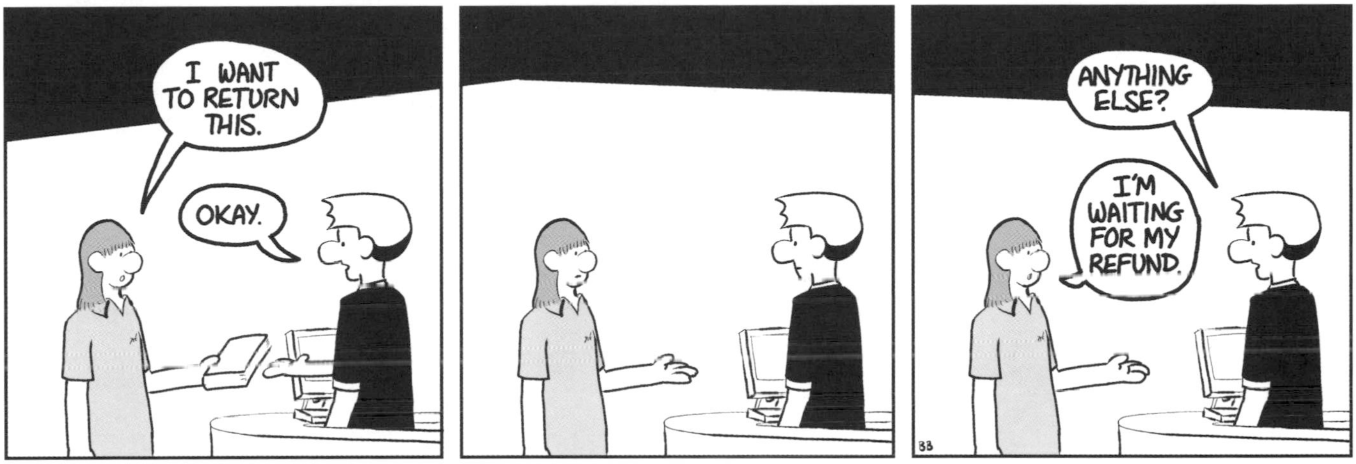
I WANT TO RETURN THIS.
OKAY.
ANYTHING ELSE?
I'M WAITING FOR MY REFUND.
BB

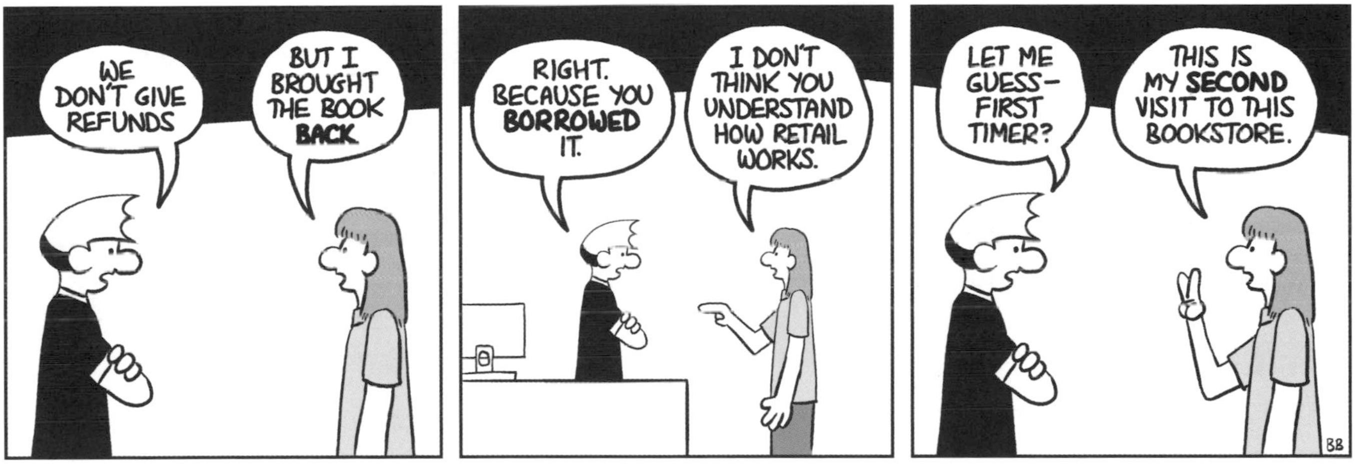
WE DON'T GIVE REFUNDS
BUT I BROUGHT THE BOOK **BACK**.
RIGHT. BECAUSE YOU **BORROWED** IT.
I DON'T THINK YOU UNDERSTAND HOW RETAIL WORKS.
LET ME GUESS– FIRST TIMER?
THIS IS MY **SECOND** VISIT TO THIS BOOKSTORE.
BB

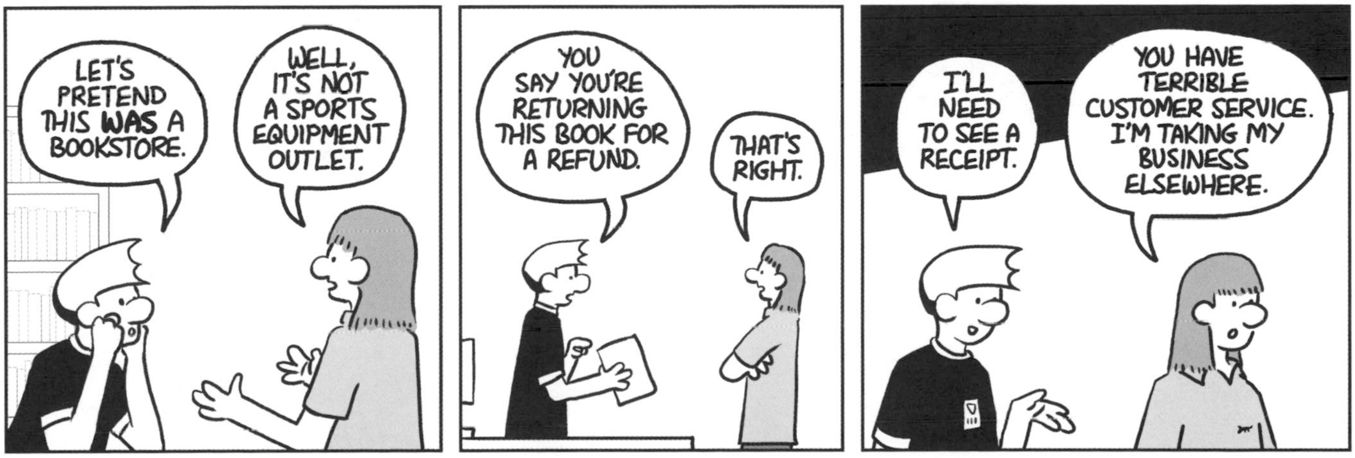
LET'S PRETEND THIS **WAS** A BOOKSTORE.
WELL, IT'S NOT A SPORTS EQUIPMENT OUTLET.
YOU SAY YOU'RE RETURNING THIS BOOK FOR A REFUND.
THAT'S RIGHT.
I'LL NEED TO SEE A RECEIPT.
YOU HAVE TERRIBLE CUSTOMER SERVICE. I'M TAKING MY BUSINESS ELSEWHERE.

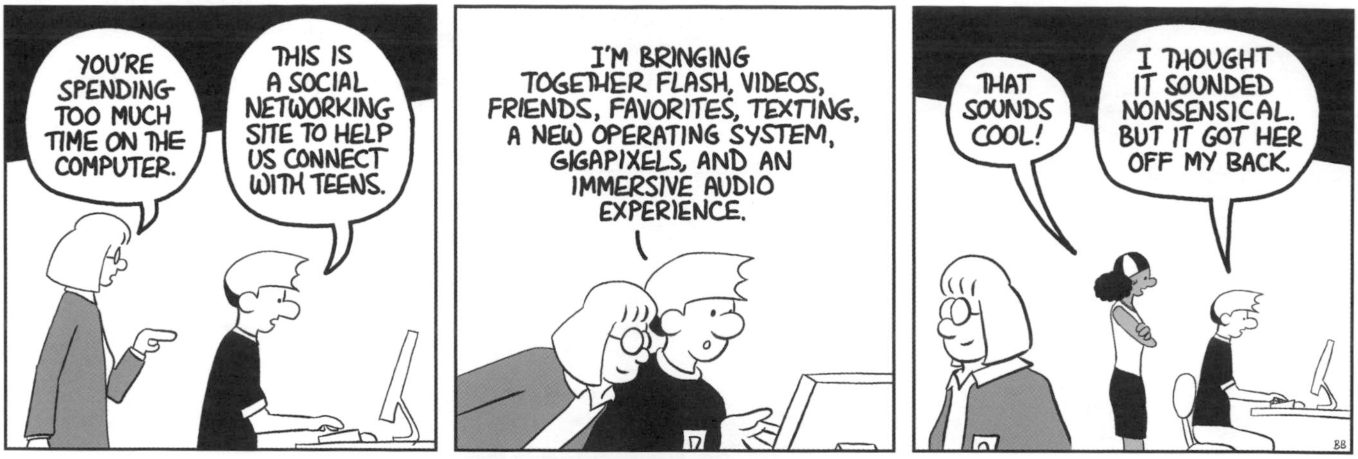
YOU'RE SPENDING TOO MUCH TIME ON THE COMPUTER.
THIS IS A SOCIAL NETWORKING SITE TO HELP US CONNECT WITH TEENS.
I'M BRINGING TOGETHER FLASH, VIDEOS, FRIENDS, FAVORITES, TEXTING, A NEW OPERATING SYSTEM, GIGAPIXELS, AND AN IMMERSIVE AUDIO EXPERIENCE.
THAT SOUNDS COOL!
I THOUGHT IT SOUNDED NONSENSICAL. BUT IT GOT HER OFF MY BACK.
BB

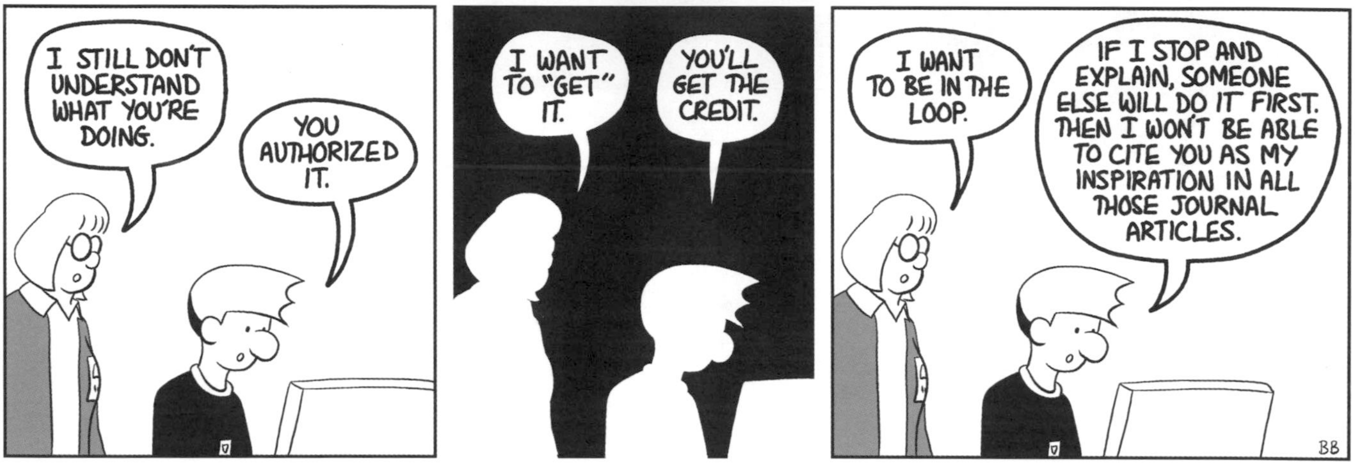
I STILL DON'T UNDERSTAND WHAT YOU'RE DOING.
YOU AUTHORIZED IT.
I WANT TO "GET" IT.
YOU'LL GET THE CREDIT.
I WANT TO BE IN THE LOOP.
IF I STOP AND EXPLAIN, SOMEONE ELSE WILL DO IT FIRST. THEN I WON'T BE ABLE TO CITE YOU AS MY INSPIRATION IN ALL THOSE JOURNAL ARTICLES.
BB

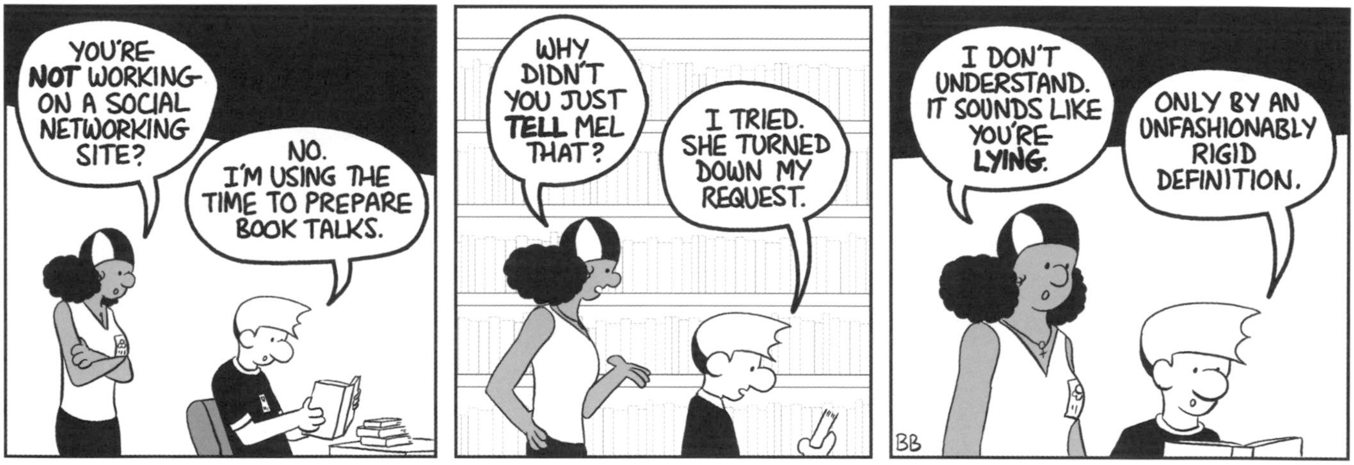
YOU'RE **NOT** WORKING ON A SOCIAL NETWORKING SITE?
NO. I'M USING THE TIME TO PREPARE BOOK TALKS.
WHY DIDN'T YOU JUST **TELL** MEL THAT?
I TRIED. SHE TURNED DOWN MY REQUEST.
I DON'T UNDERSTAND. IT SOUNDS LIKE YOU'RE **LYING**.
ONLY BY AN UNFASHIONABLY RIGID DEFINITION.
BB

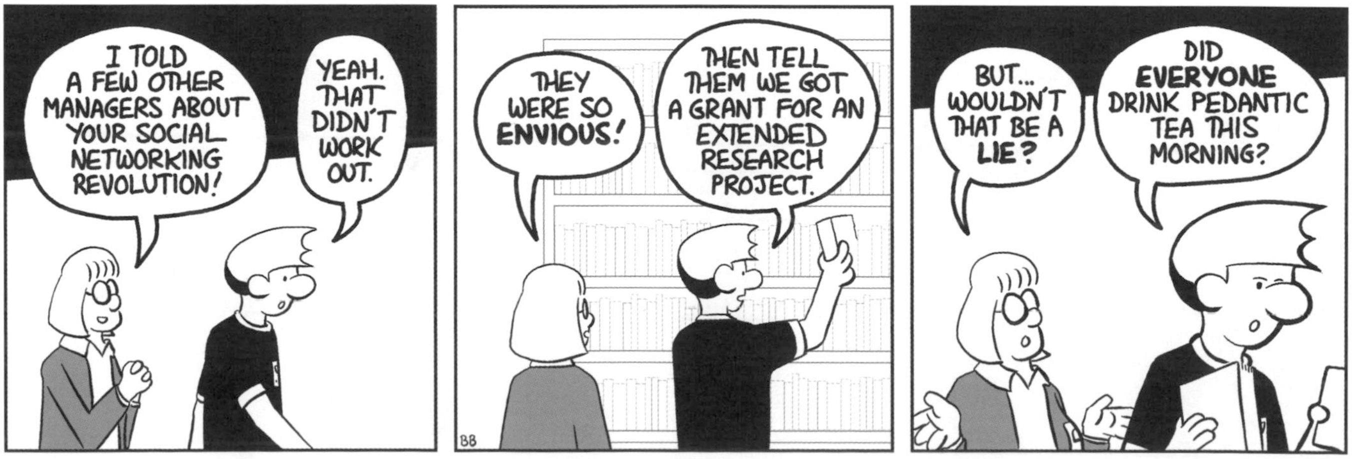
I TOLD A FEW OTHER MANAGERS ABOUT YOUR SOCIAL NETWORKING REVOLUTION!
YEAH. THAT DIDN'T WORK OUT.
THEY WERE SO **ENVIOUS**!
THEN TELL THEM WE GOT A GRANT FOR AN EXTENDED RESEARCH PROJECT.
BB
BUT... WOULDN'T THAT BE A **LIE**?
DID **EVERYONE** DRINK PEDANTIC TEA THIS MORNING?

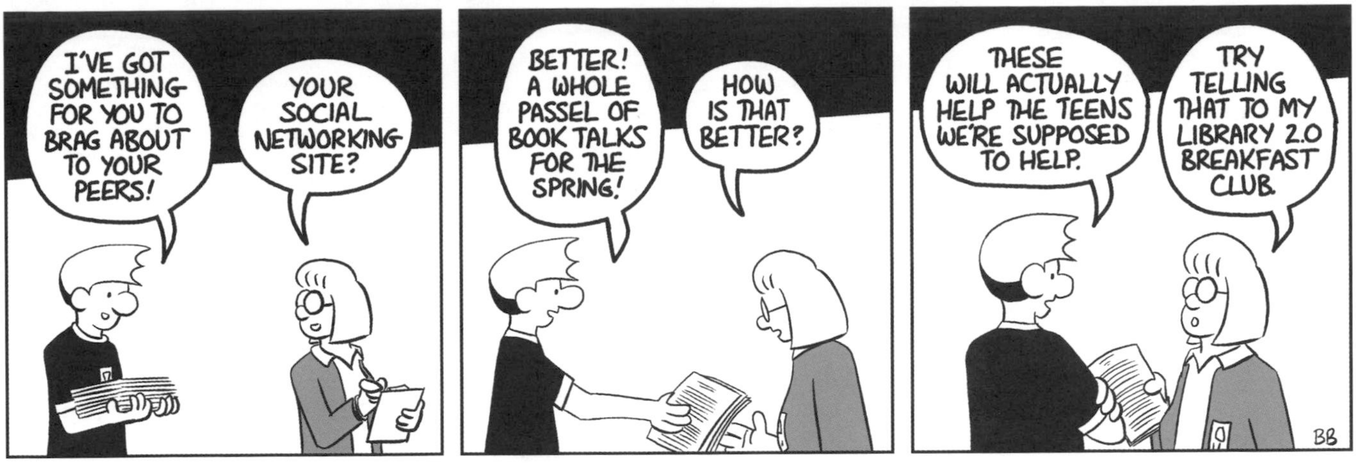
I'VE GOT SOMETHING FOR YOU TO BRAG ABOUT TO YOUR PEERS!
YOUR SOCIAL NETWORKING SITE?
BETTER! A WHOLE PASSEL OF BOOK TALKS FOR THE SPRING!
HOW IS THAT BETTER?
THESE WILL ACTUALLY HELP THE TEENS WE'RE SUPPOSED TO HELP.
TRY TELLING THAT TO MY LIBRARY 2.0 BREAKFAST CLUB.
BB

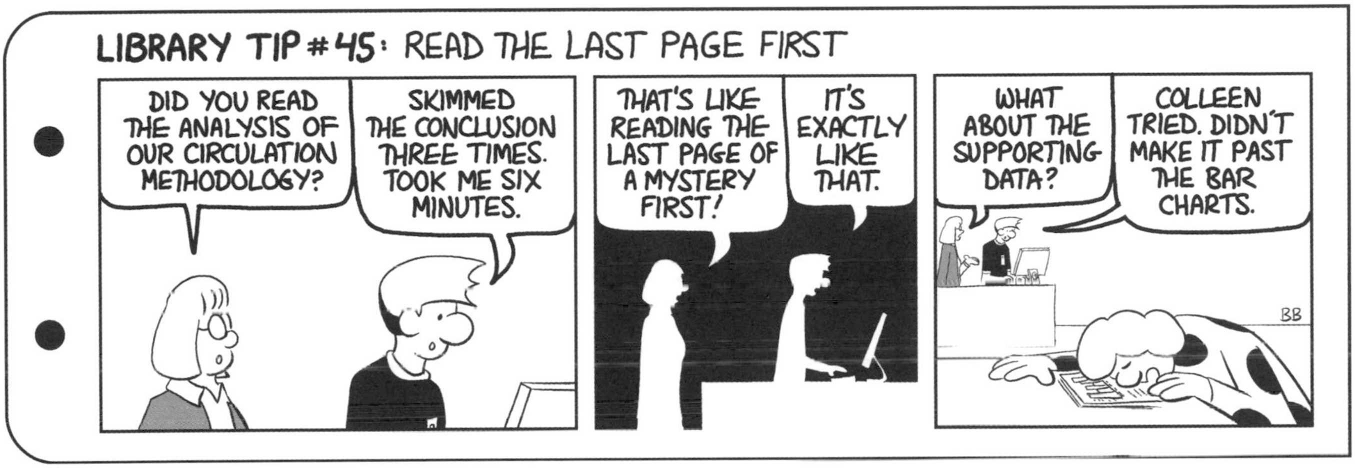
LIBRARY TIP #45: READ THE LAST PAGE FIRST
DID YOU READ THE ANALYSIS OF OUR CIRCULATION METHODOLOGY?
SKIMMED THE CONCLUSION THREE TIMES. TOOK ME SIX MINUTES.
THAT'S LIKE READING THE LAST PAGE OF A MYSTERY FIRST!
IT'S EXACTLY LIKE THAT.
WHAT ABOUT THE SUPPORTING DATA?
COLLEEN TRIED. DIDN'T MAKE IT PAST THE BAR CHARTS.
BB

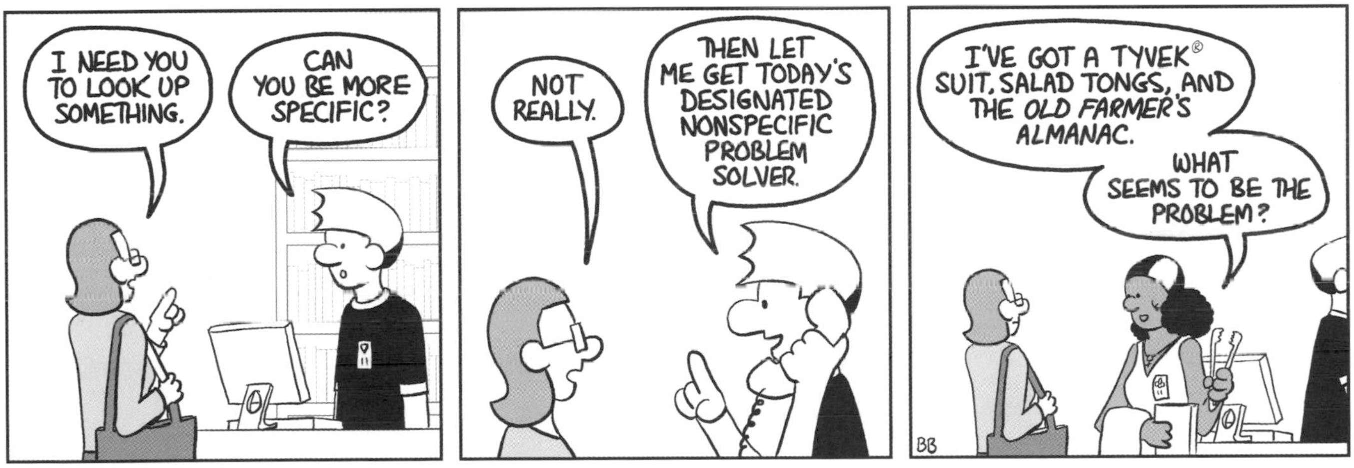
I NEED YOU TO LOOK UP SOMETHING.
CAN YOU BE MORE SPECIFIC?
NOT REALLY.
THEN LET ME GET TODAY'S DESIGNATED NONSPECIFIC PROBLEM SOLVER.
I'VE GOT A TYVEK® SUIT, SALAD TONGS, AND THE OLD FARMER'S ALMANAC.
WHAT SEEMS TO BE THE PROBLEM?
BB

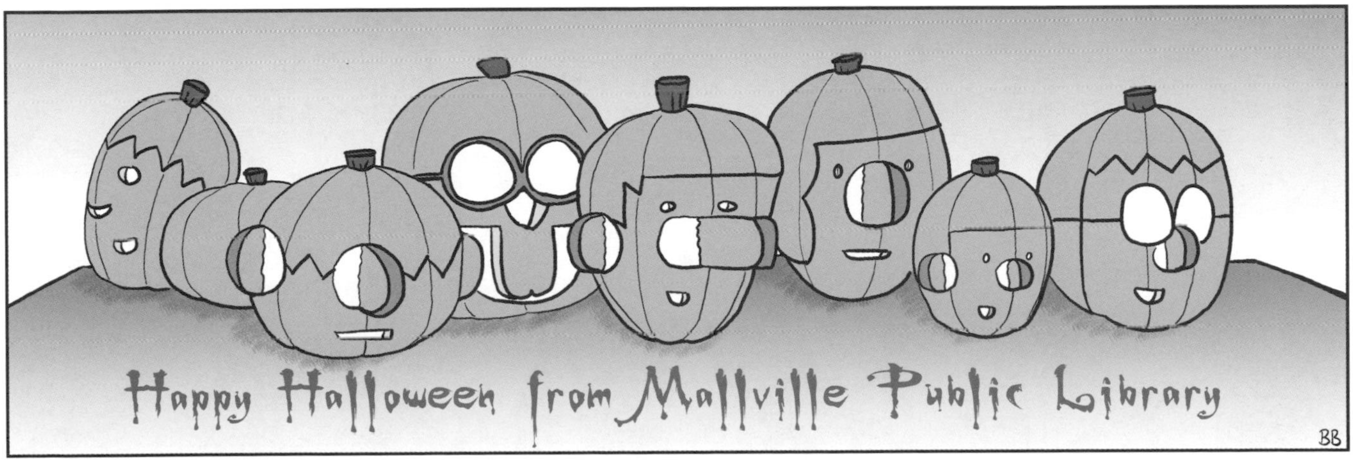
Happy Halloween from Mallville Public Library
BB

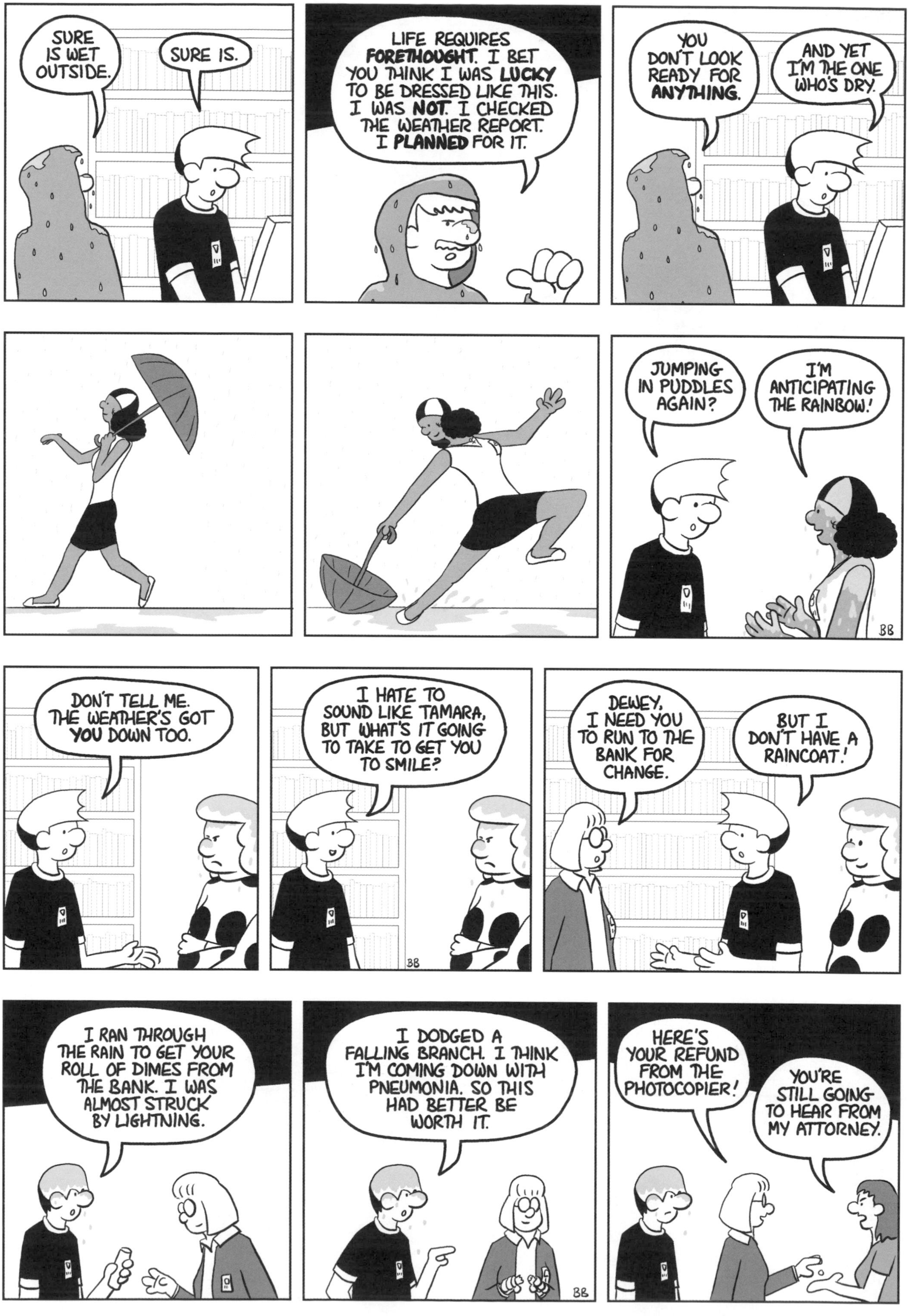
SURE IS WET OUTSIDE.
SURE IS.
LIFE REQUIRES FORETHOUGHT. I BET YOU THINK I WAS LUCKY TO BE DRESSED LIKE THIS. I WAS NOT. I CHECKED THE WEATHER REPORT. I PLANNED FOR IT.
YOU DON'T LOOK READY FOR ANYTHING.
AND YET I'M THE ONE WHO'S DRY.
JUMPING IN PUDDLES AGAIN?
I'M ANTICIPATING THE RAINBOW!
BB
DON'T TELL ME. THE WEATHER'S GOT YOU DOWN TOO.
I HATE TO SOUND LIKE TAMARA, BUT WHAT'S IT GOING TO TAKE TO GET YOU TO SMILE?
BB
DEWEY, I NEED YOU TO RUN TO THE BANK FOR CHANGE.
BUT I DON'T HAVE A RAINCOAT!
I RAN THROUGH THE RAIN TO GET YOUR ROLL OF DIMES FROM THE BANK. I WAS ALMOST STRUCK BY LIGHTNING.
I DODGED A FALLING BRANCH. I THINK I'M COMING DOWN WITH PNEUMONIA. SO THIS HAD BETTER BE WORTH IT.
BB
HERE'S YOUR REFUND FROM THE PHOTOCOPIER!
YOU'RE STILL GOING TO HEAR FROM MY ATTORNEY.

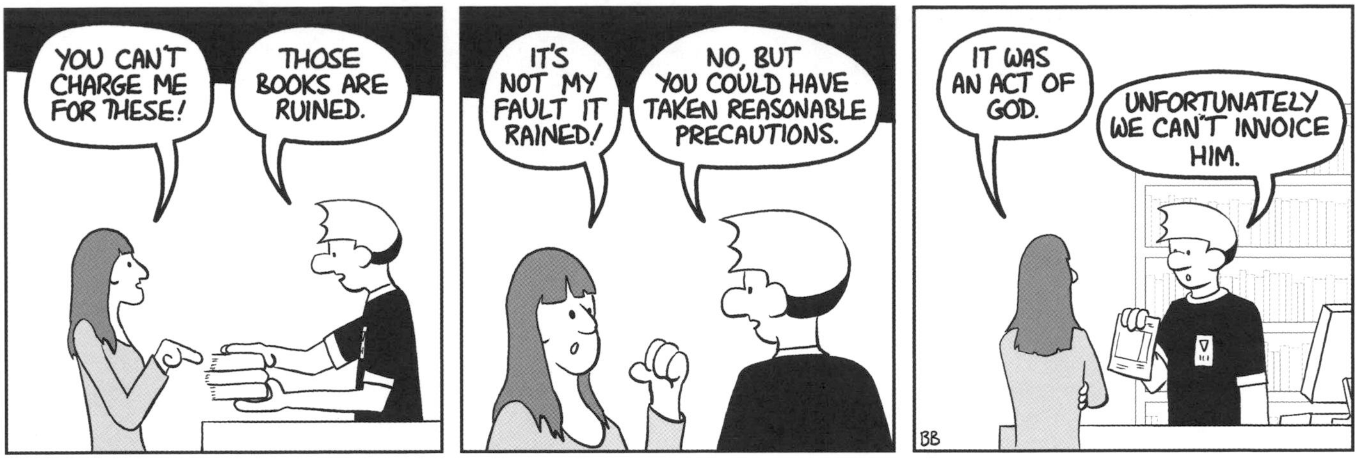
YOU CAN'T CHARGE ME FOR THESE!
THOSE BOOKS ARE RUINED.
IT'S NOT MY FAULT IT RAINED!
NO, BUT YOU COULD HAVE TAKEN REASONABLE PRECAUTIONS.
IT WAS AN ACT OF GOD.
UNFORTUNATELY WE CAN'T INVOICE HIM.
BB

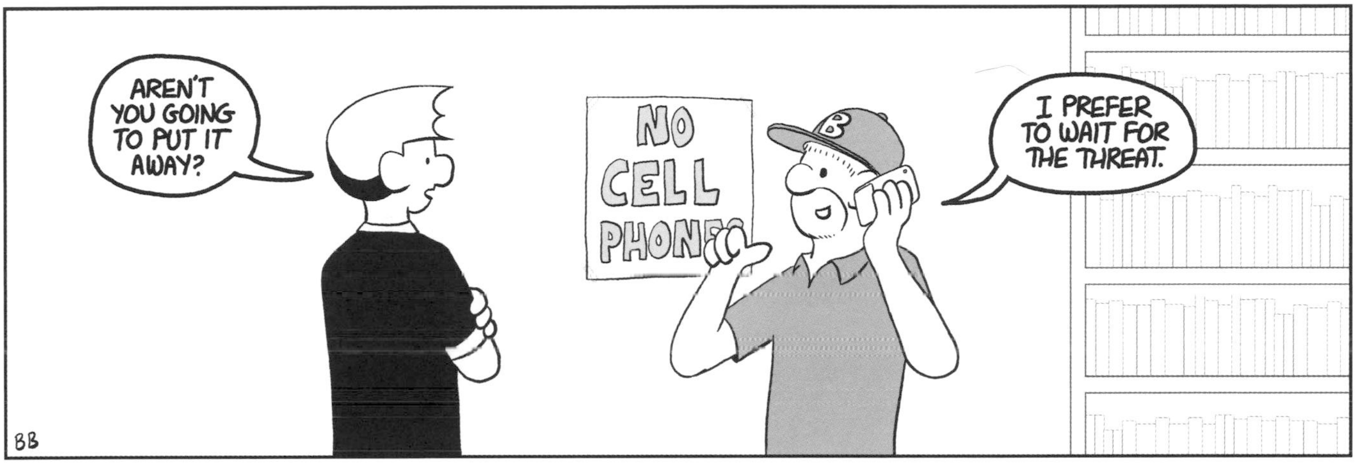
AREN'T YOU GOING TO PUT IT AWAY?
NO CELL
I PREFER TO WAIT FOR THE THREAT.
BB

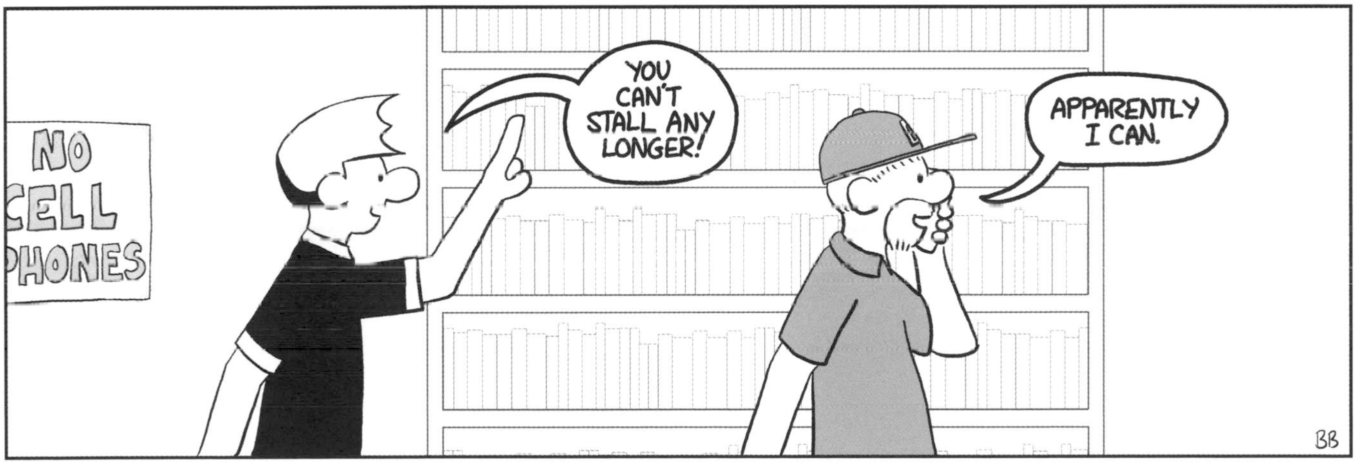
YOU CAN'T STALL ANY LONGER!
APPARENTLY I CAN.
BB

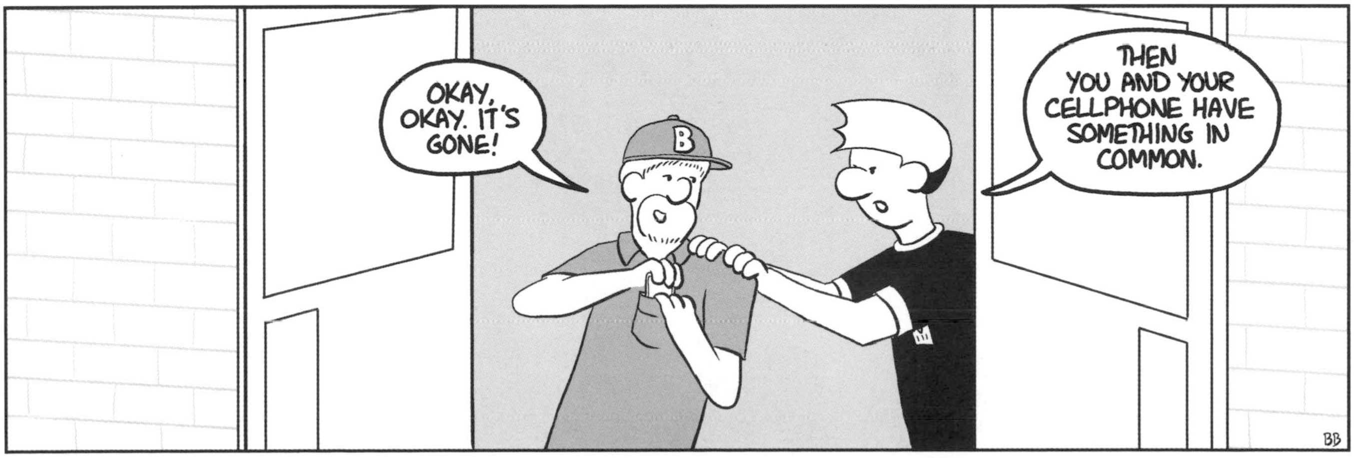
OKAY, OKAY. IT'S GONE!
THEN YOU AND YOUR CELLPHONE HAVE SOMETHING IN COMMON.
BB

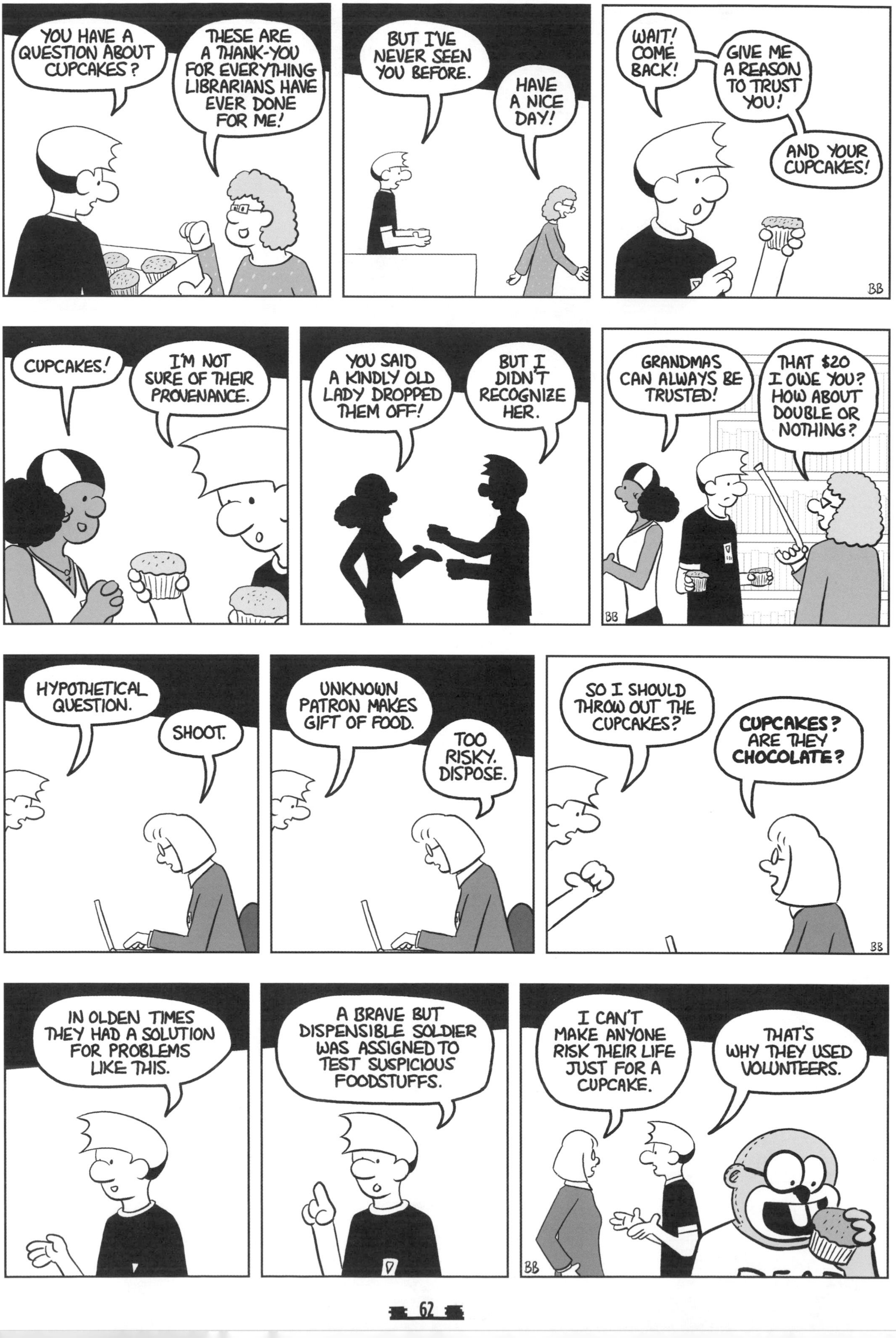
YOU HAVE A QUESTION ABOUT CUPCAKES?
THESE ARE A THANK-YOU FOR EVERYTHING LIBRARIANS HAVE EVER DONE FOR ME!
BUT I'VE NEVER SEEN YOU BEFORE.
HAVE A NICE DAY!
WAIT! COME BACK!
GIVE ME A REASON TO TRUST YOU!
AND YOUR CUPCAKES!
BB
CUPCAKES!
I'M NOT SURE OF THEIR PROVENANCE.
YOU SAID A KINDLY OLD LADY DROPPED THEM OFF!
BUT I DIDN'T RECOGNIZE HER.
GRANDMAS CAN ALWAYS BE TRUSTED!
THAT $20 I OWE YOU? HOW ABOUT DOUBLE OR NOTHING?
BB
HYPOTHETICAL QUESTION.
SHOOT.
UNKNOWN PATRON MAKES GIFT OF FOOD.
TOO RISKY. DISPOSE.
SO I SHOULD THROW OUT THE CUPCAKES?
CUPCAKES? ARE THEY CHOCOLATE?
BB
IN OLDEN TIMES THEY HAD A SOLUTION FOR PROBLEMS LIKE THIS.
A BRAVE BUT DISPENSIBLE SOLDIER WAS ASSIGNED TO TEST SUSPICIOUS FOODSTUFFS.
I CAN'T MAKE ANYONE RISK THEIR LIFE JUST FOR A CUPCAKE.
THAT'S WHY THEY USED VOLUNTEERS.
BB

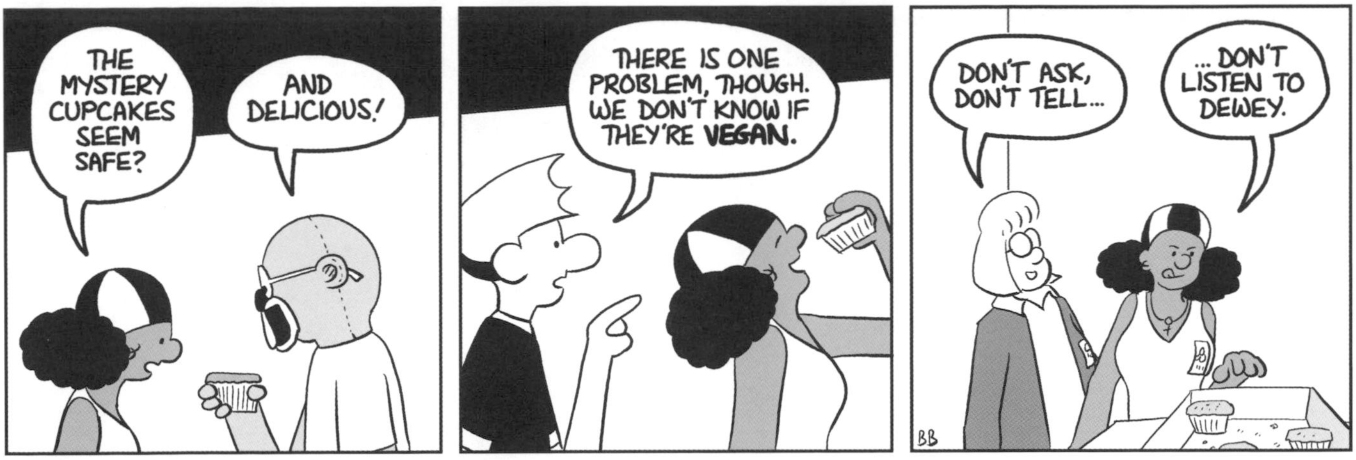
THE MYSTERY CUPCAKES SEEM SAFE?
AND DELICIOUS!
THERE IS ONE PROBLEM, THOUGH. WE DON'T KNOW IF THEY'RE **VEGAN.**
DON'T ASK, DON'T TELL...
...DON'T LISTEN TO DEWEY.
BB

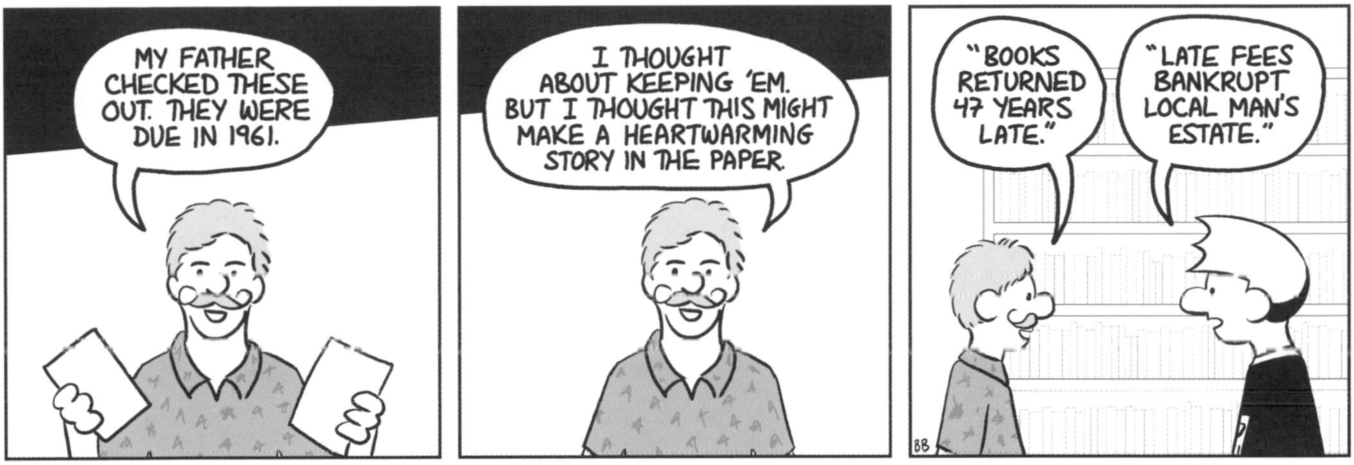
MY FATHER CHECKED THESE OUT. THEY WERE DUE IN 1961.
I THOUGHT ABOUT KEEPING 'EM. BUT I THOUGHT THIS MIGHT MAKE A HEARTWARMING STORY IN THE PAPER.
"BOOKS RETURNED 47 YEARS LATE."
"LATE FEES BANKRUPT LOCAL MAN'S ESTATE."
BB

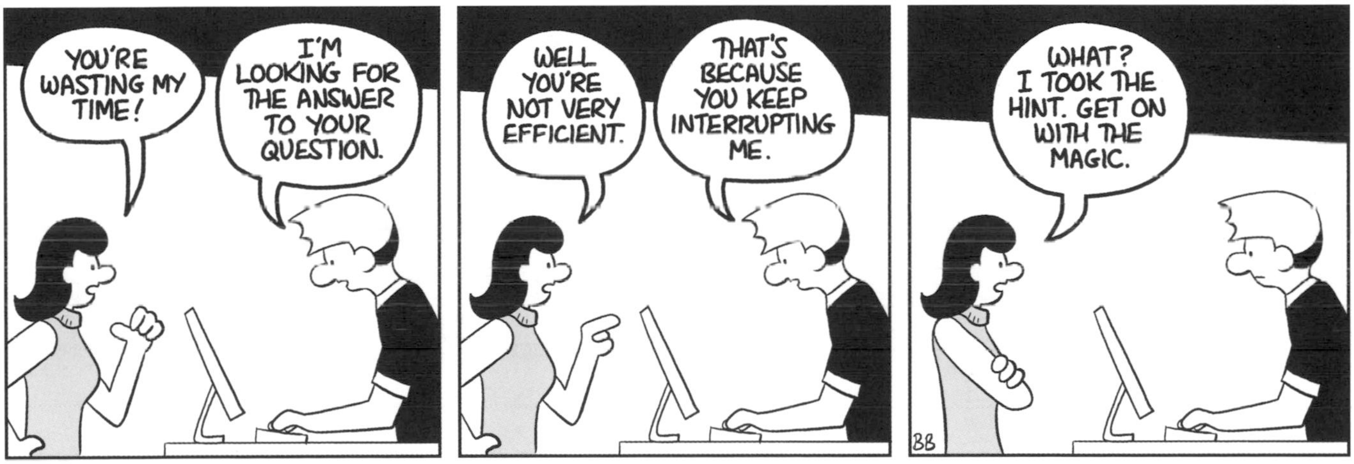
YOU'RE WASTING MY TIME!
I'M LOOKING FOR THE ANSWER TO YOUR QUESTION.
WELL YOU'RE NOT VERY EFFICIENT.
THAT'S BECAUSE YOU KEEP INTERRUPTING ME.
WHAT? I TOOK THE HINT. GET ON WITH THE MAGIC.
BB

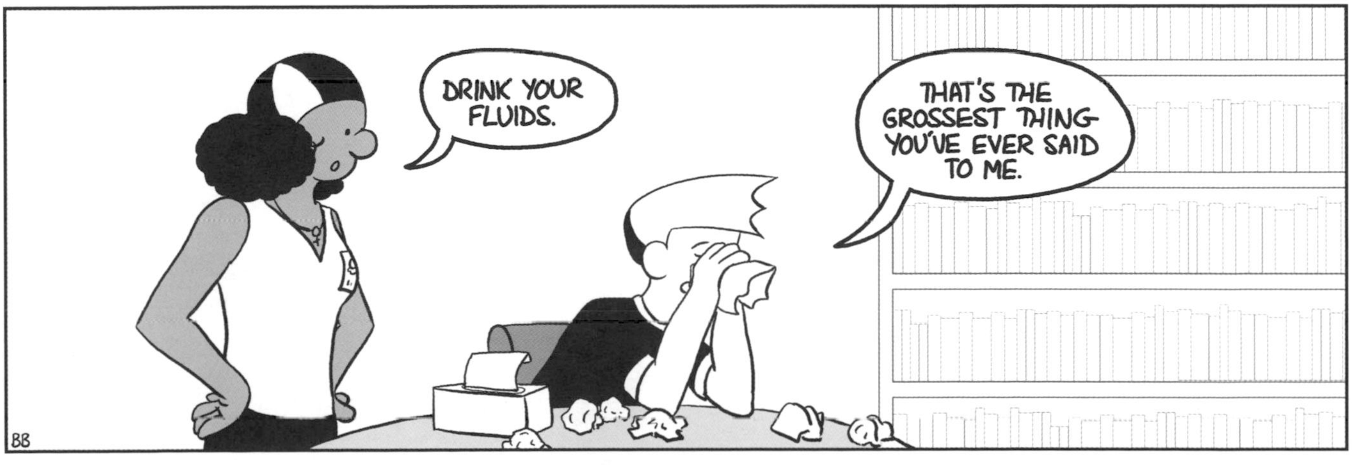
DRINK YOUR FLUIDS.
THAT'S THE GROSSEST THING YOU'VE EVER SAID TO ME.
BB

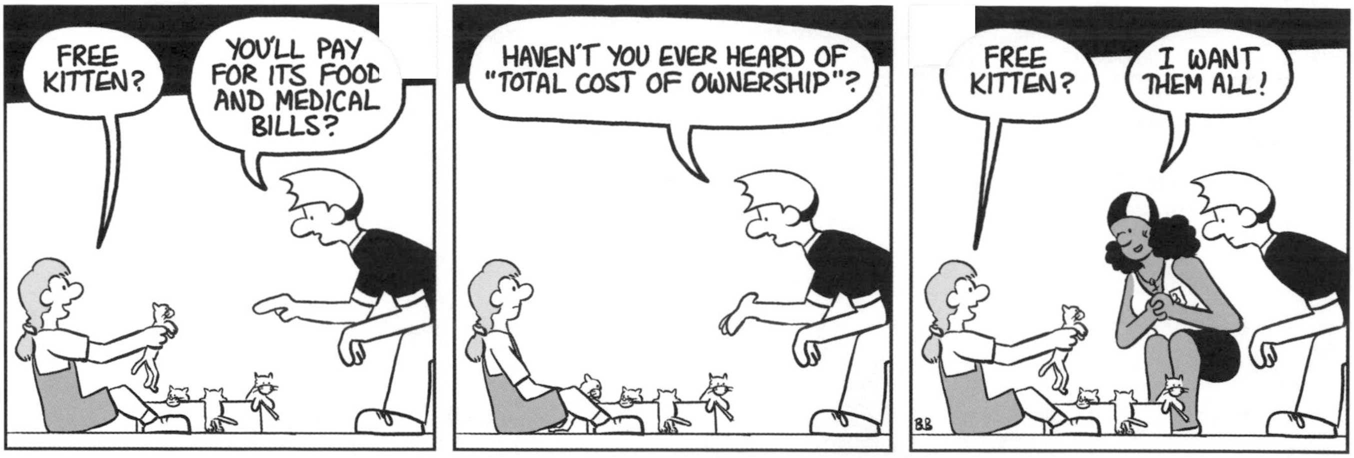
FREE KITTEN?
YOU'LL PAY FOR ITS FOOD AND MEDICAL BILLS?
HAVEN'T YOU EVER HEARD OF "TOTAL COST OF OWNERSHIP"?
FREE KITTEN?
I WANT THEM ALL!
BB

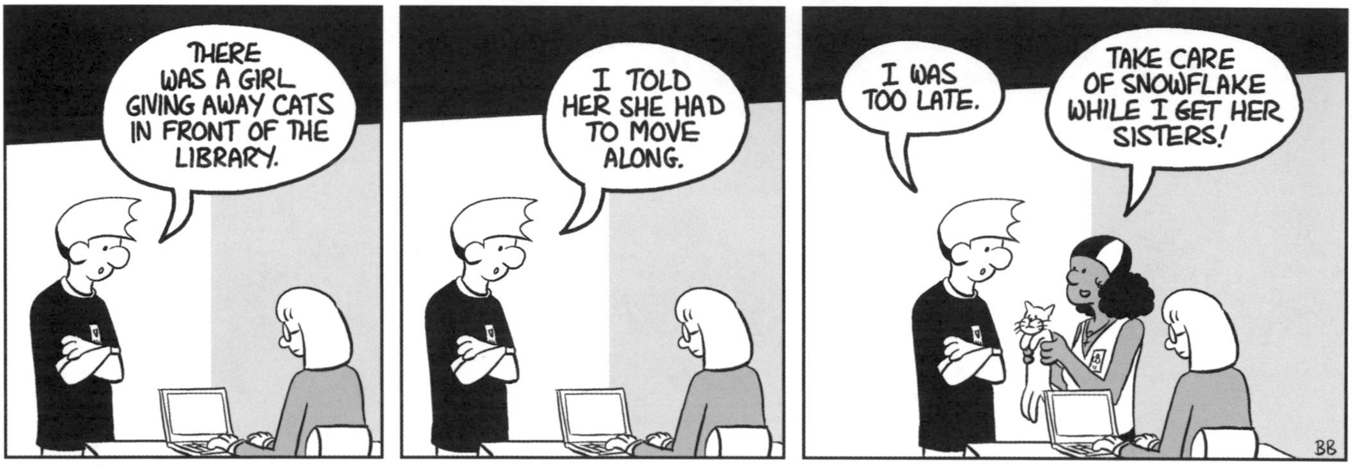
THERE WAS A GIRL GIVING AWAY CATS IN FRONT OF THE LIBRARY.
I TOLD HER SHE HAD TO MOVE ALONG.
I WAS TOO LATE.
TAKE CARE OF SNOWFLAKE WHILE I GET HER SISTERS!
BB

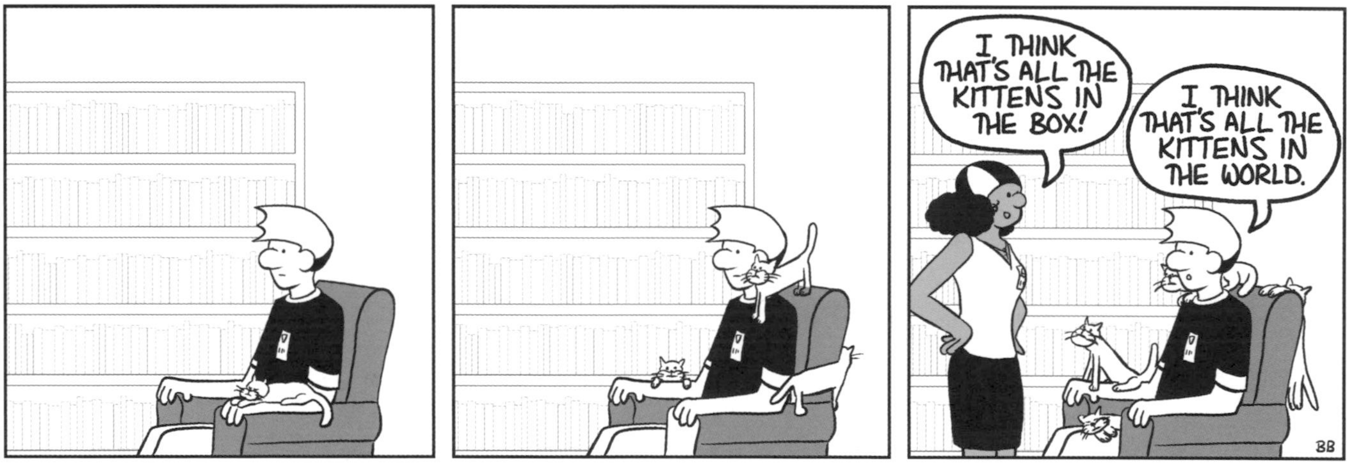
I THINK THAT'S ALL THE KITTENS IN THE BOX!
I THINK THAT'S ALL THE KITTENS IN THE WORLD.
BB

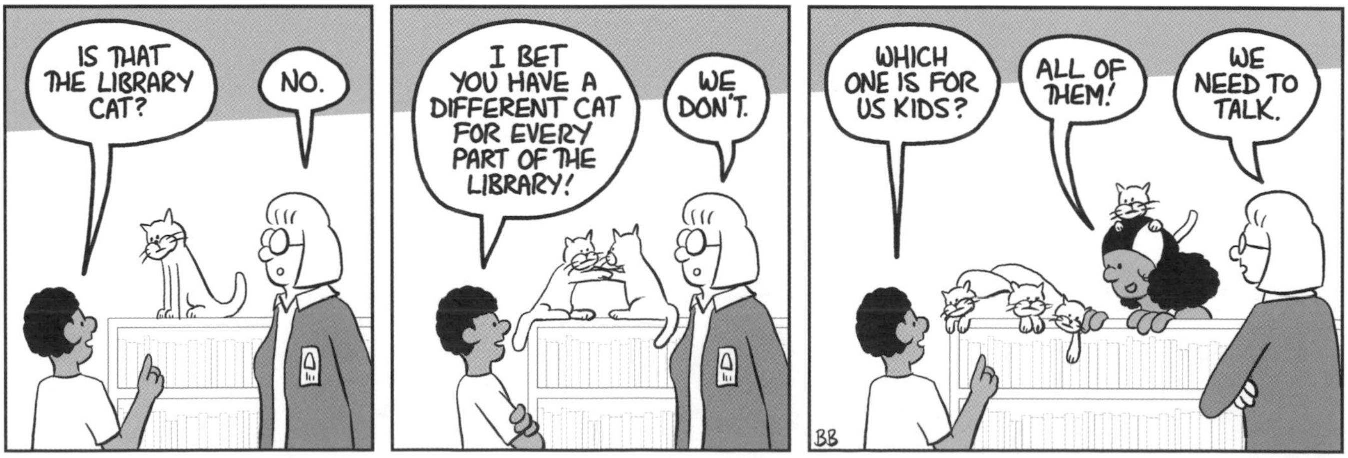
IS THAT THE LIBRARY CAT?
NO.
I BET YOU HAVE A DIFFERENT CAT FOR EVERY PART OF THE LIBRARY!
WE DON'T.
WHICH ONE IS FOR US KIDS?
ALL OF THEM!
WE NEED TO TALK.
BB

I CAN'T BELIEVE NONE OF YOU LIKE MY KITTENS!

I CAN'T BELIEVE YOU DO.

WHAT DO YOU MEAN?

WELL, YOU'RE A GERMAPHOBE. AND YOU JUST ADOPTED A POOP FACTORY.

FREE KITTENS?

WE GOT A CALL FROM SOME GUY WHO HEARD YOU'D TAKEN IN A LITTER OF KITTENS.

HE WANTED TO KNOW IF YOU'D TAKE AN INCONTINENT OLD DOG THAT NEEDS HIP REPLACEMENT SURGERY.

WELL, I MIGHT...

I KNOW. SO I EXERCISED DISCRETION ON YOUR BEHALF AND ONLY PRETENDED TO TAKE HIS NUMBER.

AH-CHOOH!

CAN YOU BELIEVE IT? THIS LITTLE THING RECORDS IN **H.D.**!

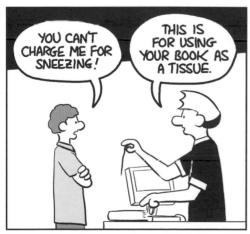

YOU CAN'T CHARGE ME FOR SNEEZING!

THIS IS FOR USING YOUR BOOK AS A TISSUE.

IT'S STILL READABLE!

SHOW ME.

I CAN'T GET THE PAGES UNSTUCK.

I'M CHARGING DOUBLE.

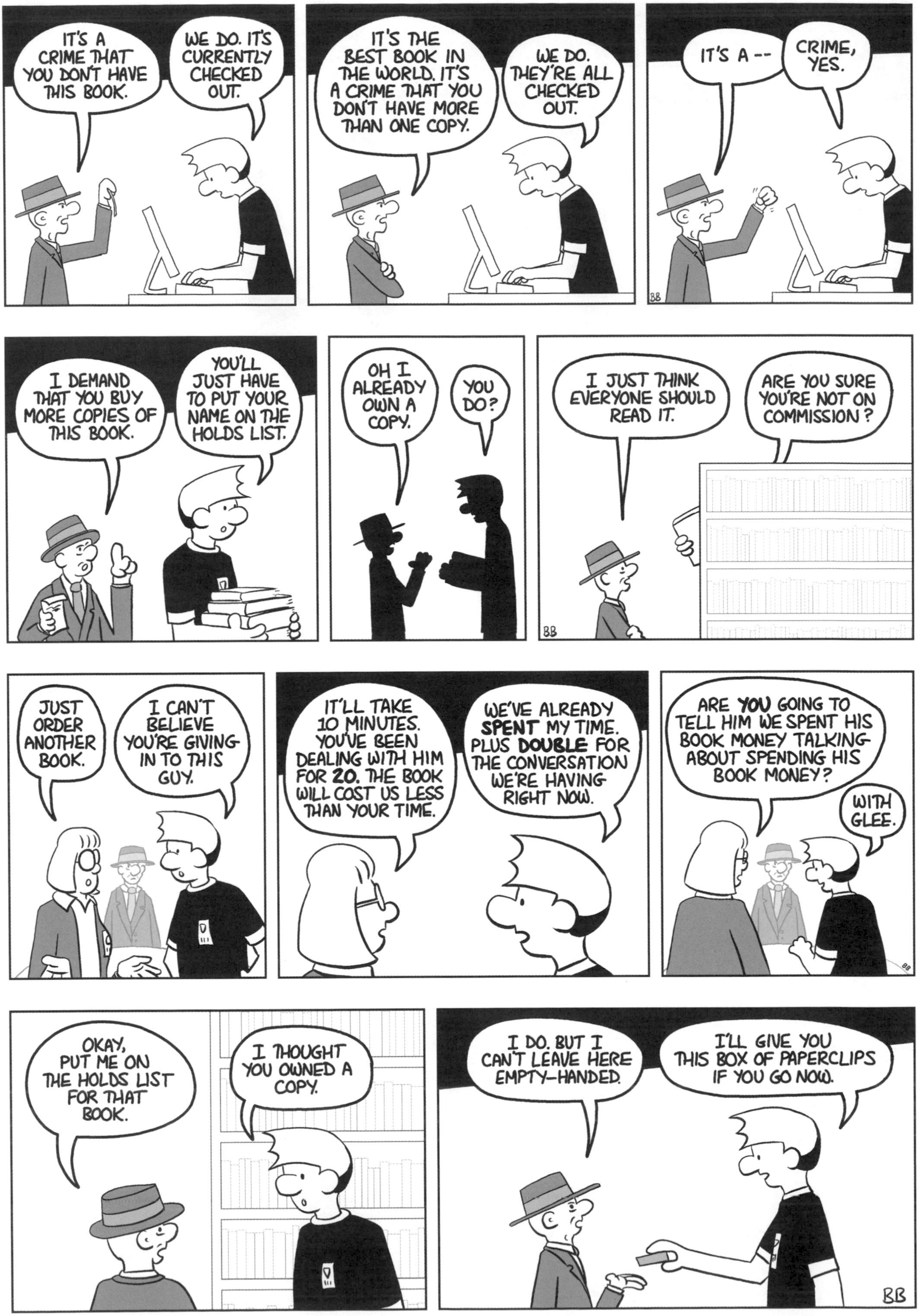
IT'S A CRIME THAT YOU DON'T HAVE THIS BOOK.
WE DO. IT'S CURRENTLY CHECKED OUT.
IT'S THE BEST BOOK IN THE WORLD. IT'S A CRIME THAT YOU DON'T HAVE MORE THAN ONE COPY.
WE DO. THEY'RE ALL CHECKED OUT.
IT'S A --
CRIME, YES.
BB
I DEMAND THAT YOU BUY MORE COPIES OF THIS BOOK.
YOU'LL JUST HAVE TO PUT YOUR NAME ON THE HOLDS LIST.
OH I ALREADY OWN A COPY.
YOU DO?
I JUST THINK EVERYONE SHOULD READ IT.
ARE YOU SURE YOU'RE NOT ON COMMISSION?
BB
JUST ORDER ANOTHER BOOK.
I CAN'T BELIEVE YOU'RE GIVING IN TO THIS GUY.
IT'LL TAKE 10 MINUTES. YOU'VE BEEN DEALING WITH HIM FOR 20. THE BOOK WILL COST US LESS THAN YOUR TIME.
WE'VE ALREADY SPENT MY TIME. PLUS DOUBLE FOR THE CONVERSATION WE'RE HAVING RIGHT NOW.
ARE YOU GOING TO TELL HIM WE SPENT HIS BOOK MONEY TALKING ABOUT SPENDING HIS BOOK MONEY?
WITH GLEE.
BB
OKAY, PUT ME ON THE HOLDS LIST FOR THAT BOOK.
I THOUGHT YOU OWNED A COPY.
I DO. BUT I CAN'T LEAVE HERE EMPTY-HANDED.
I'LL GIVE YOU THIS BOX OF PAPERCLIPS IF YOU GO NOW.
BB

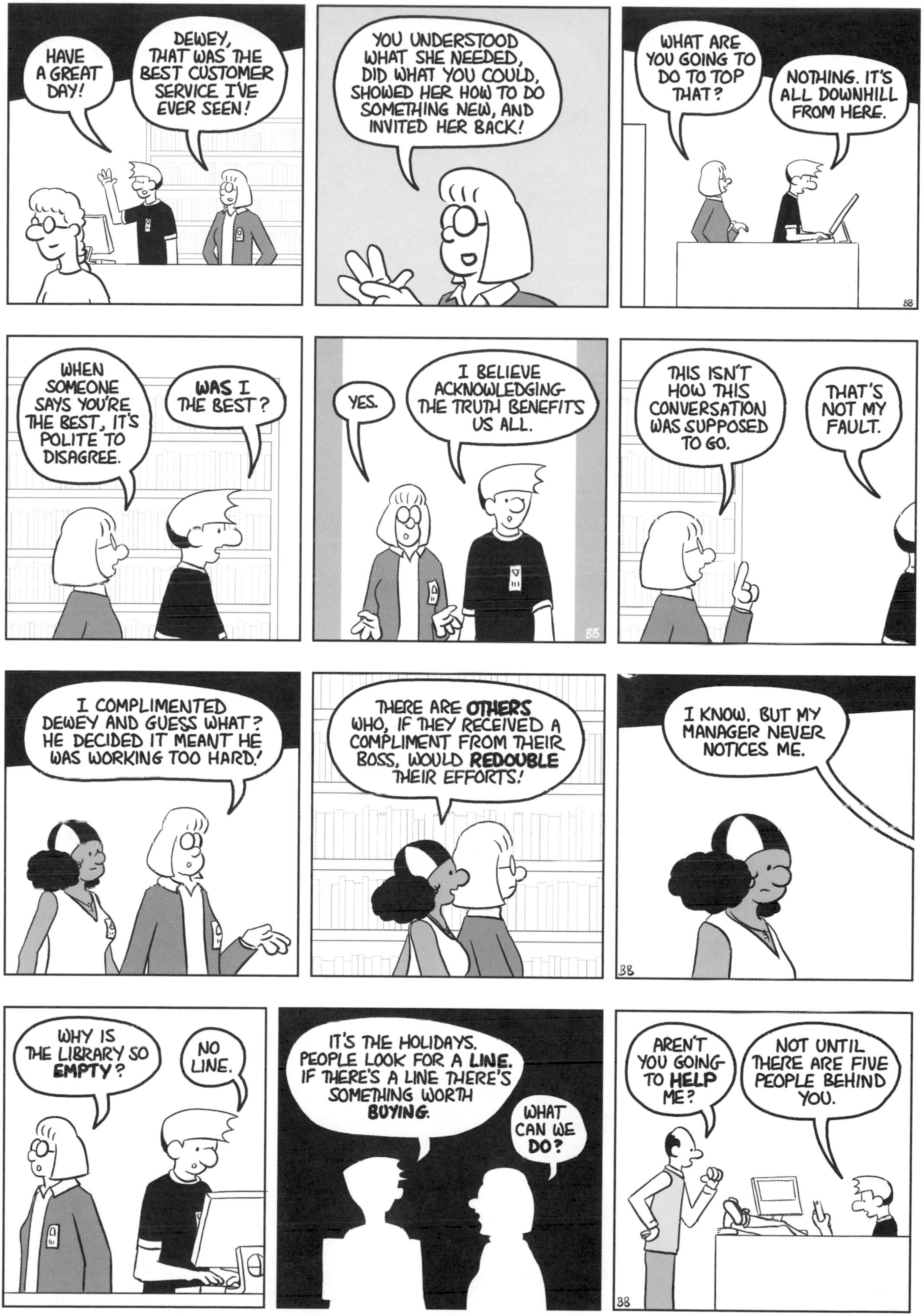
HAVE A GREAT DAY!
DEWEY, THAT WAS THE BEST CUSTOMER SERVICE I'VE EVER SEEN!
YOU UNDERSTOOD WHAT SHE NEEDED, DID WHAT YOU COULD, SHOWED HER HOW TO DO SOMETHING NEW, AND INVITED HER BACK!
WHAT ARE YOU GOING TO DO TO TOP THAT?
NOTHING. IT'S ALL DOWNHILL FROM HERE.
BB
WHEN SOMEONE SAYS YOU'RE THE BEST, IT'S POLITE TO DISAGREE.
WAS I THE BEST?
YES.
I BELIEVE ACKNOWLEDGING THE TRUTH BENEFITS US ALL.
BB
THIS ISN'T HOW THIS CONVERSATION WAS SUPPOSED TO GO.
THAT'S NOT MY FAULT.
I COMPLIMENTED DEWEY AND GUESS WHAT? HE DECIDED IT MEANT HE WAS WORKING TOO HARD!
THERE ARE **OTHERS** WHO, IF THEY RECEIVED A COMPLIMENT FROM THEIR BOSS, WOULD **REDOUBLE** THEIR EFFORTS!
I KNOW. BUT MY MANAGER NEVER NOTICES ME.
BB
WHY IS THE LIBRARY SO **EMPTY**?
NO LINE.
IT'S THE HOLIDAYS. PEOPLE LOOK FOR A **LINE**. IF THERE'S A LINE THERE'S SOMETHING WORTH **BUYING**.
WHAT CAN WE **DO**?
AREN'T YOU GOING TO **HELP** ME?
NOT UNTIL THERE ARE FIVE PEOPLE BEHIND YOU.
BB

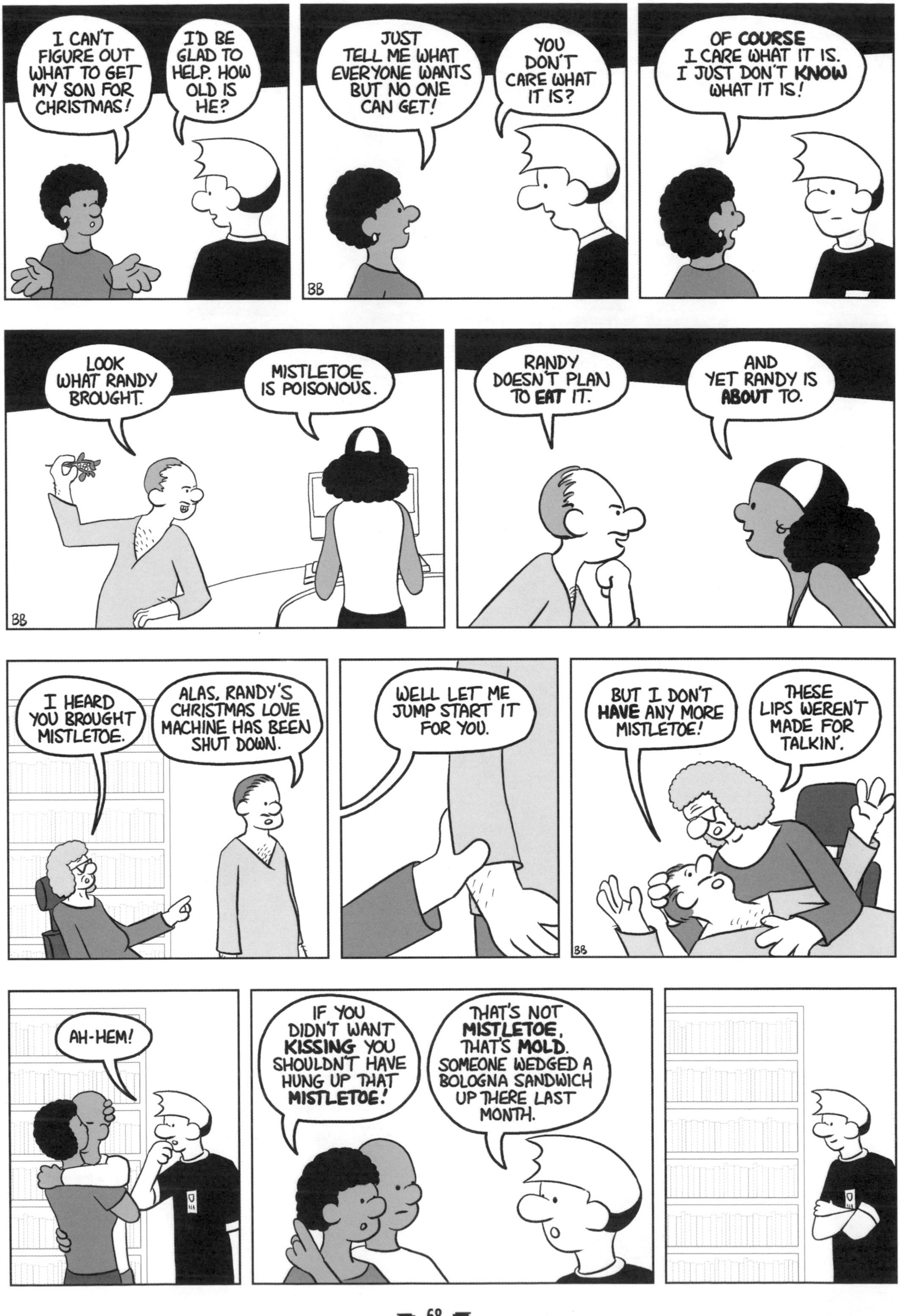

I CAN'T FIGURE OUT WHAT TO GET MY SON FOR CHRISTMAS!
I'D BE GLAD TO HELP. HOW OLD IS HE?
BB
JUST TELL ME WHAT EVERYONE WANTS BUT NO ONE CAN GET!
YOU DON'T CARE WHAT IT IS?
OF **COURSE** I CARE WHAT IT IS. I JUST DON'T **KNOW** WHAT IT IS!
LOOK WHAT RANDY BROUGHT.
MISTLETOE IS POISONOUS.
BB
RANDY DOESN'T PLAN TO **EAT** IT.
AND YET RANDY IS **ABOUT** TO.
I HEARD YOU BROUGHT MISTLETOE.
ALAS, RANDY'S CHRISTMAS LOVE MACHINE HAS BEEN SHUT DOWN.
WELL LET ME JUMP START IT FOR YOU.
BUT I DON'T **HAVE** ANY MORE MISTLETOE!
THESE LIPS WEREN'T MADE FOR TALKIN'.
BB
AH-HEM!
IF YOU DIDN'T WANT **KISSING** YOU SHOULDN'T HAVE HUNG UP THAT **MISTLETOE**!
THAT'S NOT **MISTLETOE**, THAT'S **MOLD**. SOMEONE WEDGED A BOLOGNA SANDWICH UP THERE LAST MONTH.

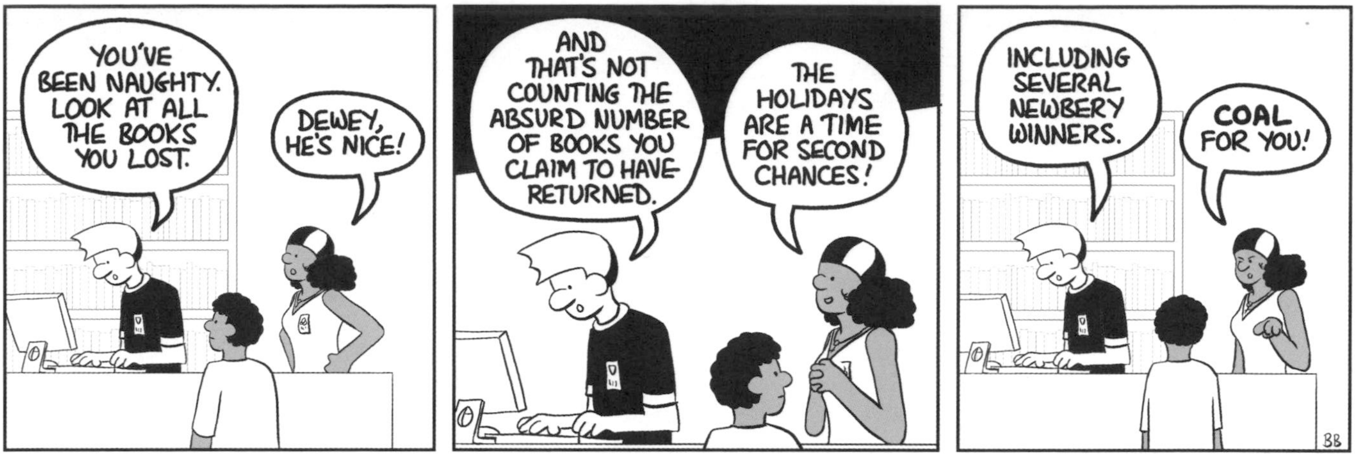
YOU'VE BEEN NAUGHTY. LOOK AT ALL THE BOOKS YOU LOST.
DEWEY, HE'S NICE!
AND THAT'S NOT COUNTING THE ABSURD NUMBER OF BOOKS YOU CLAIM TO HAVE RETURNED.
THE HOLIDAYS ARE A TIME FOR SECOND CHANCES!
INCLUDING SEVERAL NEWBERY WINNERS.
COAL FOR YOU!
BB

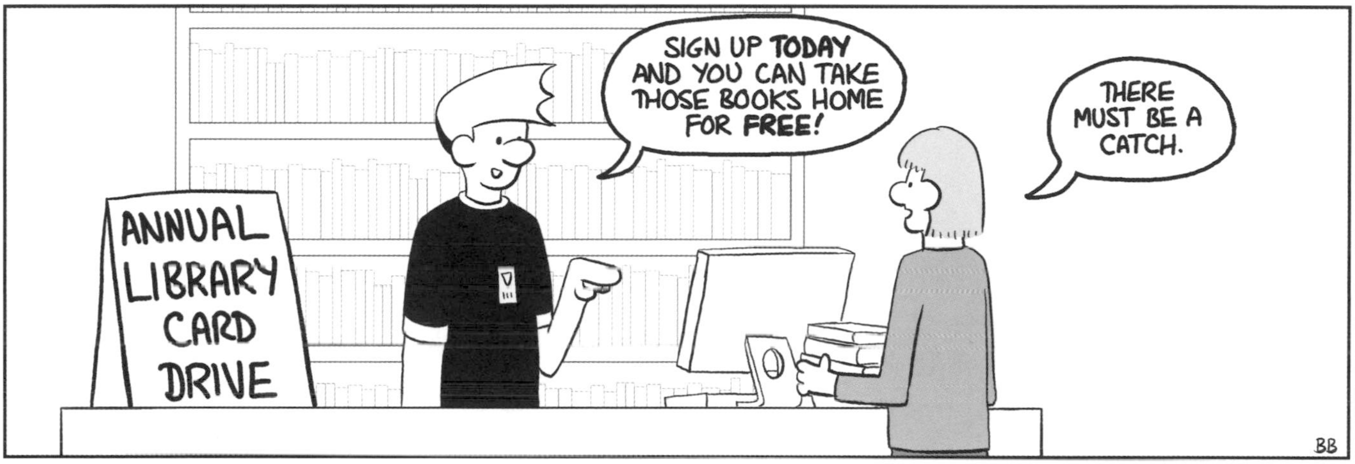
ANNUAL LIBRARY CARD DRIVE
SIGN UP **TODAY** AND YOU CAN TAKE THOSE BOOKS HOME FOR **FREE**!
THERE MUST BE A CATCH.
BB

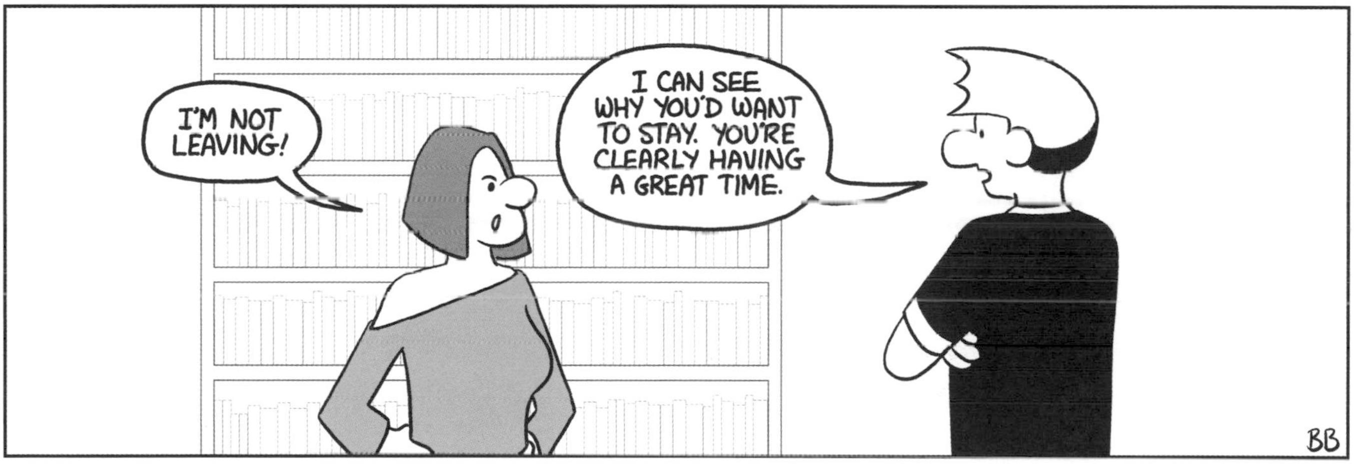
I'M NOT LEAVING!
I CAN SEE WHY YOU'D WANT TO STAY. YOU'RE CLEARLY HAVING A GREAT TIME.
BB

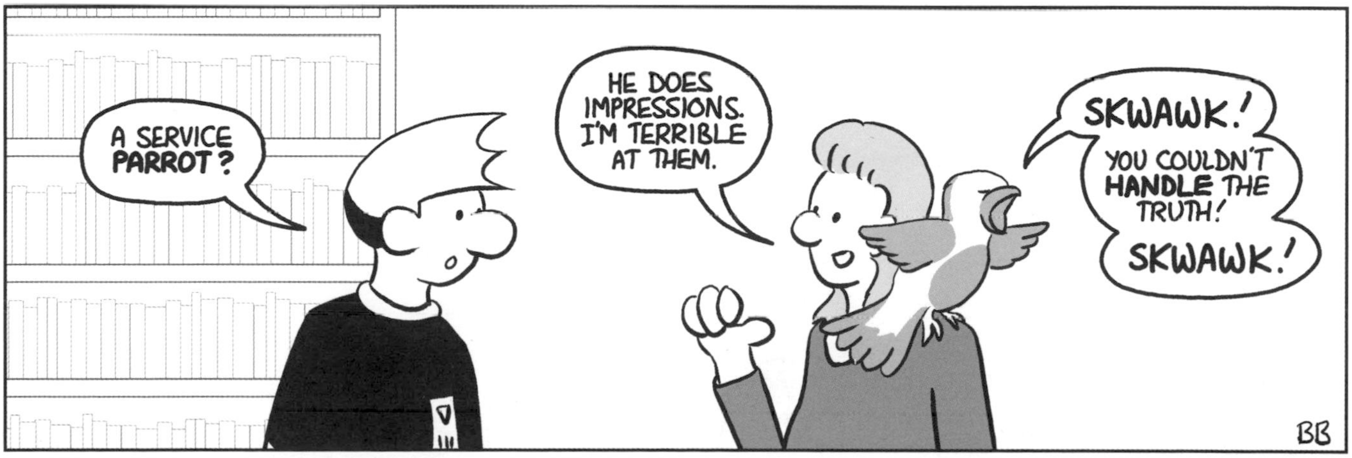
A SERVICE **PARROT**?
HE DOES IMPRESSIONS. I'M TERRIBLE AT THEM.
SKWAWK!
YOU COULDN'T **HANDLE** THE TRUTH!
SKWAWK!
BB

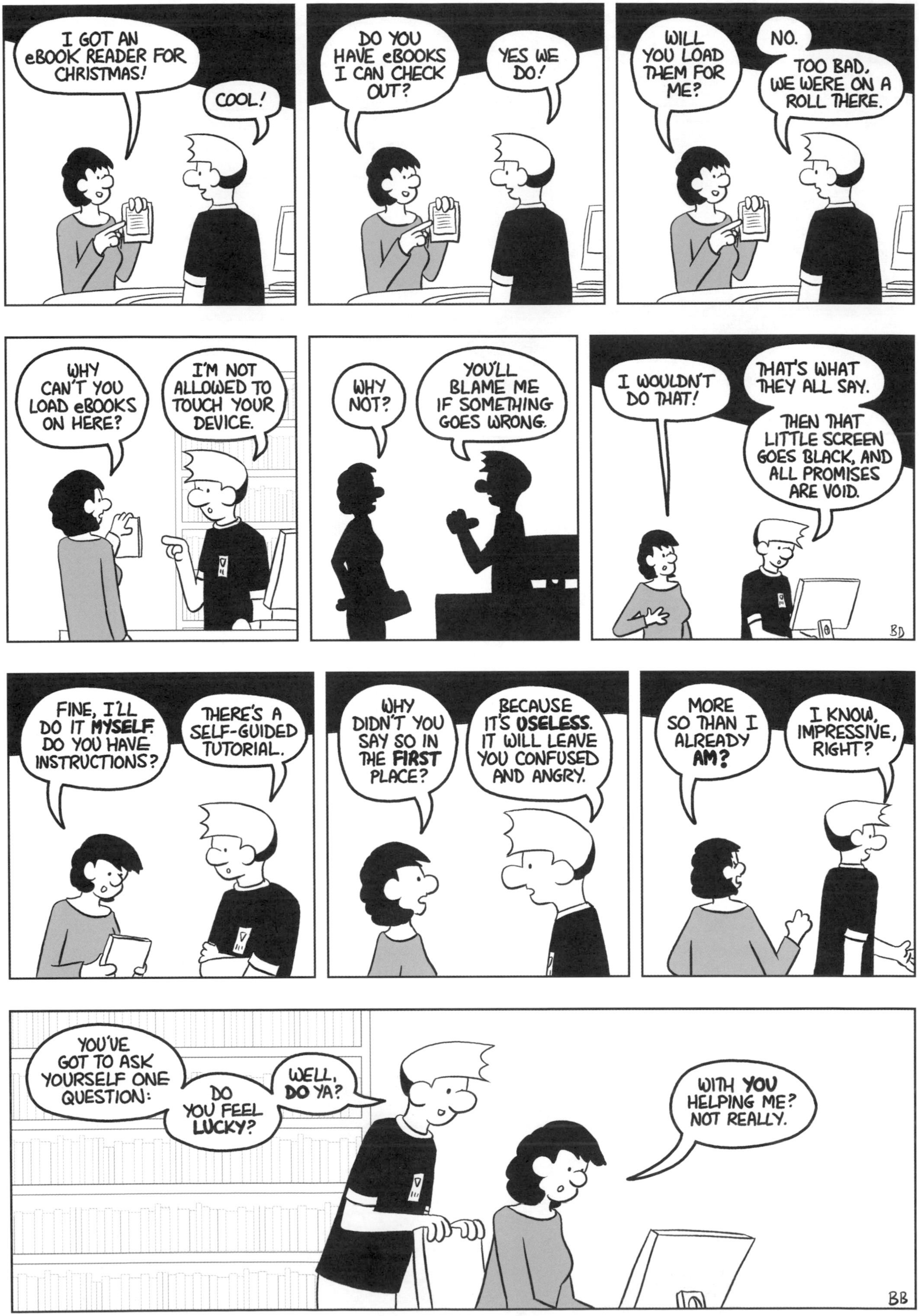
I GOT AN eBOOK READER FOR CHRISTMAS!
COOL!
DO YOU HAVE eBOOKS I CAN CHECK OUT?
YES WE DO!
WILL YOU LOAD THEM FOR ME?
NO.
TOO BAD, WE WERE ON A ROLL THERE.
WHY CAN'T YOU LOAD eBOOKS ON HERE?
I'M NOT ALLOWED TO TOUCH YOUR DEVICE.
WHY NOT?
YOU'LL BLAME ME IF SOMETHING GOES WRONG.
I WOULDN'T DO THAT!
THAT'S WHAT THEY ALL SAY.
THEN THAT LITTLE SCREEN GOES BLACK, AND ALL PROMISES ARE VOID.
BD
FINE, I'LL DO IT **MYSELF**. DO YOU HAVE INSTRUCTIONS?
THERE'S A SELF-GUIDED TUTORIAL.
WHY DIDN'T YOU SAY SO IN THE **FIRST** PLACE?
BECAUSE IT'S **USELESS**. IT WILL LEAVE YOU CONFUSED AND ANGRY.
MORE SO THAN I ALREADY **AM?**
I KNOW, IMPRESSIVE, RIGHT?
YOU'VE GOT TO ASK YOURSELF ONE QUESTION:
DO YOU FEEL **LUCKY**?
WELL, **DO** YA?
WITH **YOU** HELPING ME? NOT REALLY.
BB

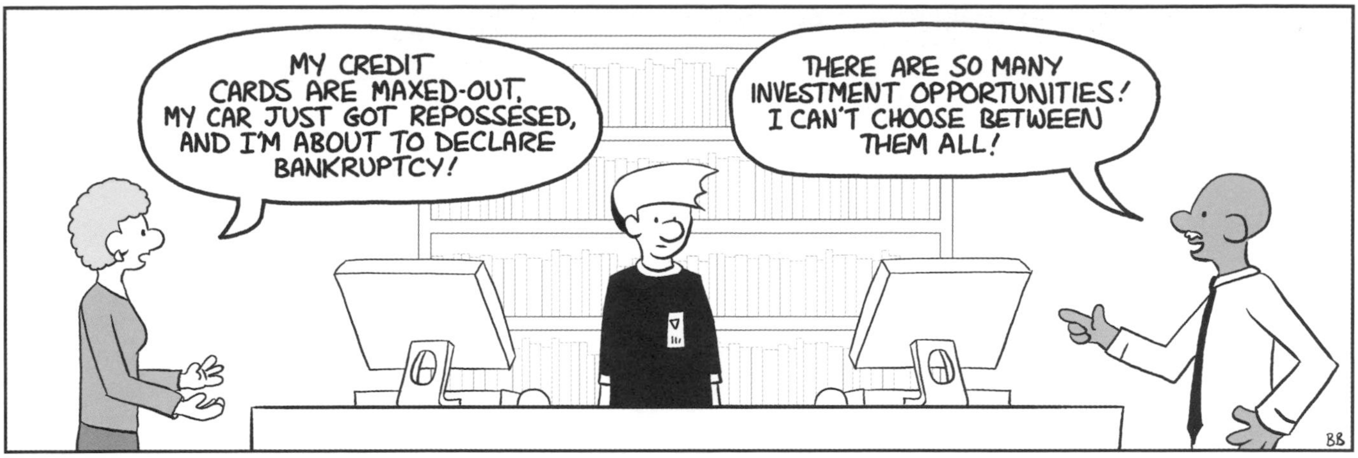
MY CREDIT CARDS ARE MAXED-OUT, MY CAR JUST GOT REPOSSESED, AND I'M ABOUT TO DECLARE BANKRUPTCY!
THERE ARE SO MANY INVESTMENT OPPORTUNITIES! I CAN'T CHOOSE BETWEEN THEM ALL!
BB

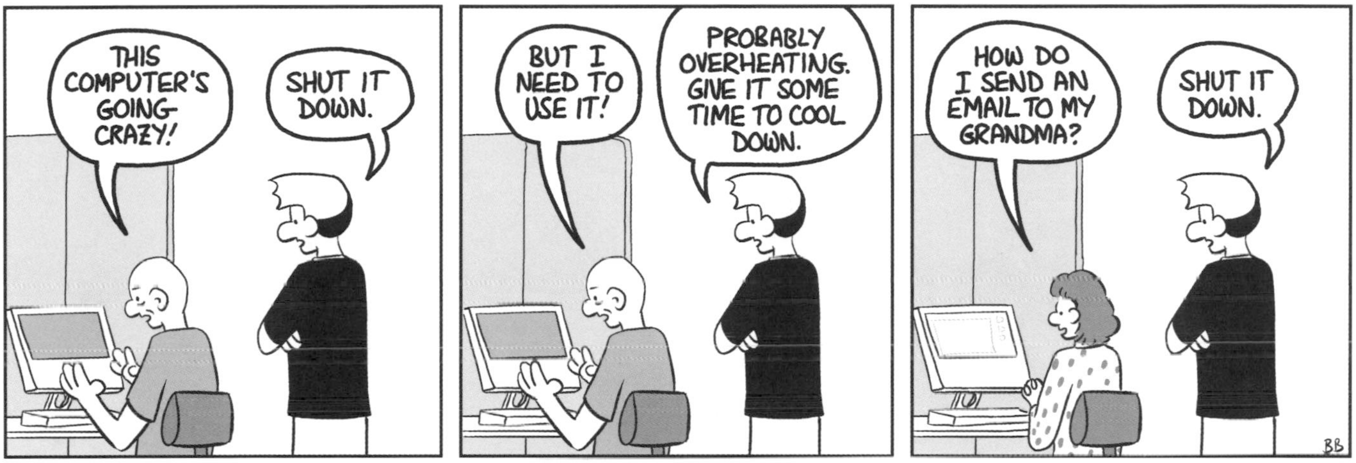
THIS COMPUTER'S GOING CRAZY!
SHUT IT DOWN.
BUT I NEED TO USE IT!
PROBABLY OVERHEATING. GIVE IT SOME TIME TO COOL DOWN.
HOW DO I SEND AN EMAIL TO MY GRANDMA?
SHUT IT DOWN.
BB

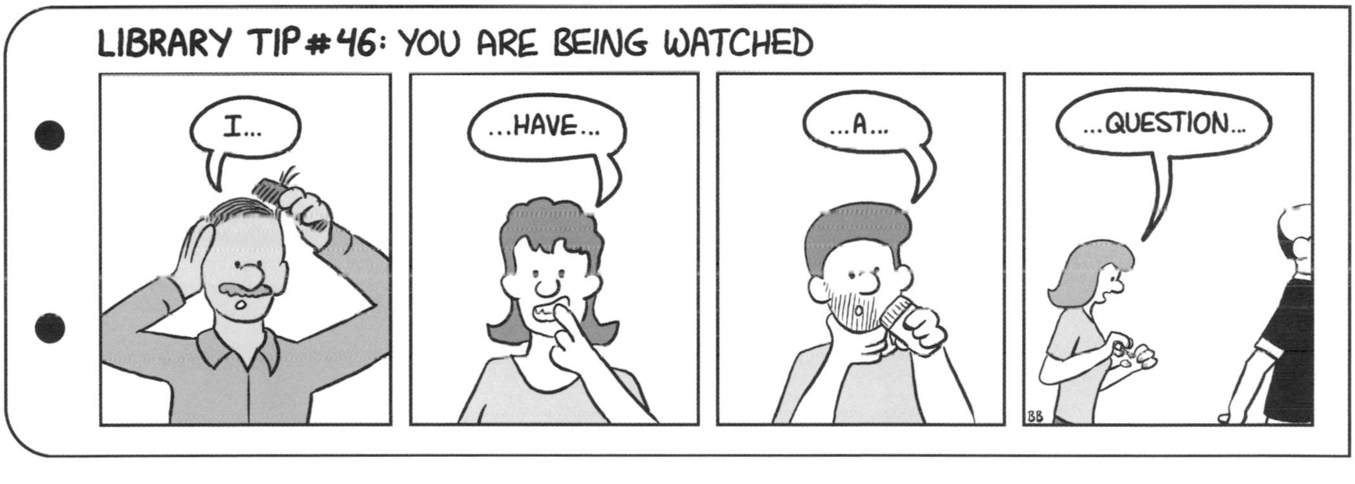
LIBRARY TIP #46: YOU ARE BEING WATCHED
I...
...HAVE...
...A...
...QUESTION...
BB

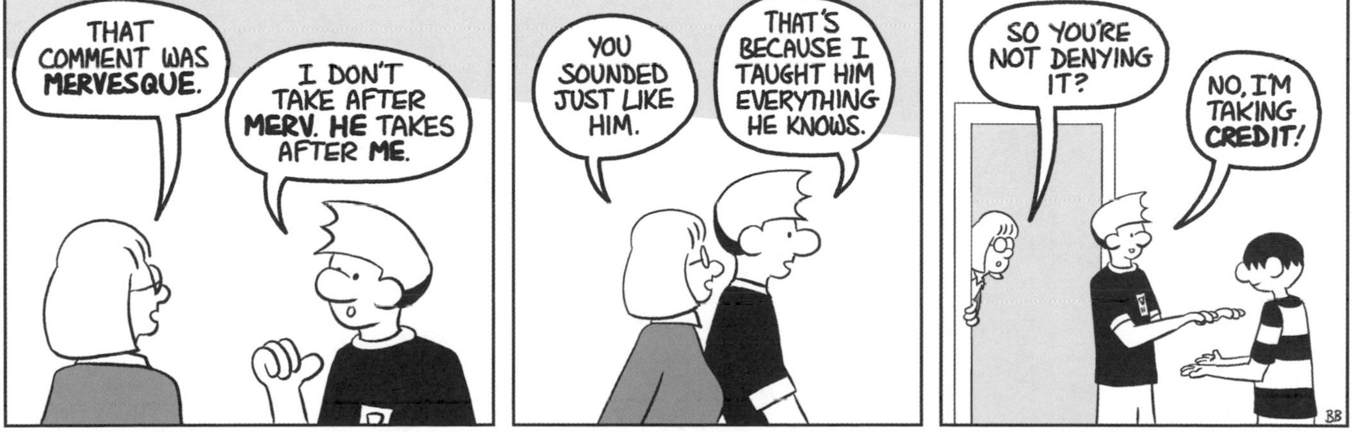
THAT COMMENT WAS **MERVESQUE**.
I DON'T TAKE AFTER **MERV. HE** TAKES AFTER **ME**.
YOU SOUNDED JUST LIKE HIM.
THAT'S BECAUSE I TAUGHT HIM EVERYTHING HE KNOWS.
SO YOU'RE NOT DENYING IT?
NO, I'M TAKING **CREDIT**!
BB

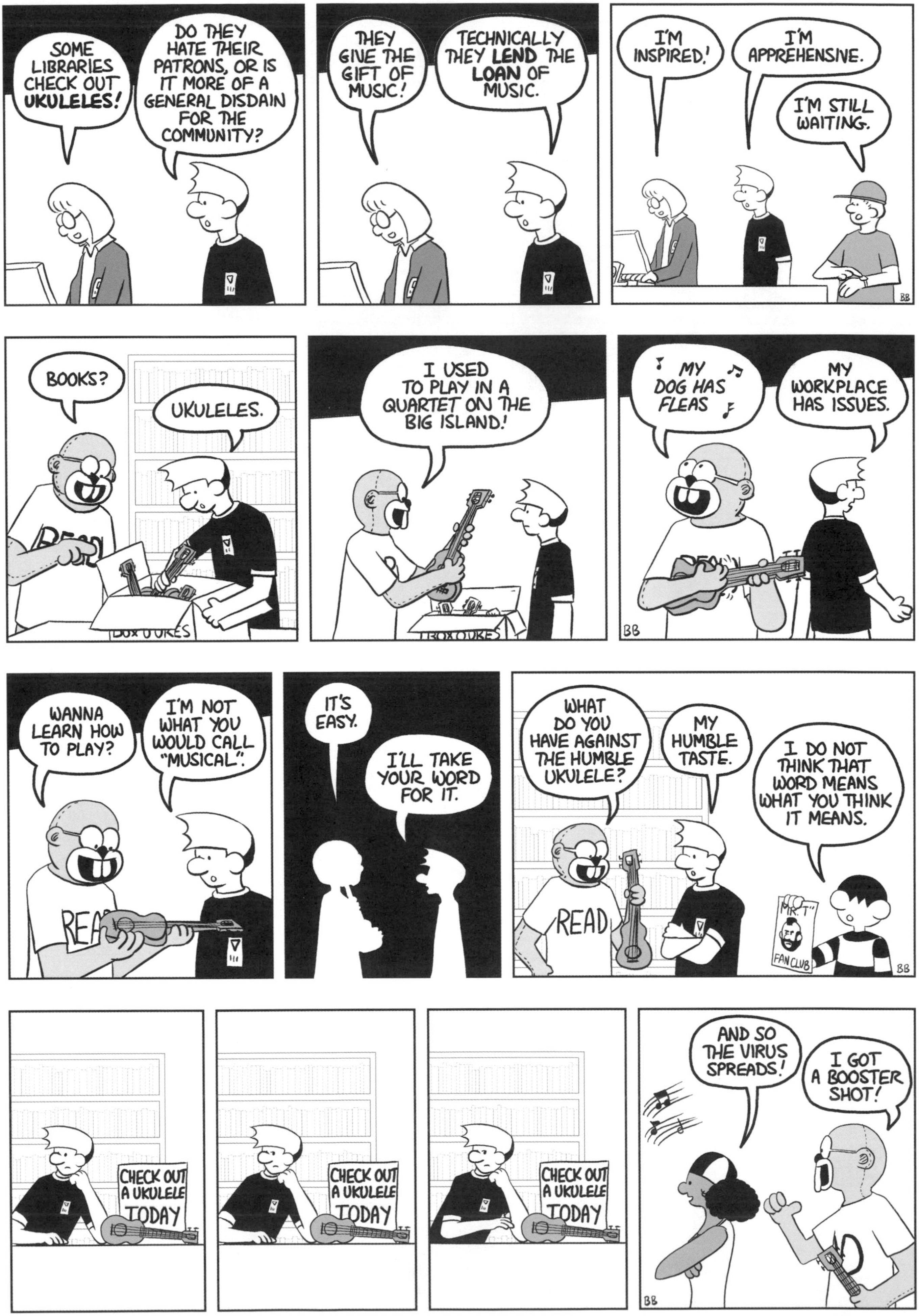
SOME LIBRARIES CHECK OUT **UKULELES**!
DO THEY HATE THEIR PATRONS, OR IS IT MORE OF A GENERAL DISDAIN FOR THE COMMUNITY?
THEY GIVE THE GIFT OF MUSIC!
TECHNICALLY THEY **LEND** THE **LOAN** OF MUSIC.
I'M INSPIRED!
I'M APPREHENSIVE.
I'M STILL WAITING.
BB
BOOKS?
UKULELES.
I USED TO PLAY IN A QUARTET ON THE BIG ISLAND!
MY DOG HAS FLEAS
MY WORKPLACE HAS ISSUES.
BB
WANNA LEARN HOW TO PLAY?
I'M NOT WHAT YOU WOULD CALL "MUSICAL".
READ
IT'S EASY.
I'LL TAKE YOUR WORD FOR IT.
WHAT DO YOU HAVE AGAINST THE HUMBLE UKULELE?
MY HUMBLE TASTE.
I DO NOT THINK THAT WORD MEANS WHAT YOU THINK IT MEANS.
READ
MR. T FAN CLUB
BB
CHECK OUT A UKULELE TODAY
CHECK OUT A UKULELE TODAY
CHECK OUT A UKULELE TODAY
AND SO THE VIRUS SPREADS!
I GOT A BOOSTER SHOT!
BB

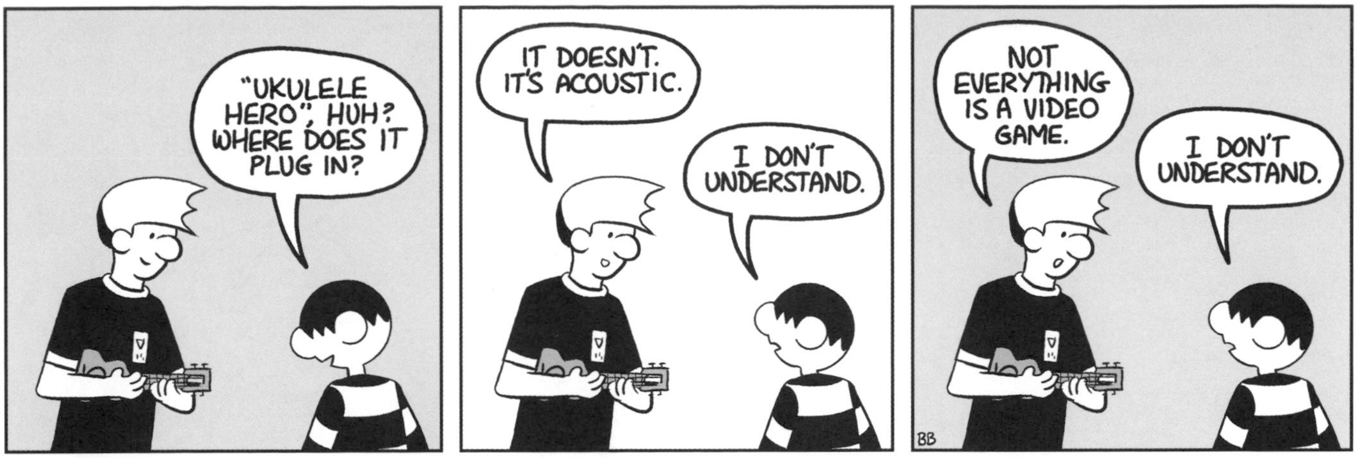
"UKULELE HERO", HUH? WHERE DOES IT PLUG IN?
IT DOESN'T. IT'S ACOUSTIC.
I DON'T UNDERSTAND.
NOT EVERYTHING IS A VIDEO GAME.
I DON'T UNDERSTAND.
BB

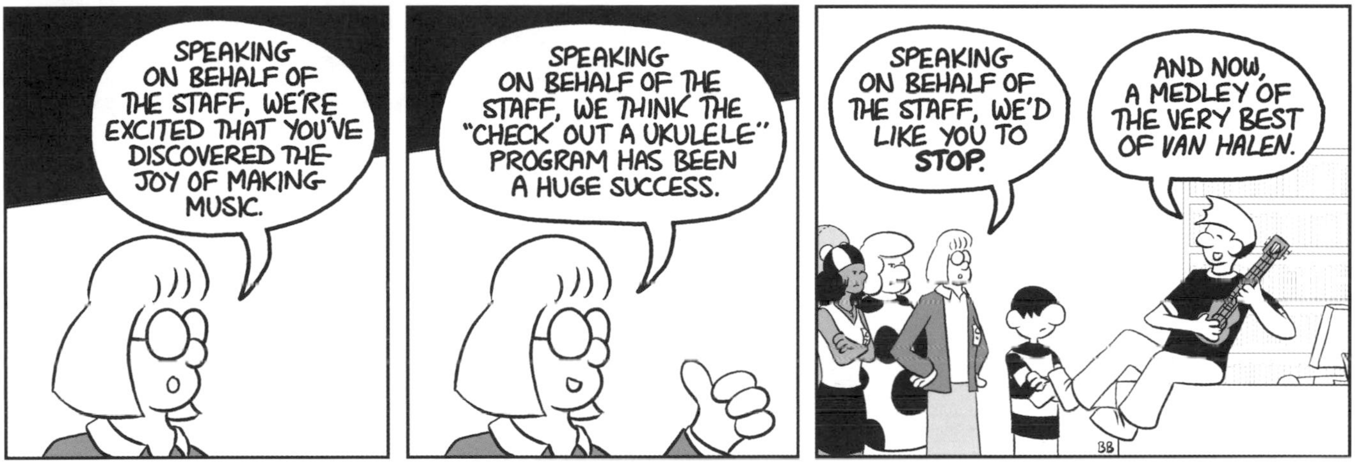
SPEAKING ON BEHALF OF THE STAFF, WE'RE EXCITED THAT YOU'VE DISCOVERED THE JOY OF MAKING MUSIC.
SPEAKING ON BEHALF OF THE STAFF, WE THINK THE "CHECK OUT A UKULELE" PROGRAM HAS BEEN A HUGE SUCCESS.
SPEAKING ON BEHALF OF THE STAFF, WE'D LIKE YOU TO **STOP.**
AND NOW, A MEDLEY OF THE VERY BEST OF *VAN HALEN*.
BB

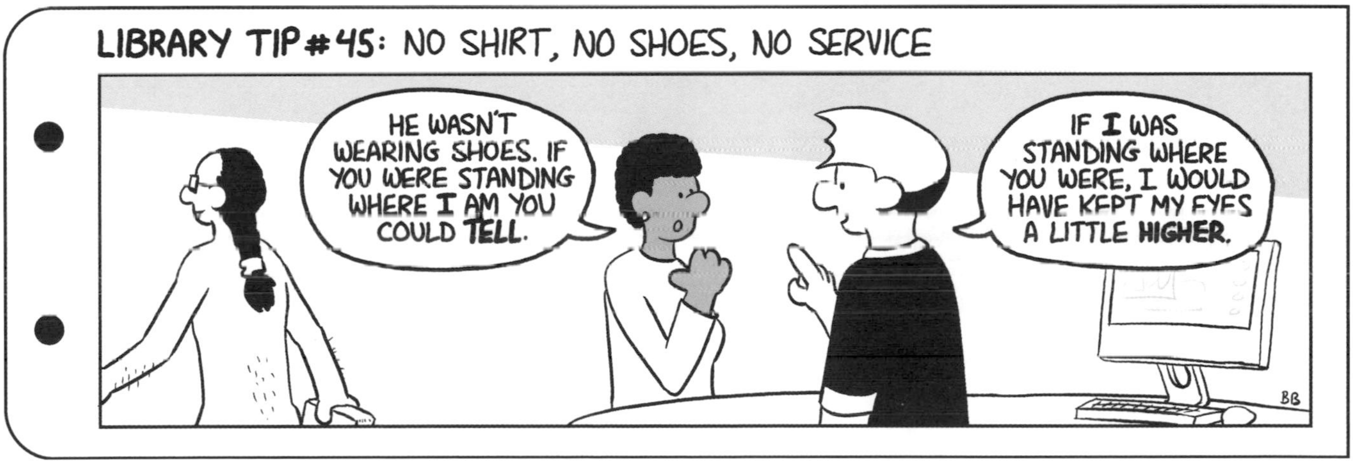
LIBRARY TIP #45: NO SHIRT, NO SHOES, NO SERVICE
HE WASN'T WEARING SHOES. IF YOU WERE STANDING WHERE **I** AM YOU COULD **TELL**.
IF **I** WAS STANDING WHERE YOU WERE, I WOULD HAVE KEPT MY EYES A LITTLE **HIGHER**.
BB

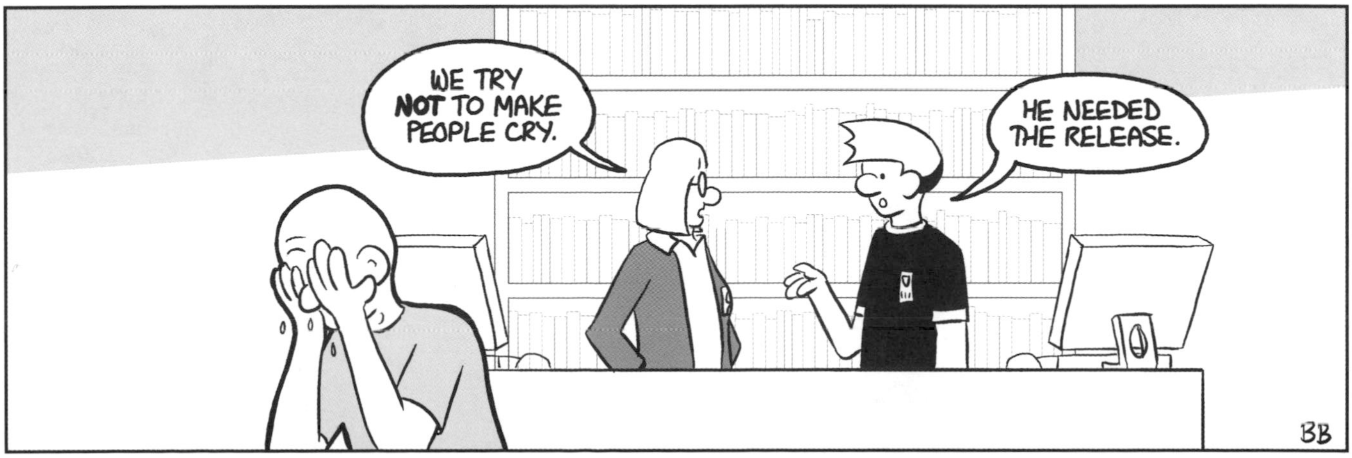
WE TRY **NOT** TO MAKE PEOPLE CRY.
HE NEEDED THE RELEASE.
BB

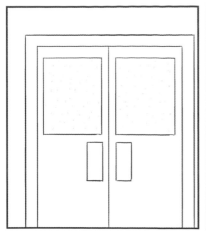

WHAM!

YOU MADE IT IN! YOU'RE MY HERO!

POLICY SAYS I ONLY GET PAID IF I SHOW UP.

YOU READ THE POLICY! YOU'RE MY HERO!

NOW WE CAN OPEN THE LIBRARY!

WHY WOULD WE DO **THAT**?

PEOPLE NEED US EVEN MORE WHEN IT'S SNOWING! THEY NEED INFORMATION ABOUT WEATHERPROOFING! SLEDDING CONDITIONS! METEOROLOGY! WHATEVER THEIR QUESTIONS WE HAVE THE ANSWERS!

WHERE'S THE BATHROOM?

WE'RE CLOSED.

NOT A SINGLE CUSTOMER ALL DAY.

THE IMPORTANT THING IS THAT WE'RE HERE.

WE'RE AN INSTITUTION! NEITHER RAIN, NOR SNOW, NOR SLEET, NOR HAIL SHALL KEEP THE LIBRARIANS FROM THEIR APPOINTED ROUNDS!

SO I'LL SEE YOU HERE AGAIN TOMORROW?

NO, IT'S MY DAY OFF. I'M GOING SKIING!

IT'S NICE TO HAVE A DAY OFF TOGETHER!

OH I DON'T HAVE THE DAY OFF.

I DON'T UNDERSTAND.

POLICY SAYS ON SNOW DAYS I GET PAID FOR THE FULL DAY EVEN IF I GET IN LATE.

IT'S FOUR O'CLOCK IN THE AFTERNOON!

YEAH I SHOULD REALLY BE GETTING READY.

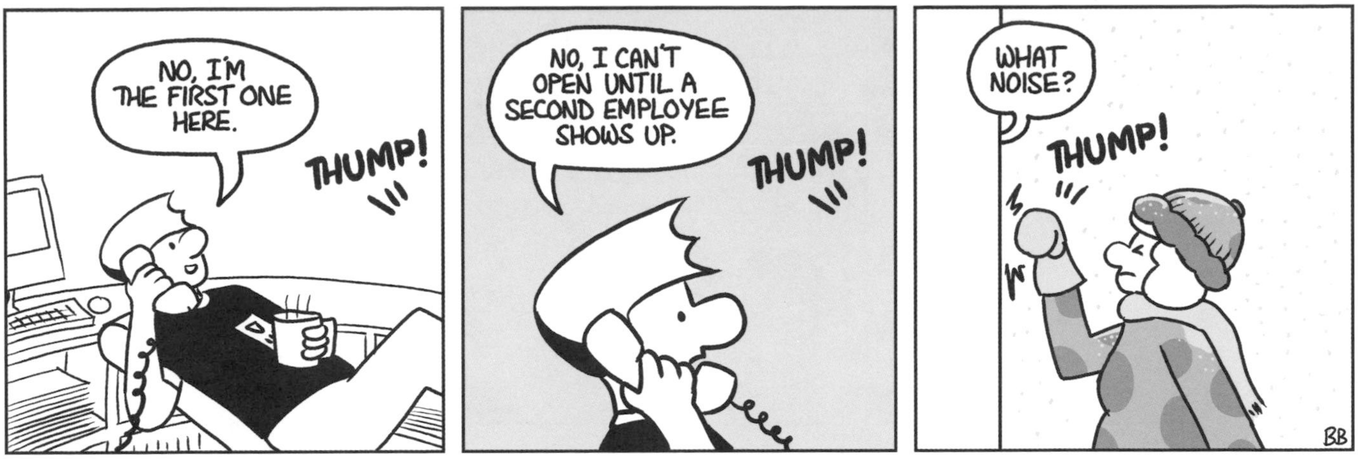
NO, I'M THE FIRST ONE HERE.
THUMP!
NO, I CAN'T OPEN UNTIL A SECOND EMPLOYEE SHOWS UP.
THUMP!
WHAT NOISE?
THUMP!
BB

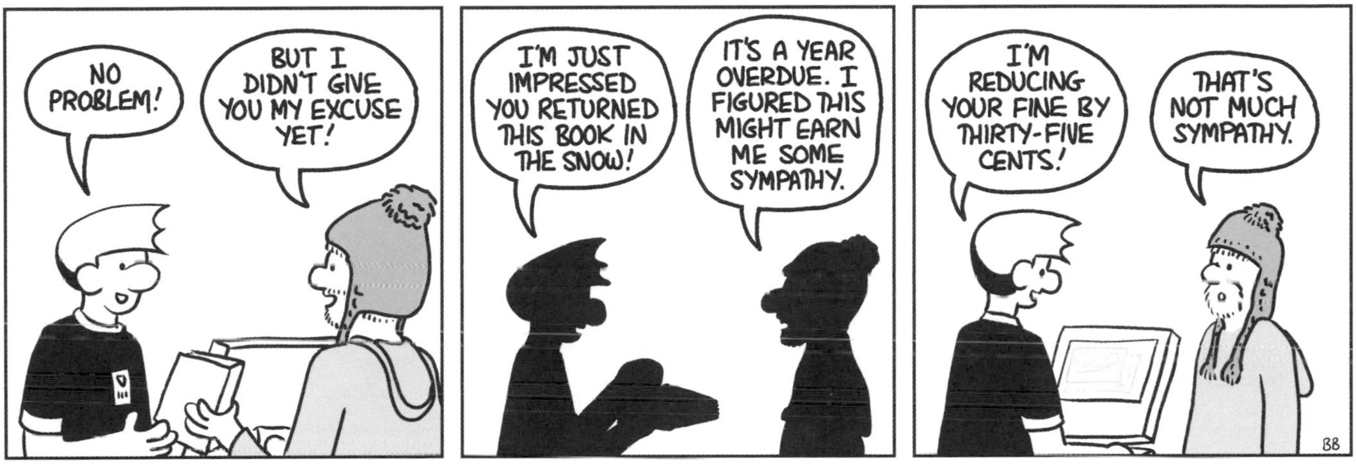
NO PROBLEM!
BUT I DIDN'T GIVE YOU MY EXCUSE YET!
I'M JUST IMPRESSED YOU RETURNED THIS BOOK IN THE SNOW!
IT'S A YEAR OVERDUE. I FIGURED THIS MIGHT EARN ME SOME SYMPATHY.
I'M REDUCING YOUR FINE BY THIRTY-FIVE CENTS!
THAT'S NOT MUCH SYMPATHY.
BB

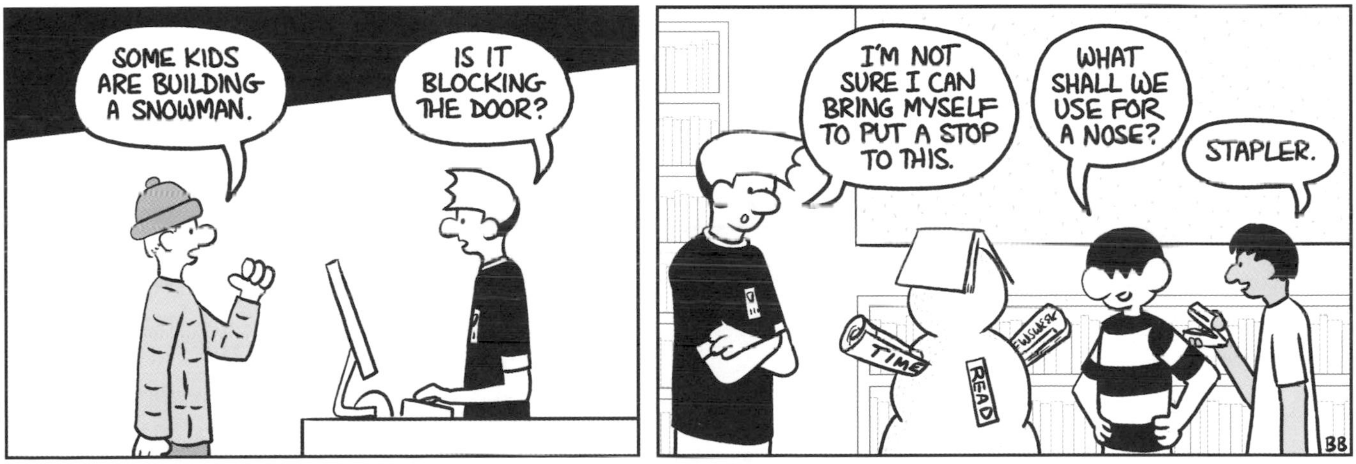
SOME KIDS ARE BUILDING A SNOWMAN.
IS IT BLOCKING THE DOOR?
I'M NOT SURE I CAN BRING MYSELF TO PUT A STOP TO THIS.
WHAT SHALL WE USE FOR A NOSE?
STAPLER.
TIME
READ
BB

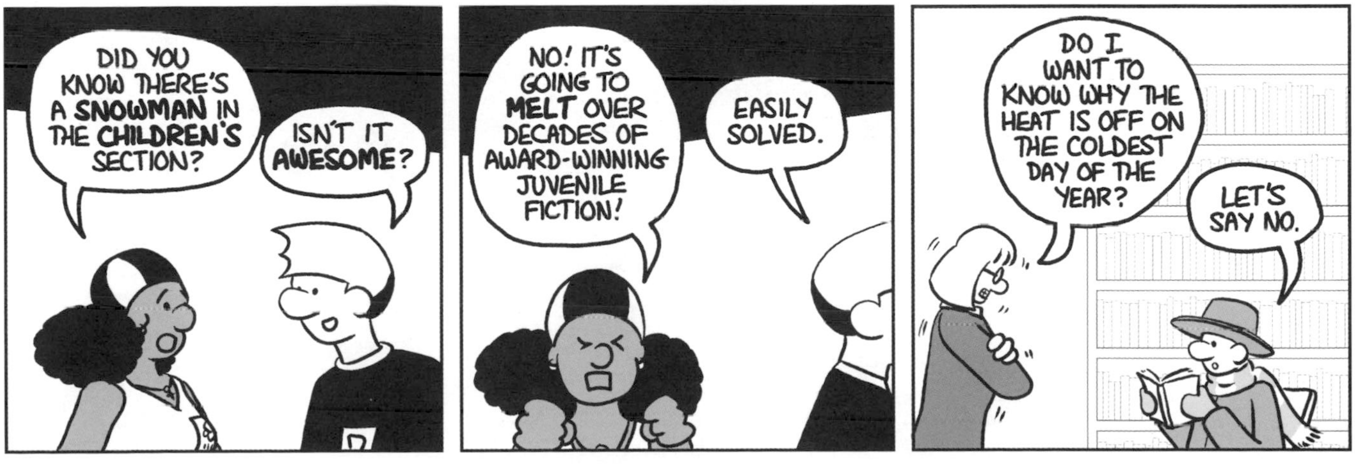
DID YOU KNOW THERE'S A **SNOWMAN** IN THE **CHILDREN'S** SECTION?
ISN'T IT **AWESOME**?
NO! IT'S GOING TO **MELT** OVER DECADES OF AWARD-WINNING JUVENILE FICTION!
EASILY SOLVED.
DO I WANT TO KNOW WHY THE HEAT IS OFF ON THE COLDEST DAY OF THE YEAR?
LET'S SAY NO.

LIBRARY TIP # 47: WE MAKE A LIVING READING PEOPLE'S FACES

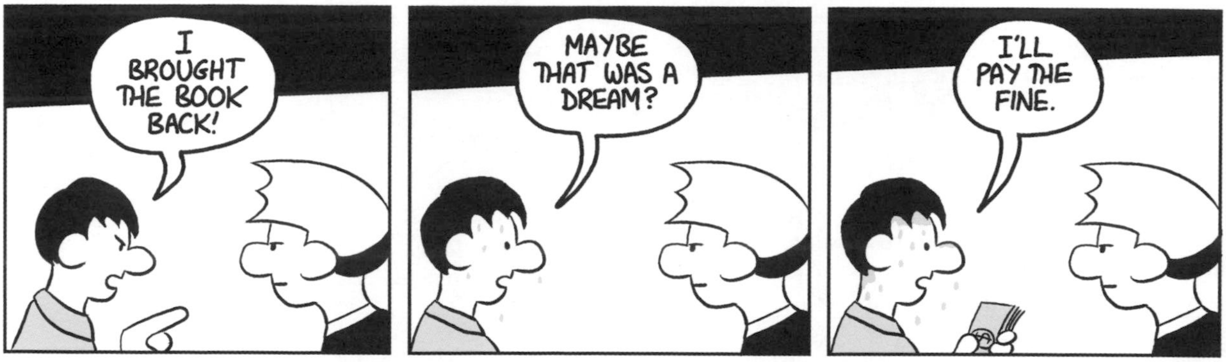
I BROUGHT THE BOOK BACK!
MAYBE THAT WAS A DREAM?
I'LL PAY THE FINE.

LIBRARY TIP # 48: IF YOU'RE GONNA PLAY THE GAME, LEARN TO DO IT RIGHT

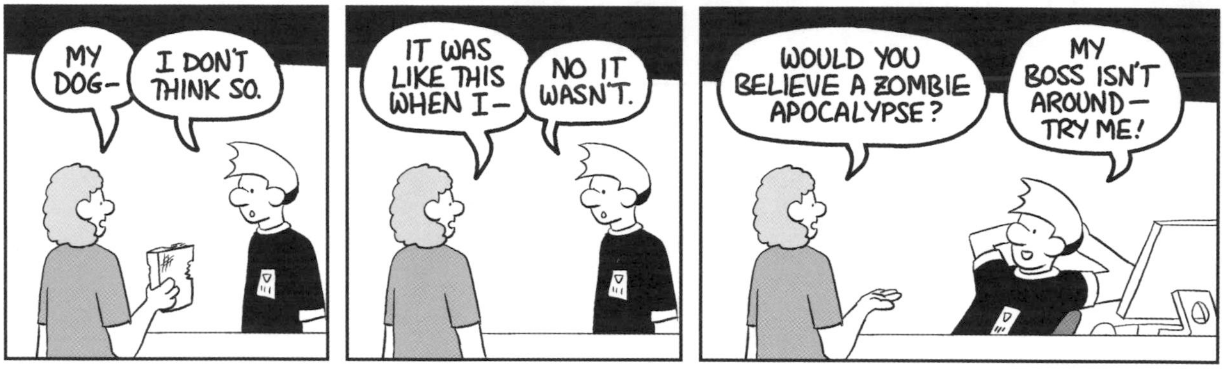
MY DOG-
I DON'T THINK SO.
IT WAS LIKE THIS WHEN I-
NO IT WASN'T.
WOULD YOU BELIEVE A ZOMBIE APOCALYPSE?
MY BOSS ISN'T AROUND— TRY ME!

LIBRARY TIP # 49: KNOW WHAT TO THROW AWAY, KNOW WHAT TO KEEP

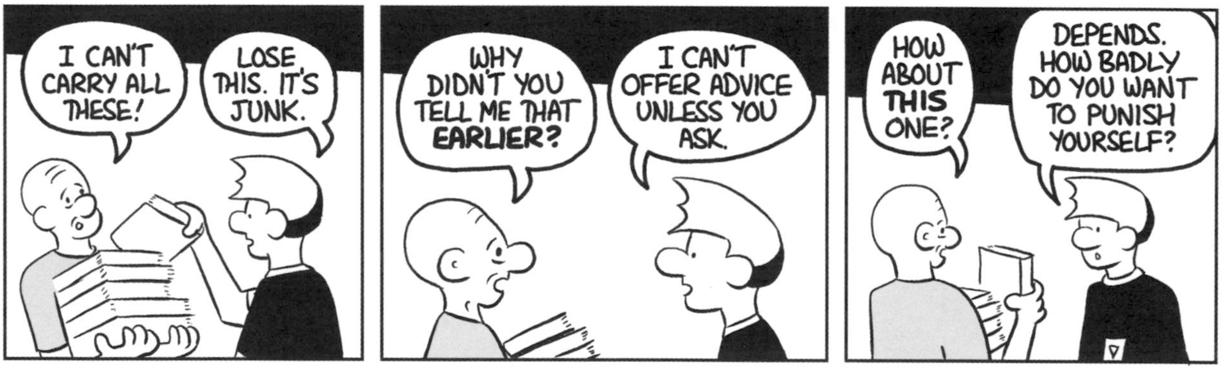
I CAN'T CARRY ALL THESE!
LOSE THIS. IT'S JUNK.
WHY DIDN'T YOU TELL ME THAT **EARLIER?**
I CAN'T OFFER ADVICE UNLESS YOU ASK.
HOW ABOUT **THIS** ONE?
DEPENDS. HOW BADLY DO YOU WANT TO PUNISH YOURSELF?

LIBRARY TIP # 50: KNOW WHEN TO HOLD 'EM

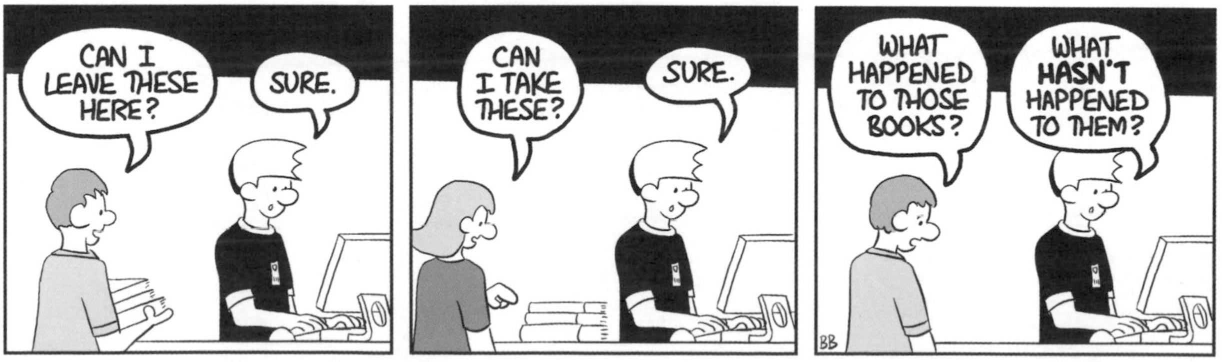
CAN I LEAVE THESE HERE?
SURE.
CAN I TAKE THESE?
SURE.
WHAT HAPPENED TO THOSE BOOKS?
WHAT **HASN'T** HAPPENED TO THEM?
BB

LIBRARY TIP #51: KNOW WHEN TO FOLD 'EM

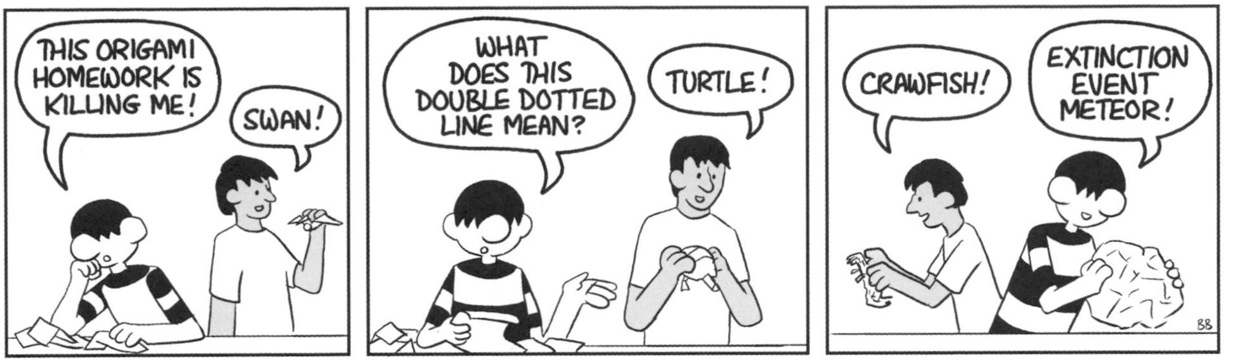
THIS ORIGAMI HOMEWORK IS KILLING ME!
SWAN!
WHAT DOES THIS DOUBLE DOTTED LINE MEAN?
TURTLE!
CRAWFISH!
EXTINCTION EVENT METEOR!
BB

LIBRARY TIP #52: KNOW WHEN TO WALK AWAY

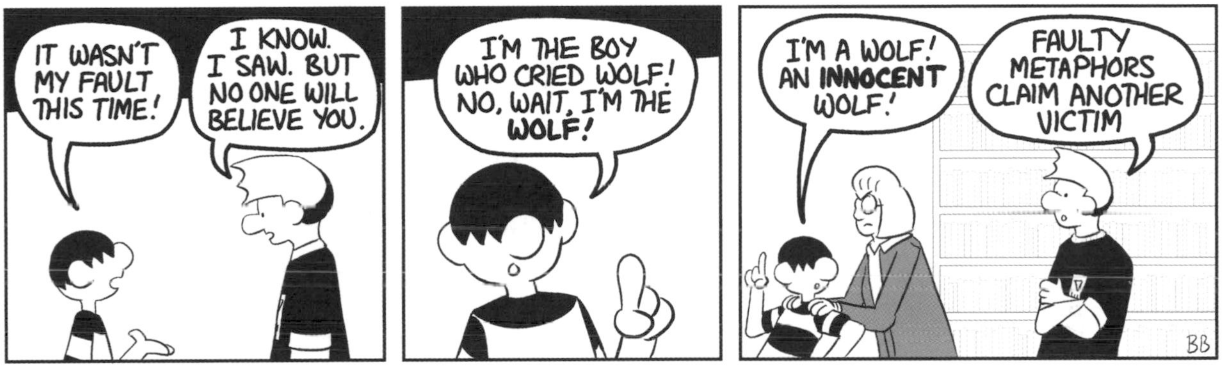
IT WASN'T MY FAULT THIS TIME!
I KNOW. I SAW. BUT NO ONE WILL BELIEVE YOU.
I'M THE BOY WHO CRIED WOLF! NO, WAIT, I'M THE **WOLF**!
I'M A WOLF! AN **INNOCENT** WOLF!
FAULTY METAPHORS CLAIM ANOTHER VICTIM
BB

LIBRARY TIP #53: KNOW WHEN TO RUN

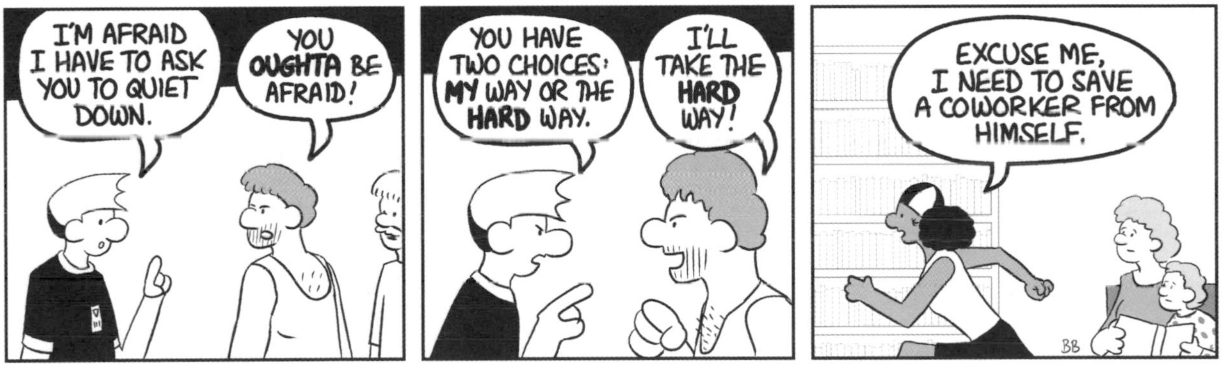
I'M AFRAID I HAVE TO ASK YOU TO QUIET DOWN.
YOU **OUGHTA** BE AFRAID!
YOU HAVE TWO CHOICES: **MY** WAY OR THE **HARD** WAY.
I'LL TAKE THE **HARD** WAY!
EXCUSE ME, I NEED TO SAVE A COWORKER FROM HIMSELF.
BB

LIBRARY TIP #54: NEVER COUNT YOUR MONEY WHEN YOU'RE SITTING AT THE TABLE

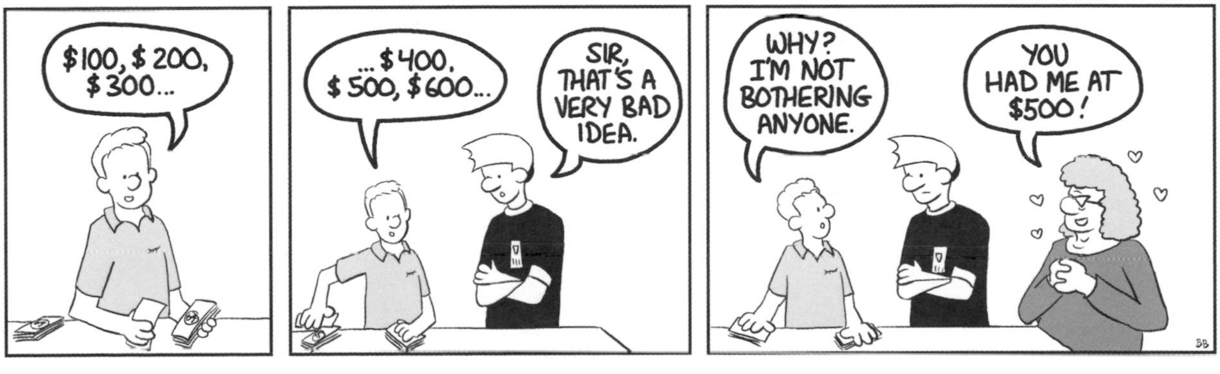
$100, $200, $300...
...$400, $500, $600...
SIR, THAT'S A VERY BAD IDEA.
WHY? I'M NOT BOTHERING ANYONE.
YOU HAD ME AT $500!
BB

LIBRARY TIP #55: THERE'LL BE TIME ENOUGH FOR COUNTING WHEN THE DEALING'S DONE

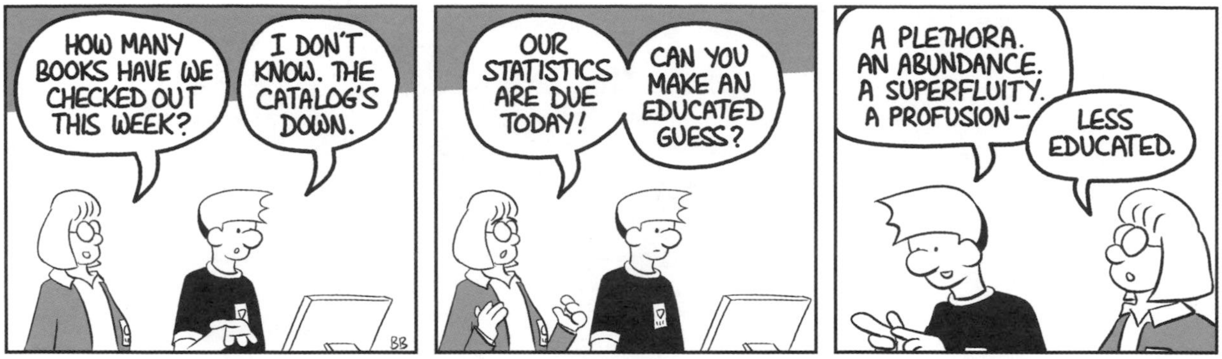
HOW MANY BOOKS HAVE WE CHECKED OUT THIS WEEK?
I DON'T KNOW. THE CATALOG'S DOWN.
OUR STATISTICS ARE DUE TODAY!
CAN YOU MAKE AN EDUCATED GUESS?
A PLETHORA. AN ABUNDANCE. A SUPERFLUITY. A PROFUSION—
LESS EDUCATED.
BB

CONFERENCE TIP: ENERGIZE YOUR PROFESSIONAL LIFE

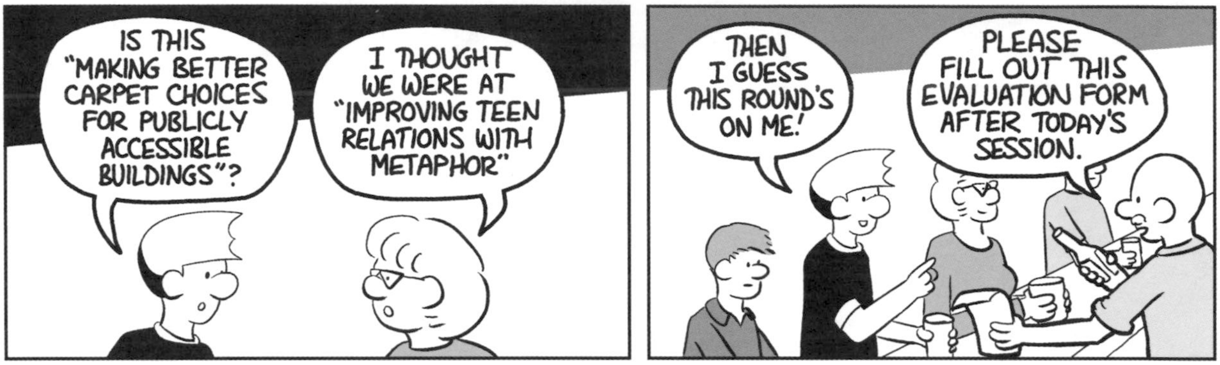
IS THIS "MAKING BETTER CARPET CHOICES FOR PUBLICLY ACCESSIBLE BUILDINGS"?
I THOUGHT WE WERE AT "IMPROVING TEEN RELATIONS WITH METAPHOR"
THEN I GUESS THIS ROUND'S ON ME!
PLEASE FILL OUT THIS EVALUATION FORM AFTER TODAY'S SESSION.

CONFERENCE TIP: TAKE INTERVIEWS SERIOUSLY

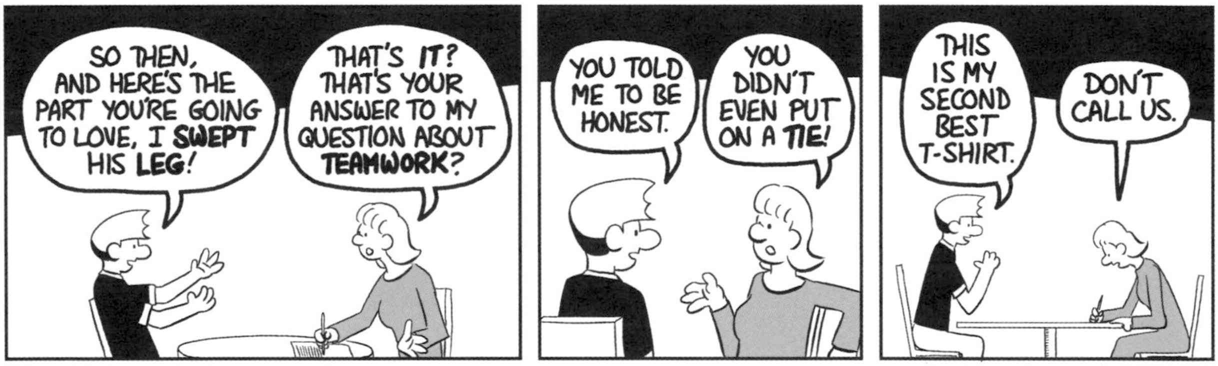
SO THEN, AND HERE'S THE PART YOU'RE GOING TO LOVE, I **SWEPT** HIS **LEG**!
THAT'S **IT**? THAT'S YOUR ANSWER TO MY QUESTION ABOUT **TEAMWORK**?
YOU TOLD ME TO BE HONEST.
YOU DIDN'T EVEN PUT ON A **TIE**!
THIS IS MY SECOND BEST T-SHIRT.
DON'T CALL US.

CONFERENCE TIP: SAVE YOUR RECEIPTS

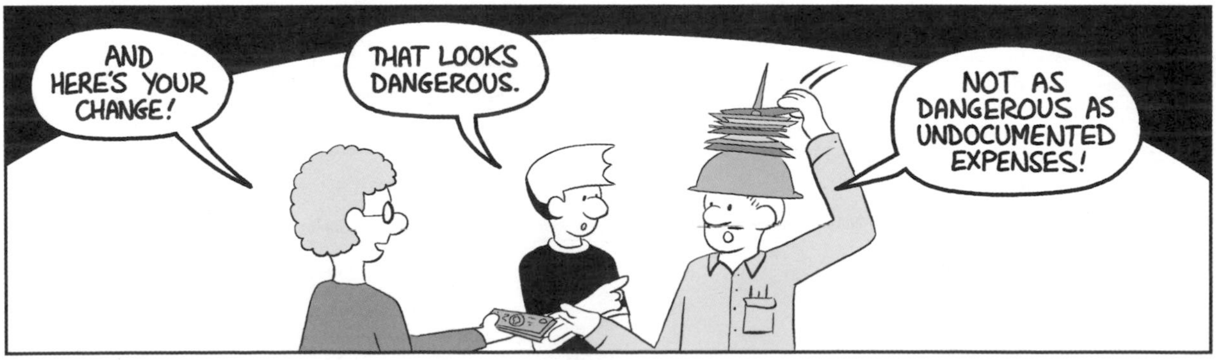
AND HERE'S YOUR CHANGE!
THAT LOOKS DANGEROUS.
NOT AS DANGEROUS AS UNDOCUMENTED EXPENSES!

CONFERENCE TIP: SO MANY BOOKS...

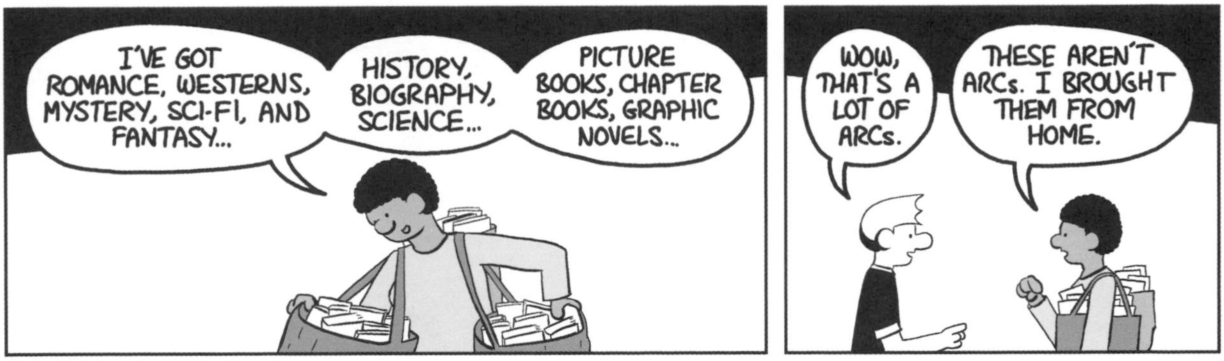
I'VE GOT ROMANCE, WESTERNS, MYSTERY, SCI-FI, AND FANTASY...
HISTORY, BIOGRAPHY, SCIENCE...
PICTURE BOOKS, CHAPTER BOOKS, GRAPHIC NOVELS...
WOW, THAT'S A LOT OF ARCs.
THESE AREN'T ARCs. I BROUGHT THEM FROM HOME.

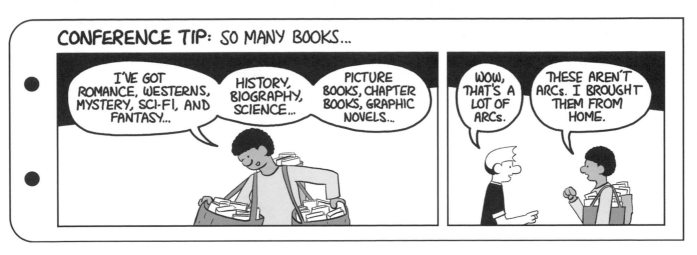

CONFERENCE TIP: BEWARE THE LOCUSTS

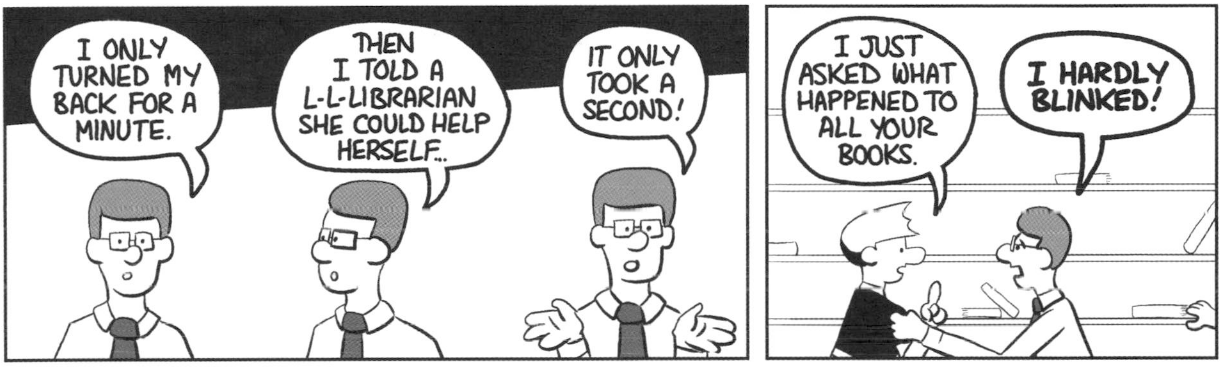
I ONLY TURNED MY BACK FOR A MINUTE.
THEN I TOLD A L-L-LIBRARIAN SHE COULD HELP HERSELF...
IT ONLY TOOK A SECOND!
I JUST ASKED WHAT HAPPENED TO ALL YOUR BOOKS.
I HARDLY BLINKED!

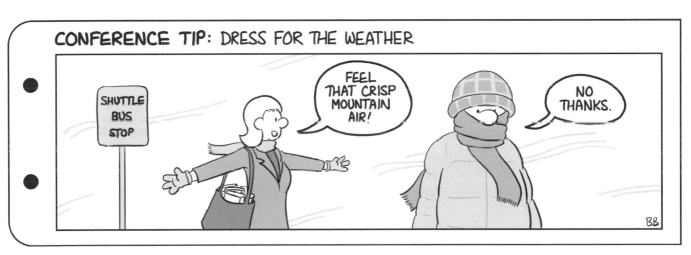

CONFERENCE TIP: DRESS FOR THE WEATHER

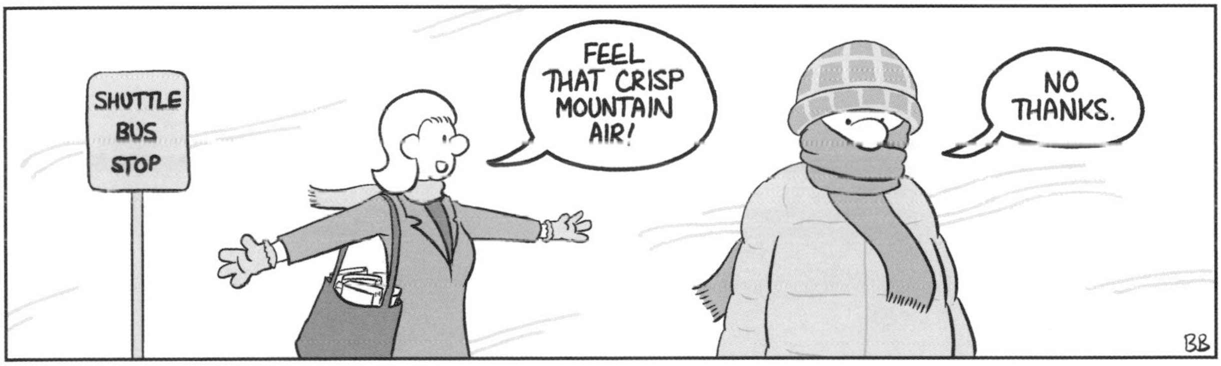
SHUTTLE BUS STOP
FEEL THAT CRISP MOUNTAIN AIR!
NO THANKS.
BB

CONFERENCE TIP: RIDE THE WAVE

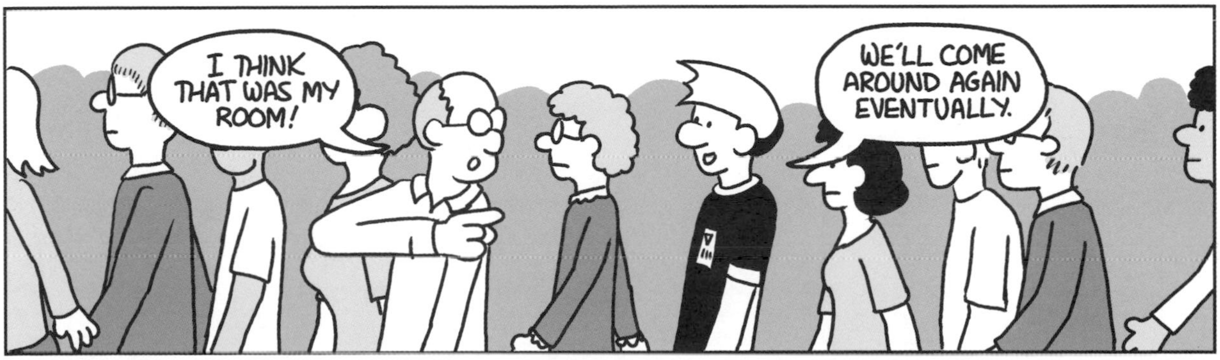
I THINK THAT WAS MY ROOM!
WE'LL COME AROUND AGAIN EVENTUALLY.

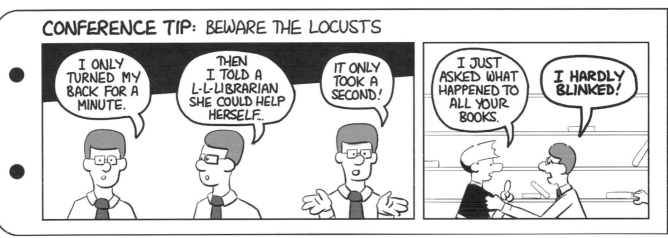

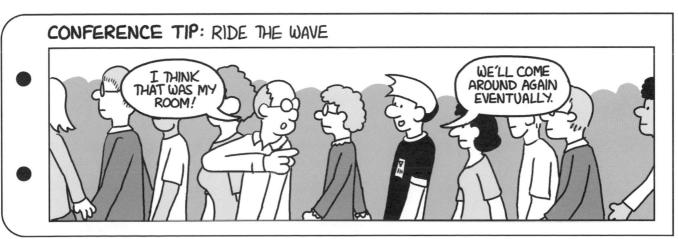

CONFERENCE TIP: FIGHT THE BAGGAGE SURCHARGE

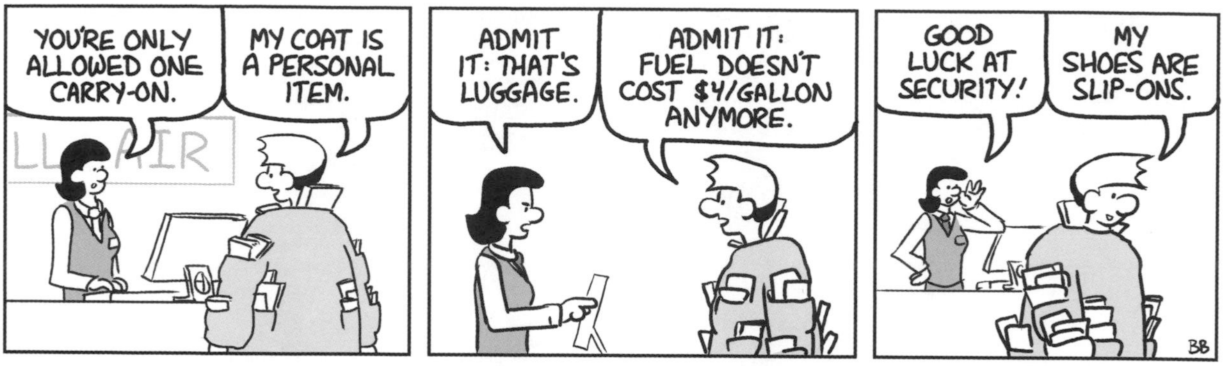
YOU'RE ONLY ALLOWED ONE CARRY-ON.
MY COAT IS A PERSONAL ITEM.
LL AIR
ADMIT IT: THAT'S LUGGAGE.
ADMIT IT: FUEL DOESN'T COST $4/GALLON ANYMORE.
GOOD LUCK AT SECURITY!
MY SHOES ARE SLIP-ONS.
BB

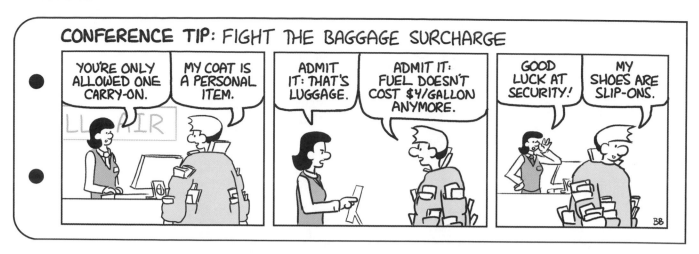

CONFERENCE TIP: KNOW THE REAL COST OF YOUR TRIP.

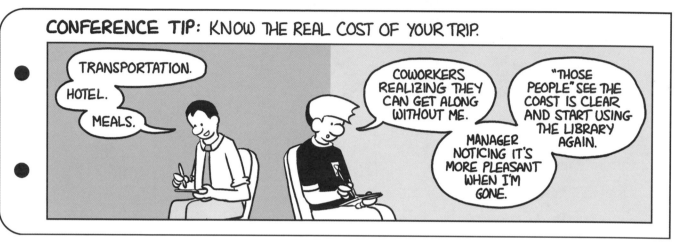

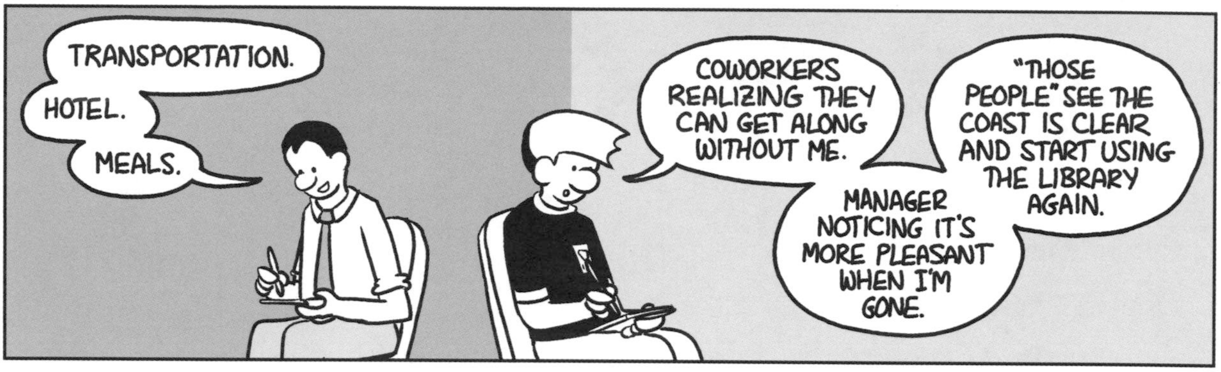
TRANSPORTATION.
HOTEL.
MEALS.
COWORKERS REALIZING THEY CAN GET ALONG WITHOUT ME.
MANAGER NOTICING IT'S MORE PLEASANT WHEN I'M GONE.
"THOSE PEOPLE" SEE THE COAST IS CLEAR AND START USING THE LIBRARY AGAIN.

CONFERENCE TIP: FIGHT FOR YOUR ARMREST

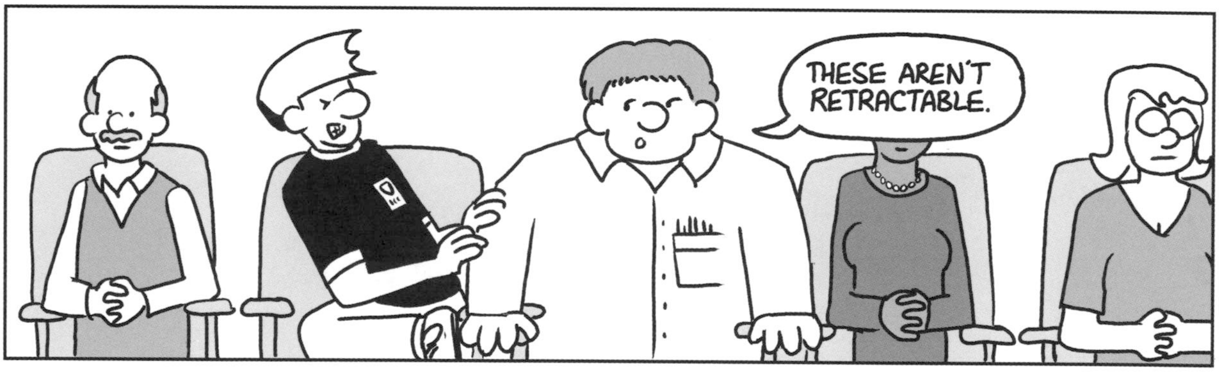
THESE AREN'T RETRACTABLE.

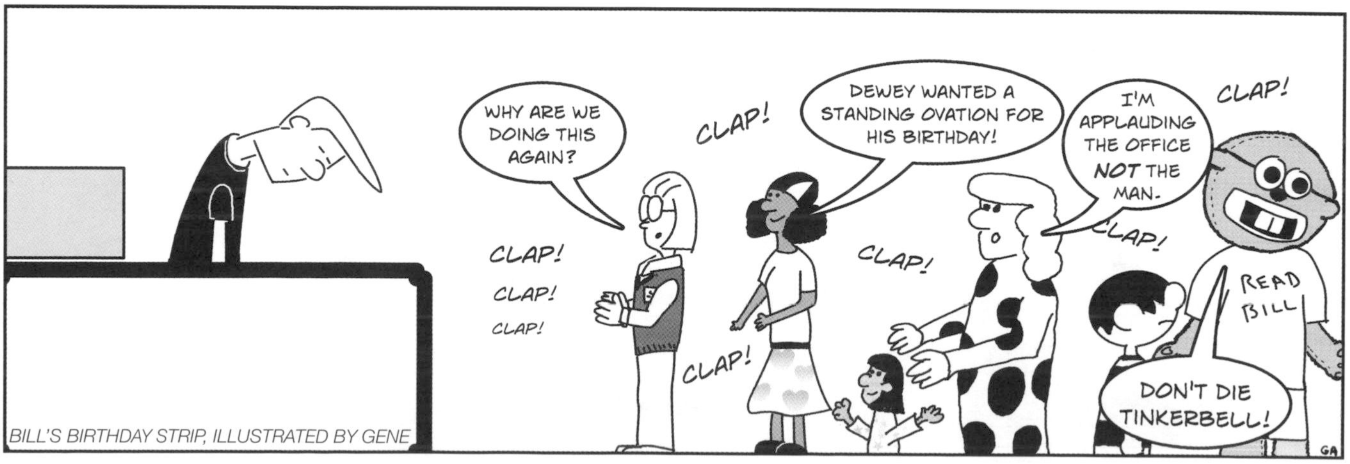
WHY ARE WE DOING THIS AGAIN?
CLAP!
DEWEY WANTED A STANDING OVATION FOR HIS BIRTHDAY!
I'M APPLAUDING THE OFFICE NOT THE MAN.
CLAP!
CLAP!
CLAP!
CLAP!
CLAP!
CLAP!
CLAP!
READ BILL
DON'T DIE TINKERBELL!
GA

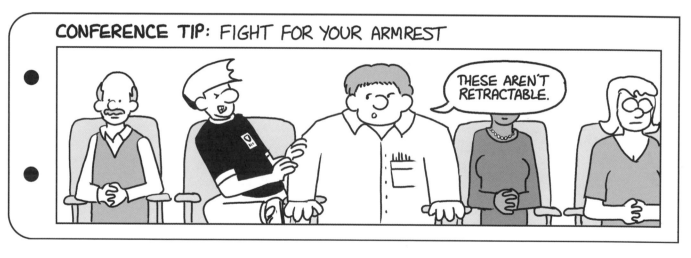

BILL'S BIRTHDAY STRIP, ILLUSTRATED BY GENE

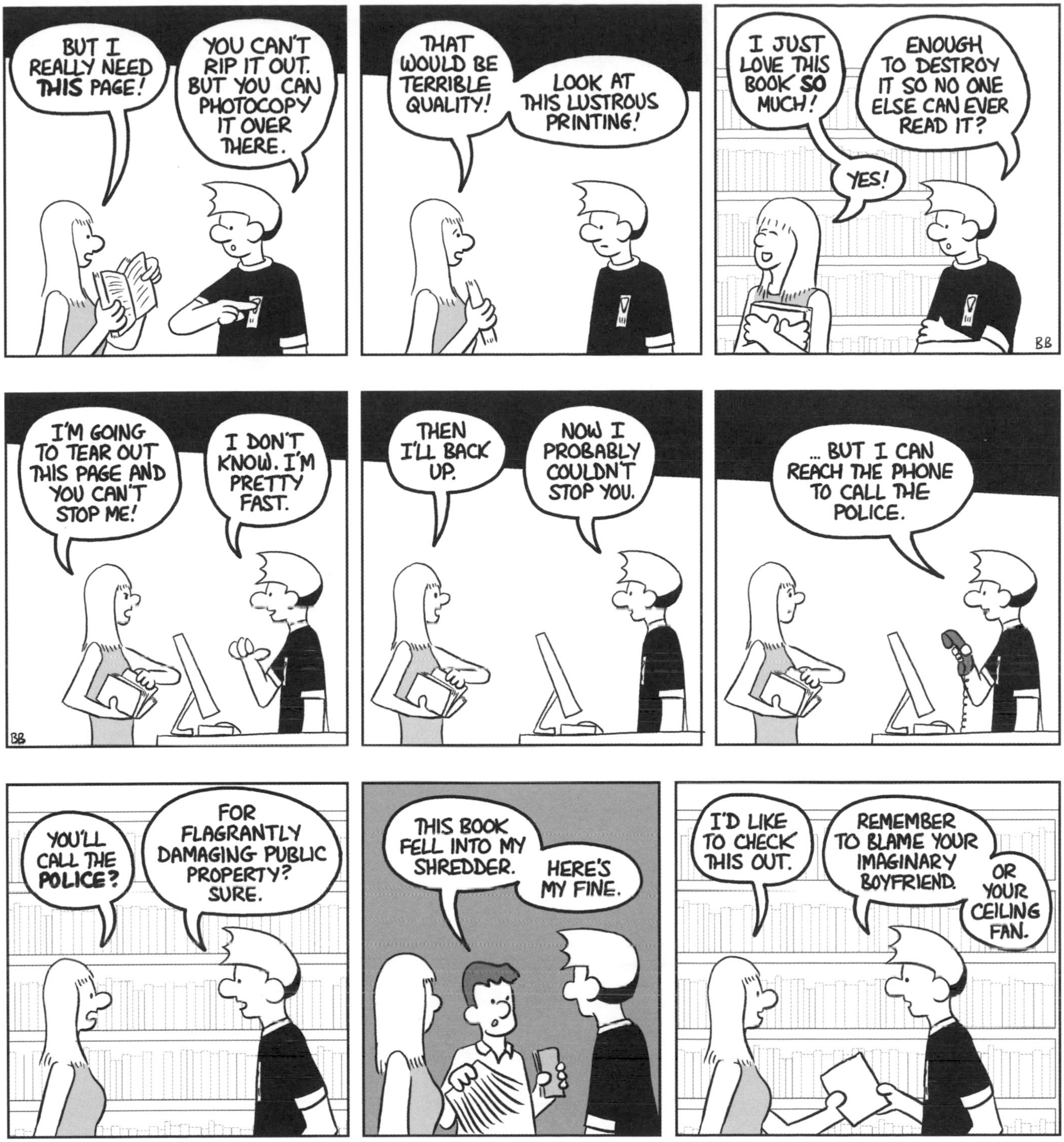
BUT I REALLY NEED THIS PAGE!
YOU CAN'T RIP IT OUT. BUT YOU CAN PHOTOCOPY IT OVER THERE.
THAT WOULD BE TERRIBLE QUALITY!
LOOK AT THIS LUSTROUS PRINTING!
I JUST LOVE THIS BOOK SO MUCH!
ENOUGH TO DESTROY IT SO NO ONE ELSE CAN EVER READ IT?
YES!
BB
I'M GOING TO TEAR OUT THIS PAGE AND YOU CAN'T STOP ME!
I DON'T KNOW. I'M PRETTY FAST.
BB
THEN I'LL BACK UP.
NOW I PROBABLY COULDN'T STOP YOU.
... BUT I CAN REACH THE PHONE TO CALL THE POLICE.
YOU'LL CALL THE POLICE?
FOR FLAGRANTLY DAMAGING PUBLIC PROPERTY? SURE.
THIS BOOK FELL INTO MY SHREDDER.
HERE'S MY FINE.
I'D LIKE TO CHECK THIS OUT.
REMEMBER TO BLAME YOUR IMAGINARY BOYFRIEND.
OR YOUR CEILING FAN.

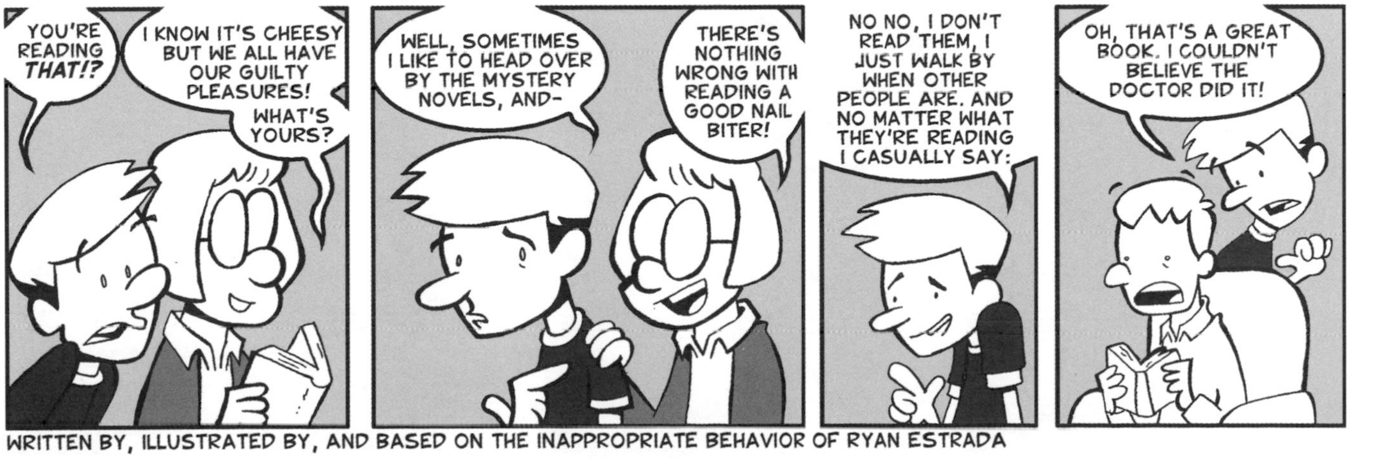
YOU'RE READING THAT!?
I KNOW IT'S CHEESY BUT WE ALL HAVE OUR GUILTY PLEASURES!
WHAT'S YOURS?
WELL, SOMETIMES I LIKE TO HEAD OVER BY THE MYSTERY NOVELS, AND-
THERE'S NOTHING WRONG WITH READING A GOOD NAIL BITER!
NO NO, I DON'T READ THEM, I JUST WALK BY WHEN OTHER PEOPLE ARE. AND NO MATTER WHAT THEY'RE READING I CASUALLY SAY:
OH, THAT'S A GREAT BOOK. I COULDN'T BELIEVE THE DOCTOR DID IT!

WRITTEN BY, ILLUSTRATED BY, AND BASED ON THE INAPPROPRIATE BEHAVIOR OF RYAN ESTRADA

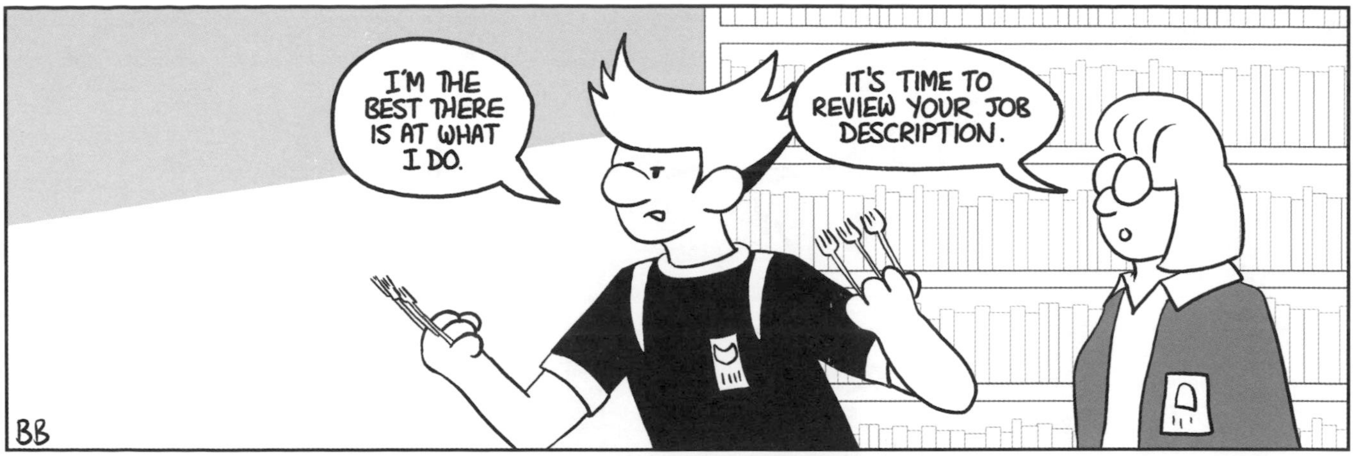
I'M THE BEST THERE IS AT WHAT I DO.
IT'S TIME TO REVIEW YOUR JOB DESCRIPTION.
BB

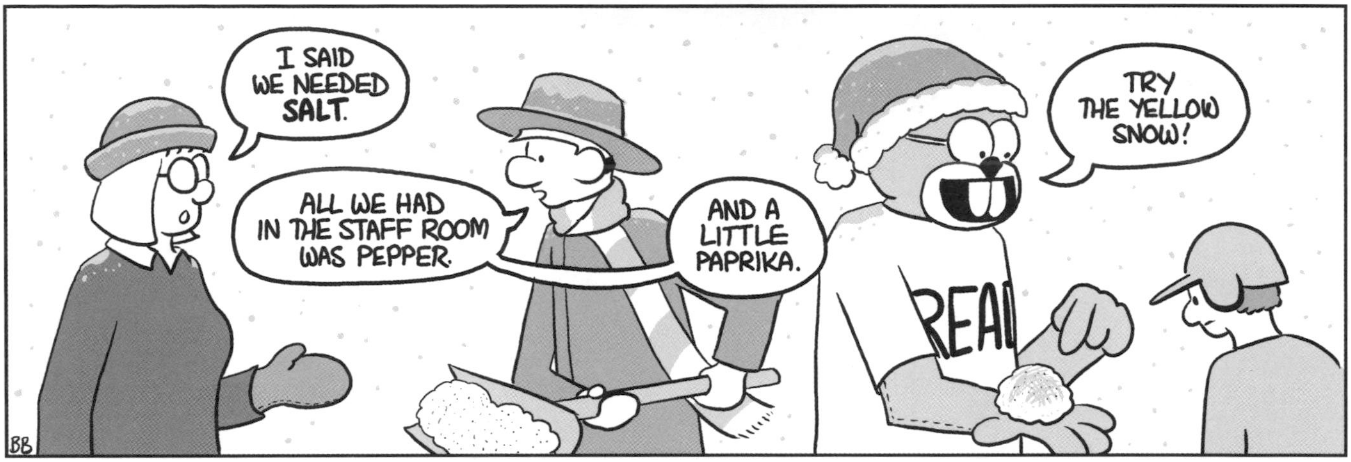
I SAID WE NEEDED **SALT**.
ALL WE HAD IN THE STAFF ROOM WAS PEPPER.
AND A LITTLE PAPRIKA.
TRY THE YELLOW SNOW!
READ
BB

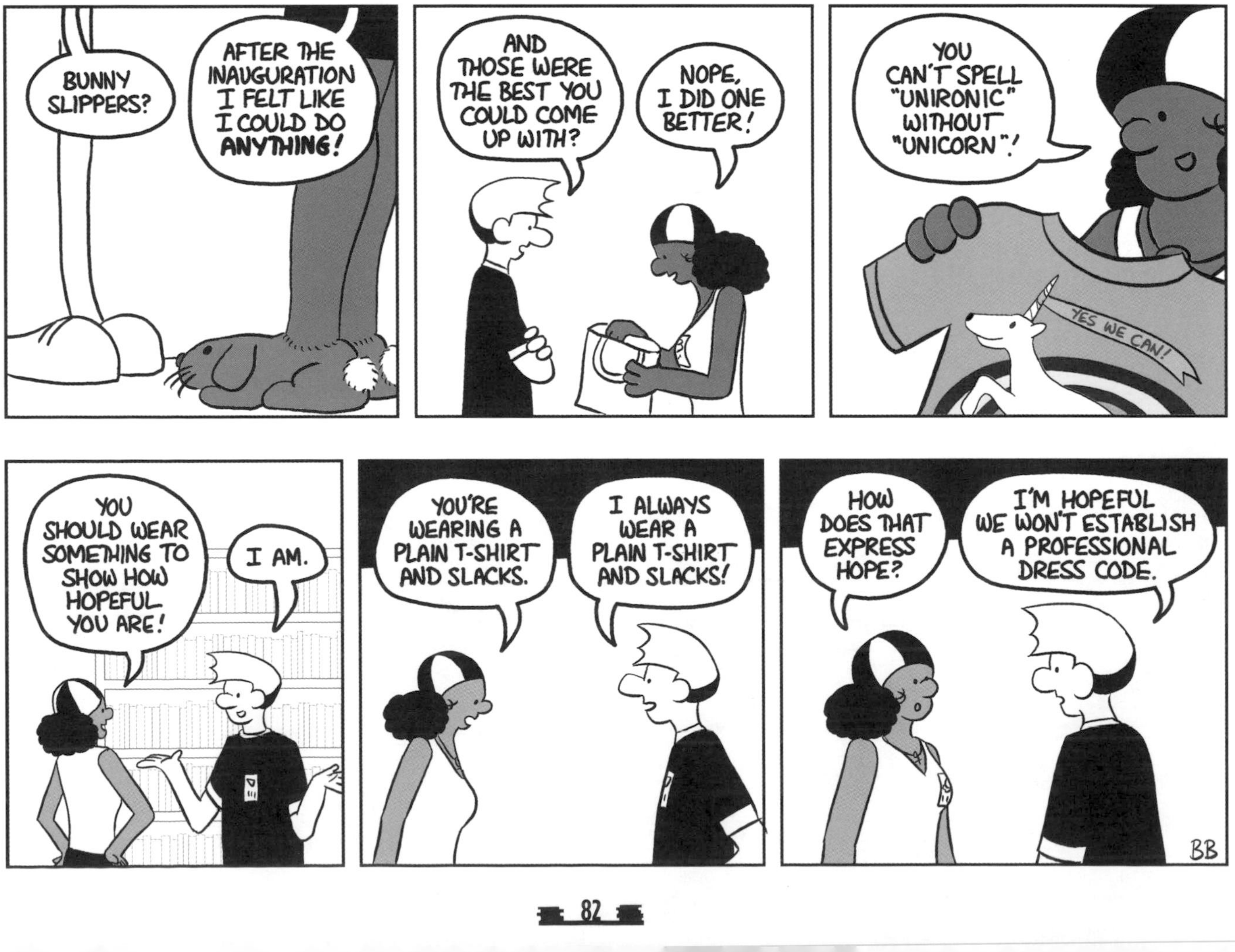
BUNNY SLIPPERS?
AFTER THE INAUGURATION I FELT LIKE I COULD DO **ANYTHING!**
AND THOSE WERE THE BEST YOU COULD COME UP WITH?
NOPE, I DID ONE BETTER!
YOU CAN'T SPELL "UNIRONIC" WITHOUT "UNICORN"!
YES WE CAN!
YOU SHOULD WEAR SOMETHING TO SHOW HOW HOPEFUL YOU ARE!
I AM.
YOU'RE WEARING A PLAIN T-SHIRT AND SLACKS.
I ALWAYS WEAR A PLAIN T-SHIRT AND SLACKS!
HOW DOES THAT EXPRESS HOPE?
I'M HOPEFUL WE WON'T ESTABLISH A PROFESSIONAL DRESS CODE.
BB

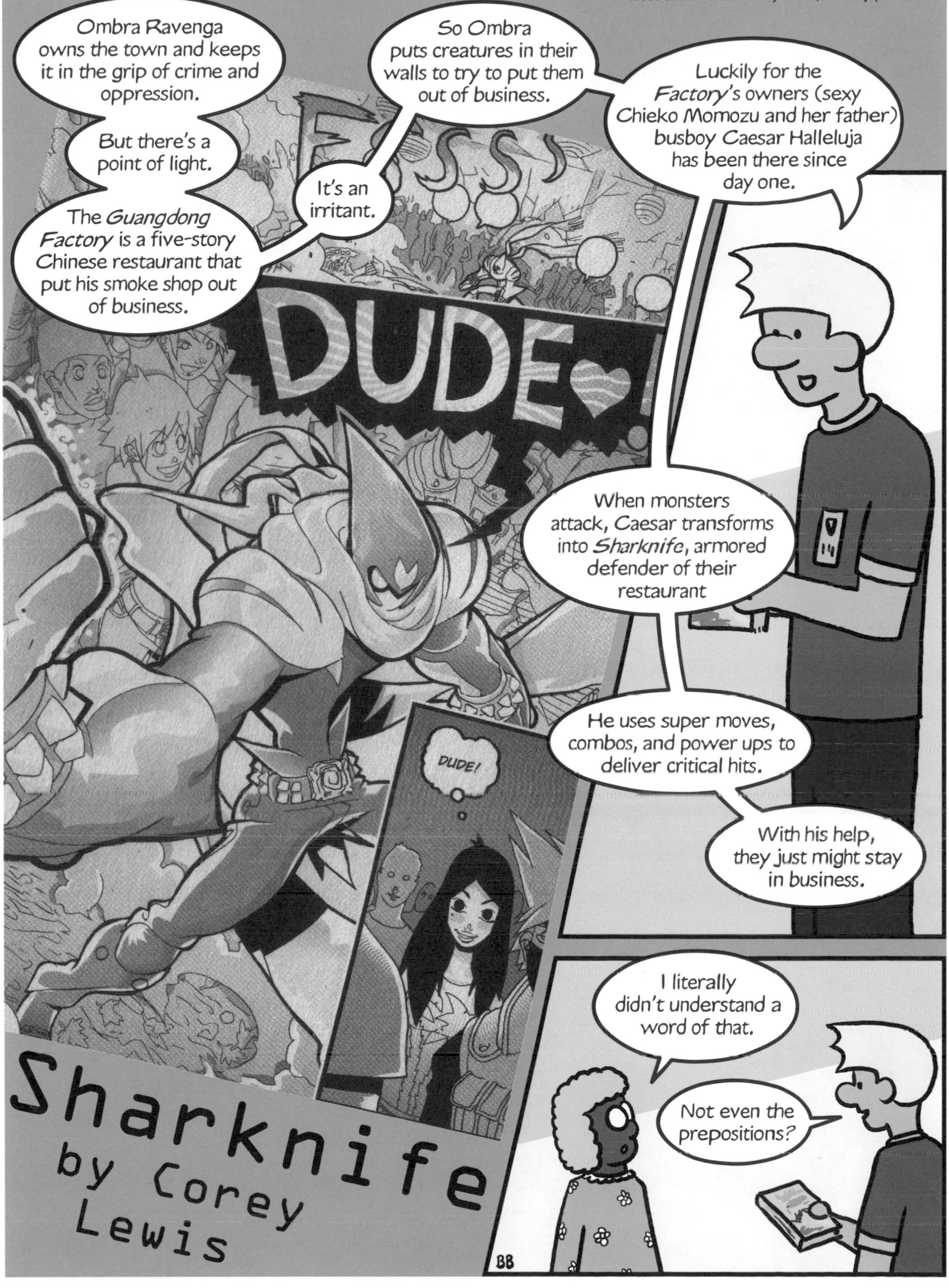
Ombra Ravenga owns the town and keeps it in the grip of crime and oppression.
But there's a point of light.
The *Guangdong Factory* is a five-story Chinese restaurant that put his smoke shop out of business.
It's an irritant.
So Ombra puts creatures in their walls to try to put them out of business.
Luckily for the *Factory*'s owners (sexy Chieko Momozu and her father) busboy Caesar Halleluja has been there since day one.
DUDE
When monsters attack, Caesar transforms into *Sharknife*, armored defender of their restaurant
He uses super moves, combos, and power ups to deliver critical hits.
With his help, they just might stay in business.
DUDE!
Sharknife by Corey Lewis
I literally didn't understand a word of that.
Not even the prepositions?
BB

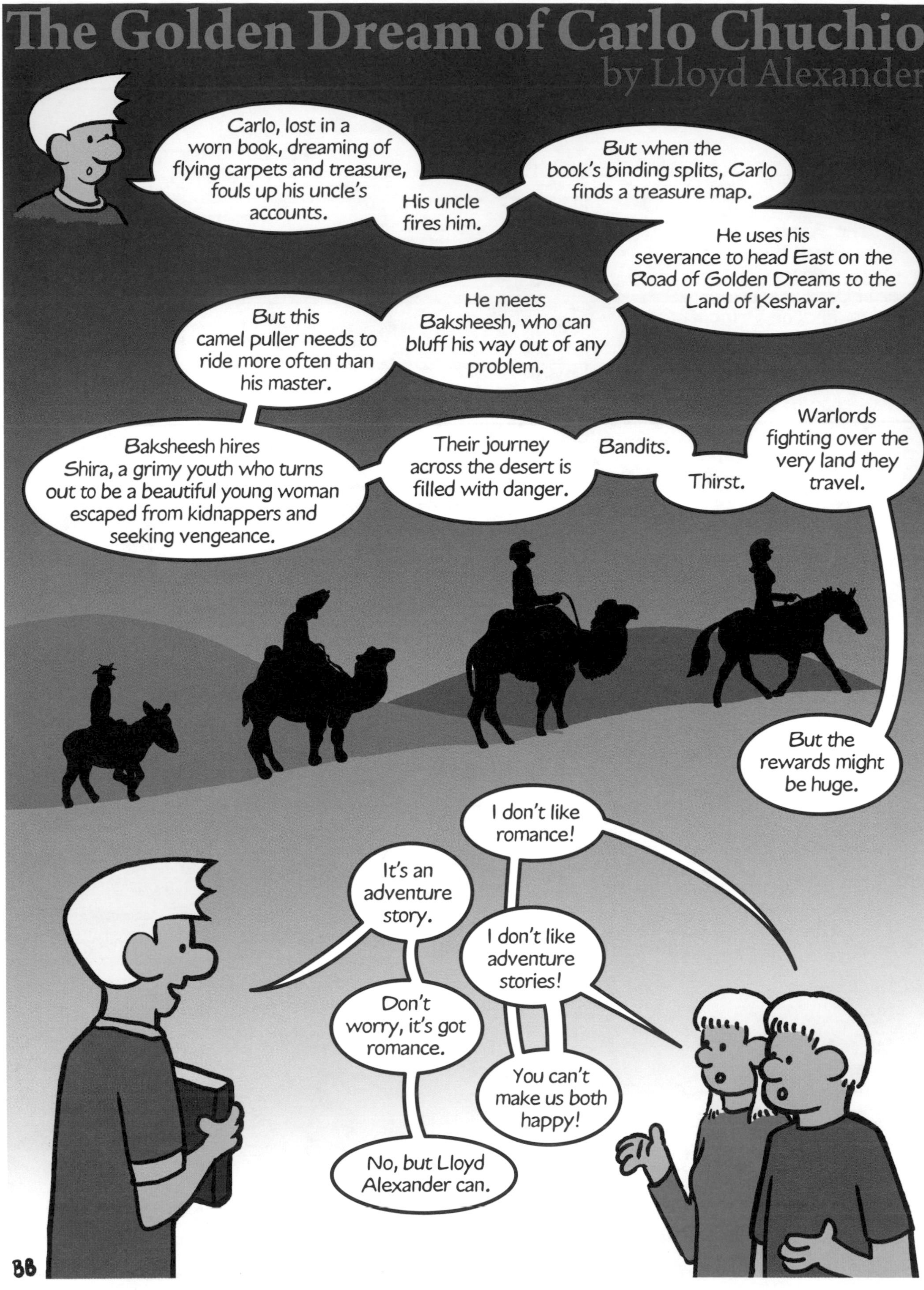
The Golden Dream of Carlo Chuchio
by Lloyd Alexander
Carlo, lost in a worn book, dreaming of flying carpets and treasure, fouls up his uncle's accounts.
His uncle fires him.
But when the book's binding splits, Carlo finds a treasure map.
He uses his severance to head East on the Road of Golden Dreams to the Land of Keshavar.
He meets Baksheesh, who can bluff his way out of any problem.
But this camel puller needs to ride more often than his master.
Baksheesh hires Shira, a grimy youth who turns out to be a beautiful young woman escaped from kidnappers and seeking vengeance.
Their journey across the desert is filled with danger.
Bandits.
Thirst.
Warlords fighting over the very land they travel.
But the rewards might be huge.
It's an adventure story.
I don't like romance!
I don't like adventure stories!
Don't worry, it's got romance.
You can't make us both happy!
No, but Lloyd Alexander can.
BB

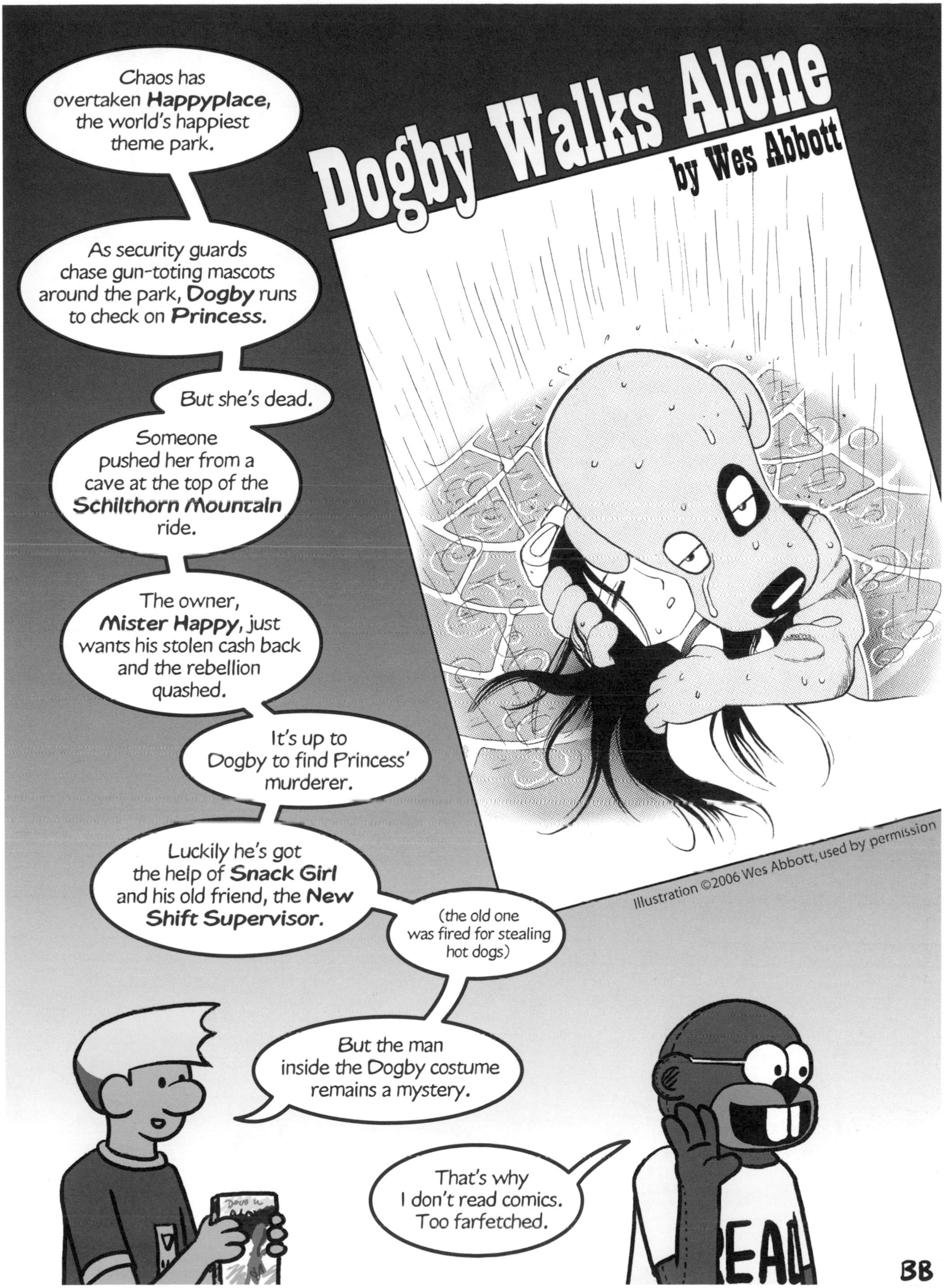
Dogby Walks Alone
by Wes Abbott
Chaos has overtaken Happyplace, the world's happiest theme park.
As security guards chase gun-toting mascots around the park, Dogby runs to check on Princess.
But she's dead.
Someone pushed her from a cave at the top of the Schilthorn Mountain ride.
The owner, Mister Happy, just wants his stolen cash back and the rebellion quashed.
It's up to Dogby to find Princess' murderer.
Luckily he's got the help of Snack Girl and his old friend, the New Shift Supervisor.
(the old one was fired for stealing hot dogs)
Illustration ©2006 Wes Abbott, used by permission
But the man inside the Dogby costume remains a mystery.
That's why I don't read comics. Too farfetched.
BB

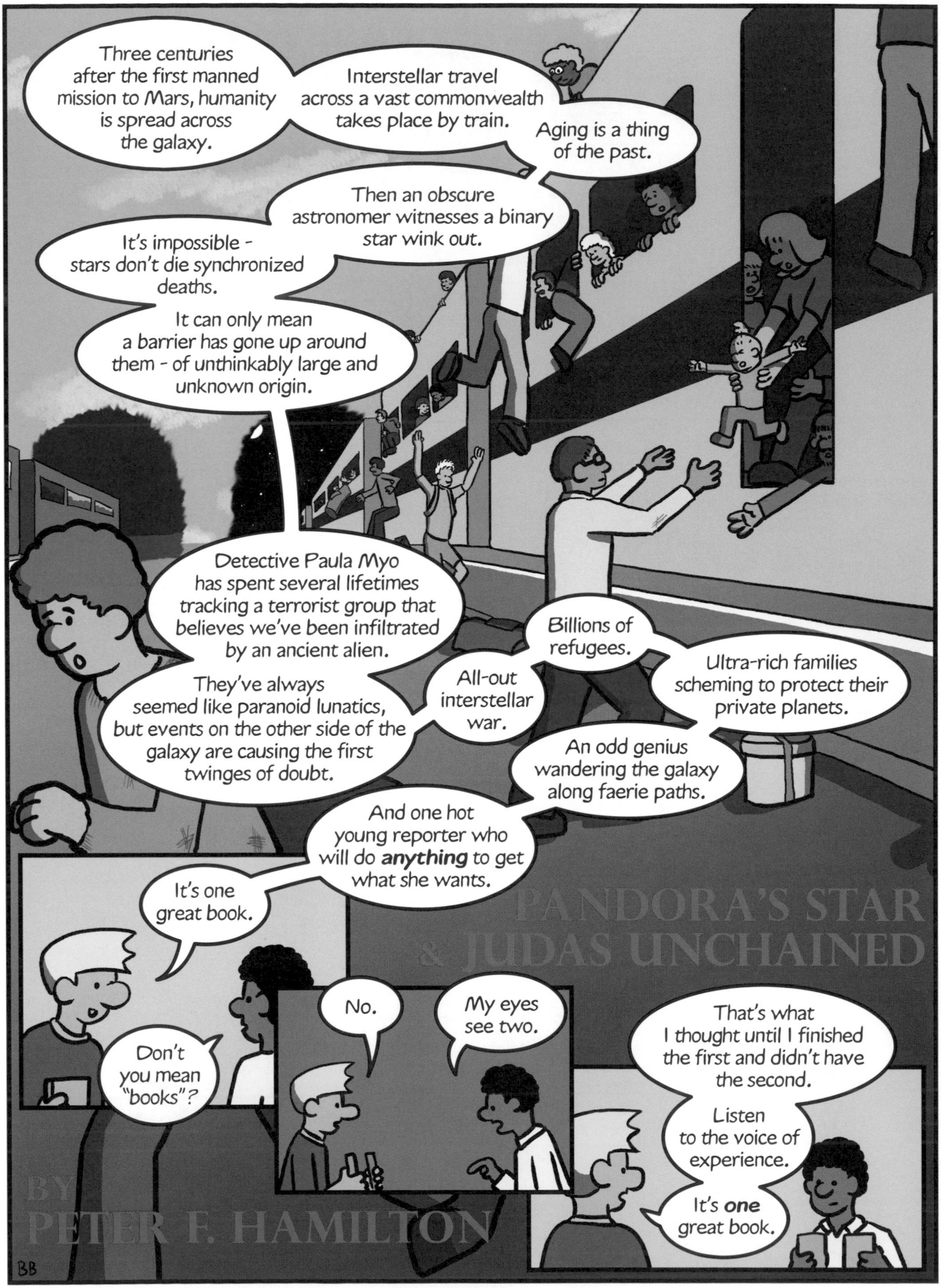
Three centuries after the first manned mission to Mars, humanity is spread across the galaxy.
Interstellar travel across a vast commonwealth takes place by train.
Aging is a thing of the past.
Then an obscure astronomer witnesses a binary star wink out.
It's impossible - stars don't die synchronized deaths.
It can only mean a barrier has gone up around them - of unthinkably large and unknown origin.
Detective Paula Myo has spent several lifetimes tracking a terrorist group that believes we've been infiltrated by an ancient alien.
They've always seemed like paranoid lunatics, but events on the other side of the galaxy are causing the first twinges of doubt.
All-out interstellar war.
Billions of refugees.
Ultra-rich families scheming to protect their private planets.
An odd genius wandering the galaxy along faerie paths.
And one hot young reporter who will do **anything** to get what she wants.
PANDORA'S STAR & JUDAS UNCHAINED
It's one great book.
Don't you mean "books"?
No.
My eyes see two.
That's what I thought until I finished the first and didn't have the second.
Listen to the voice of experience.
It's *one* great book.
BY PETER F. HAMILTON
BB

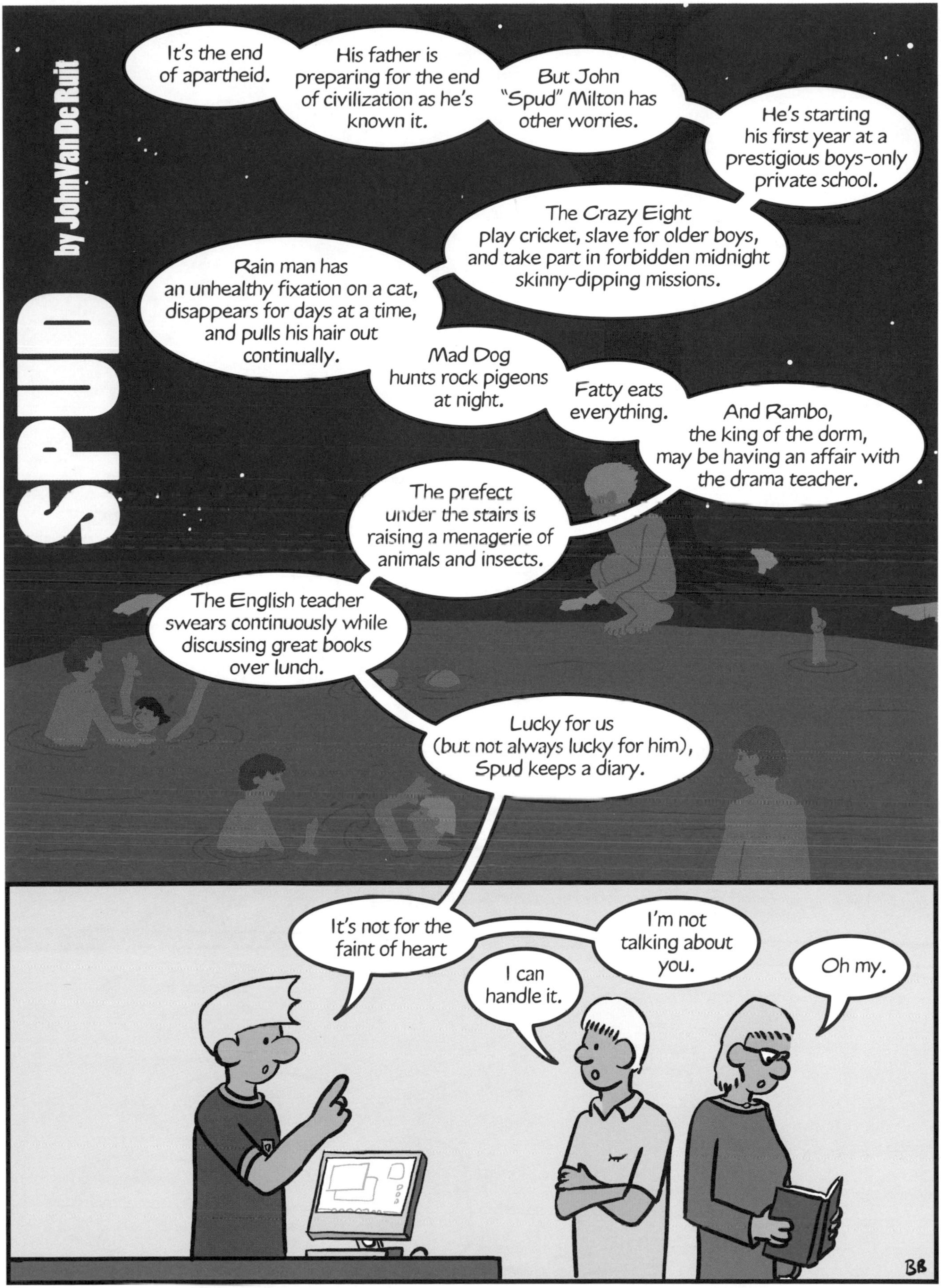
SPUD
by John Van De Ruit
It's the end of apartheid.
His father is preparing for the end of civilization as he's known it.
But John "Spud" Milton has other worries.
He's starting his first year at a prestigious boys-only private school.
The Crazy Eight play cricket, slave for older boys, and take part in forbidden midnight skinny-dipping missions.
Rain man has an unhealthy fixation on a cat, disappears for days at a time, and pulls his hair out continually.
Mad Dog hunts rock pigeons at night.
Fatty eats everything.
And Rambo, the king of the dorm, may be having an affair with the drama teacher.
The prefect under the stairs is raising a menagerie of animals and insects.
The English teacher swears continuously while discussing great books over lunch.
Lucky for us (but not always lucky for him), Spud keeps a diary.
It's not for the faint of heart
I'm not talking about you.
I can handle it.
Oh my.
BB

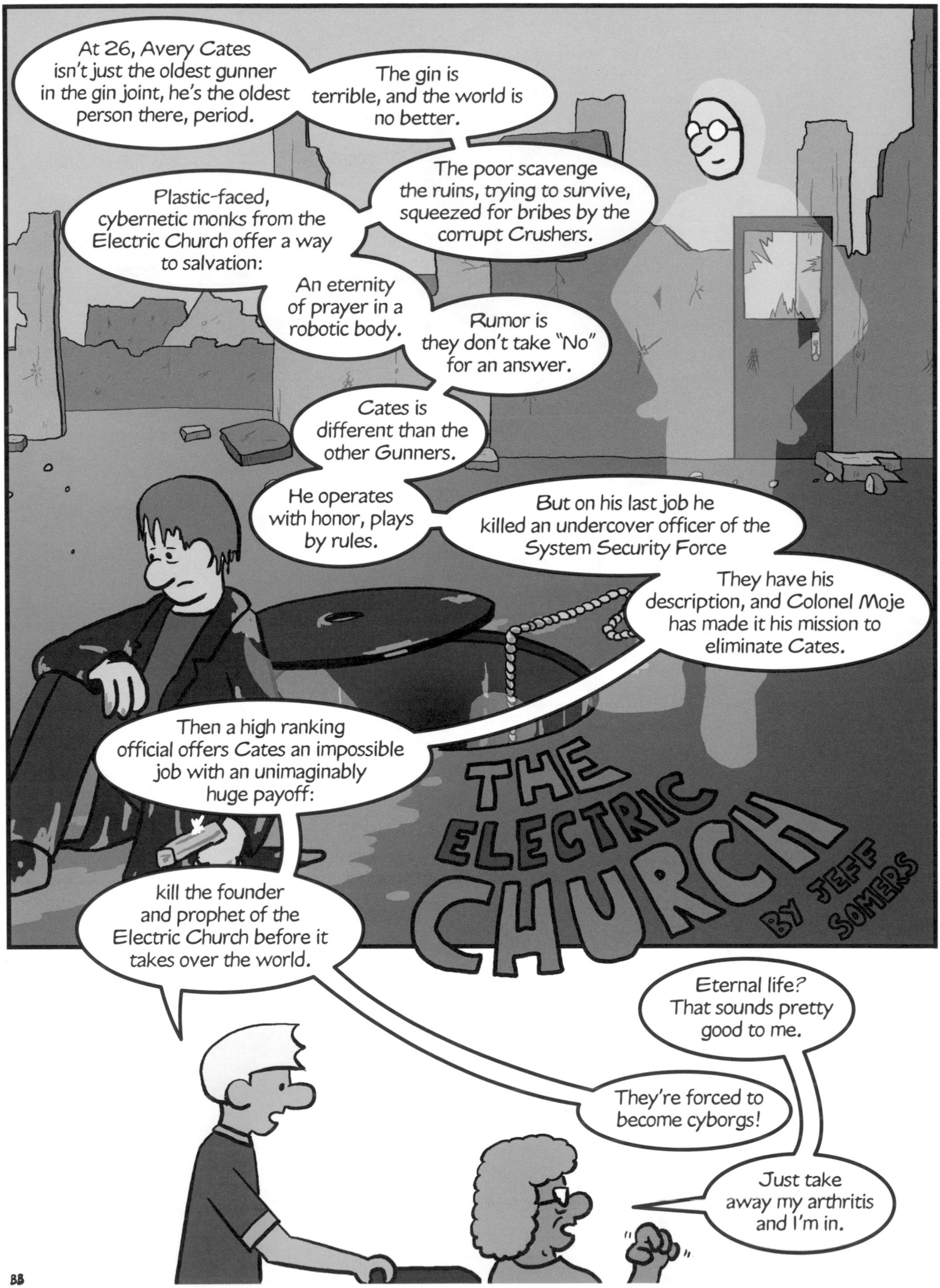
At 26, Avery Cates isn't just the oldest gunner in the gin joint, he's the oldest person there, period.
The gin is terrible, and the world is no better.
The poor scavenge the ruins, trying to survive, squeezed for bribes by the corrupt Crushers.
Plastic-faced, cybernetic monks from the Electric Church offer a way to salvation:
An eternity of prayer in a robotic body.
Rumor is they don't take "No" for an answer.
Cates is different than the other Gunners.
He operates with honor, plays by rules.
But on his last job he killed an undercover officer of the System Security Force
They have his description, and Colonel Moje has made it his mission to eliminate Cates.
Then a high ranking official offers Cates an impossible job with an unimaginably huge payoff:
kill the founder and prophet of the Electric Church before it takes over the world.
THE ELECTRIC CHURCH
BY JEFF SOMERS
Eternal life? That sounds pretty good to me.
They're forced to become cyborgs!
Just take away my arthritis and I'm in.
BB

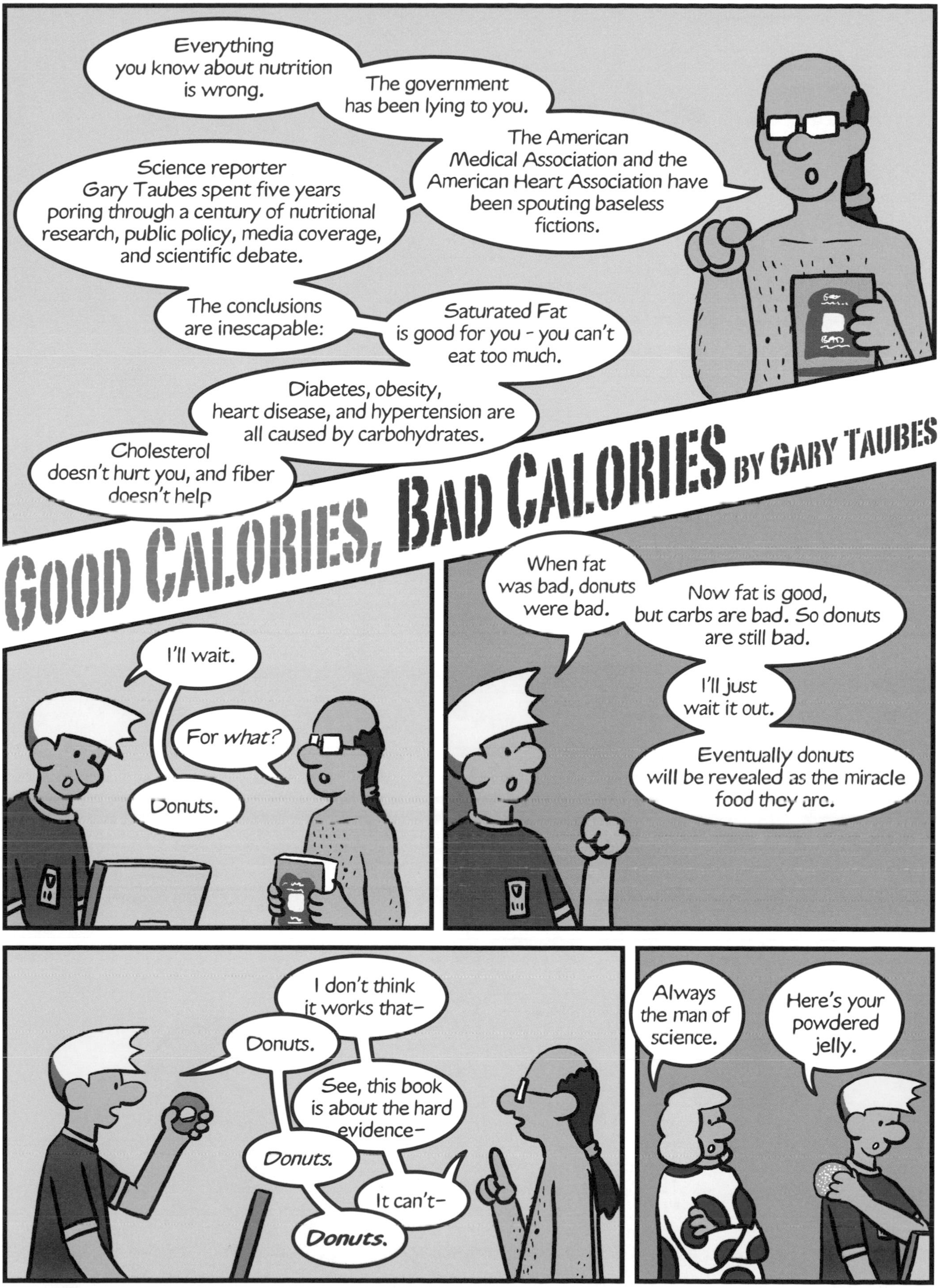

Everything you know about nutrition is wrong.
The government has been lying to you.
The American Medical Association and the American Heart Association have been spouting baseless fictions.
Science reporter Gary Taubes spent five years poring through a century of nutritional research, public policy, media coverage, and scientific debate.
The conclusions are inescapable:
Saturated Fat is good for you - you can't eat too much.
Diabetes, obesity, heart disease, and hypertension are all caused by carbohydrates.
Cholesterol doesn't hurt you, and fiber doesn't help
GOOD CALORIES, BAD CALORIES BY GARY TAUBES
I'll wait.
For *what?*
Donuts.
When fat was bad, donuts were bad.
Now fat is good, but carbs are bad. So donuts are still bad.
I'll just wait it out.
Eventually donuts will be revealed as the miracle food they are.
I don't think it works that-
Donuts.
See, this book is about the hard evidence-
Donuts.
It can't-
Donuts.
Always the man of science.
Here's your powdered jelly.

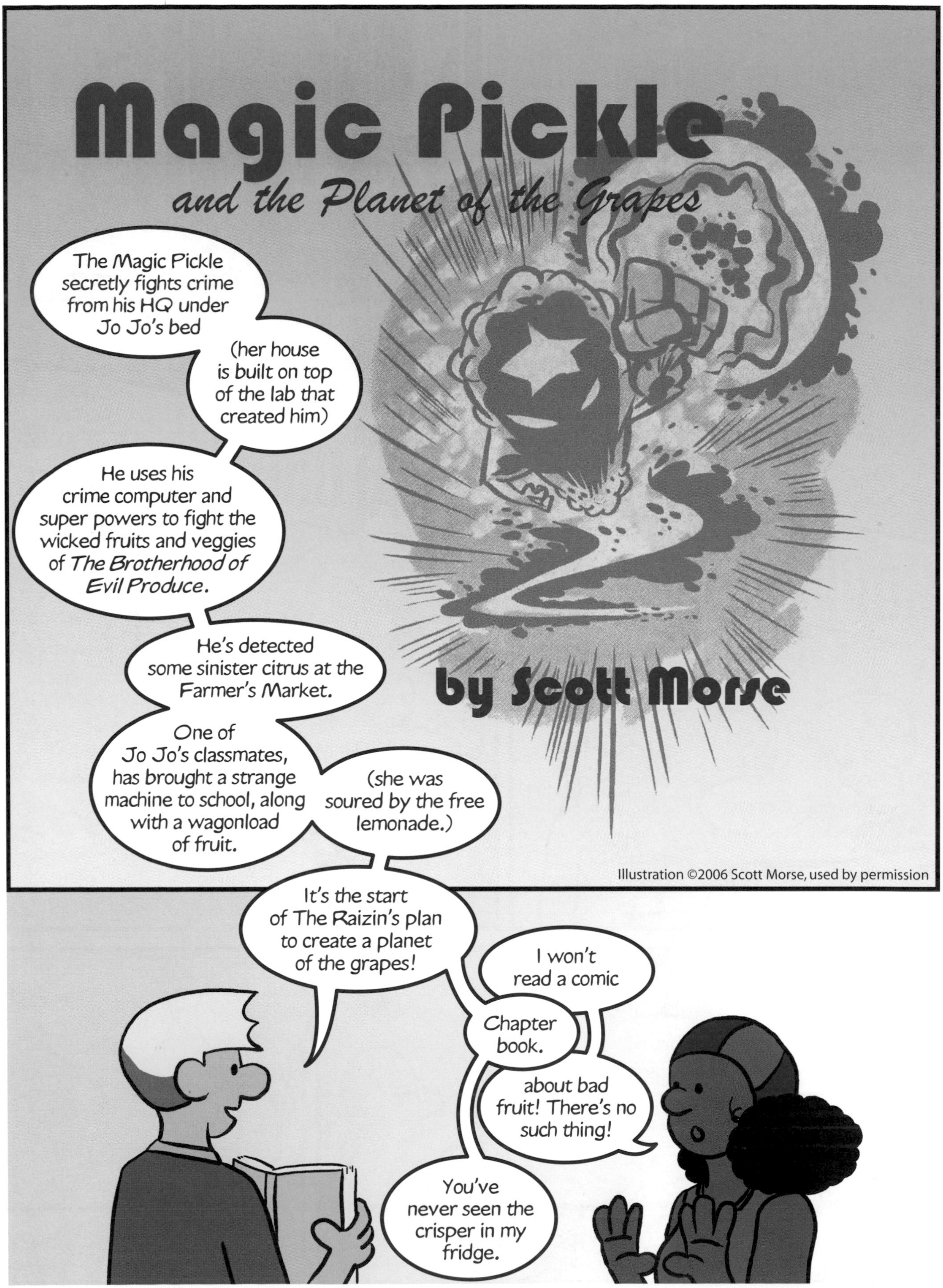
Magic Pickle
and the Planet of the Grapes
The Magic Pickle secretly fights crime from his HQ under Jo Jo's bed
(her house is built on top of the lab that created him)
He uses his crime computer and super powers to fight the wicked fruits and veggies of *The Brotherhood of Evil Produce*.
He's detected some sinister citrus at the Farmer's Market.
by Scott Morse
One of Jo Jo's classmates, has brought a strange machine to school, along with a wagonload of fruit.
(she was soured by the free lemonade.)
It's the start of The Raizin's plan to create a planet of the grapes!
I won't read a comic
Chapter book.
about bad fruit! There's no such thing!
You've never seen the crisper in my fridge.

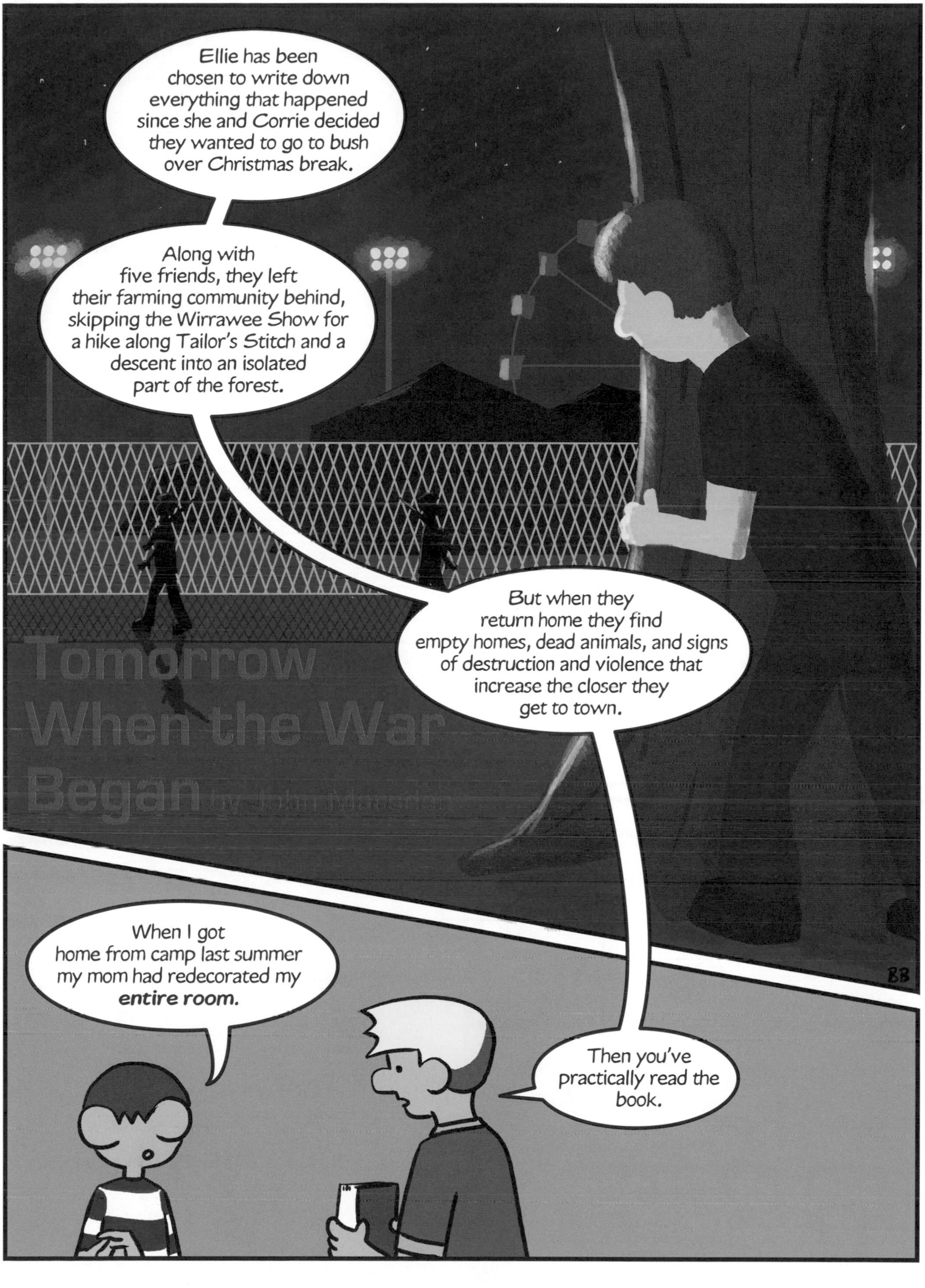
Ellie has been chosen to write down everything that happened since she and Corrie decided they wanted to go to bush over Christmas break.
Along with five friends, they left their farming community behind, skipping the Wirrawee Show for a hike along Tailor's Stitch and a descent into an isolated part of the forest.
Tomorrow When the War Began by John Marsden
But when they return home they find empty homes, dead animals, and signs of destruction and violence that increase the closer they get to town.
BB
When I got home from camp last summer my mom had redecorated my **entire room.**
Then you've practically read the book.

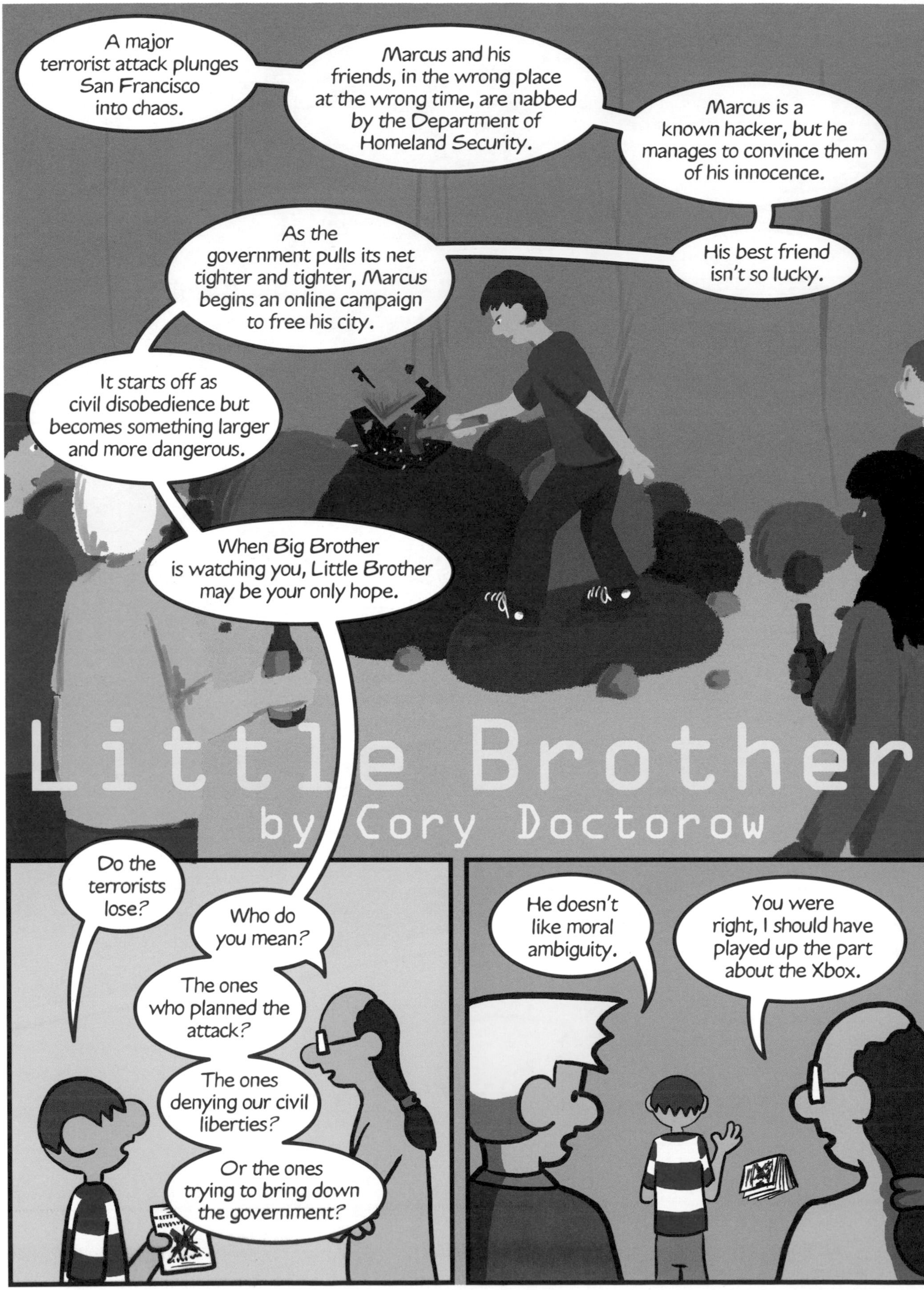
A major terrorist attack plunges San Francisco into chaos.
Marcus and his friends, in the wrong place at the wrong time, are nabbed by the Department of Homeland Security.
Marcus is a known hacker, but he manages to convince them of his innocence.
His best friend isn't so lucky.
As the government pulls its net tighter and tighter, Marcus begins an online campaign to free his city.
It starts off as civil disobedience but becomes something larger and more dangerous.
When Big Brother is watching you, Little Brother may be your only hope.
Little Brother
by Cory Doctorow
Do the terrorists lose?
Who do you mean?
The ones who planned the attack?
The ones denying our civil liberties?
Or the ones trying to bring down the government?
He doesn't like moral ambiguity.
You were right, I should have played up the part about the Xbox.

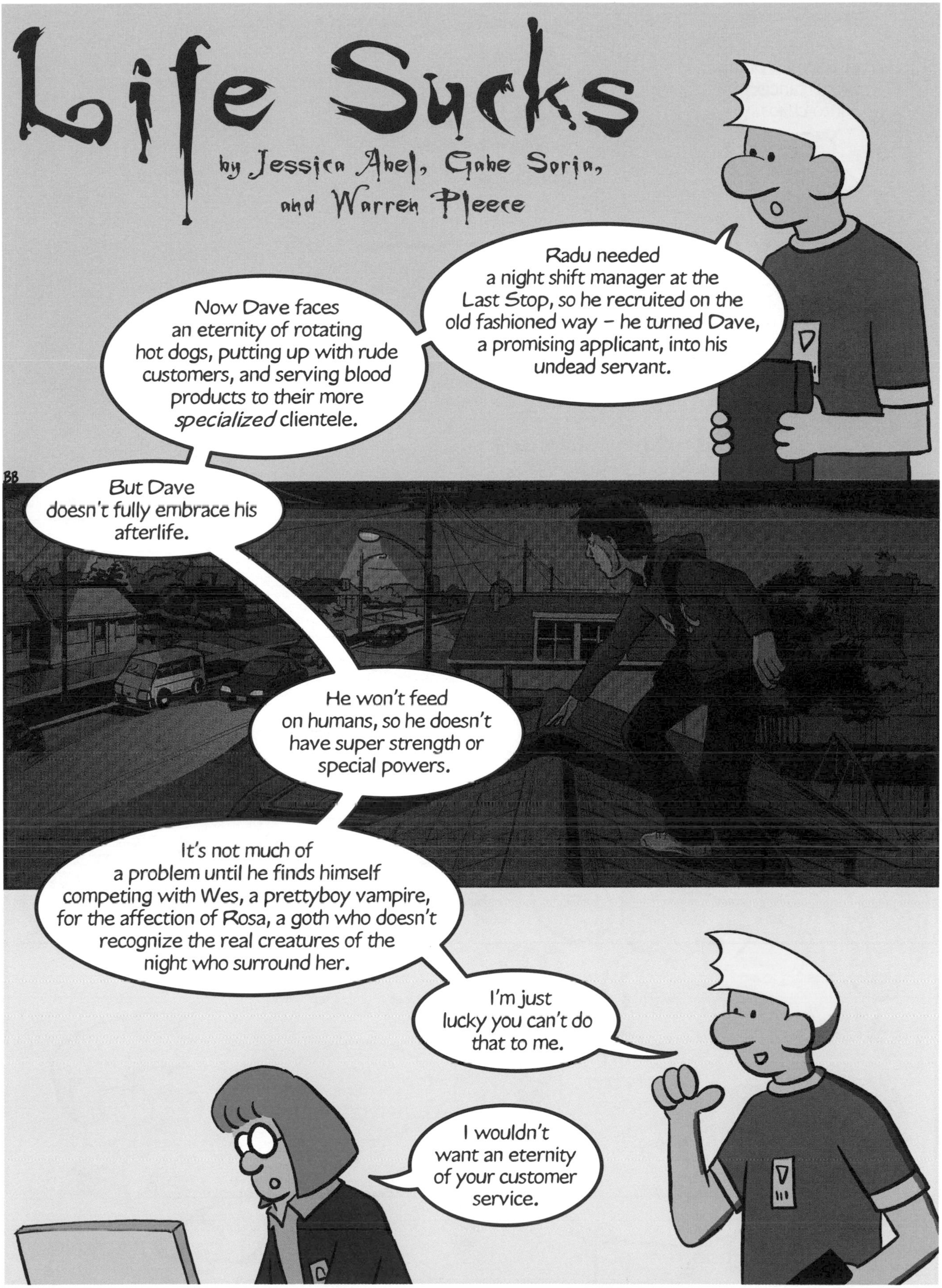
Life Sucks
by Jessica Abel, Gabe Soria, and Warren Pleece
Radu needed a night shift manager at the Last Stop, so he recruited on the old fashioned way – he turned Dave, a promising applicant, into his undead servant.
Now Dave faces an eternity of rotating hot dogs, putting up with rude customers, and serving blood products to their more *specialized* clientele.
But Dave doesn't fully embrace his afterlife.
He won't feed on humans, so he doesn't have super strength or special powers.
It's not much of a problem until he finds himself competing with Wes, a prettyboy vampire, for the affection of Rosa, a goth who doesn't recognize the real creatures of the night who surround her.
I'm just lucky you can't do that to me.
I wouldn't want an eternity of your customer service.

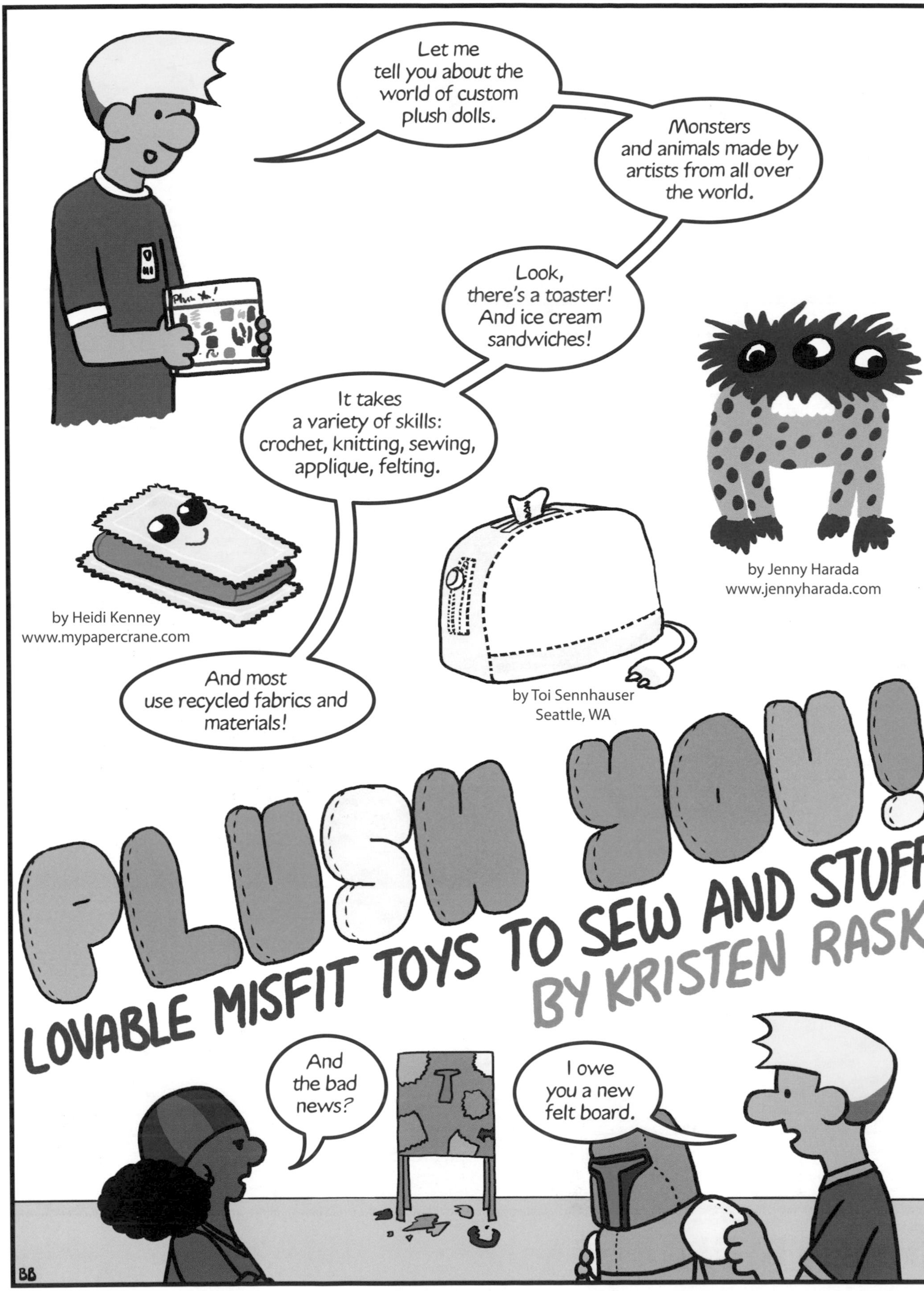
Let me tell you about the world of custom plush dolls.
Monsters and animals made by artists from all over the world.
Look, there's a toaster! And ice cream sandwiches!
It takes a variety of skills: crochet, knitting, sewing, applique, felting.
And most use recycled fabrics and materials!
by Heidi Kenney
www.mypapercrane.com
by Toi Sennhauser
Seattle, WA
by Jenny Harada
www.jennyharada.com
PLUSH YOU!
LOVABLE MISFIT TOYS TO SEW AND STUFF
BY KRISTEN RASK
And the bad news?
I owe you a new felt board.
BB

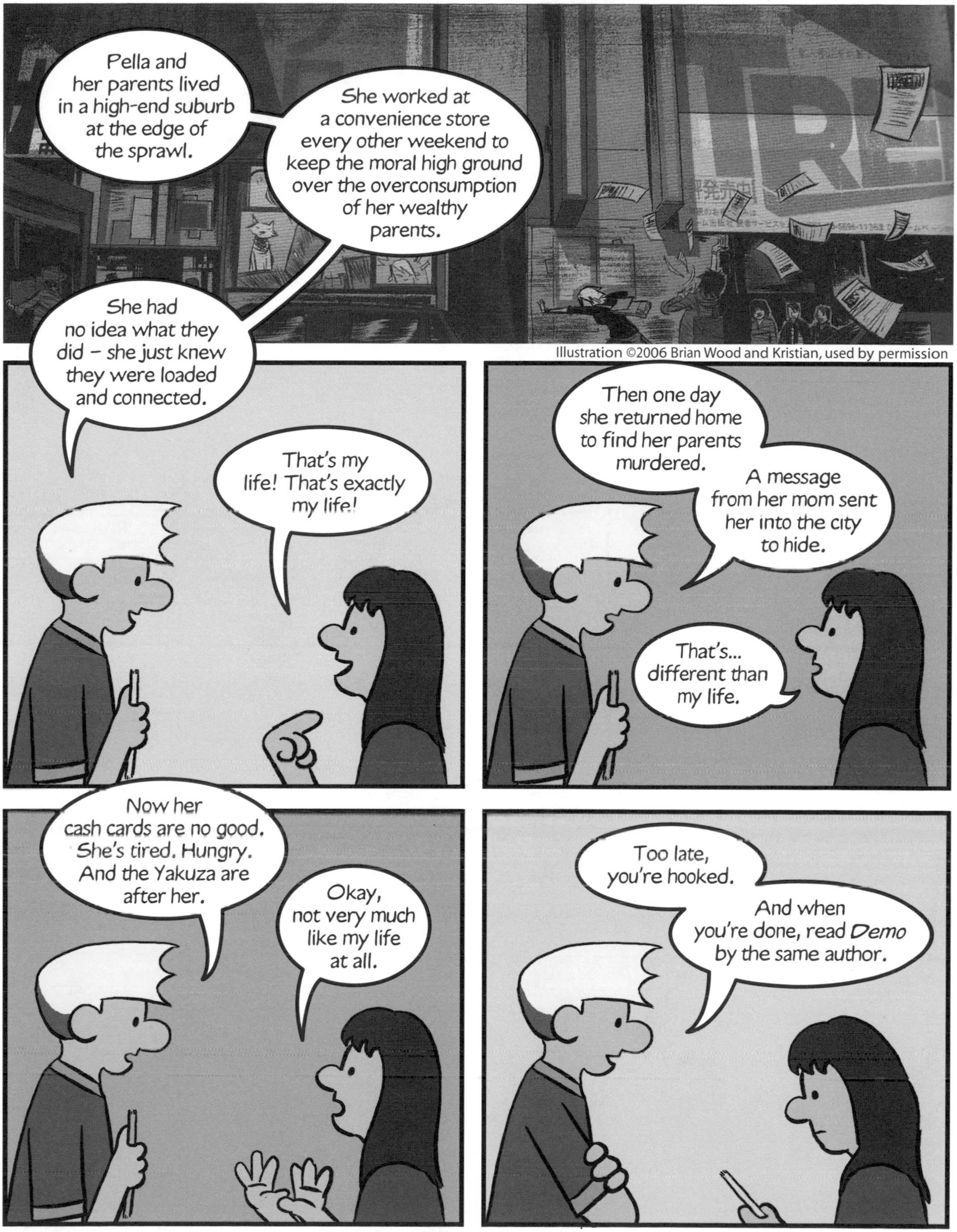
Pella and her parents lived in a high-end suburb at the edge of the sprawl.
She worked at a convenience store every other weekend to keep the moral high ground over the overconsumption of her wealthy parents.
She had no idea what they did – she just knew they were loaded and connected.
That's my life! That's exactly my life!
Then one day she returned home to find her parents murdered.
A message from her mom sent her into the city to hide.
That's... different than my life.
Now her cash cards are no good. She's tired. Hungry. And the Yakuza are after her.
Okay, not very much like my life at all.
Too late, you're hooked.
And when you're done, read *Demo* by the same author.
Illustration ©2006 Brian Wood and Kristian, used by permission

Supermarket by Brian Wood and Kristian

The Day My Butt Went Psycho

by Andy Griffiths

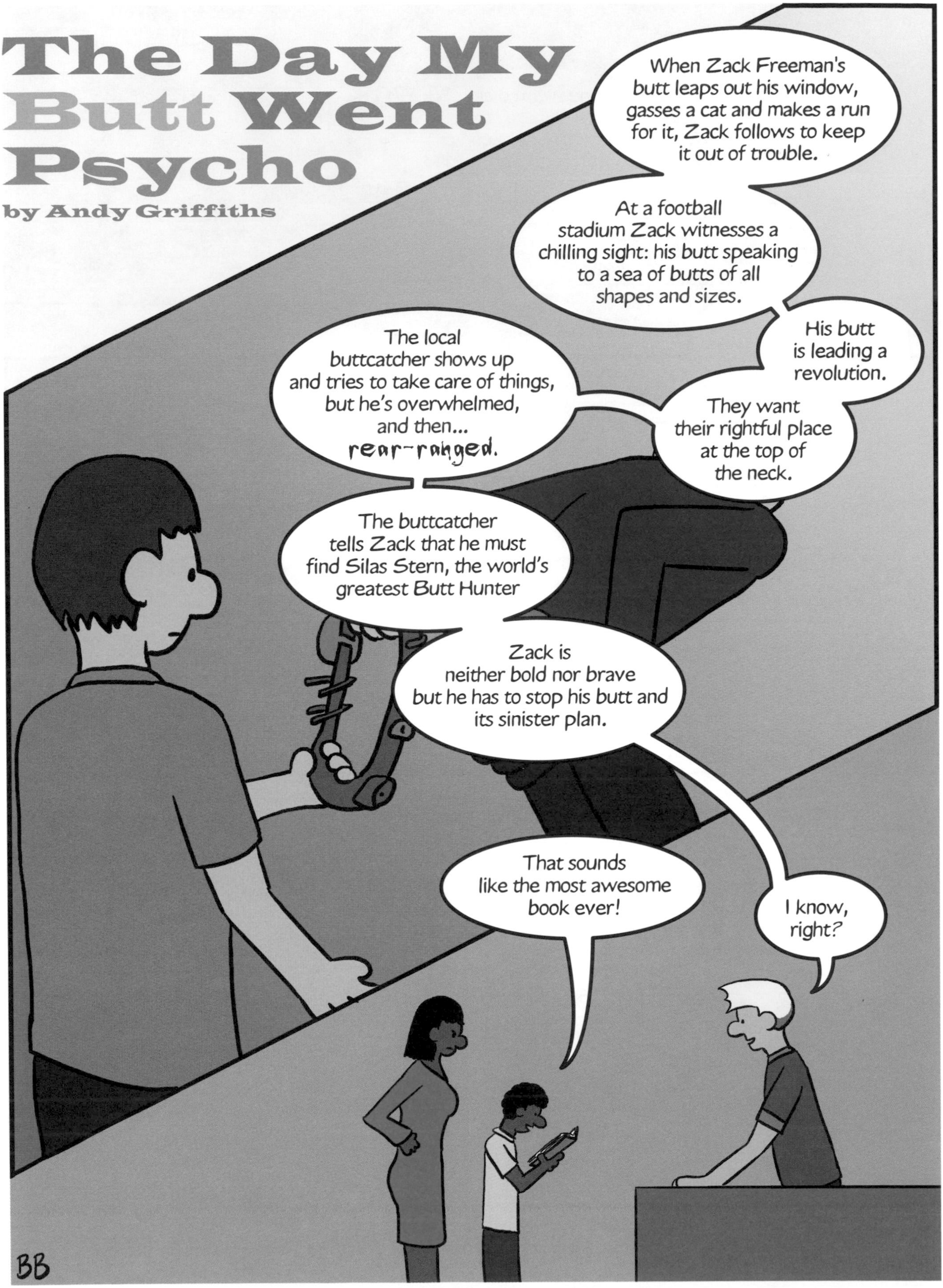

When Zack Freeman's butt leaps out his window, gasses a cat and makes a run for it, Zack follows to keep it out of trouble.
At a football stadium Zack witnesses a chilling sight: his butt speaking to a sea of butts of all shapes and sizes.
His butt is leading a revolution.
They want their rightful place at the top of the neck.
The local buttcatcher shows up and tries to take care of things, but he's overwhelmed, and then... rear-ranged.
The buttcatcher tells Zack that he must find Silas Stern, the world's greatest Butt Hunter
Zack is neither bold nor brave but he has to stop his butt and its sinister plan.
That sounds like the most awesome book ever!
I know, right?
BB

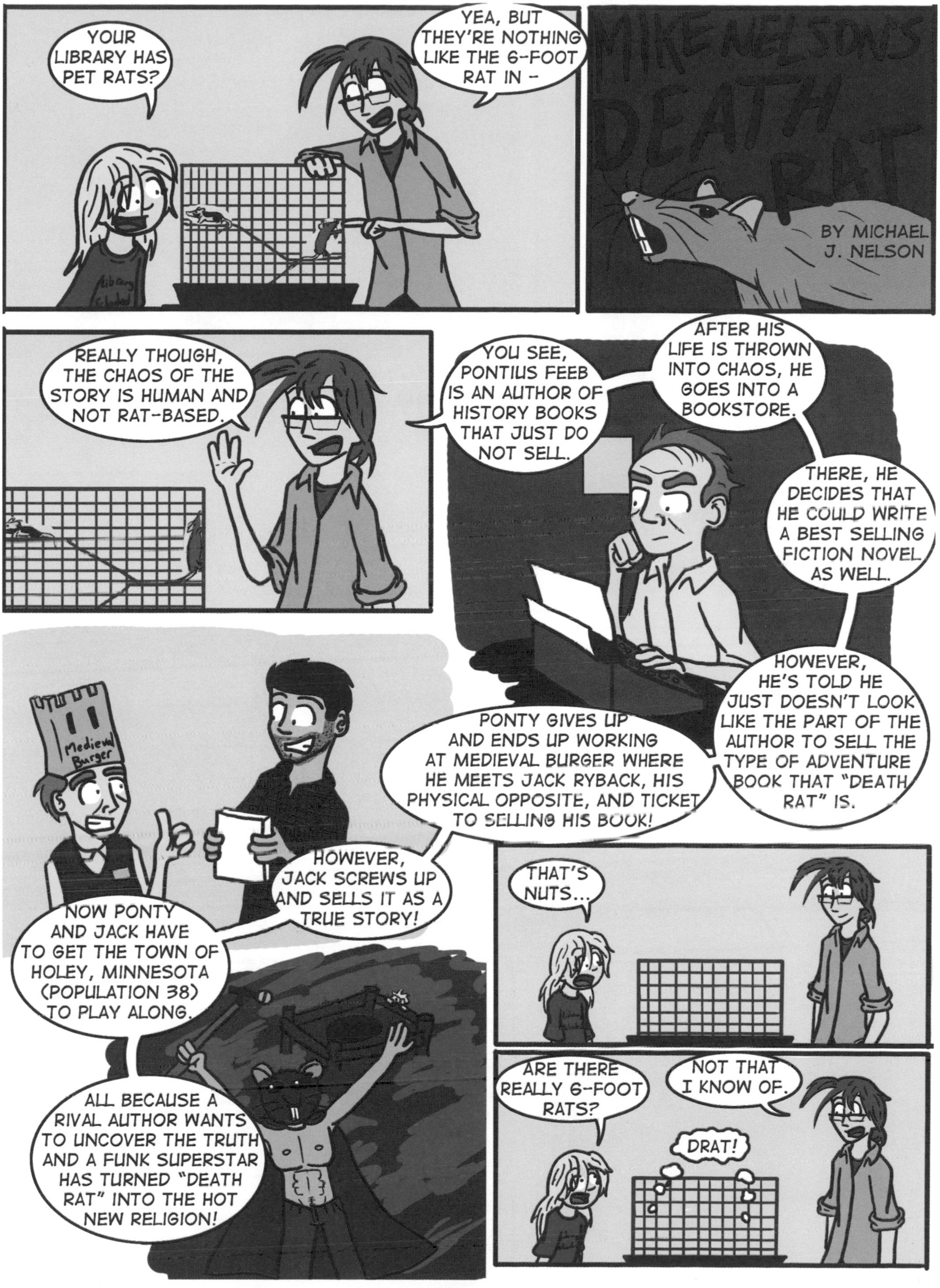
YOUR LIBRARY HAS PET RATS?
YEA, BUT THEY'RE NOTHING LIKE THE 6-FOOT RAT IN -
MIKE NELSON'S DEATH RAT
BY MICHAEL J. NELSON
REALLY THOUGH, THE CHAOS OF THE STORY IS HUMAN AND NOT RAT-BASED.
YOU SEE, PONTIUS FEEB IS AN AUTHOR OF HISTORY BOOKS THAT JUST DO NOT SELL.
AFTER HIS LIFE IS THROWN INTO CHAOS, HE GOES INTO A BOOKSTORE.
THERE, HE DECIDES THAT HE COULD WRITE A BEST SELLING FICTION NOVEL AS WELL.
HOWEVER, HE'S TOLD HE JUST DOESN'T LOOK LIKE THE PART OF THE AUTHOR TO SELL THE TYPE OF ADVENTURE BOOK THAT "DEATH RAT" IS.
PONTY GIVES UP AND ENDS UP WORKING AT MEDIEVAL BURGER WHERE HE MEETS JACK RYBACK, HIS PHYSICAL OPPOSITE, AND TICKET TO SELLING HIS BOOK!
Medieval Burger
HOWEVER, JACK SCREWS UP AND SELLS IT AS A TRUE STORY!
NOW PONTY AND JACK HAVE TO GET THE TOWN OF HOLEY, MINNESOTA (POPULATION 38) TO PLAY ALONG.
ALL BECAUSE A RIVAL AUTHOR WANTS TO UNCOVER THE TRUTH AND A FUNK SUPERSTAR HAS TURNED "DEATH RAT" INTO THE HOT NEW RELIGION!
THAT'S NUTS...
ARE THERE REALLY 6-FOOT RATS?
NOT THAT I KNOW OF.
DRAT!

Guest Book Club by Carl Sjostrand @ www.crazycstudios.com

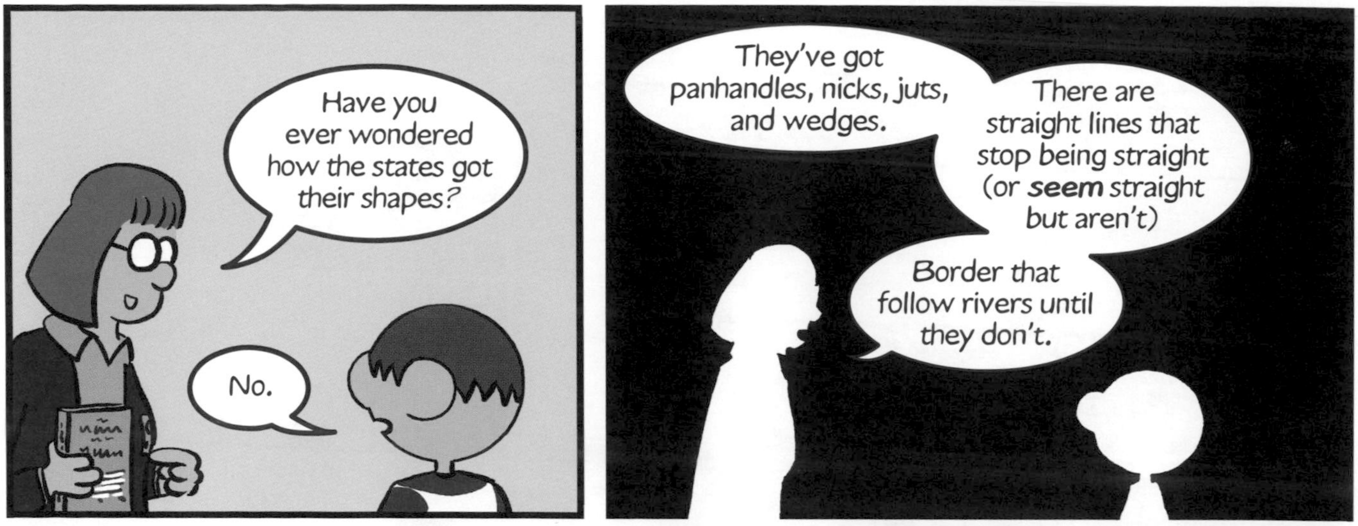
Have you ever wondered how the states got their shapes?
No.
They've got panhandles, nicks, juts, and wedges.
There are straight lines that stop being straight (or **seem** straight but aren't)
Border that follow rivers until they don't.

How the States Got Their Shapes

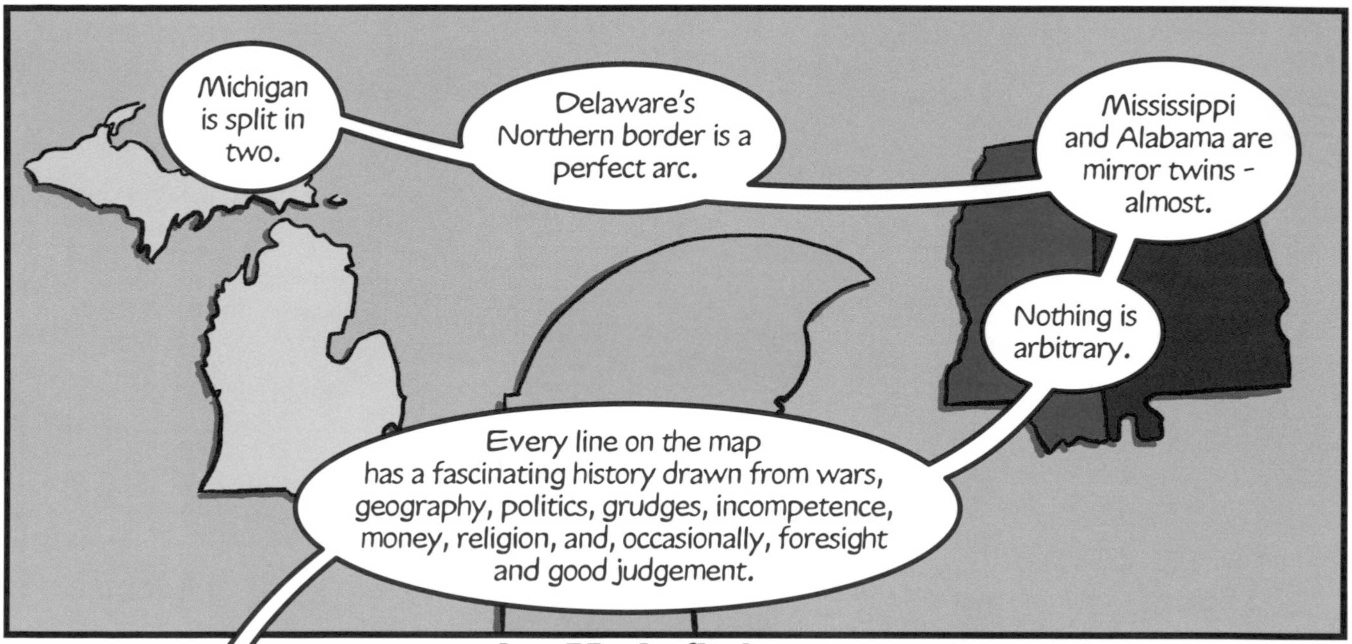
Michigan is split in two.
Delaware's Northern border is a perfect arc.
Mississippi and Alabama are mirror twins - almost.
Nothing is arbitrary.
Every line on the map has a fascinating history drawn from wars, geography, politics, grudges, incompetence, money, religion, and, occasionally, foresight and good judgement.

by Mark Stein

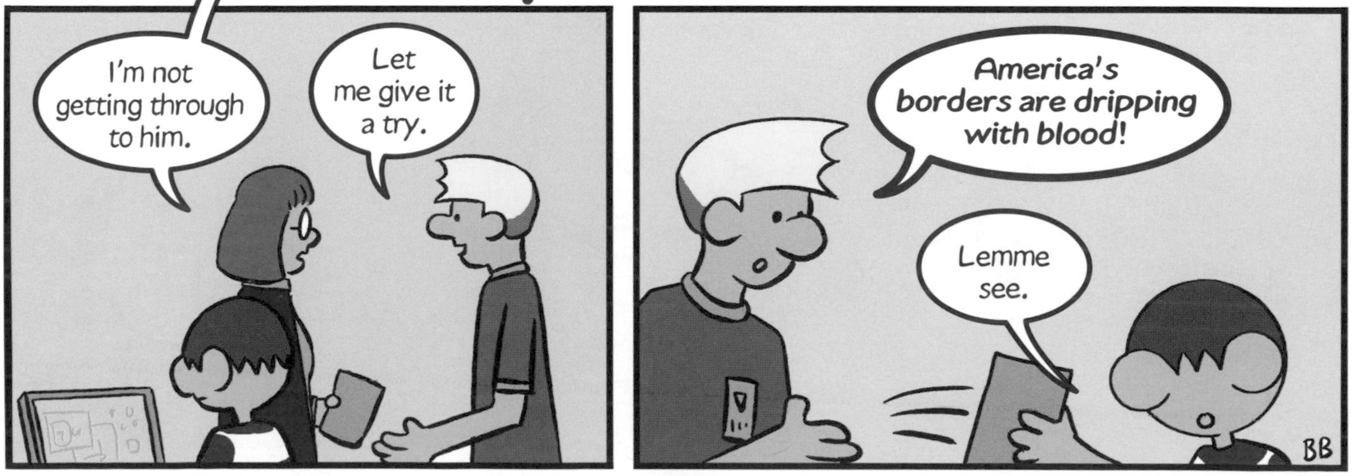
I'm not getting through to him.
Let me give it a try.
America's borders are dripping with blood!
Lemme see.
BB

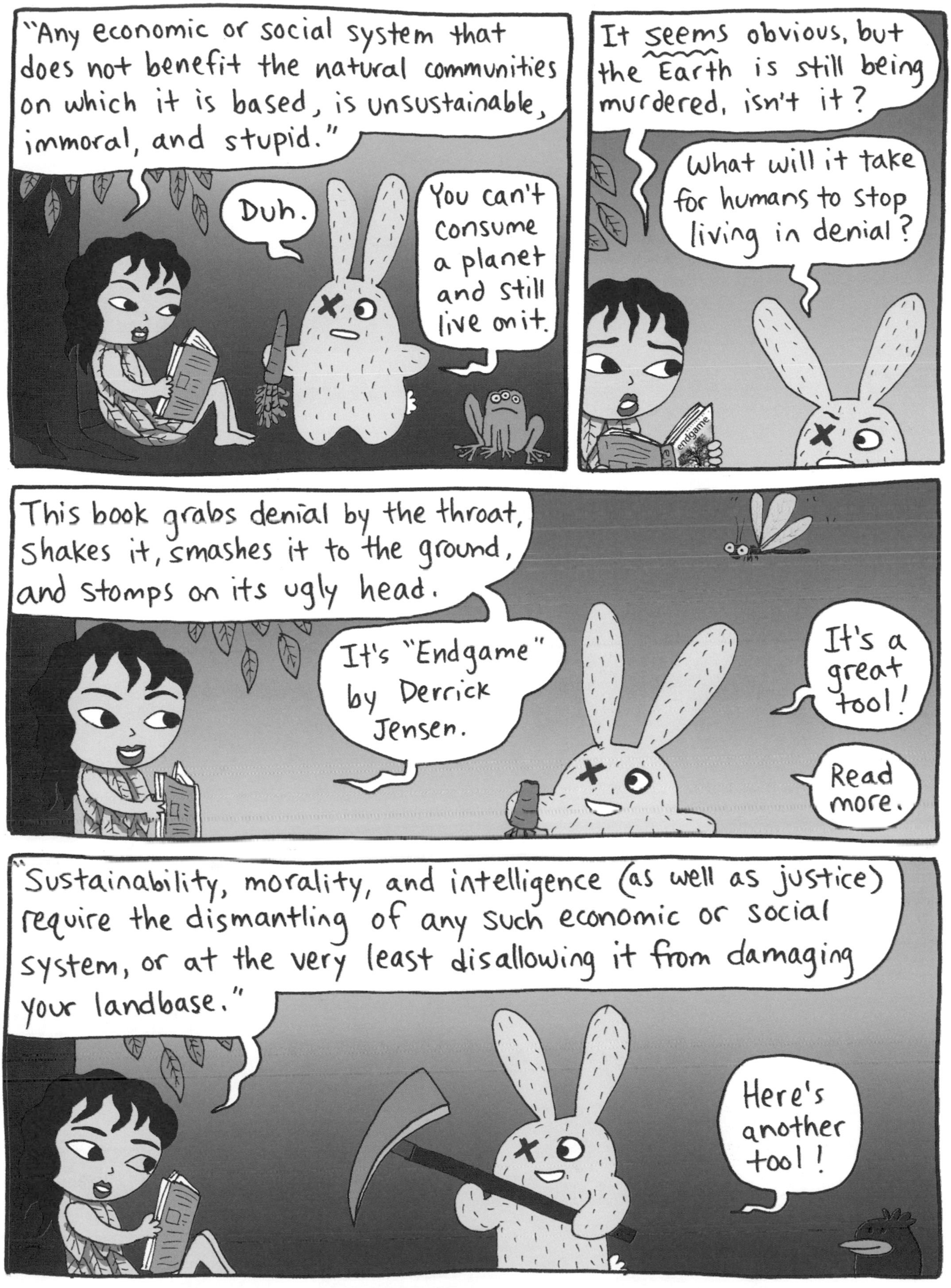
"Any economic or social system that does not benefit the natural communities on which it is based, is unsustainable, immoral, and stupid."
Duh.
You can't consume a planet and still live on it.
It seems obvious, but the Earth is still being murdered, isn't it?
What will it take for humans to stop living in denial?
endgame
This book grabs denial by the throat, shakes it, smashes it to the ground, and stomps on its ugly head.
It's "Endgame" by Derrick Jensen.
It's a great tool!
Read more.
"Sustainability, morality, and intelligence (as well as justice) require the dismantling of any such economic or social system, or at the very least disallowing it from damaging your landbase."
Here's another tool!

Guest Book Club by Stephanie McMillan @ www.minimumsecurity.net

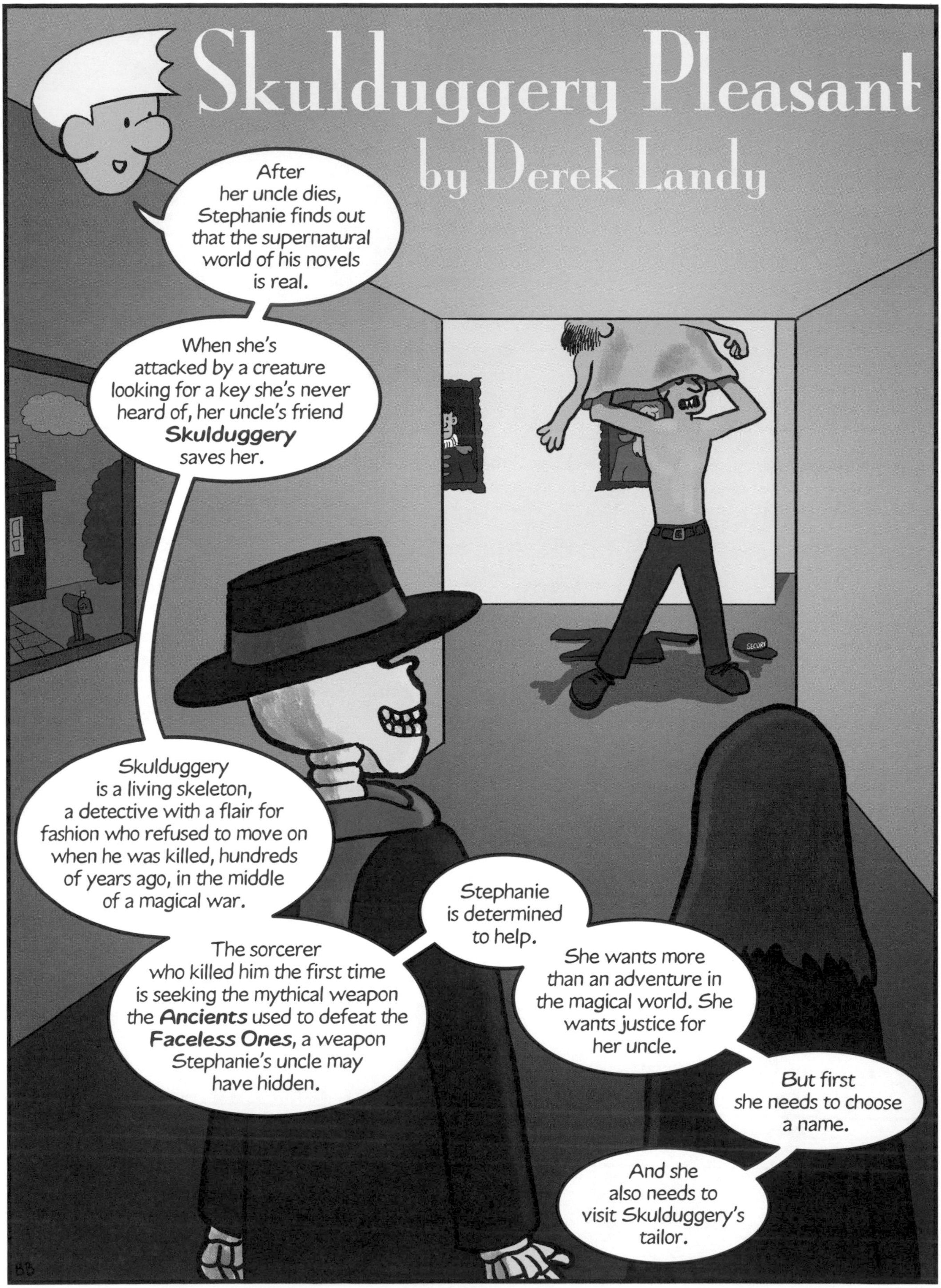
Skulduggery Pleasant
by Derek Landy
After her uncle dies, Stephanie finds out that the supernatural world of his novels is real.
When she's attacked by a creature looking for a key she's never heard of, her uncle's friend **Skulduggery** saves her.
Skulduggery is a living skeleton, a detective with a flair for fashion who refused to move on when he was killed, hundreds of years ago, in the middle of a magical war.
The sorcerer who killed him the first time is seeking the mythical weapon the ***Ancients*** used to defeat the ***Faceless Ones***, a weapon Stephanie's uncle may have hidden.
Stephanie is determined to help.
She wants more than an adventure in the magical world. She wants justice for her uncle.
But first she needs to choose a name.
And she also needs to visit Skulduggery's tailor.

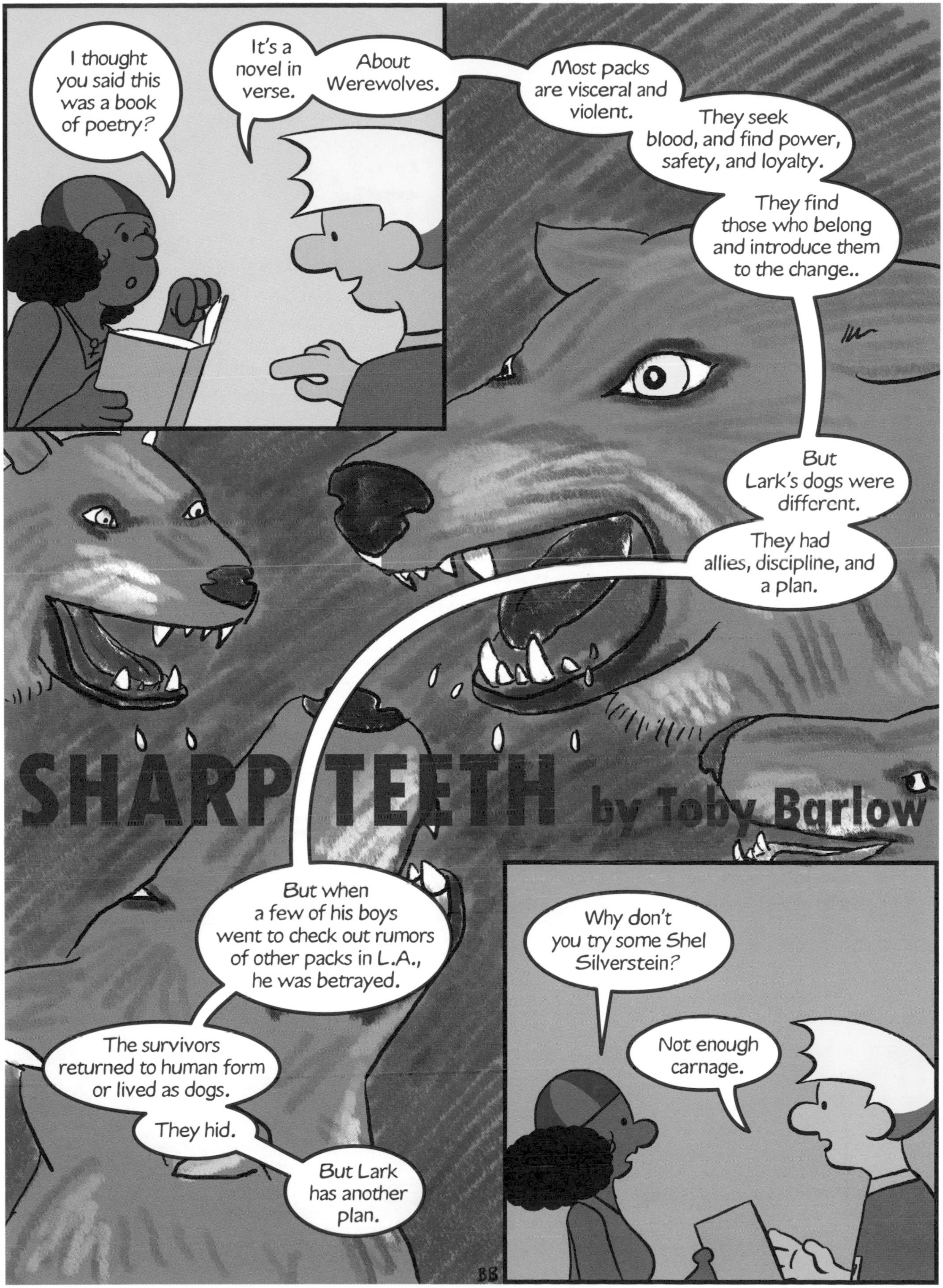
I thought you said this was a book of poetry?
It's a novel in verse.
About Werewolves.
Most packs are visceral and violent.
They seek blood, and find power, safety, and loyalty.
They find those who belong and introduce them to the change..
But Lark's dogs were different.
They had allies, discipline, and a plan.
SHARP TEETH by Toby Barlow
But when a few of his boys went to check out rumors of other packs in L.A., he was betrayed.
The survivors returned to human form or lived as dogs.
They hid.
But Lark has another plan.
Why don't you try some Shel Silverstein?
Not enough carnage.
BB

Emmy and the Incredible Shrinking Rat by Lynne Jonell

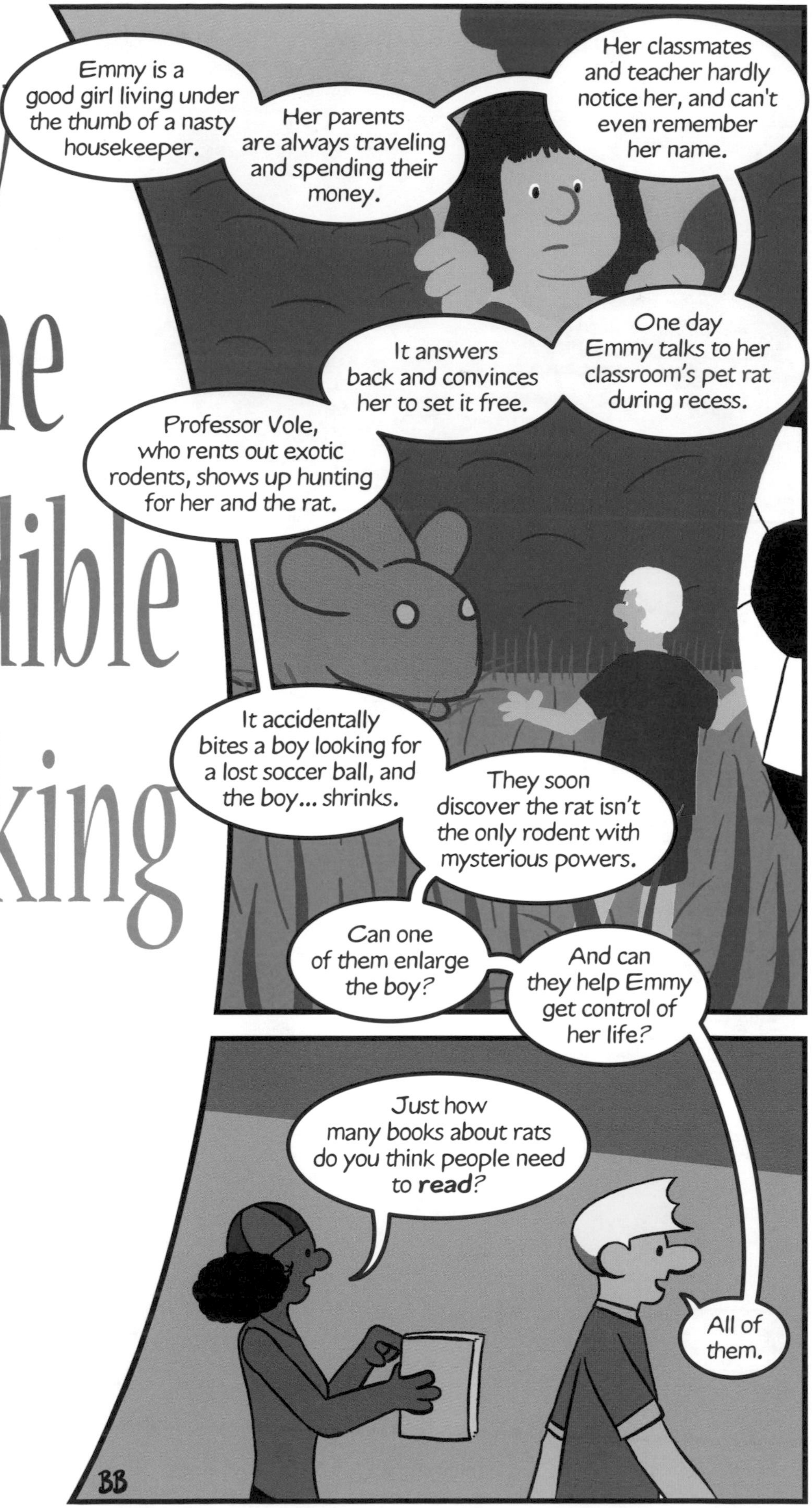
Emmy is a good girl living under the thumb of a nasty housekeeper.
Her parents are always traveling and spending their money.
Her classmates and teacher hardly notice her, and can't even remember her name.
One day Emmy talks to her classroom's pet rat during recess.
It answers back and convinces her to set it free.
Professor Vole, who rents out exotic rodents, shows up hunting for her and the rat.
It accidentally bites a boy looking for a lost soccer ball, and the boy... shrinks.
They soon discover the rat isn't the only rodent with mysterious powers.
Can one of them enlarge the boy?
And can they help Emmy get control of her life?
Just how many books about rats do you think people need to **read**?
All of them.
BB

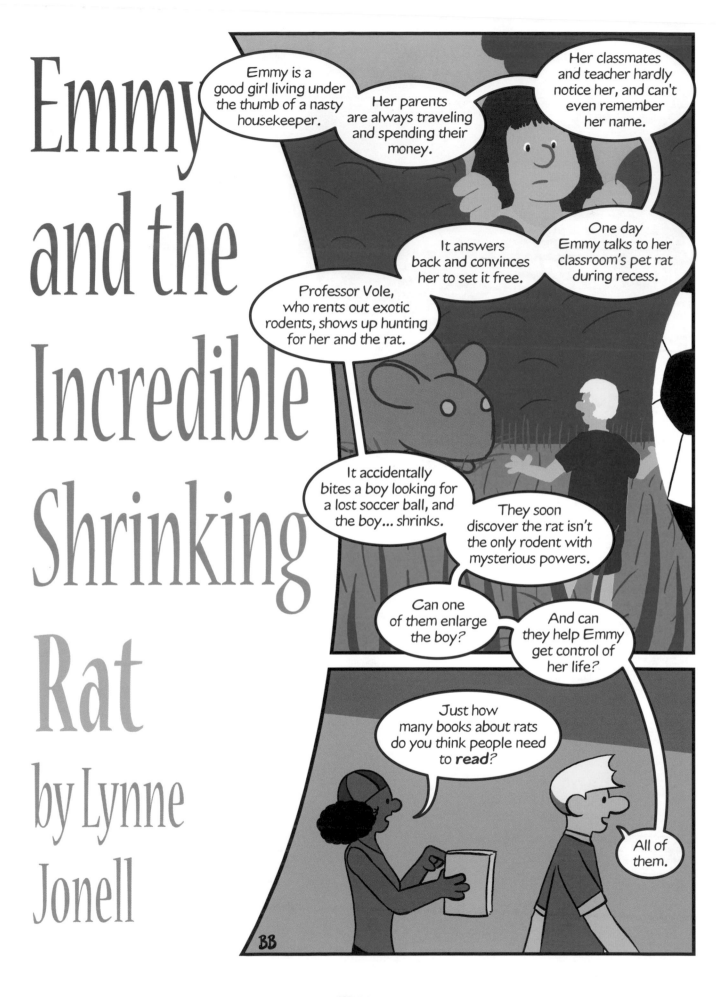

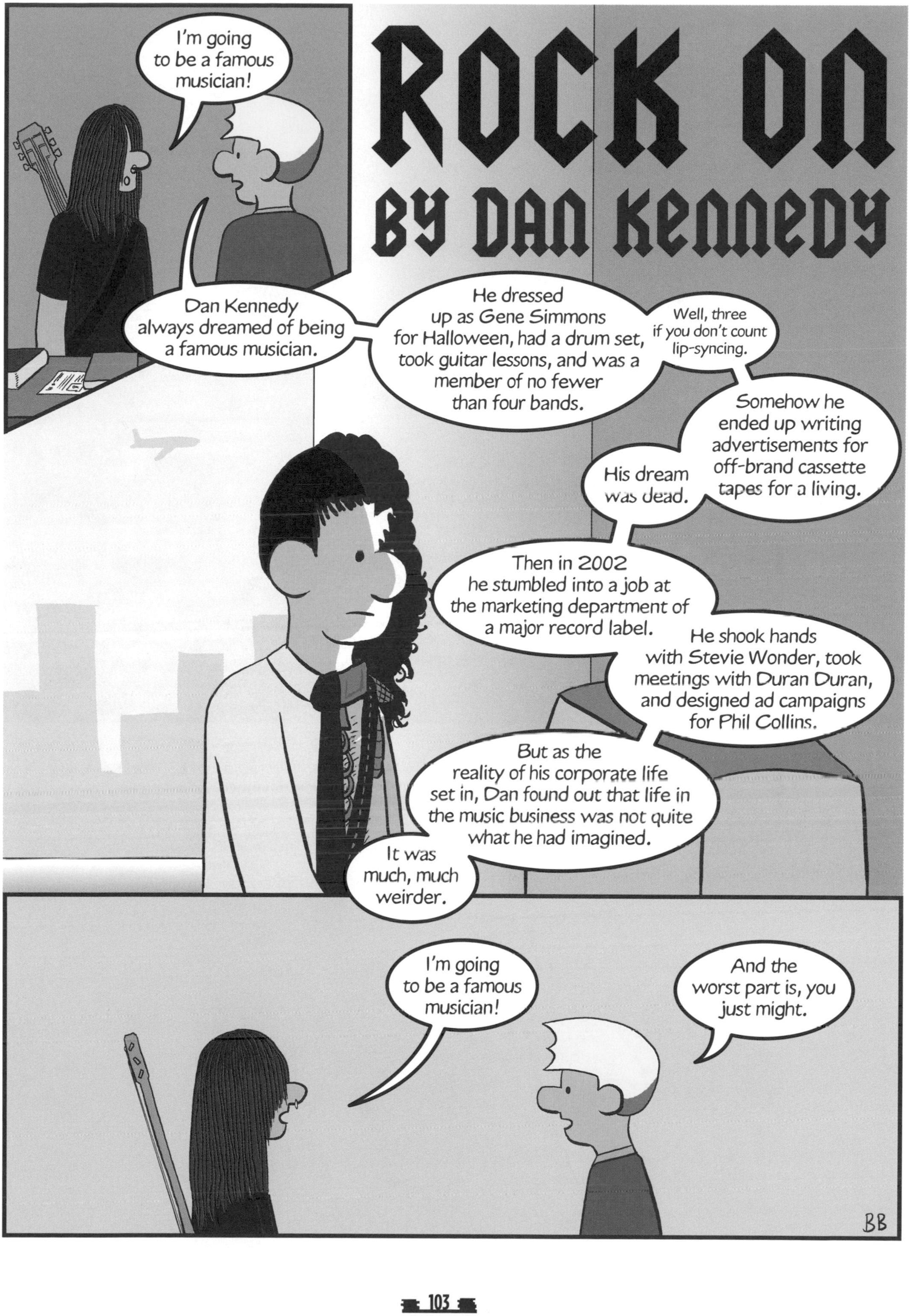
I'm going to be a famous musician!
ROCK ON
BY DAN KENNEDY
Dan Kennedy always dreamed of being a famous musician.
He dressed up as Gene Simmons for Halloween, had a drum set, took guitar lessons, and was a member of no fewer than four bands.
Well, three if you don't count lip-syncing.
Somehow he ended up writing advertisements for off-brand cassette tapes for a living.
His dream was dead.
Then in 2002 he stumbled into a job at the marketing department of a major record label.
He shook hands with Stevie Wonder, took meetings with Duran Duran, and designed ad campaigns for Phil Collins.
But as the reality of his corporate life set in, Dan found out that life in the music business was not quite what he had imagined.
It was much, much weirder.
I'm going to be a famous musician!
And the worst part is, you just might.
BB

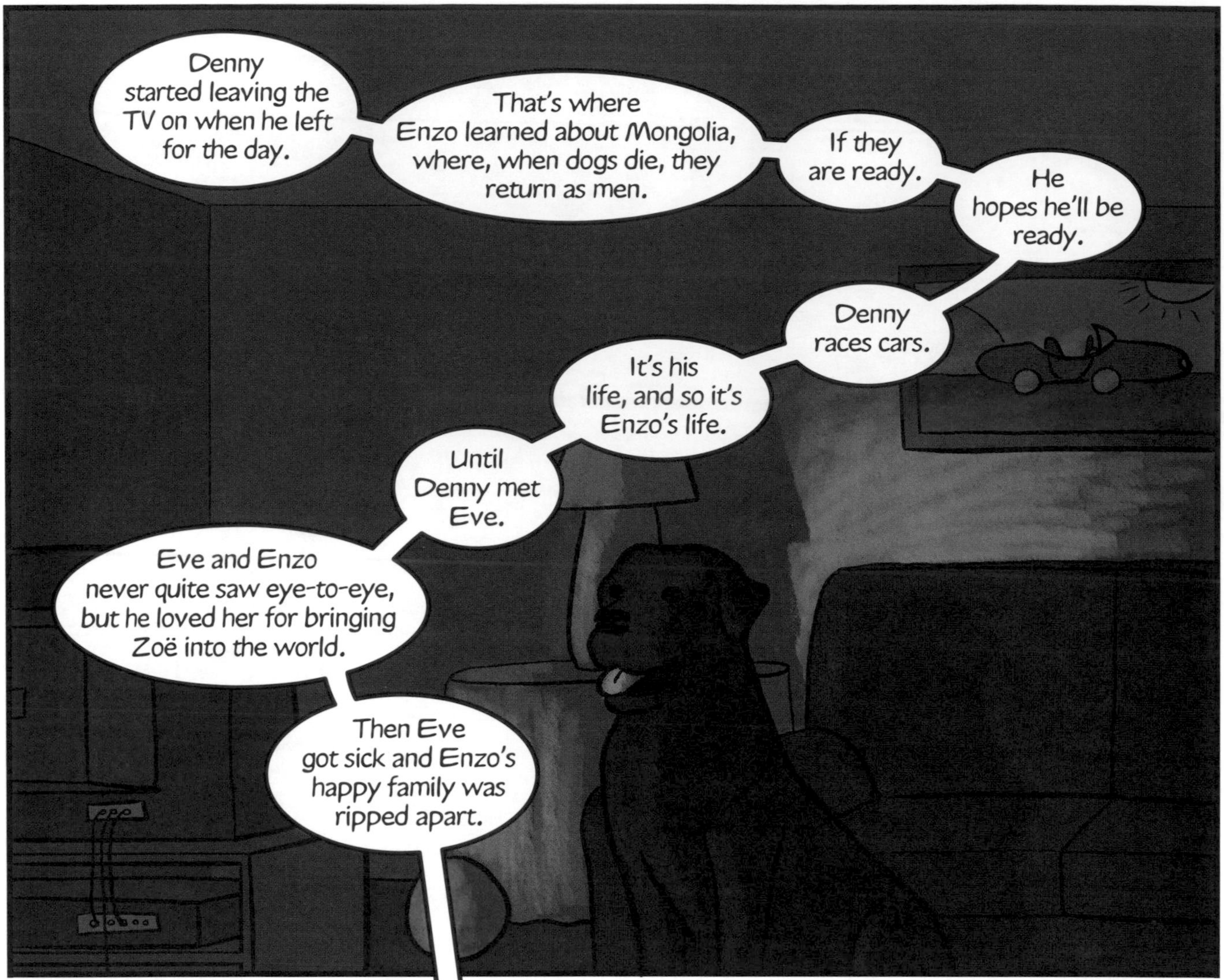
Denny started leaving the TV on when he left for the day.
That's where Enzo learned about Mongolia, where, when dogs die, they return as men.
If they are ready.
He hopes he'll be ready.
Denny races cars.
It's his life, and so it's Enzo's life.
Until Denny met Eve.
Eve and Enzo never quite saw eye-to-eye, but he loved her for bringing Zoë into the world.
Then Eve got sick and Enzo's happy family was ripped apart.

The Art of Racing in the Rain

by Garth Stein

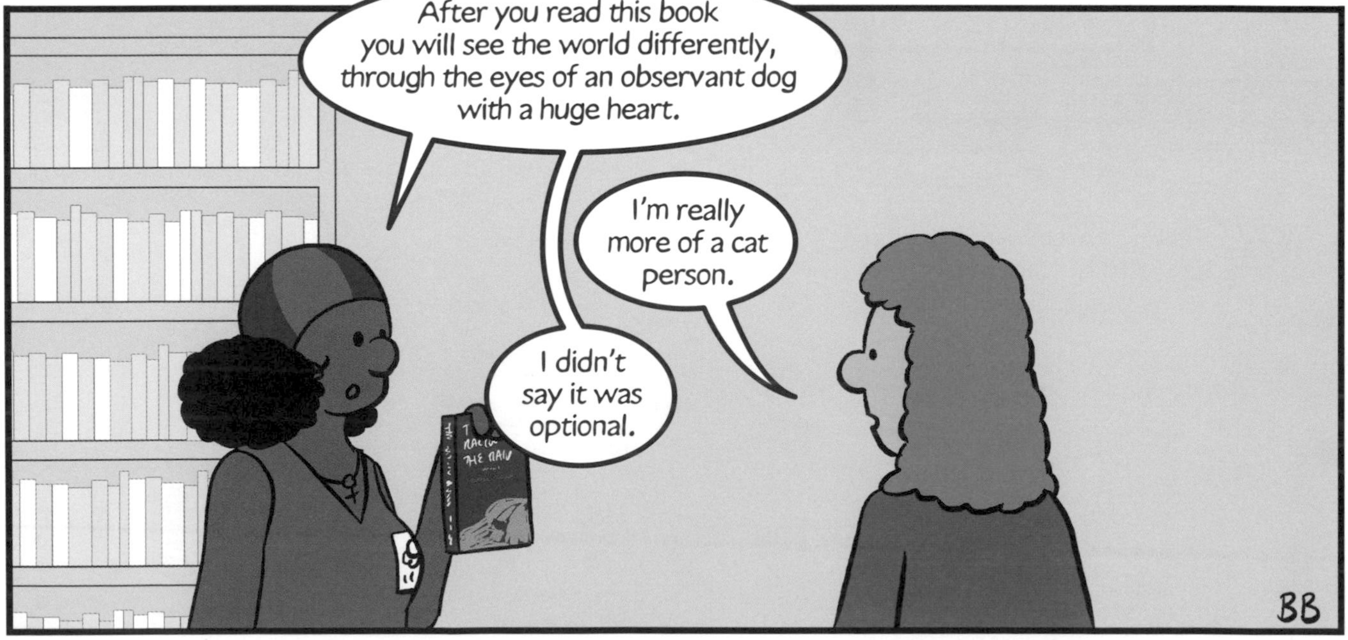
After you read this book you will see the world differently, through the eyes of an observant dog with a huge heart.
I'm really more of a cat person.
I didn't say it was optional.
BB

The Gargoyle

by Andrew Davidson

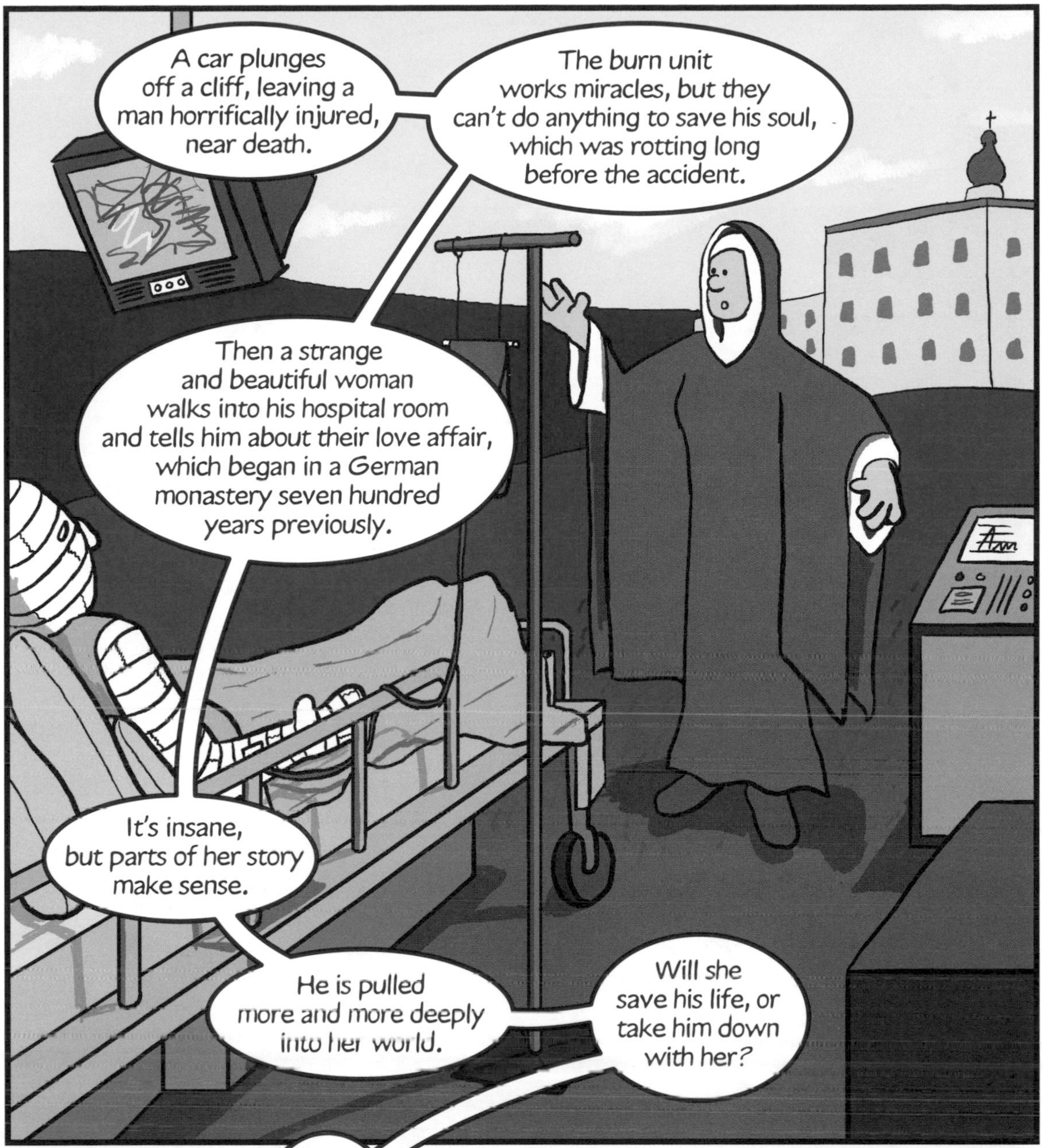

A car plunges off a cliff, leaving a man horrifically injured, near death.
The burn unit works miracles, but they can't do anything to save his soul, which was rotting long before the accident.
Then a strange and beautiful woman walks into his hospital room and tells him about their love affair, which began in a German monastery seven hundred years previously.
It's insane, but parts of her story make sense.
He is pulled more and more deeply into her world.
Will she save his life, or take him down with her?

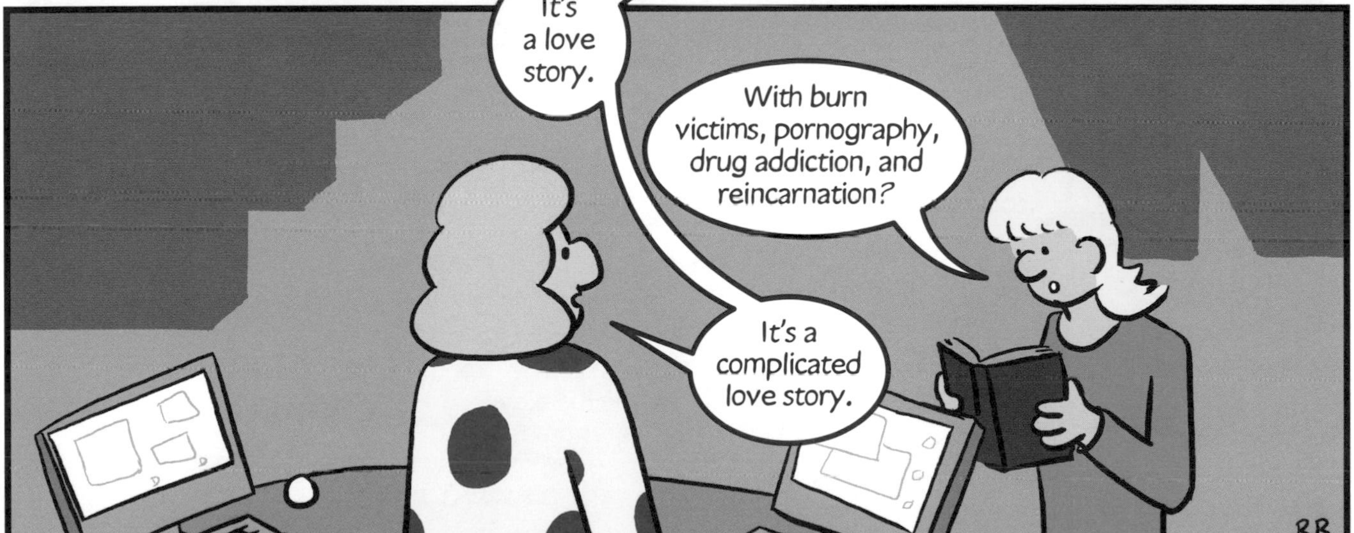

It's a love story.
With burn victims, pornography, drug addiction, and reincarnation?
It's a complicated love story.
BB

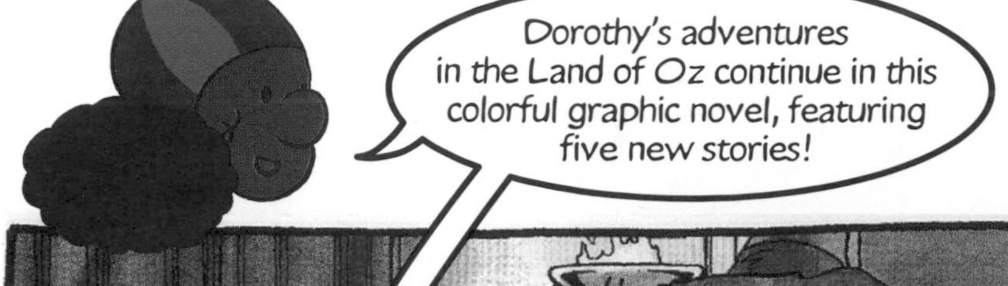
Dorothy's adventures in the Land of Oz continue in this colorful graphic novel, featuring five new stories!

Illustration (c)2006 Eric Shanower, used by permission

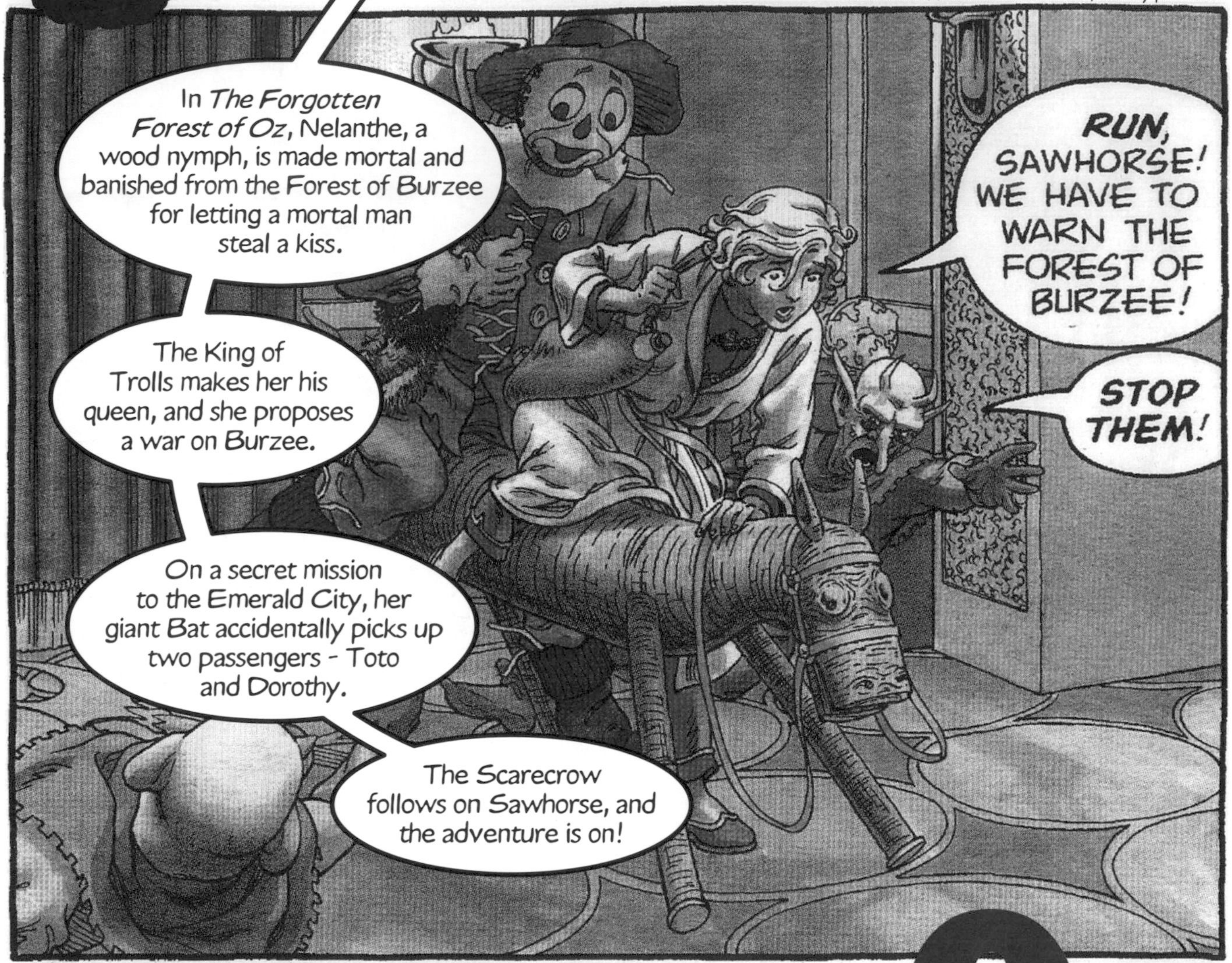
In *The Forgotten Forest of Oz*, Nelanthe, a wood nymph, is made mortal and banished from the Forest of Burzee for letting a mortal man steal a kiss.
The King of Trolls makes her his queen, and she proposes a war on Burzee.
On a secret mission to the Emerald City, her giant Bat accidentally picks up two passengers - Toto and Dorothy.
The Scarecrow follows on Sawhorse, and the adventure is on!
RUN, SAWHORSE! WE HAVE TO WARN THE FOREST OF BURZEE!
STOP THEM!

Adventures in Oz

by Eric Shanower

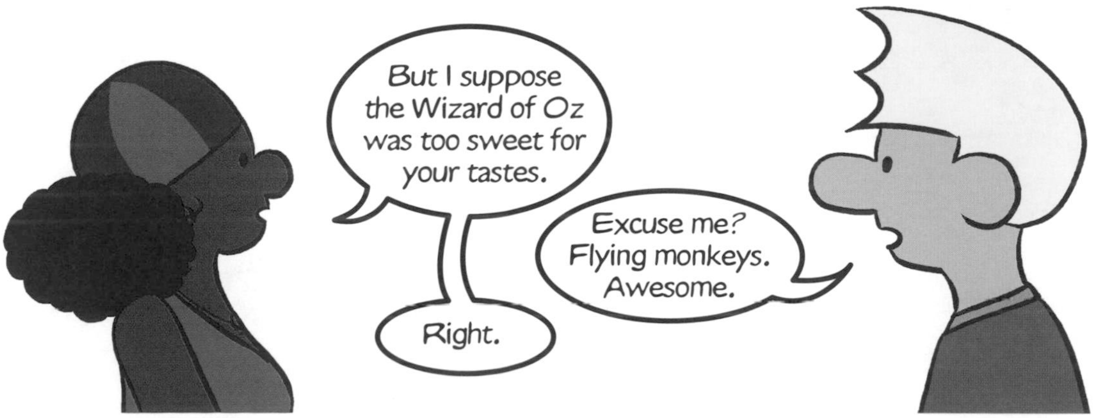
But I suppose the Wizard of Oz was too sweet for your tastes.
Excuse me? Flying monkeys. Awesome.
Right.

THE SOMNAMBULIST
BY JONATHAN BARNES

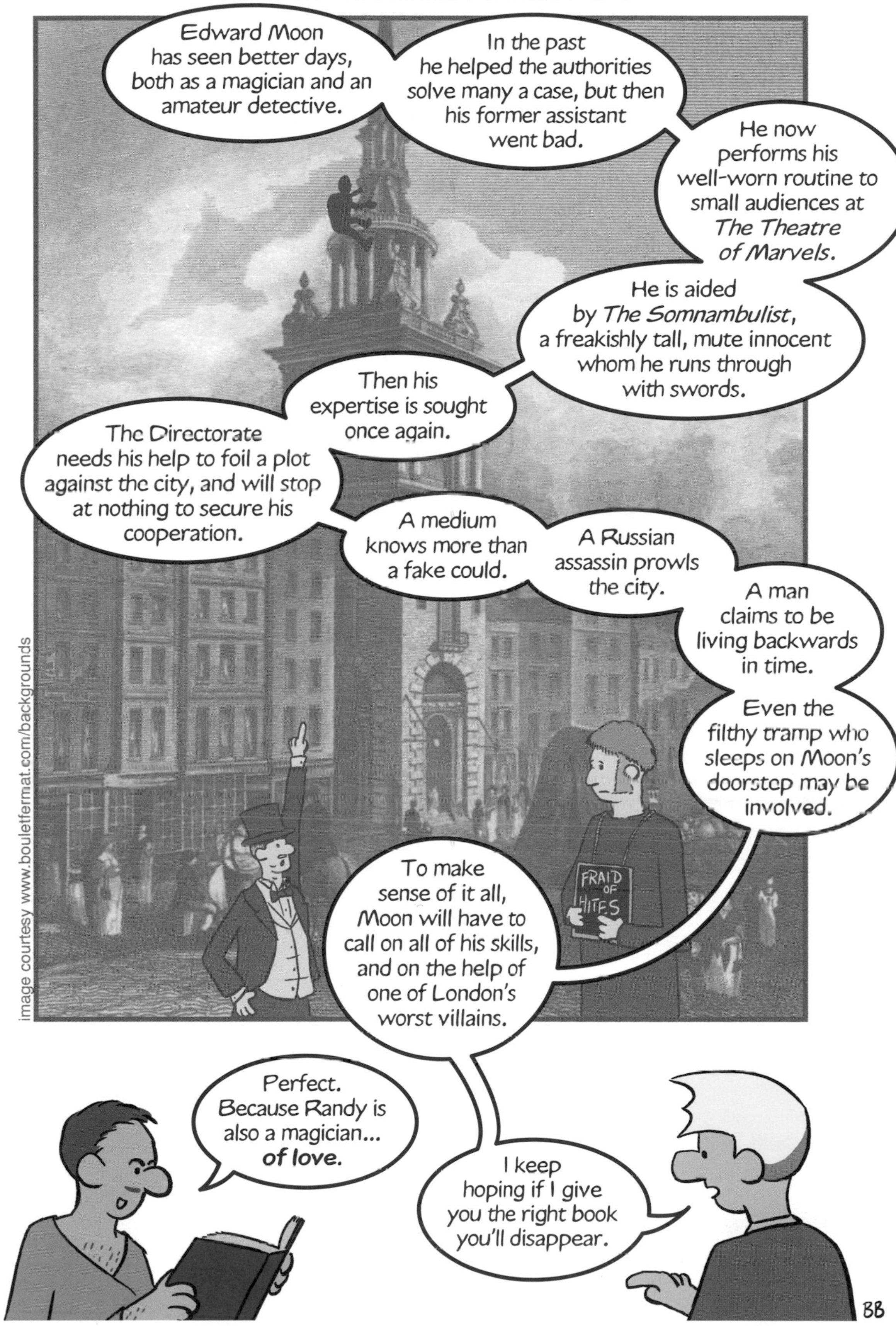
Edward Moon has seen better days, both as a magician and an amateur detective.
In the past he helped the authorities solve many a case, but then his former assistant went bad.
He now performs his well-worn routine to small audiences at *The Theatre of Marvels*.
He is aided by *The Somnambulist*, a freakishly tall, mute innocent whom he runs through with swords.
Then his expertise is sought once again.
The Directorate needs his help to foil a plot against the city, and will stop at nothing to secure his cooperation.
A medium knows more than a fake could.
A Russian assassin prowls the city.
A man claims to be living backwards in time.
Even the filthy tramp who sleeps on Moon's doorstep may be involved.
To make sense of it all, Moon will have to call on all of his skills, and on the help of one of London's worst villains.
Perfect. Because Randy is also a magician... **of love.**
I keep hoping if I give you the right book you'll disappear.
image courtesy www.bouletfermat.com/backgrounds
BB

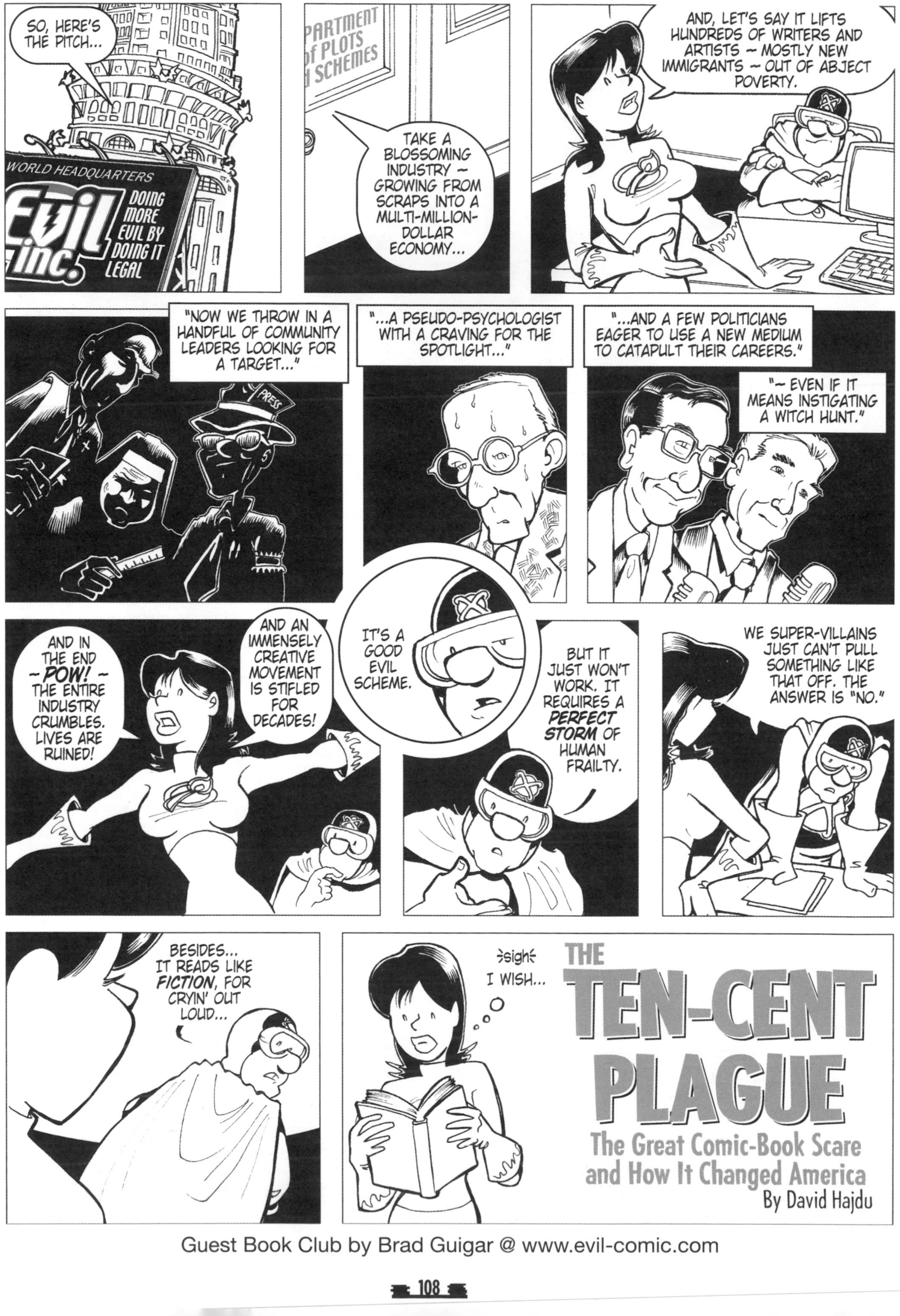
SO, HERE'S THE PITCH...
WORLD HEADQUARTERS
Evil inc.
DOING MORE EVIL BY DOING IT LEGAL
TAKE A BLOSSOMING INDUSTRY -- GROWING FROM SCRAPS INTO A MULTI-MILLION-DOLLAR ECONOMY...
PARTMENT OF PLOTS SCHEMES
AND, LET'S SAY IT LIFTS HUNDREDS OF WRITERS AND ARTISTS -- MOSTLY NEW IMMIGRANTS -- OUT OF ABJECT POVERTY.
"NOW WE THROW IN A HANDFUL OF COMMUNITY LEADERS LOOKING FOR A TARGET..."
PRESS
"...A PSEUDO-PSYCHOLOGIST WITH A CRAVING FOR THE SPOTLIGHT..."
"...AND A FEW POLITICIANS EAGER TO USE A NEW MEDIUM TO CATAPULT THEIR CAREERS."
"-- EVEN IF IT MEANS INSTIGATING A WITCH HUNT."
AND IN THE END -- POW! -- THE ENTIRE INDUSTRY CRUMBLES. LIVES ARE RUINED!
AND AN IMMENSELY CREATIVE MOVEMENT IS STIFLED FOR DECADES!
IT'S A GOOD EVIL SCHEME.
BUT IT JUST WON'T WORK. IT REQUIRES A PERFECT STORM OF HUMAN FRAILTY.
WE SUPER-VILLAINS JUST CAN'T PULL SOMETHING LIKE THAT OFF. THE ANSWER IS "NO."
BESIDES... IT READS LIKE FICTION, FOR CRYIN' OUT LOUD...
sigh
I WISH...
THE TEN-CENT PLAGUE
The Great Comic-Book Scare and How It Changed America
By David Hajdu

Guest Book Club by Brad Guigar @ www.evil-comic.com

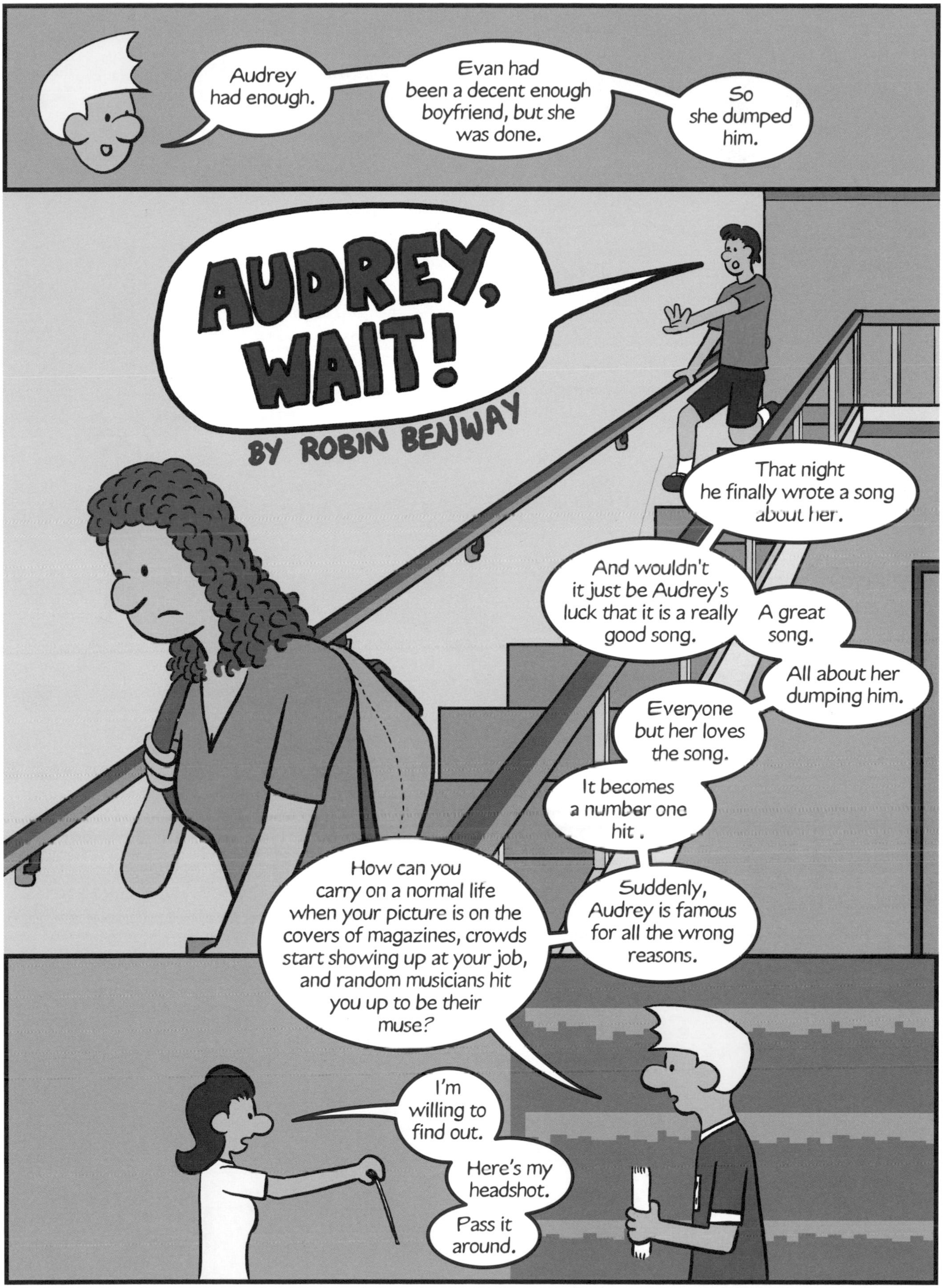

Audrey had enough.
Evan had been a decent enough boyfriend, but she was done.
So she dumped him.
AUDREY, WAIT!
BY ROBIN BENWAY
That night he finally wrote a song about her.
And wouldn't it just be Audrey's luck that it is a really good song.
A great song.
All about her dumping him.
Everyone but her loves the song.
It becomes a number one hit.
Suddenly, Audrey is famous for all the wrong reasons.
How can you carry on a normal life when your picture is on the covers of magazines, crowds start showing up at your job, and random musicians hit you up to be their muse?
I'm willing to find out.
Here's my headshot.
Pass it around.

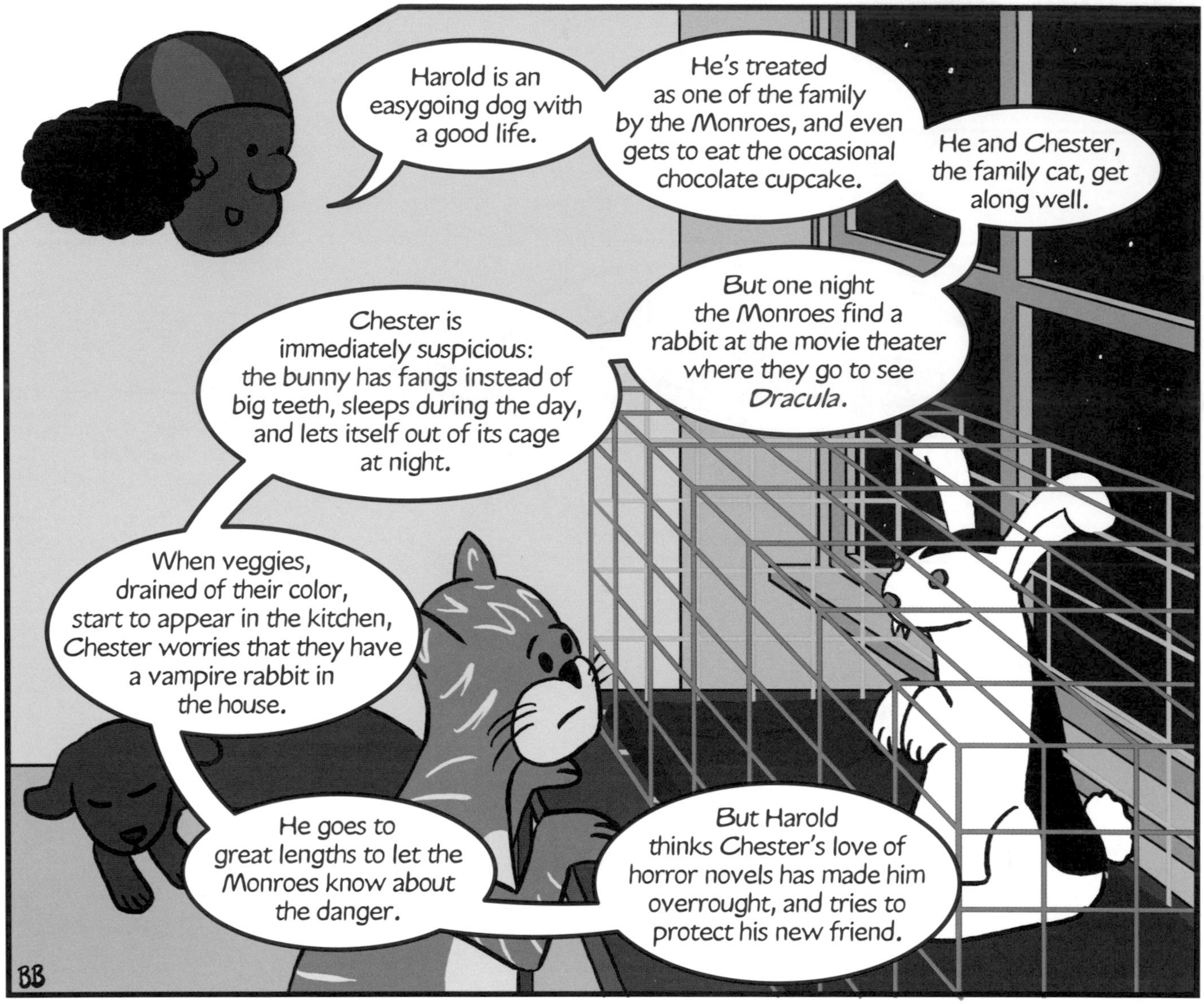
Harold is an easygoing dog with a good life.
He's treated as one of the family by the Monroes, and even gets to eat the occasional chocolate cupcake.
He and Chester, the family cat, get along well.
But one night the Monroes find a rabbit at the movie theater where they go to see *Dracula*.
Chester is immediately suspicious: the bunny has fangs instead of big teeth, sleeps during the day, and lets itself out of its cage at night.
When veggies, drained of their color, start to appear in the kitchen, Chester worries that they have a vampire rabbit in the house.
He goes to great lengths to let the Monroes know about the danger.
But Harold thinks Chester's love of horror novels has made him overrought, and tries to protect his new friend.
BB

BUNNICULA

A RABBIT TALE OF MYSTERY
BY DEBORAH & JAMES HOWE
ILLUSTRATED BY ALAN DANIEL

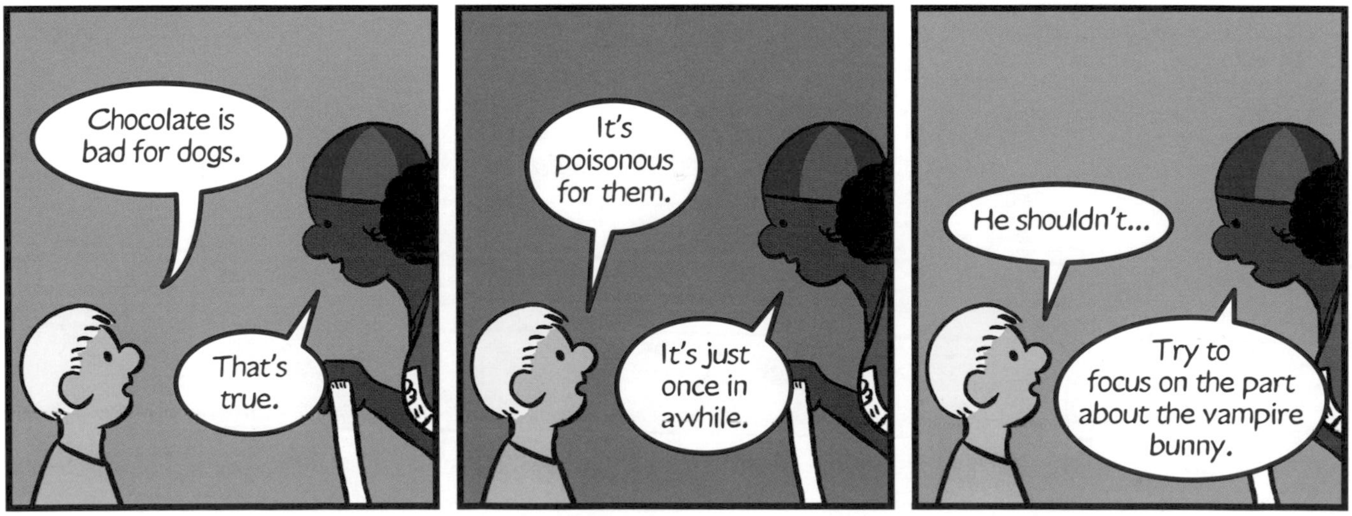
Chocolate is bad for dogs.
That's true.
It's poisonous for them.
It's just once in awhile.
He shouldn't...
Try to focus on the part about the vampire bunny.

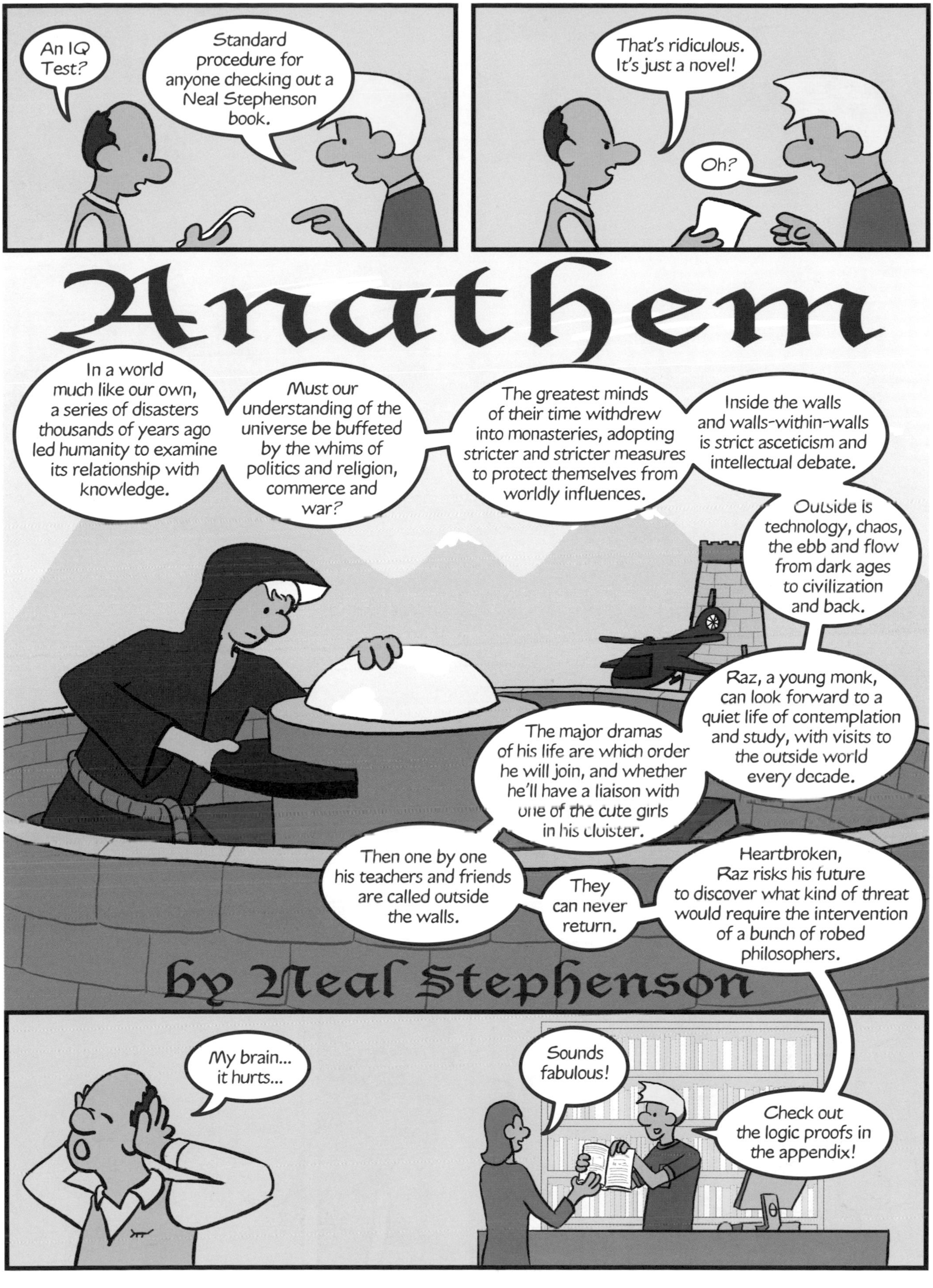
An IQ Test?
Standard procedure for anyone checking out a Neal Stephenson book.
That's ridiculous. It's just a novel!
Oh?
Anathem
In a world much like our own, a series of disasters thousands of years ago led humanity to examine its relationship with knowledge.
Must our understanding of the universe be buffeted by the whims of politics and religion, commerce and war?
The greatest minds of their time withdrew into monasteries, adopting stricter and stricter measures to protect themselves from worldly influences.
Inside the walls and walls-within-walls is strict asceticism and intellectual debate.
Outside is technology, chaos, the ebb and flow from dark ages to civilization and back.
Raz, a young monk, can look forward to a quiet life of contemplation and study, with visits to the outside world every decade.
The major dramas of his life are which order he will join, and whether he'll have a liaison with one of the cute girls in his cloister.
Then one by one his teachers and friends are called outside the walls.
They can never return.
Heartbroken, Raz risks his future to discover what kind of threat would require the intervention of a bunch of robed philosophers.
by Neal Stephenson
My brain... it hurts...
Sounds fabulous!
Check out the logic proofs in the appendix!

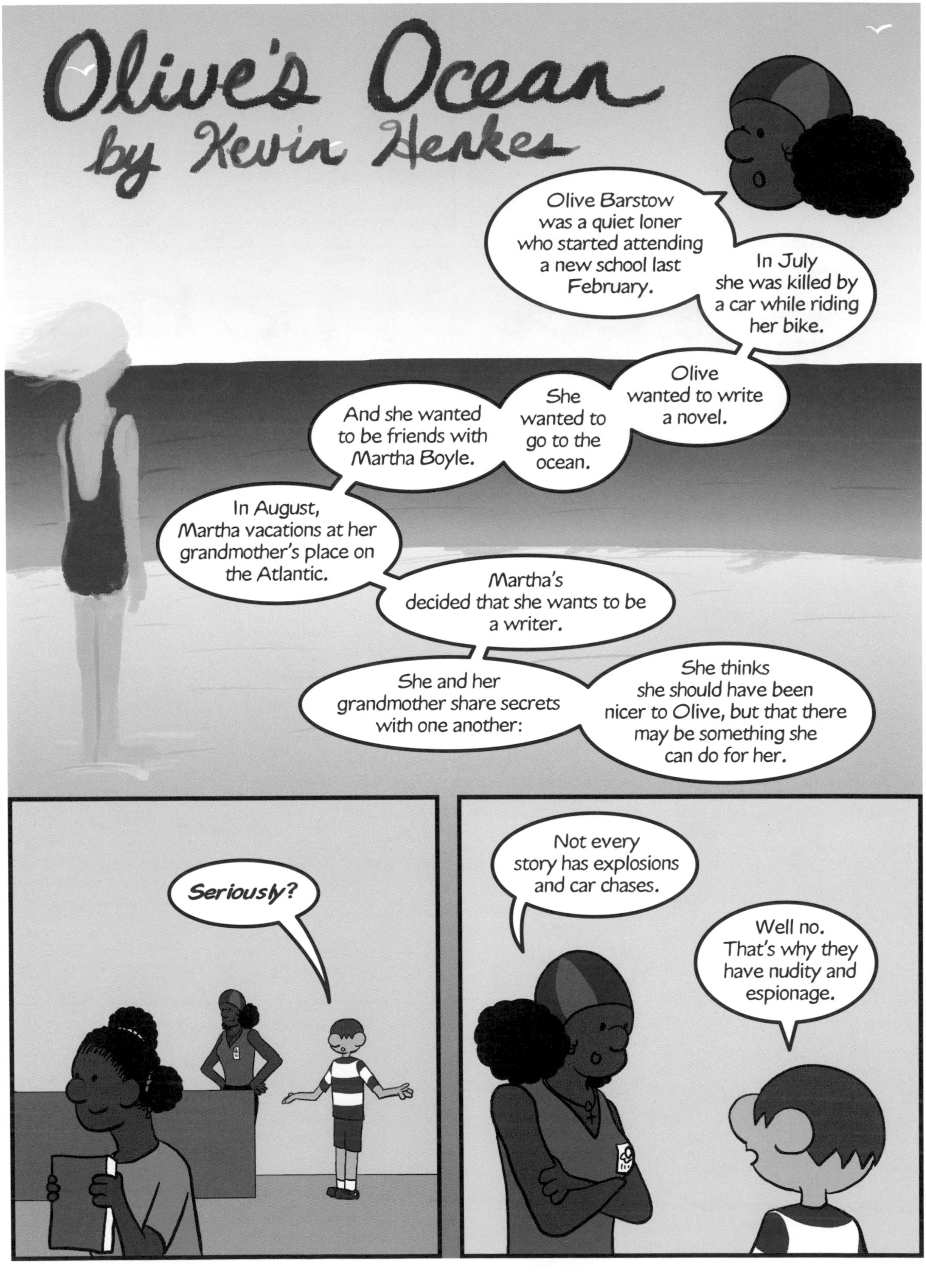
Olive's Ocean
by Kevin Henkes
Olive Barstow was a quiet loner who started attending a new school last February.
In July she was killed by a car while riding her bike.
Olive wanted to write a novel.
She wanted to go to the ocean.
And she wanted to be friends with Martha Boyle.
In August, Martha vacations at her grandmother's place on the Atlantic.
Martha's decided that she wants to be a writer.
She and her grandmother share secrets with one another:
She thinks she should have been nicer to Olive, but that there may be something she can do for her.
Seriously?
Not every story has explosions and car chases.
Well no. That's why they have nudity and espionage.

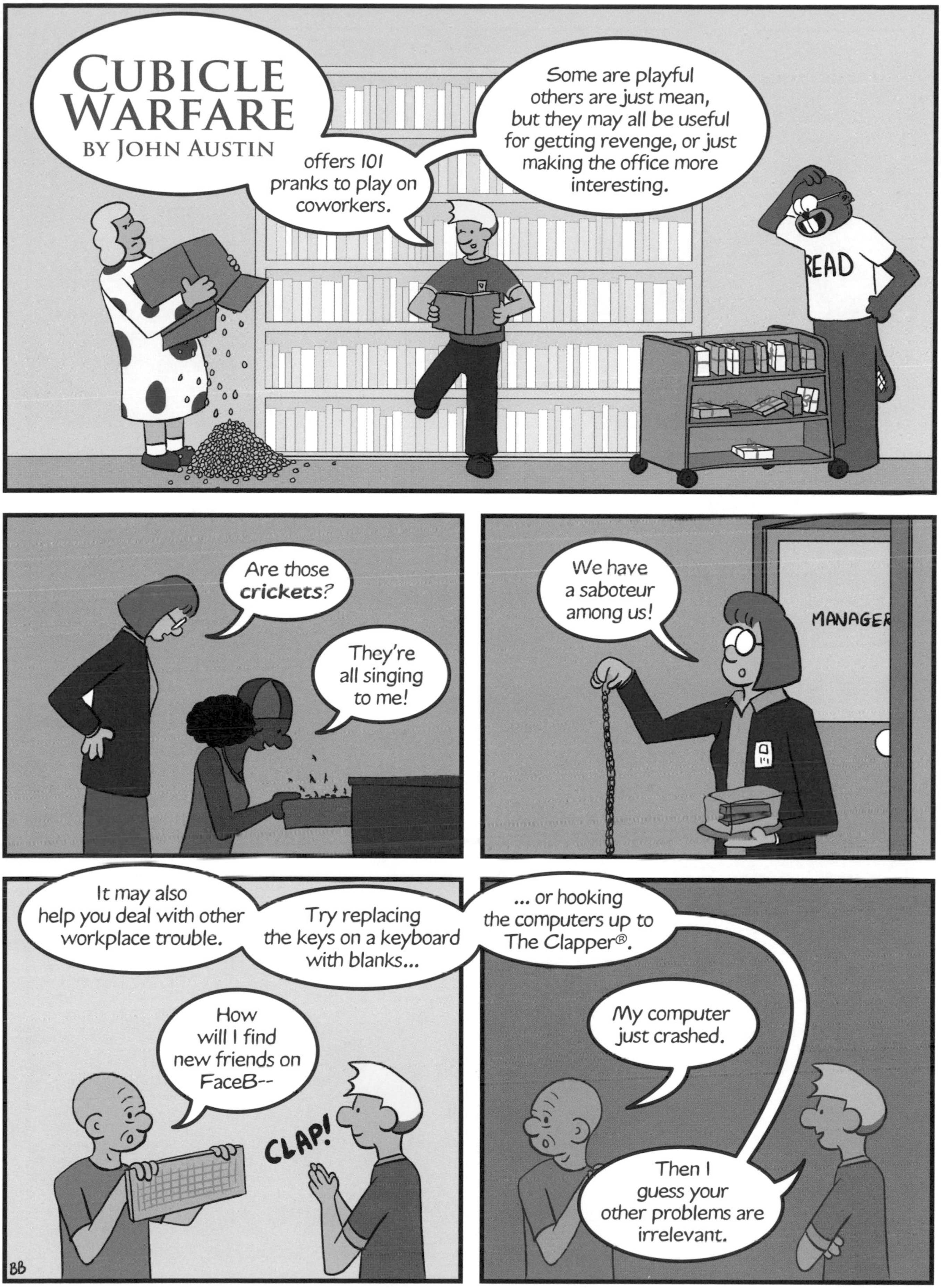

CUBICLE WARFARE BY JOHN AUSTIN
offers 101 pranks to play on coworkers.
Some are playful others are just mean, but they may all be useful for getting revenge, or just making the office more interesting.
READ
Are those **crickets**?
They're all singing to me!
We have a saboteur among us!
MANAGER
It may also help you deal with other workplace trouble.
Try replacing the keys on a keyboard with blanks...
... or hooking the computers up to The Clapper®.
How will I find new friends on FaceB--
CLAP!
My computer just crashed.
Then I guess your other problems are irrelevant.
BB

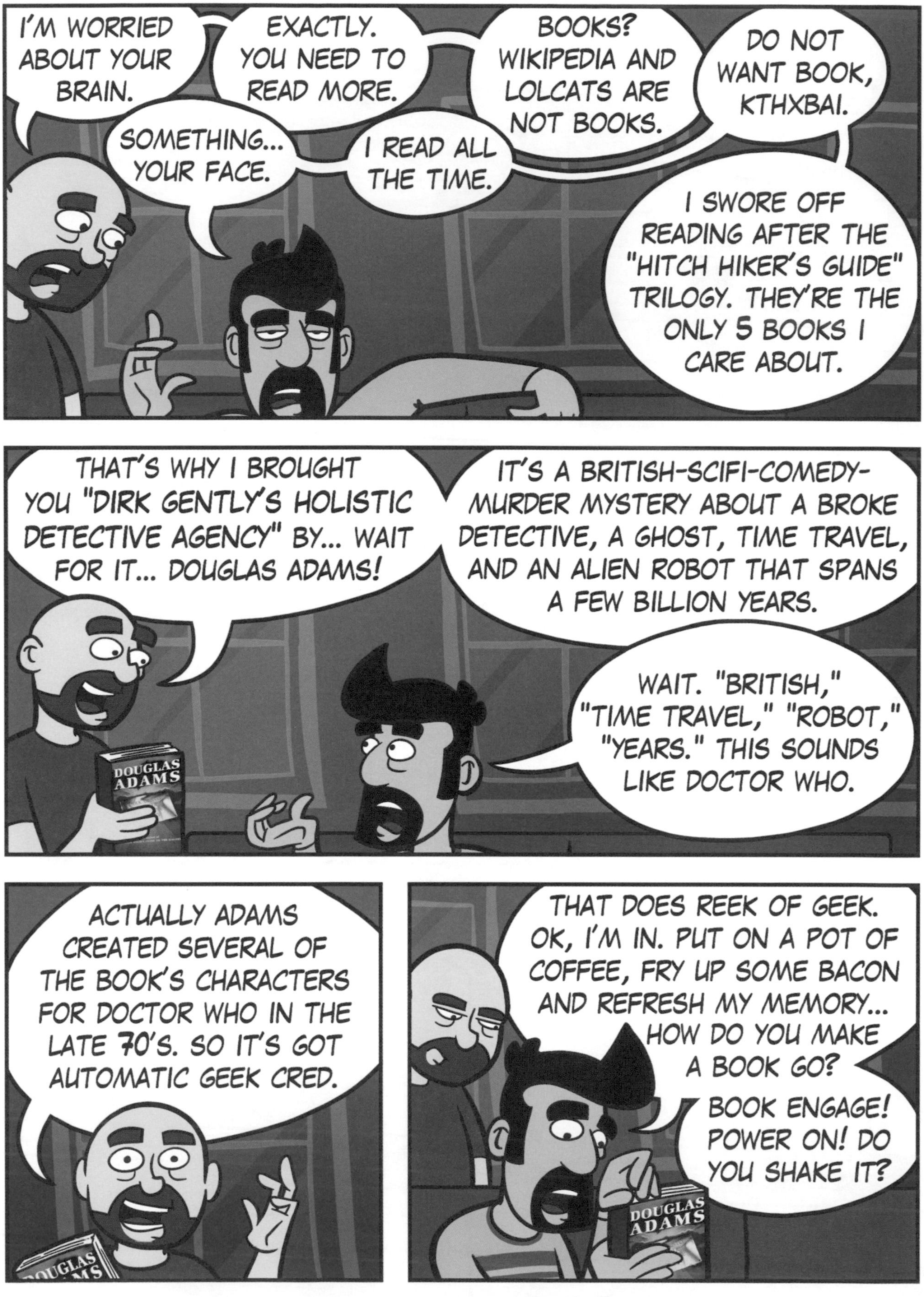
I'M WORRIED ABOUT YOUR BRAIN.
SOMETHING... YOUR FACE.
EXACTLY. YOU NEED TO READ MORE.
I READ ALL THE TIME.
BOOKS? WIKIPEDIA AND LOLCATS ARE NOT BOOKS.
DO NOT WANT BOOK, KTHXBAI.
I SWORE OFF READING AFTER THE "HITCH HIKER'S GUIDE" TRILOGY. THEY'RE THE ONLY 5 BOOKS I CARE ABOUT.
THAT'S WHY I BROUGHT YOU "DIRK GENTLY'S HOLISTIC DETECTIVE AGENCY" BY... WAIT FOR IT... DOUGLAS ADAMS!
IT'S A BRITISH-SCIFI-COMEDY-MURDER MYSTERY ABOUT A BROKE DETECTIVE, A GHOST, TIME TRAVEL, AND AN ALIEN ROBOT THAT SPANS A FEW BILLION YEARS.
DOUGLAS ADAMS
WAIT. "BRITISH," "TIME TRAVEL," "ROBOT," "YEARS." THIS SOUNDS LIKE DOCTOR WHO.
ACTUALLY ADAMS CREATED SEVERAL OF THE BOOK'S CHARACTERS FOR DOCTOR WHO IN THE LATE 70'S. SO IT'S GOT AUTOMATIC GEEK CRED.
THAT DOES REEK OF GEEK. OK, I'M IN. PUT ON A POT OF COFFEE, FRY UP SOME BACON AND REFRESH MY MEMORY... HOW DO YOU MAKE A BOOK GO?
BOOK ENGAGE! POWER ON! DO YOU SHAKE IT?
DOUGLAS ADAMS

Guest Book Club by Joel Watson @ www.hijinksensue.com

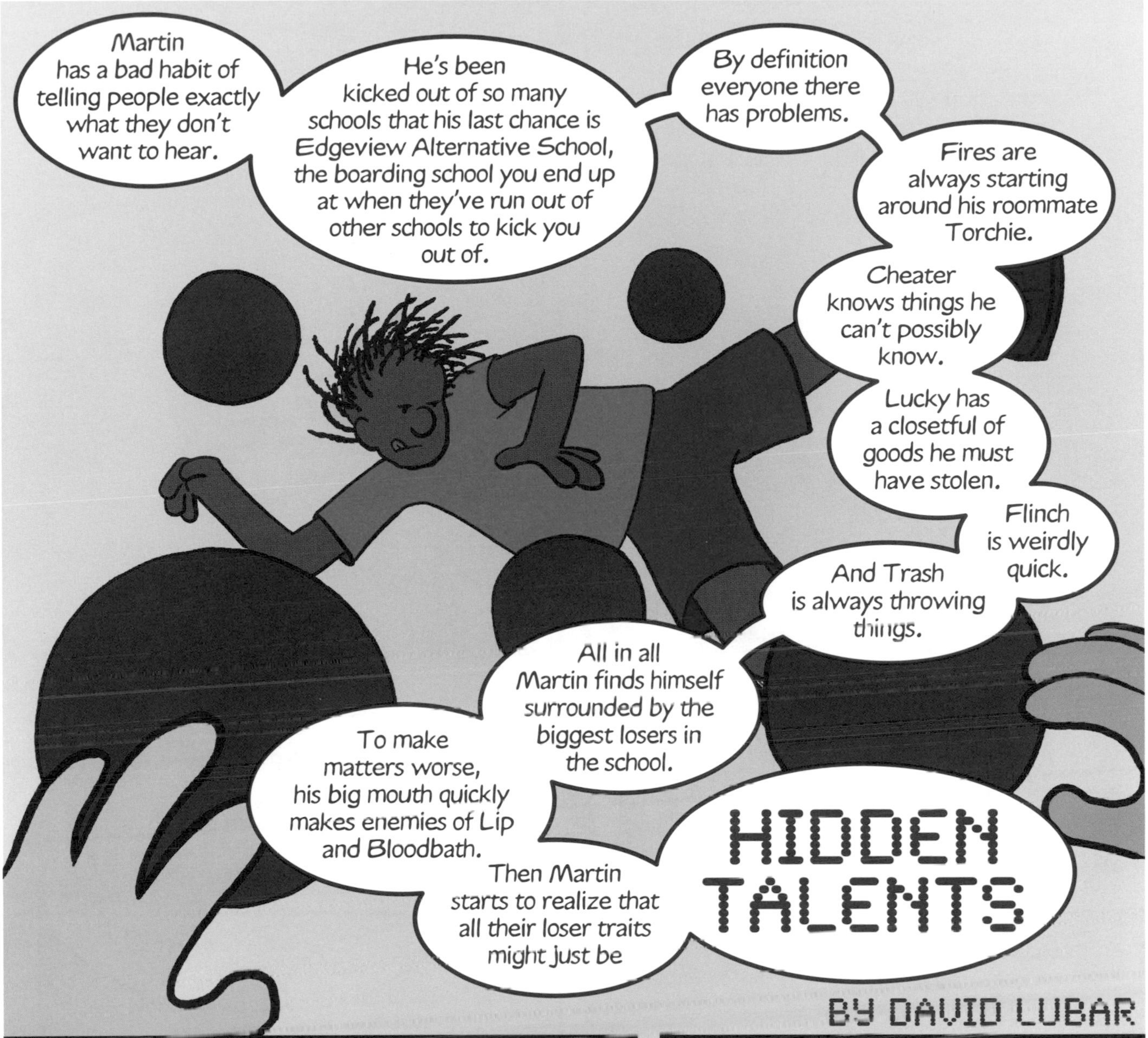
Martin has a bad habit of telling people exactly what they don't want to hear.
He's been kicked out of so many schools that his last chance is Edgeview Alternative School, the boarding school you end up at when they've run out of other schools to kick you out of.
By definition everyone there has problems.
Fires are always starting around his roommate Torchie.
Cheater knows things he can't possibly know.
Lucky has a closetful of goods he must have stolen.
Flinch is weirdly quick.
And Trash is always throwing things.
All in all Martin finds himself surrounded by the biggest losers in the school.
To make matters worse, his big mouth quickly makes enemies of Lip and Bloodbath.
Then Martin starts to realize that all their loser traits might just be
HIDDEN TALENTS
BY DAVID LUBAR

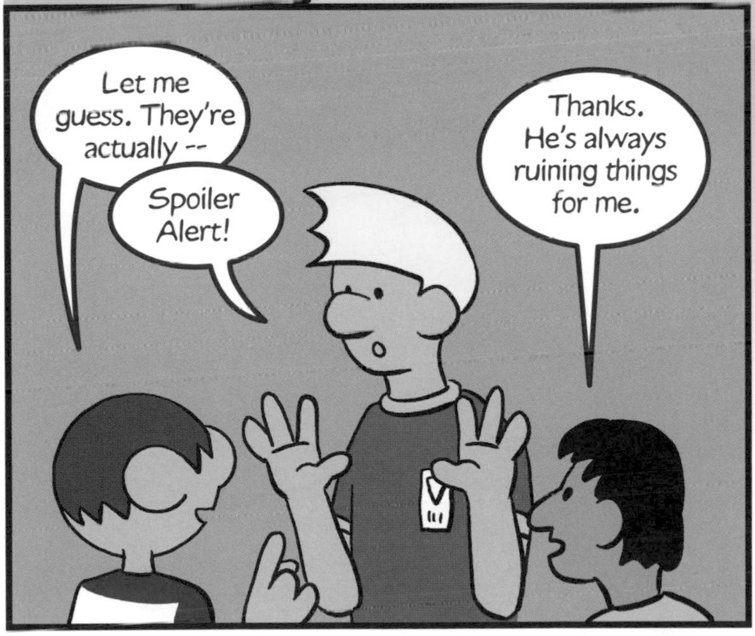
Let me guess. They're actually --
Spoiler Alert!
Thanks. He's always ruining things for me.

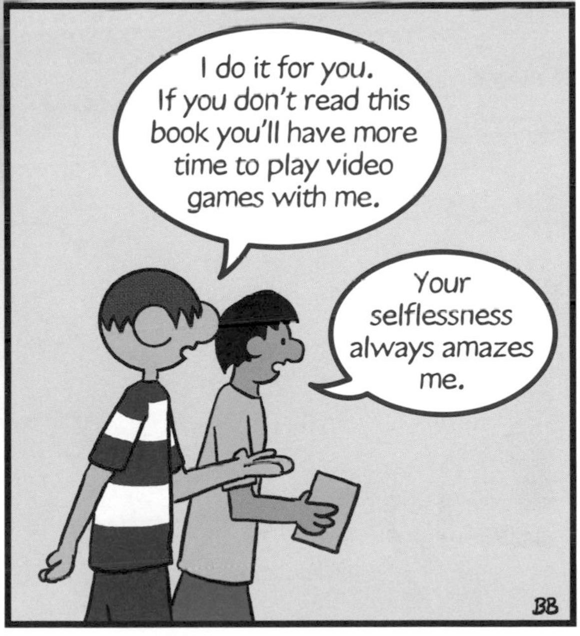
I do it for you. If you don't read this book you'll have more time to play video games with me.
Your selflessness always amazes me.
BB

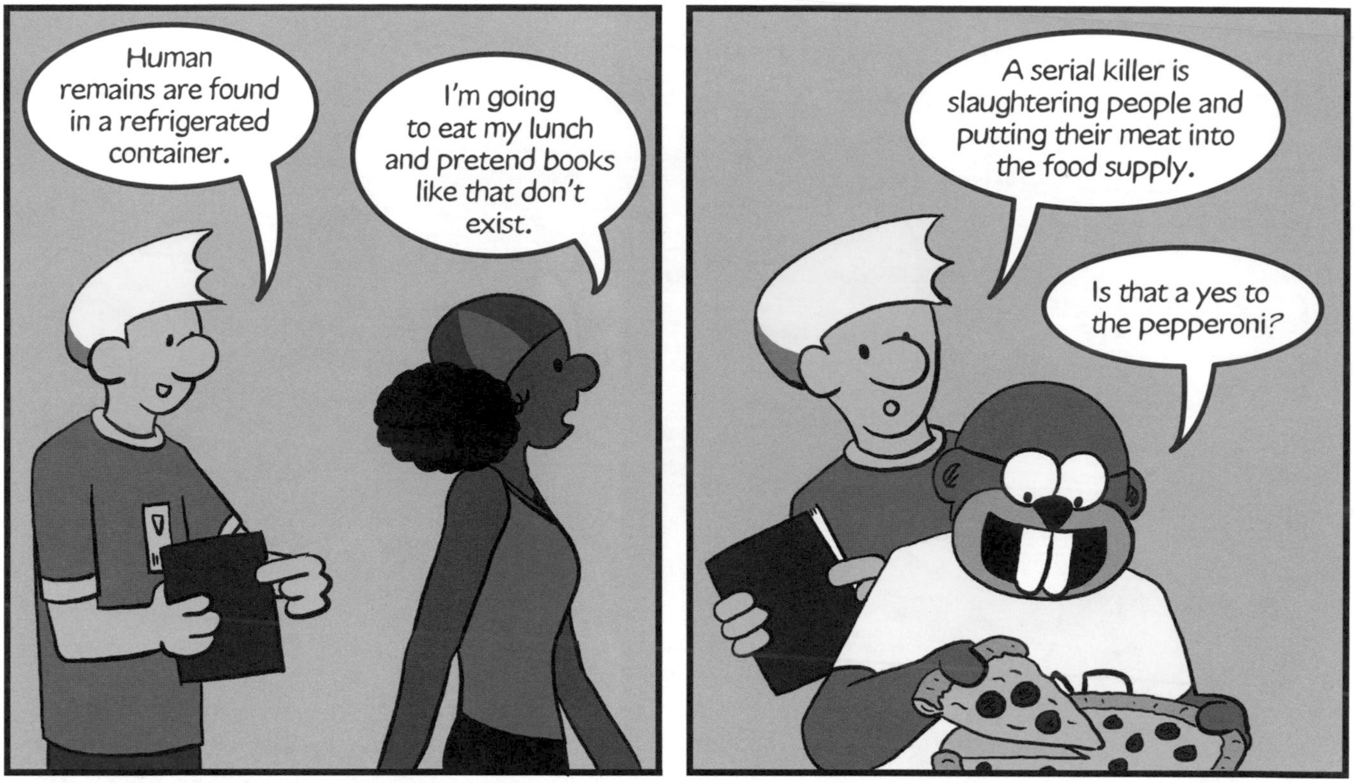
Human remains are found in a refrigerated container.
I'm going to eat my lunch and pretend books like that don't exist.
A serial killer is slaughtering people and putting their meat into the food supply.
Is that a yes to the pepperoni?

FLESH HOUSE by Stuart MacBride

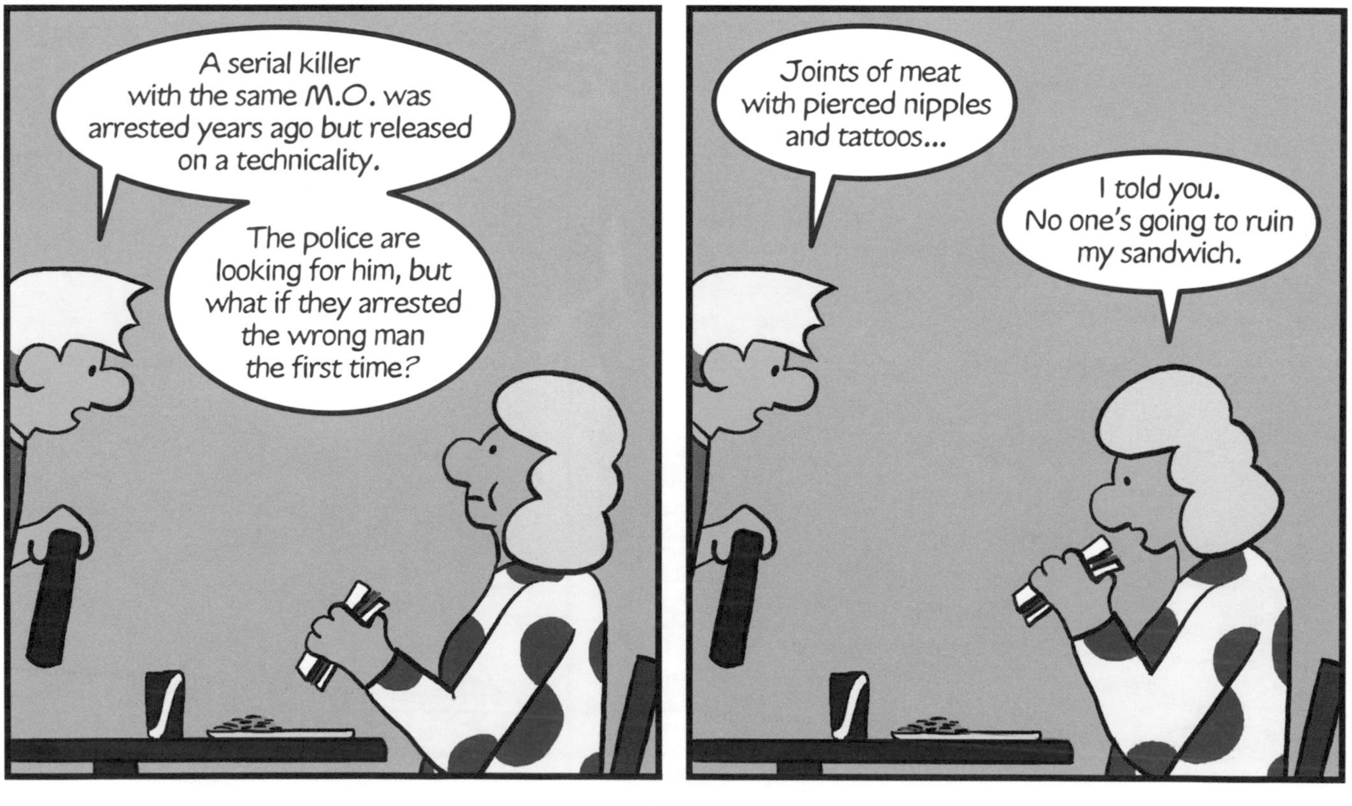
A serial killer with the same M.O. was arrested years ago but released on a technicality.
The police are looking for him, but what if they arrested the wrong man the first time?
Joints of meat with pierced nipples and tattoos...
I told you. No one's going to ruin my sandwich.

After the end of the world, a man and his young son struggle to survive their journey across a stark, unforgiving post-apocalyptic wasteland...

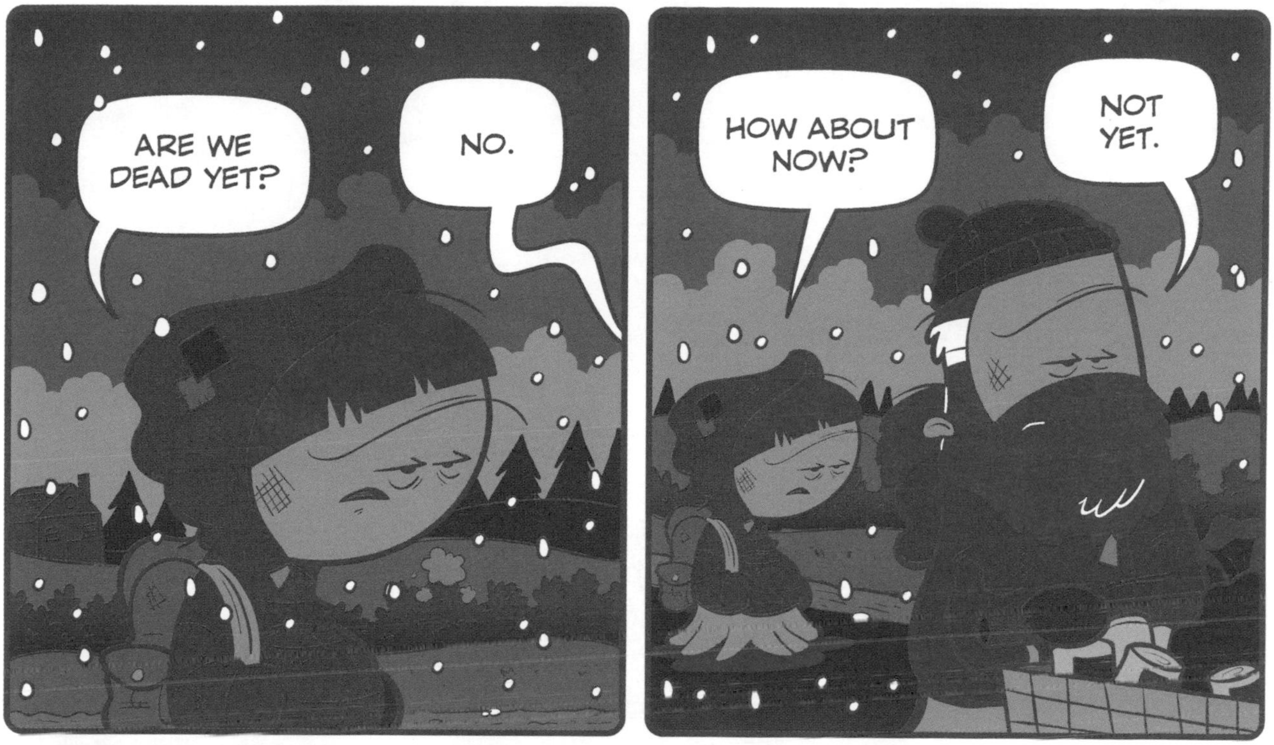
ARE WE DEAD YET?
NO.
HOW ABOUT NOW?
NOT YET.

THE ROAD

By Cormac McCarthy

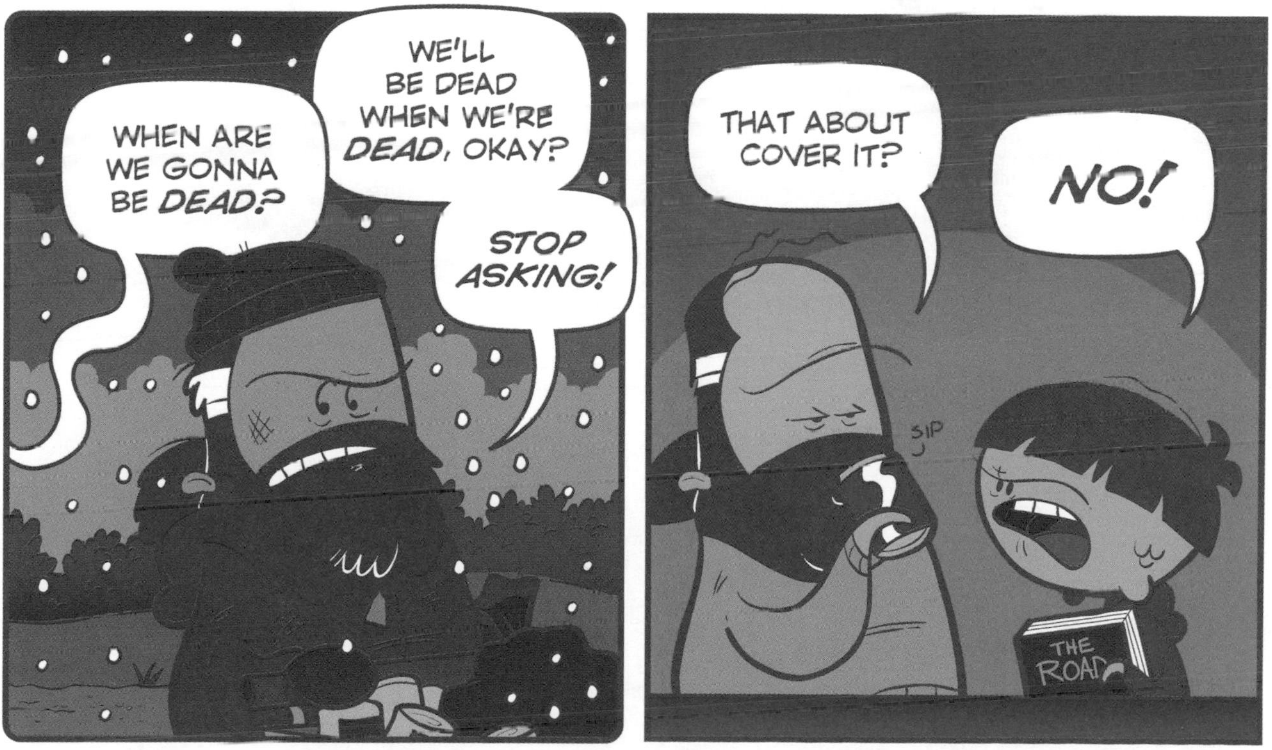
WHEN ARE WE GONNA BE *DEAD*?
WE'LL BE DEAD WHEN WE'RE *DEAD*, OKAY?
STOP ASKING!
THAT ABOUT COVER IT?
SIP
NO!
THE ROAD

Guest Book Club by Paul Southworth @ www.uglyhill.com

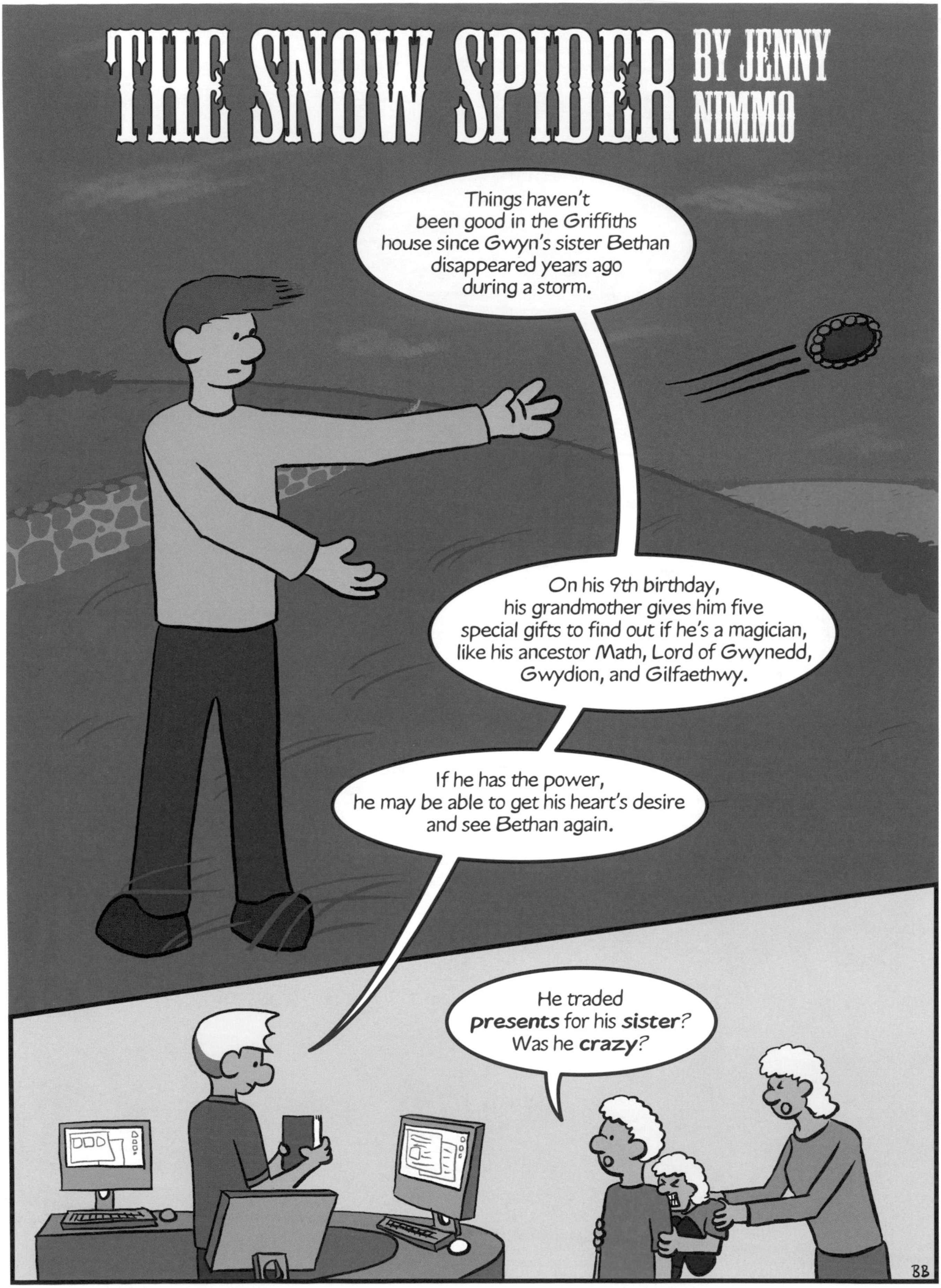
THE SNOW SPIDER BY JENNY NIMMO
Things haven't been good in the Griffiths house since Gwyn's sister Bethan disappeared years ago during a storm.
On his 9th birthday, his grandmother gives him five special gifts to find out if he's a magician, like his ancestor Math, Lord of Gwynedd, Gwydion, and Gilfaethwy.
If he has the power, he may be able to get his heart's desire and see Bethan again.
He traded **presents** for his ***sister***? Was he ***crazy***?
BB

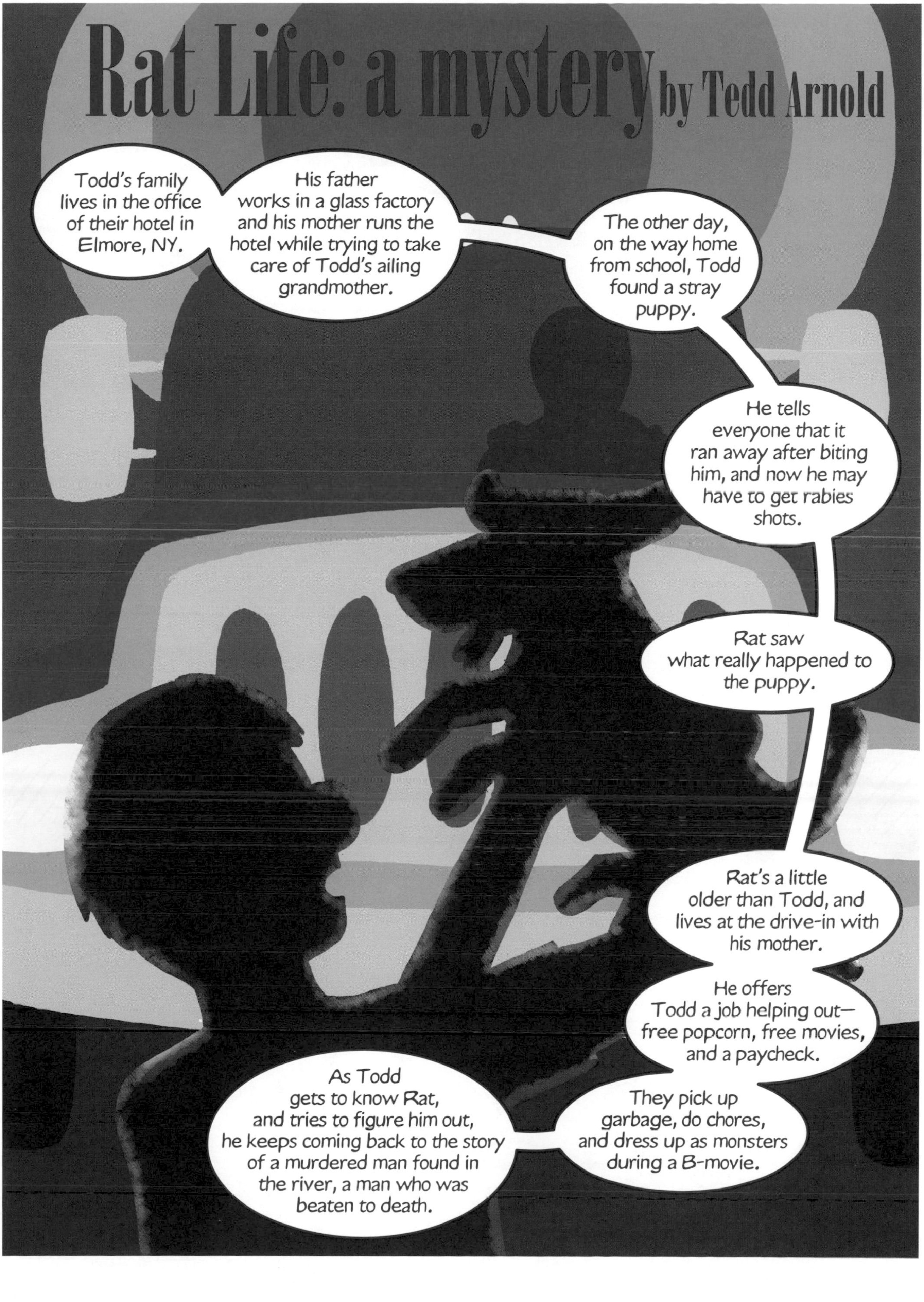
Rat Life: a mystery by Tedd Arnold
Todd's family lives in the office of their hotel in Elmore, NY.
His father works in a glass factory and his mother runs the hotel while trying to take care of Todd's ailing grandmother.
The other day, on the way home from school, Todd found a stray puppy.
He tells everyone that it ran away after biting him, and now he may have to get rabies shots.
Rat saw what really happened to the puppy.
Rat's a little older than Todd, and lives at the drive-in with his mother.
He offers Todd a job helping out—free popcorn, free movies, and a paycheck.
They pick up garbage, do chores, and dress up as monsters during a B-movie.
As Todd gets to know Rat, and tries to figure him out, he keeps coming back to the story of a murdered man found in the river, a man who was beaten to death.

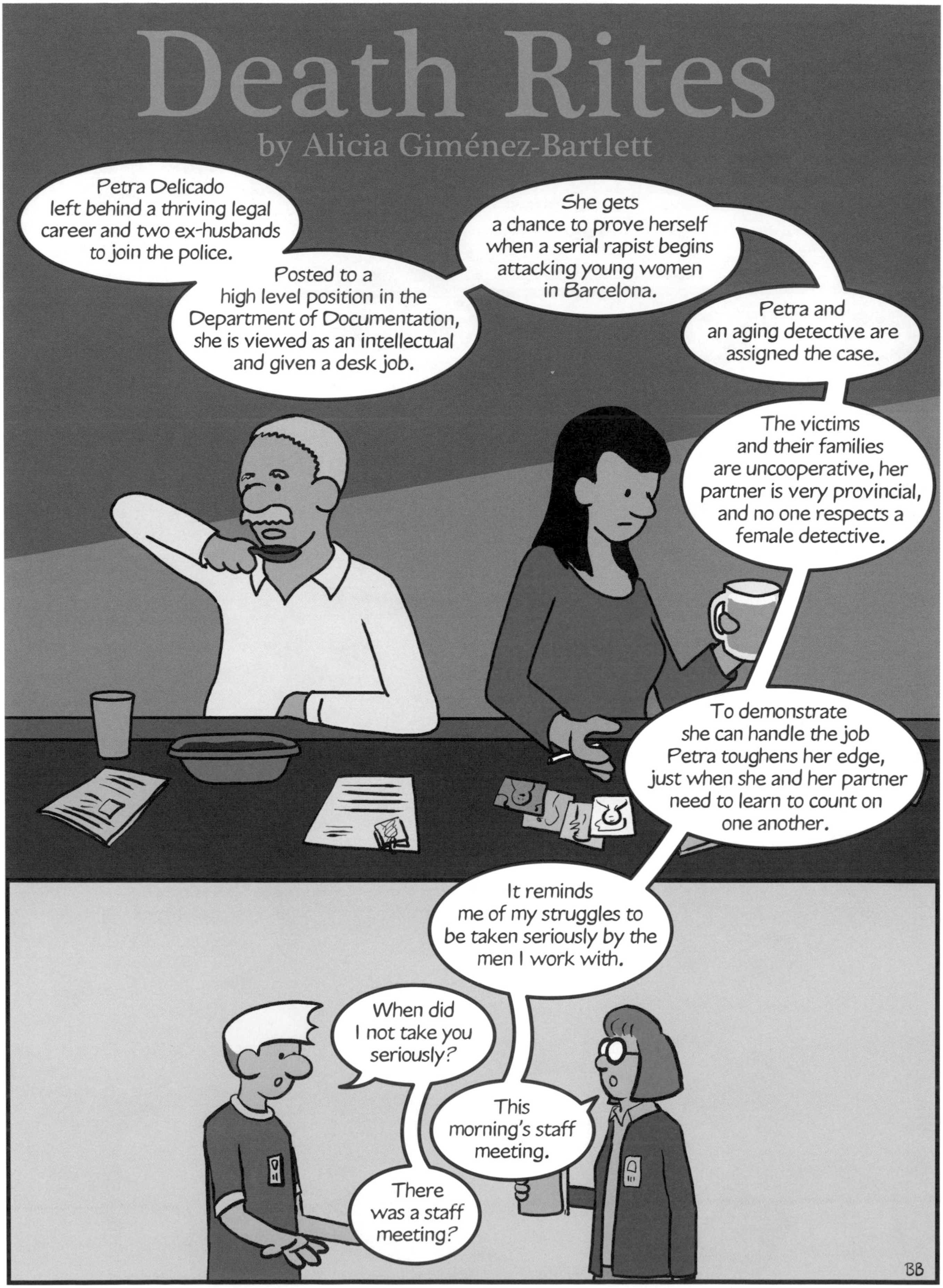
Death Rites
by Alicia Giménez-Bartlett
Petra Delicado left behind a thriving legal career and two ex-husbands to join the police.
Posted to a high level position in the Department of Documentation, she is viewed as an intellectual and given a desk job.
She gets a chance to prove herself when a serial rapist begins attacking young women in Barcelona.
Petra and an aging detective are assigned the case.
The victims and their families are uncooperative, her partner is very provincial, and no one respects a female detective.
To demonstrate she can handle the job Petra toughens her edge, just when she and her partner need to learn to count on one another.
It reminds me of my struggles to be taken seriously by the men I work with.
When did I not take you seriously?
This morning's staff meeting.
There was a staff meeting?
BB

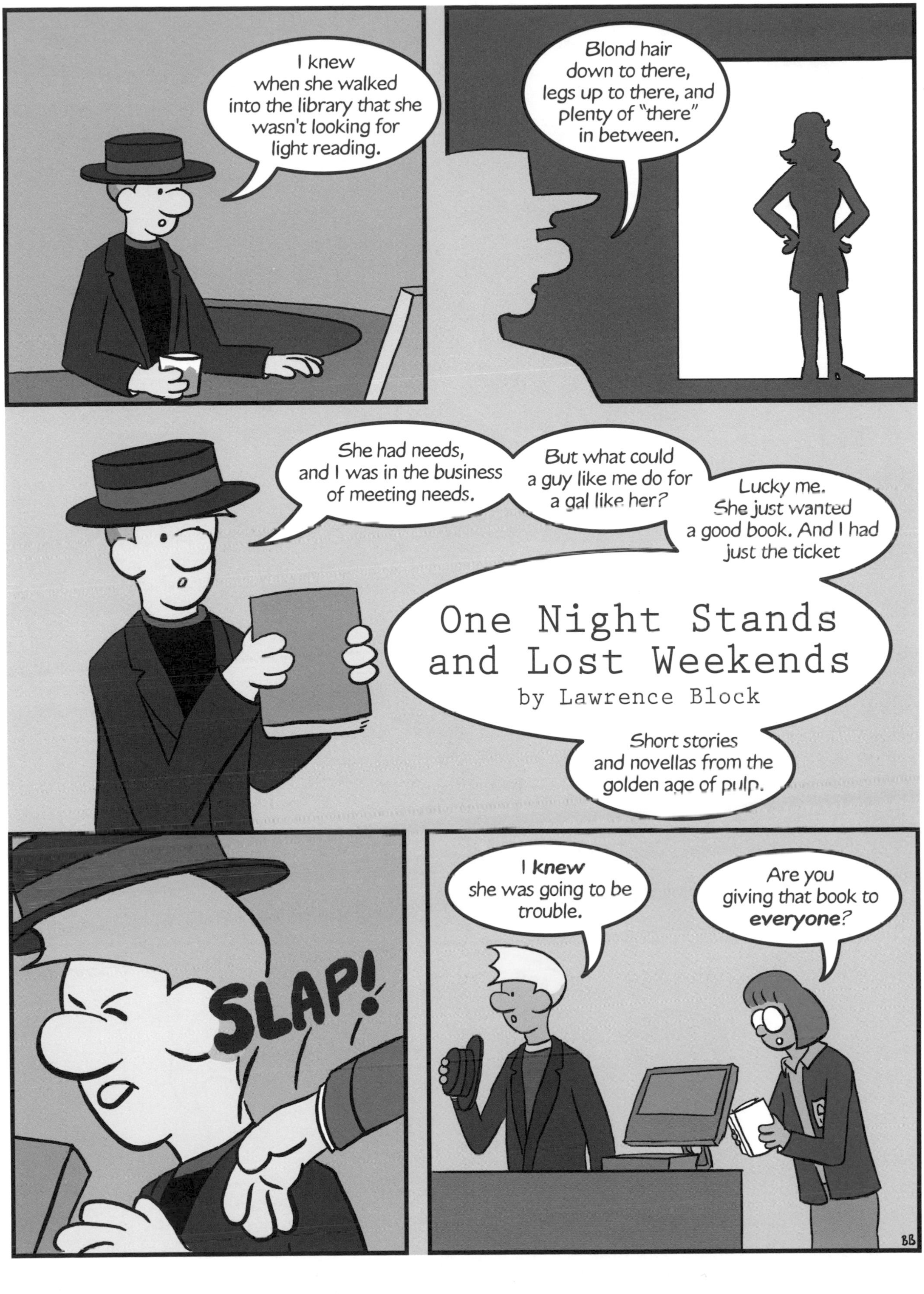
I knew when she walked into the library that she wasn't looking for light reading.
Blond hair down to there, legs up to there, and plenty of "there" in between.
She had needs, and I was in the business of meeting needs.
But what could a guy like me do for a gal like her?
Lucky me. She just wanted a good book. And I had just the ticket
One Night Stands and Lost Weekends
by Lawrence Block
Short stories and novellas from the golden age of pulp.
SLAP!
I **knew** she was going to be trouble.
Are you giving that book to **everyone**?
BB

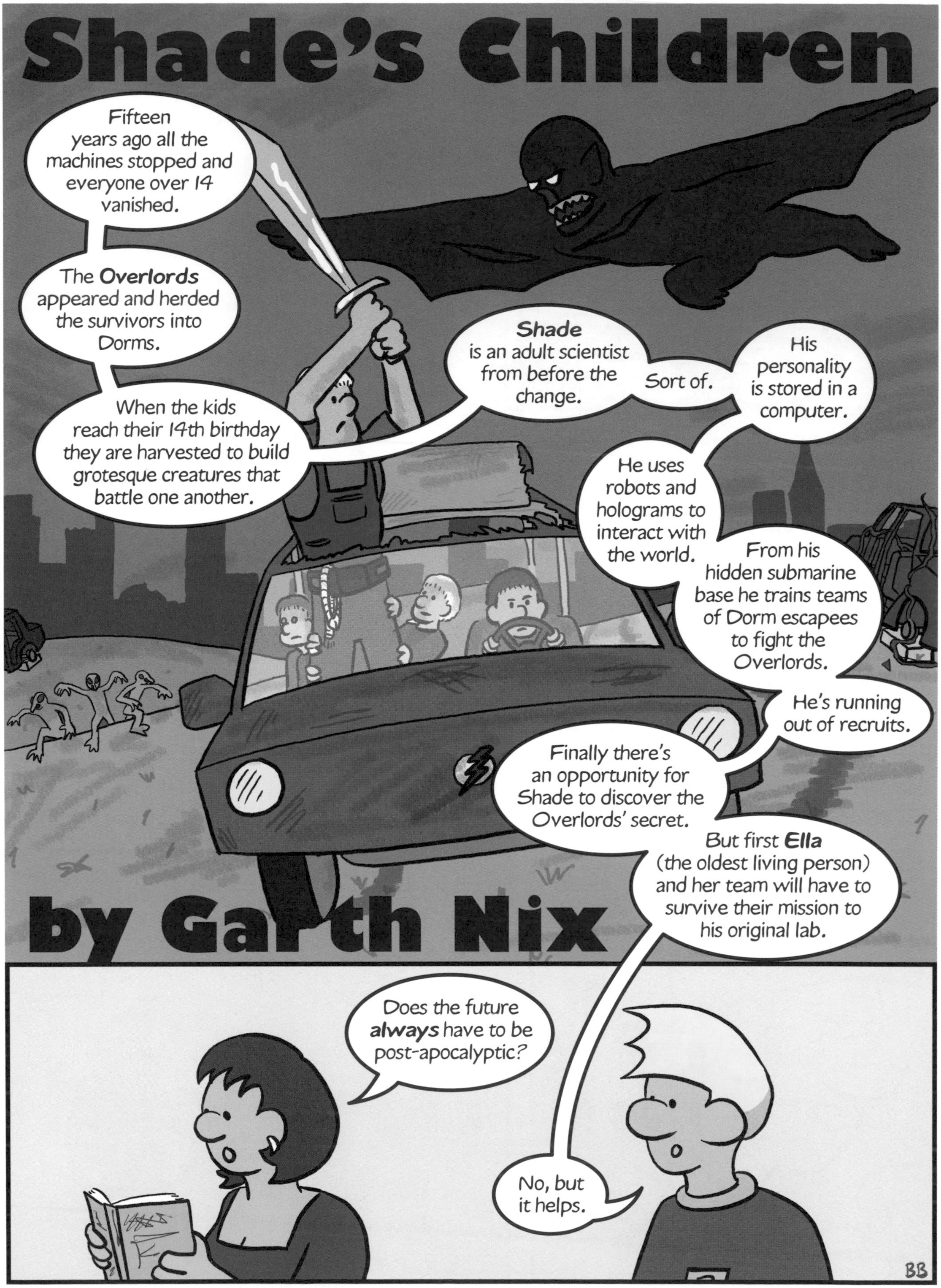

Shade's Children
Fifteen years ago all the machines stopped and everyone over 14 vanished.
The **Overlords** appeared and herded the survivors into Dorms.
When the kids reach their 14th birthday they are harvested to build grotesque creatures that battle one another.
Shade is an adult scientist from before the change.
Sort of.
His personality is stored in a computer.
He uses robots and holograms to interact with the world.
From his hidden submarine base he trains teams of Dorm escapees to fight the Overlords.
He's running out of recruits.
Finally there's an opportunity for Shade to discover the Overlords' secret.
But first **Ella** (the oldest living person) and her team will have to survive their mission to his original lab.
by Garth Nix
Does the future **always** have to be post-apocalyptic?
No, but it helps.
BB

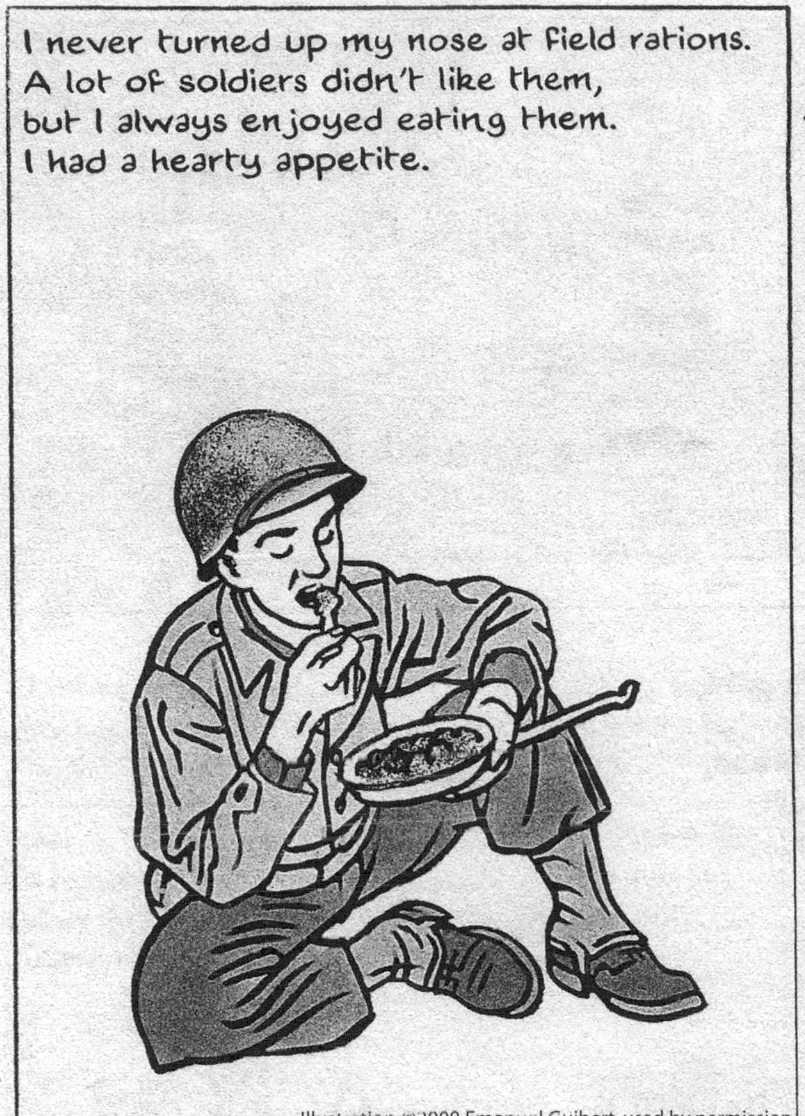
I never turned up my nose at field rations.
A lot of soldiers didn't like them,
but I always enjoyed eating them.
I had a hearty appetite.

Illustration ©2008 Emanuel Guibert, used by permission

ALAN'S WAR

THE MEMORIES OF G.I. ALAN COPE BY EMANUAL GUIBERT

ALAN COPE WAS BORN IN A LOS ANGELES SUBURB IN 1925 AND SERVED IN EUROPE DURING WW II. HIS SERVICE WAS UNEVENTFUL, A SERIES OF JOBS PUNCTUATED BY SURREAL WARTIME EXPERIENCES. THERE WAS FREQUENT BOREDOM AND RARE TERROR.

IN 1994, FIVE YEARS BEFORE HIS DEATH, ALAN MET CARTOONIST EMANUEL GUILBERT AND THE TWO BECAME CLOSE FRIENDS. THEY DECIDED TO TELL HIS STORY TOGETHER.

ALAN'S WAR ISN'T ABOUT THE WAR. IT'S ABOUT THE DETAILS: FRIENDS, LIVING CONDITIONS, THE PEOPLE HE MET. ALAN QUIETLY FOUND THE PASSIONS THAT WOULD DEFINE THE REST OF HIS LIFE.

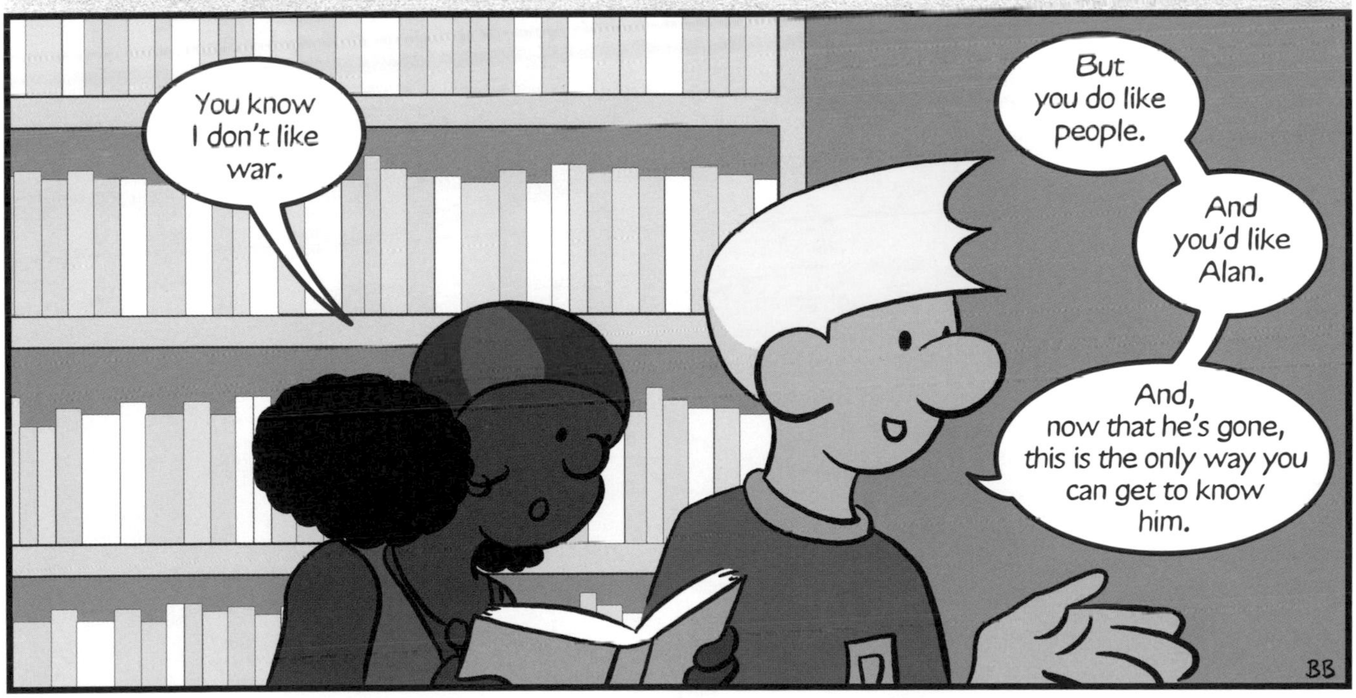
You know I don't like war.
But you do like people.
And you'd like Alan.
And, now that he's gone, this is the only way you can get to know him.
BB

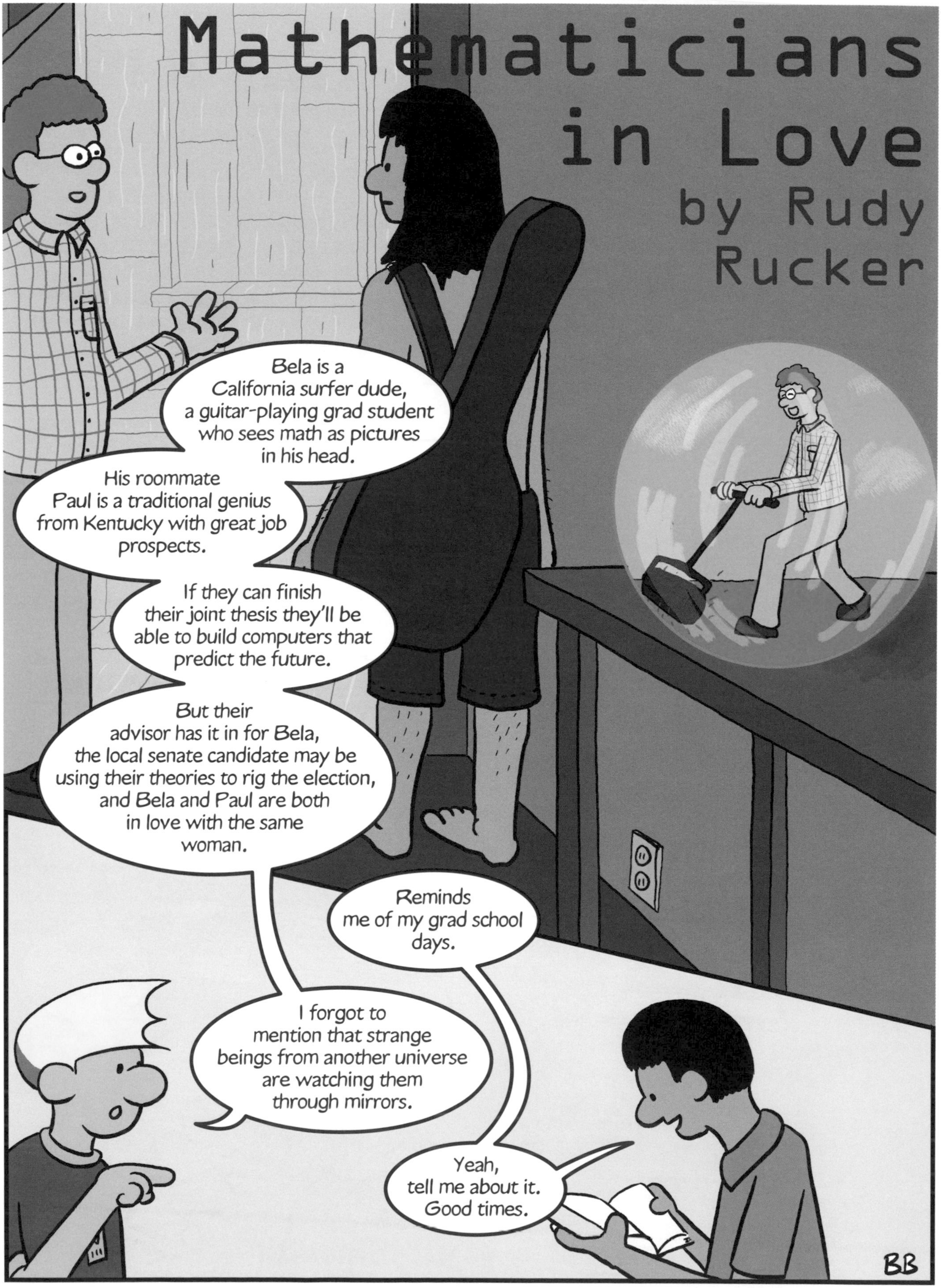
Mathematicians in Love
by Rudy Rucker
Bela is a California surfer dude, a guitar-playing grad student who sees math as pictures in his head.
His roommate Paul is a traditional genius from Kentucky with great job prospects.
If they can finish their joint thesis they'll be able to build computers that predict the future.
But their advisor has it in for Bela, the local senate candidate may be using their theories to rig the election, and Bela and Paul are both in love with the same woman.
Reminds me of my grad school days.
I forgot to mention that strange beings from another universe are watching them through mirrors.
Yeah, tell me about it. Good times.
BB

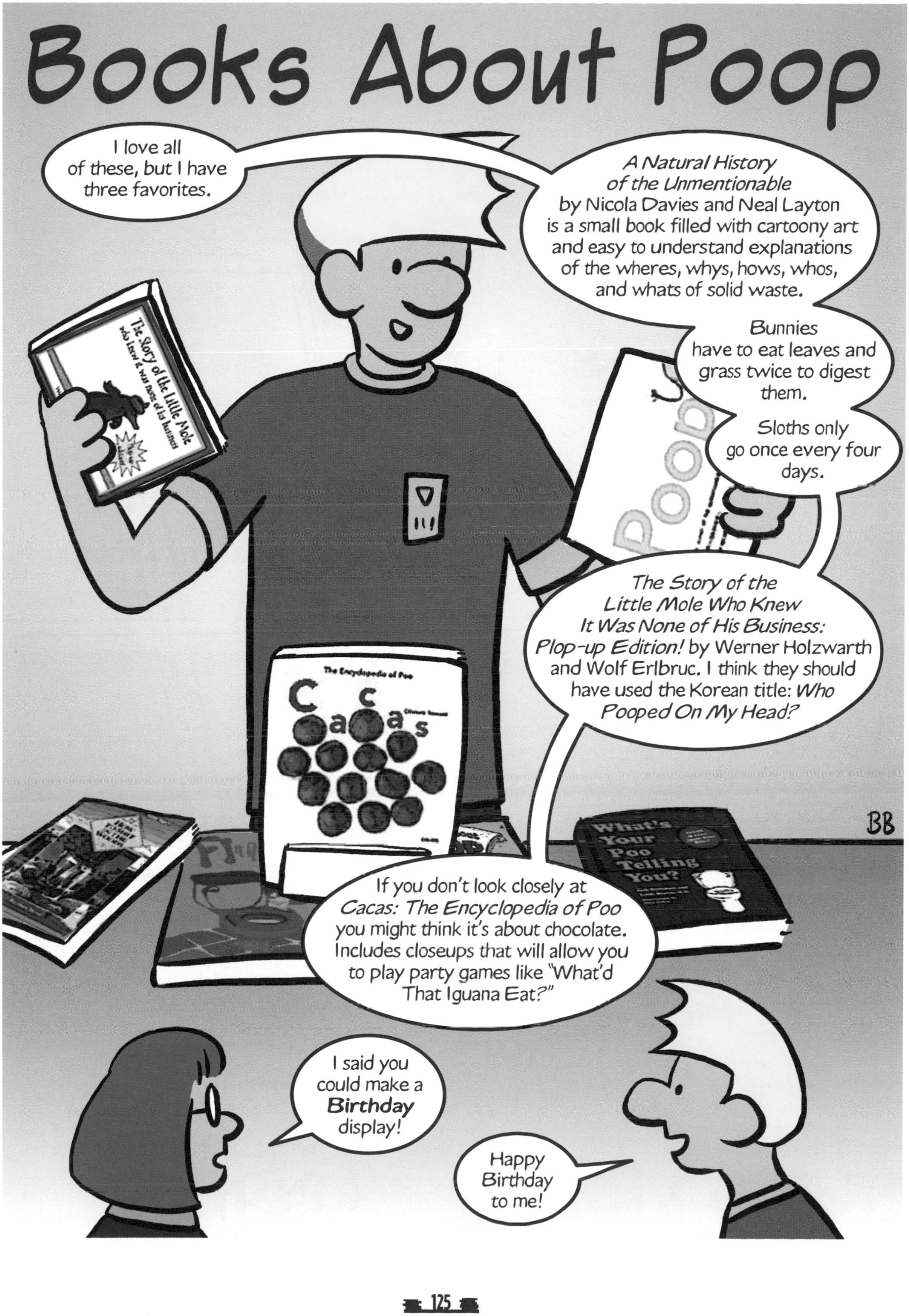
Books About Poop
I love all of these, but I have three favorites.
A Natural History of the Unmentionable by Nicola Davies and Neal Layton is a small book filled with cartoony art and easy to understand explanations of the wheres, whys, hows, whos, and whats of solid waste.
Bunnies have to eat leaves and grass twice to digest them.
Sloths only go once every four days.
The Story of the Little Mole Who Knew It Was None of His Business: Plop-up Edition! by Werner Holzwarth and Wolf Erlbruc. I think they should have used the Korean title: *Who Pooped On My Head?*
If you don't look closely at *Cacas: The Encyclopedia of Poo* you might think it's about chocolate. Includes closeups that will allow you to play party games like "What'd That Iguana Eat?"
I said you could make a **Birthday** display!
Happy Birthday to me!
The Encyclopedia of Poo
Cacas
What's Your Poo Telling You?
BB

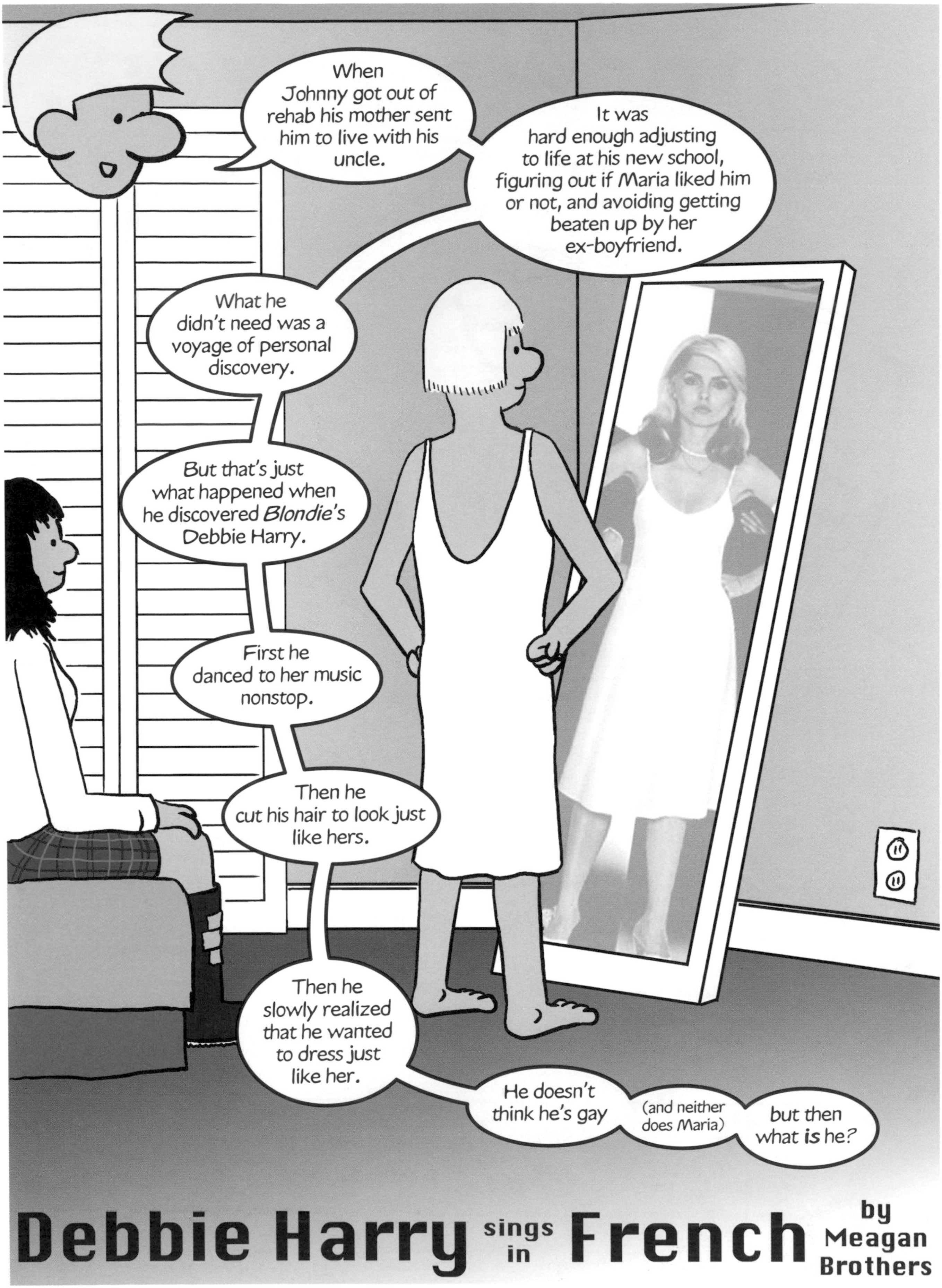
When Johnny got out of rehab his mother sent him to live with his uncle.
It was hard enough adjusting to life at his new school, figuring out if Maria liked him or not, and avoiding getting beaten up by her ex-boyfriend.
What he didn't need was a voyage of personal discovery.
But that's just what happened when he discovered *Blondie*'s Debbie Harry.
First he danced to her music nonstop.
Then he cut his hair to look just like hers.
Then he slowly realized that he wanted to dress just like her.
He doesn't think he's gay
(and neither does Maria)
but then what ***is*** he?

Debbie Harry sings in French

by Meagan Brothers

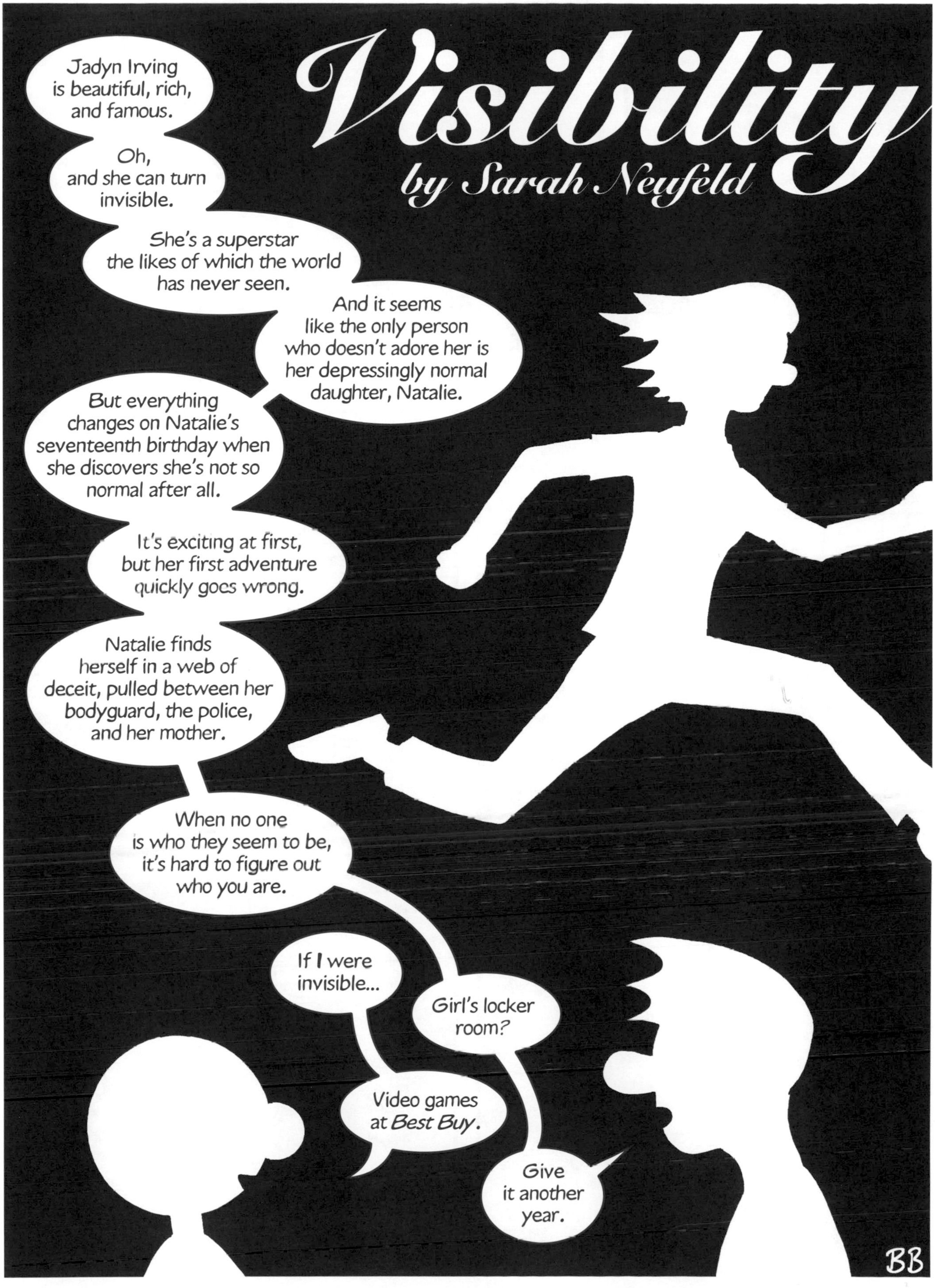
Visibility
by Sarah Neufeld
Jadyn Irving is beautiful, rich, and famous.
Oh, and she can turn invisible.
She's a superstar the likes of which the world has never seen.
And it seems like the only person who doesn't adore her is her depressingly normal daughter, Natalie.
But everything changes on Natalie's seventeenth birthday when she discovers she's not so normal after all.
It's exciting at first, but her first adventure quickly goes wrong.
Natalie finds herself in a web of deceit, pulled between her bodyguard, the police, and her mother.
When no one is who they seem to be, it's hard to figure out who you are.
If I were invisible...
Girl's locker room?
Video games at *Best Buy*.
Give it another year.
BB

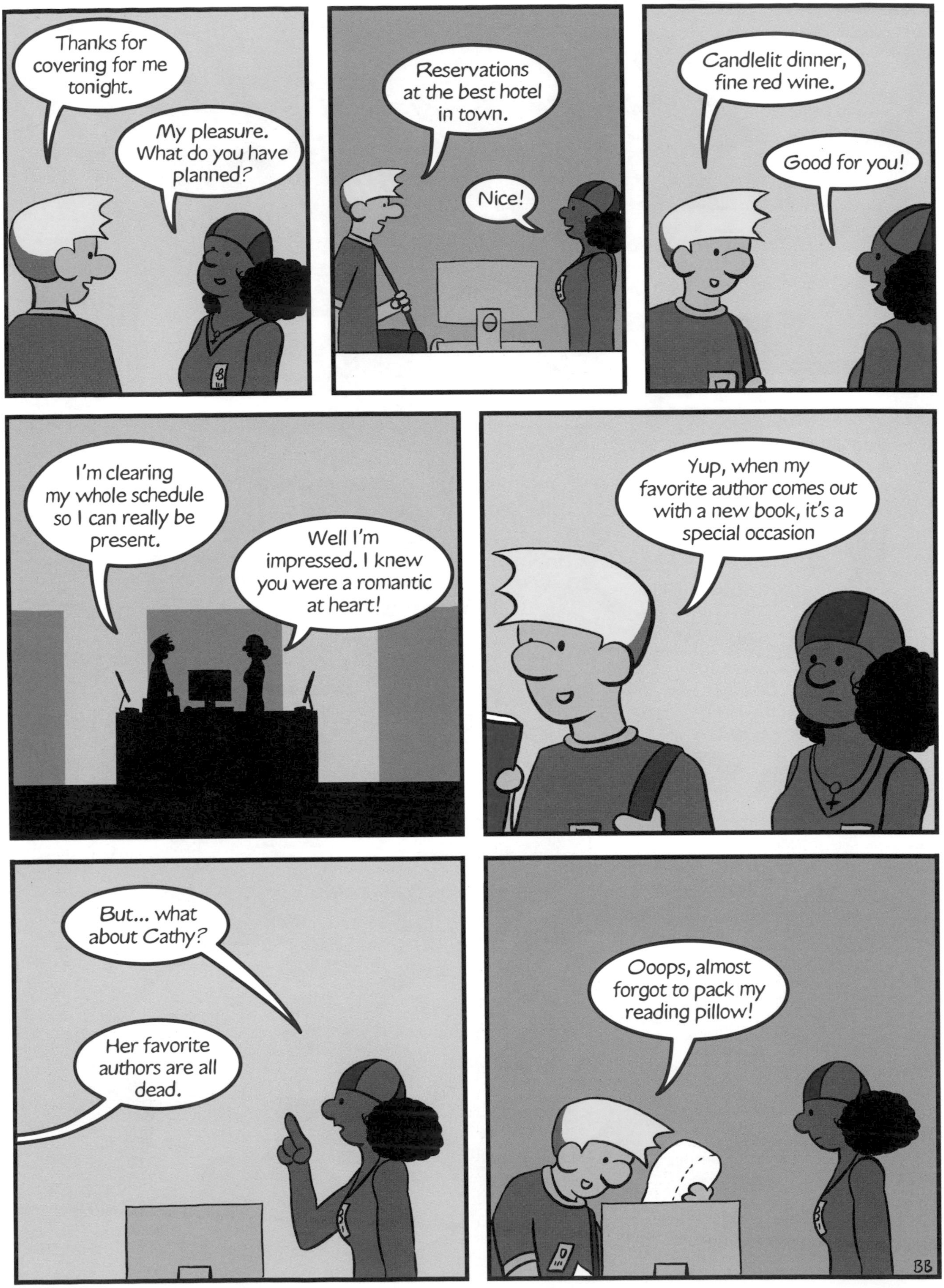
Thanks for covering for me tonight.
My pleasure. What do you have planned?
Reservations at the best hotel in town.
Nice!
Candlelit dinner, fine red wine.
Good for you!
I'm clearing my whole schedule so I can really be present.
Well I'm impressed. I knew you were a romantic at heart!
Yup, when my favorite author comes out with a new book, it's a special occasion
But... what about Cathy?
Her favorite authors are all dead.
Ooops, almost forgot to pack my reading pillow!
BB